Information Retrieval

THE KLUWER INTERNATIONAL SERIES ON INFORMATION RETRIEVAL

Series Editor:
W. Bruce Croft
University of Massachusetts, Amherst

Also in the Series:

INFORMATION RETRIEVAL SYSTEMS: ***Theory and Implementation,*** *by Gerald Kowalski;* ISBN: 0-7923-9926-9

CROSS-LANGUAGE INFORMATION RETRIEVAL, *edited by Gregory Grefenstette;* ISBN: 0-7923-8122-X

TEXT RETRIEVAL AND FILTERING: ***Analytic Models of Performance***, *by Robert M. Losee;* ISBN: 0-7923-8177-7

INFORMATION RETRIEVAL: UNCERTAINTY AND LOGICS: ***Advanced Models for the Representation and Retrieval of Information***, *by Fabio Crestani, Mounia Lalmas, and Cornelis Joost van Rijsbergen;* ISBN: 0-7923-8302-8

DOCUMENT COMPUTING: ***Technologies for Managing Electronic Document Collections***, *by Ross Wilkinson, Timothy Arnold-Moore, Michael Fuller, Ron Sacks-Davis, James Thom, and Justin Zobel;* ISBN: 0-7923-8357-5

AUTOMATIC INDEXING AND ABSTRACTING OF DOCUMENT TEXTS, *by Marie-Francine Moens*; ISBN 0-7923-7793-1

ADVANCES IN INFORMATIONAL RETRIEVAL: ***Recent Research from the Center for Intelligent Information Retrieval***, *by W. Bruce Croft*; ISBN 0-7923-7812-1

INFORMATION RETRIEVAL SYSTEMS: ***Theory and Implementation,*** **Second Edition**, *by Gerald J. Kowalski and Mark T. Maybury;* ISBN: 0-7923-7924-1

PERSPECTIVES ON CONTENT-BASED MULTIMEDIA SYSTEMS, *by Jian Kang Wu; Mohan S. Kankanhalli;Joo-Hwee Lim;Dezhong Hong;* ISBN: 0-7923-7944-6

MINING THE WORLD WIDE WEB: ***An Information Search Approach***, *by George Chang, Marcus J. Healey, James A. M. McHugh, Jason T. L. Wang;* ISBN: 0-7923-7349-9

INTEGRATED REGION-BASED IMAGE RETRIEVAL, *by James Z. Wang;* ISBN: 0-7923-7350-2

TOPIC DETECTION AND TRACKING: **Event-based Information Organization**, *edited by James Allan;* ISBN: 0-7923-7664-1

LANGUAGE MODELING FOR INFORMATION RETRIEVAL, *edited by W. Bruce Croft, John Lafferty;* ISBN: 1-4020-1216-0

Information Retrieval
Algorithms and Heuristics
Second Edition

by

David A. Grossman
Illinois Institute of Technology,
Chicago, IL, U.S.A.

and

Ophir Frieder
Illinois Institute of Technology,
Chicago, IL, U.S.A.

A C.I.P. Catalogue record for this book is available from the Library of Congress.

ISBN 1-4020-3004-5 (PB)
ISBN 1-4020-3003-7 (HB)
ISBN 1-4020-3005-3 (e-book)

Published by Springer,
P.O. Box 17, 3300 AA Dordrecht, The Netherlands.

Sold and distributed in North, Central and South America
by Springer,
101 Philip Drive, Norwell, MA 02061, U.S.A.

In all other countries, sold and distributed
by Springer,
P.O. Box 322, 3300 AH Dordrecht, The Netherlands.

Printed on acid-free paper

springeronline.com

Printed in the Netherlands.

For our wives:
Mary Catherine and Nazli
and of course, for
Isaac Sean Grossman,
born 2/2/04.

Contents

List of Figures

Foreword

The past five years, as Grossman and Frieder acknowledge in their preface, have been a period of considerable progress for the field of information retrieval (IR). To the general public, this is reflected in the maturing of commercial Web search engines. To the IR practitioner, research has led to an improved understanding of the scope and limitations of the Web search problem, new insights into the retrieval process through the development of the formal underpinnings and models for IR, and a variety of exciting new applications such as cross-language retrieval, peer-to-peer search, and music retrieval, which have expanded the horizons of the research landscape. In addition, there has been an increasing realization on the part of the database and IR communities that solving the information problems of the future will involve the integration of techniques for unstructured and structured data. The revised edition of this book addresses many of these important new developments, and is currently the only textbook that does so.

Two particular examples that stood out for me are the descriptions of language models for IR and cross-language retrieval. Language models have become an important topic at the major IR conferences and many researchers are adapting this framework due to its power and simplicity, as well as the availability of tools for experimentation and application building. Grossman and Frieder provide an excellent overview of the topic in the retrieval strategies chapter, together with examples of different smoothing techniques. Cross-language retrieval, which involves the retrieval of text in different languages than the query source language, has been driven by government interest in Europe and the U.S. A number of approaches have been developed that can exploit available resources such as parallel and comparable corpora, and the effectiveness of these systems now approaches (or even surpasses in some cases) monolingual retrieval. The revised version of this book contains a chapter on cross-language retrieval that clearly describes the major approaches and gives examples of how the algorithms involved work with real data. The combination of up-to-date coverage, straightforward treatment, and the frequent use of examples makes this book an excellent choice for undergraduate or graduate IR courses.

W. Bruce Croft
August 2004

Preface

When we wrote the first edition of this book in 1998, the Web was relatively new, and information retrieval was an old field but it lacked popular appeal. Today the word *Google* has joined the popular lexicon, and *Google* indexes more than four billion Web pages. In 1998, only a few schools taught graduate courses in information retrieval; today, the subject is commonly offered at the undergraduate level. Our experience with teaching information retrieval at the undergraduate level, as well as a detailed analysis of the topics covered and the effectiveness of the class, are given in [Goharian et al., 2004].

The term *Information Retrieval* refers to a search that may cover any form of information: structured data, text, video, image, sound, musical scores, DNA sequences, etc. The reality is that for many years, database systems existed to search structured data, and information retrieval meant the search of documents. The authors come originally from the world of structured search, but for much of the last ten years, we have worked in the area of document retrieval. To us, the world should be data type agnostic. There is no need for a special delineation between structured and unstructured data. In 1998, we included a chapter on data integration, and reviews suggested the only reason it was there was because it covered some of our recent research. Today, such an allegation makes no sense, since information *mediators* have been developed which operate with both structured and unstructured data. Furthermore, the eXtensible Markup Language (XML) has become prolific in both the database and information retrieval domains.

We focus on the ad hoc information retrieval problem. Simply put, ad hoc information retrieval allows users to search for documents that are relevant to user-provided queries. It may appear that systems such as *Google* have solved this problem, but effectiveness measures for *Google* have not been published. Typical systems still have an effectiveness (accuracy) of, at best, forty percent [TREC, 2003]. This leaves ample room for improvement, with the prerequisite of a firm understanding of existing approaches.

Information retrieval textbooks on the market are relatively unfocused, and we were uncomfortable using them in our classes. They tend to leave out details of a variety of key retrieval models. Few books detail inference networks, yet an inference network is a core model used by a variety of systems. Additionally, many books lack much detail on efficiency, namely, the execution speed of a query. Efficiency is potentially of limited interest to those who focus only on effectiveness, but for the practitioner, efficiency concerns can override all others.

Additionally, for each strategy, we provide a detailed running example. When presenting strategies, it is easy to gloss over the details, but examples keep us honest. We find that students benefit from a single example that runs through the whole book. Furthermore, every section of this book that describes a core retrieval strategy was reviewed by either the inventor of the strategy (and we thank them profusely; more thanks are in the acknowledgments!) or someone intimately familiar with it. Hence, to our knowledge, this book contains some of the gory details of some strategies that cannot be found anywhere else in print.

Our goal is to provide a book that is sharply focused on ad hoc information retrieval. To do this, we developed a taxonomy of the field based on a model that a *strategy* compares a document to a query and a utility can be plugged into any strategy to improve the performance of the given strategy. We cover all of the basic strategies, not just a couple of them, and a variety of utilities. We provide sufficient detail so that a student or practitioner who reads our book can implement any particular strategy or utility. The book, *Managing Gigabytes* [Witten et al., 1999], does an excellent job of describing a variety of detailed inverted index compression strategies. We include the most recently developed and the most efficient of these, but we certainly recommend Managing Gigabytes as an excellent side reference.

So what is new in this second edition? Much of the core retrieval strategies remain unchanged. Since 1998, numerous papers were written about the use of language models for information retrieval. We have added a new section on language models. Furthermore, cross-lingual information retrieval, that is, the posting of a query in one language and finding documents in another language, was just in its infancy at the time of the first version. We have added an entire chapter on the topic that incorporates information from over 100 recent references.

Naturally, we have included some discussion on current topics such as XML, peer-to-peer information retrieval, duplicate document detection, parallel document clustering, fusion of disparate retrieval strategies, and information mediators.

Finally, we fixed a number of bugs found by our alert undergraduate and graduate students. We thank them all for their efforts.

This book is intended primarily as a textbook for an undergraduate or graduate level course in Information Retrieval. It has been used in a graduate course, and we incorporated student feedback when we developed a set of overhead transparencies that can be used when teaching with our text. The presentation is available at *www.ir.iit.edu*.

Additionally, practitioners who build information retrieval systems or applications that use information retrieval systems will find this book useful when selecting retrieval strategies and utilities to deploy for production use. We have heard from several practitioners that the first edition was helpful, and we incorporated their comments and suggested additions into this edition.

We emphasize that the focus of the book is on algorithms, not on commercial products, but, to our knowledge, the basic strategies used by the majority of commercial products are described in the book. We believe practitioners may find that a commercial product is using a given strategy and can then use this book as a reference to learn what is known about the techniques used by the product.

Finally, we note that the information retrieval field changes daily. For the most up to date coverage of the field, the best sources include journals like the *ACM Transactions on Information Systems*, the *Journal of the American Society for Information Science and Technology*, *Information Processing and Management*, and *Information Retrieval*. Other relevant papers are found in the various information retrieval conferences such as ACM SIGIR *www.sigir.org*, NIST TREC *trec.nist.gov*, and the ACM CIKM *www.cikm.org*.

Acknowledgments

The first edition of this book was published in 1998. Since then, numerous advancements in Information Retrieval have occurred.

For help with most of the material for the first edition, we are still deeply indebted to Paul Kantor and Don Kraft for their insightful comments during some of the early stages of the development of the book. We also greatly thank Steve Robertson, K.L. Kwok, and Jamie Callan for critically reviewing the sections describing their efforts, and Warren Greiff whose extreme patience taught and retaught us the details of inference networks.

With the addition of language models and cross-language information retrieval we are extremely thankful for the insightful comments and suggestions from ChengXiang Zhai, Doug Oard, and James Mayfield.

General critical feedback came from multiple individuals. Readability for classroom use was enhanced by feedback given from the students in our undergraduate Information Retrieval course and our graduate Advanced Information Retrieval. John Juilfs spent countless hours checking all of the new examples for this edition and checking our math (we take full responsibility for any remaining errors, but he saved us from lots of them). Abdur Chowdhury carefully reviewed and provided input for our new section on duplicate document detection. Wei Gen Yee provided significant input to our modifications in the distributed information retrieval chapter. Steve Beitzel and Eric Jensen provided significant input to updates in our efficiency and parallel processing sections. Rebecca Cathey provided examples for our new language modeling and cross-language sections. Michael Saelee produced and refined our figures. Finally, Wei Guan carefully and repeatedly checked all of our examples and notation.

We also thank Wendy Grossman, Ben Goldfarb, David Roberts, and Jordan Wilberding for detailed comments. We also thank all others who read the book and provided excellent feedback, and our friends and colleagues who provided moral support.

Finally, we would not have ever finished the book without constant moral support from our families and close friends. Special thanks go to Mary Catherine McCabe and Nazli Goharian who made countless sacrifices of their time and gave us constant encouragement and support.

From both of us to all of you, THANKS.

Chapter 1

INTRODUCTION

Since the near beginnings of civilization, human beings have focused on written communication. From cave drawings to scroll writings, from printing presses to electronic libraries, communicating was of primary concern to man's existence. Today, with the emergence of digital libraries and electronic information exchange there is clear need for improved techniques to organize large quantities of information. Applied and theoretical research and development in the areas of information authorship, processing, storage, and retrieval is of interest to all sectors of the community. In this book, we survey recent research efforts that focus on the electronic searching and retrieving of documents.

Our focus is strictly on the retrieval of information in response to user queries. That is, we discuss algorithms and approaches for ad hoc information retrieval, or simply, information retrieval. Figure 1.1 illustrates the basic process of ad hoc information retrieval. A static, or relatively static, document collection is indexed prior to any user query. A query is issued and a set of documents that are deemed relevant to the query are ranked based on their computed similarity to the query and presented to the user. Numerous techniques exist to identify how these documents are ranked, and that is a key focus of this book (effectiveness). Other techniques also exist to rank documents quickly, and these are also discussed (efficiency).

Information Retrieval (IR) is devoted to finding *relevant* documents, not finding simple matches to patterns. Yet, often when information retrieval systems are evaluated, they are found to miss numerous relevant documents [Blair and Maron, 1985]. Moreover, users have become complacent in their expectation of accuracy of information retrieval systems [Gordon, 1997].

A related problem is that of document routing or filtering. Here, the queries are static and the document collection constantly changes. An environment where corporate e-mail is routed based on predefined queries to different parts

Figure 1.1. Document Retrieval

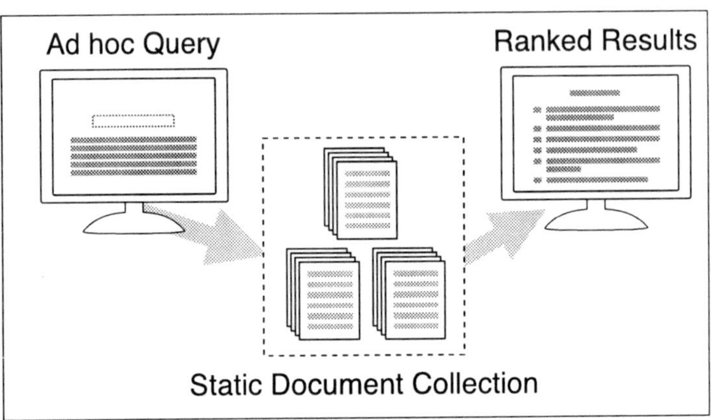

of the organization (i.e., e-mail about sales is routed to the sales department, marketing e-mail goes to marketing, etc.) is an example of an application of document routing. Figure 1.2 illustrates document routing. Document routing algorithms and approaches also widely appear in the literature, but are not addressed in this book.

In Figure 1.3, we illustrate the critical document categories that correspond to any issued query. Namely, in the collection there are documents which are retrieved, and there are those documents that are relevant. In a perfect system, these two sets would be equivalent; we would only retrieve relevant documents. In reality, systems retrieve many non-relevant documents. To measure effectiveness, two ratios are used: *precision* and *recall*. Precision is the ratio of the number of relevant documents retrieved to the total number retrieved. Precision provides an indication of the quality of the answer set. However, this does not consider the total number of relevant documents. A system might have good precision by retrieving ten documents and finding that nine are relevant (a 0.9 precision), but the total number of relevant documents also matters. If there were only nine relevant documents, the system would be a huge success — however if millions of documents were relevant and desired, this would not be a good result set.

Recall considers the total number of relevant documents; it is the ratio of the number of relevant documents retrieved to the total number of documents in the collection that are believed to be relevant. Computing the total number of relevant documents is non-trivial. The only sure means of doing this is to read the entire document collection. Since this is clearly not feasible, an approximation of the number is obtained (see Chapter 9). A good survey of

Figure 1.2. Document Routing

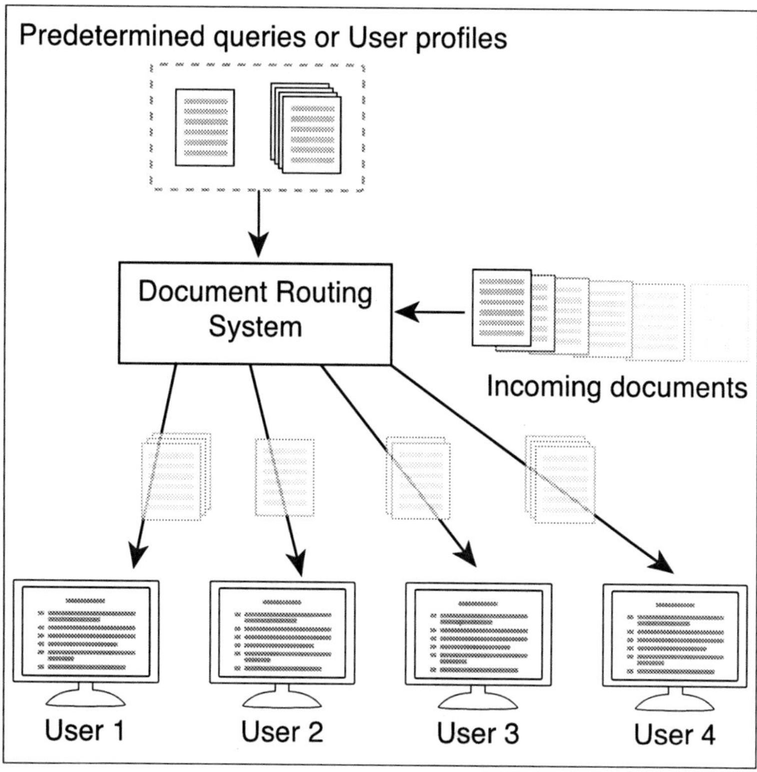

effectiveness measures, as well as a brief overview of information retrieval, is found in [Kantor, 1994].

Precision can be computed at various points of recall. Consider an example query q. For this query, we have estimated that there are two relevant documents. Now assume that when the user submits query q that ten documents are retrieved, including the two relevant documents. In our example, documents two and five are relevant. The sloped line in Figure 1.4 shows that after retrieving two documents, we have found one relevant document, and hence have achieved fifty percent *recall*. At this point, *precision* is fifty percent as we have retrieved two documents and one of them is relevant.

To reach one hundred percent recall, we must continue to retrieve documents until both relevant documents are retrieved. For our example, it is necessary to retrieve five documents to find both relevant documents. At this point, precision is forty percent because two out of five retrieved documents are relevant. Hence, for any desired level of recall, it is possible to compute precision.

Figure 1.3. Result Set: Relevant Retrieved, Relevant, and Retrieved

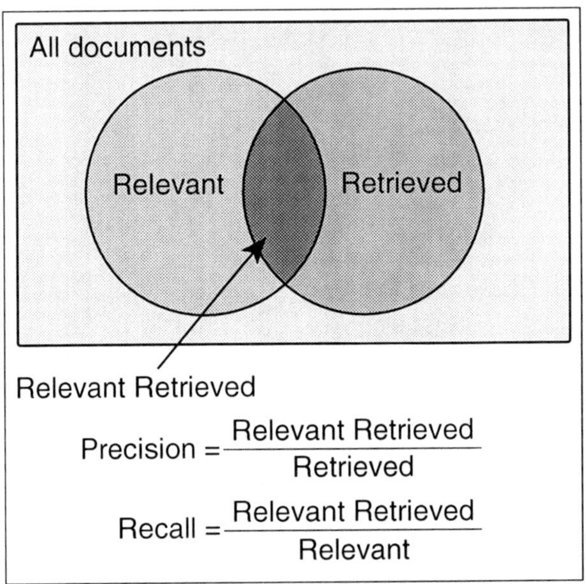

Graphing precision at various points of recall is referred to as a *precision/recall curve*.

A typical precision/recall curve is shown in Figure 1.5. Typically, as higher recall is desired, more documents must be retrieved to obtain the desired level of recall. In a perfect system, only relevant documents are retrieved. This means that at any level of recall, precision would be 1.0. The optimal precision/recall line is shown in Figure 1.5.

Average precision refers to an average of precision at various points of recall. Many systems today, when run on a standard document collection, report an average precision of between 0.2 and 0.3. Certainly, there is some element of fuzziness here because relevance is not a clearly defined concept, but it is clear that there is significant room for improvement in the area of effectiveness.

Finding relevant documents is not enough. The goal is to identify relevant documents within an acceptable response time. This book describes the current strategies to find relevant documents *quickly*. The quest to find efficient and effective information retrieval algorithms continues.

We explain each algorithm in detail, and for each topic, include examples for the most crucial algorithms. We then switch gears into survey mode and provide references to related and follow-on work. We explain the key aspects of the algorithms and then provide references for those interested in further

Figure 1.4. Precision and Two Points of Recall

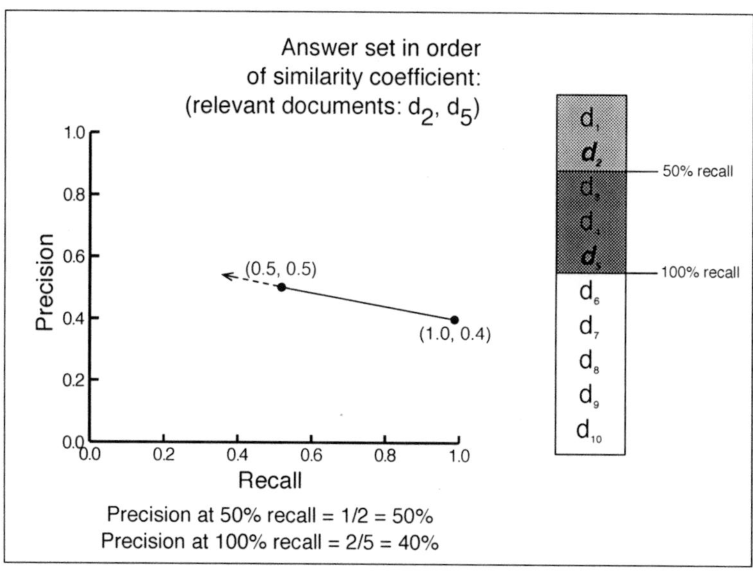

Figure 1.5. Typical and Optimal Precision/Recall Graph

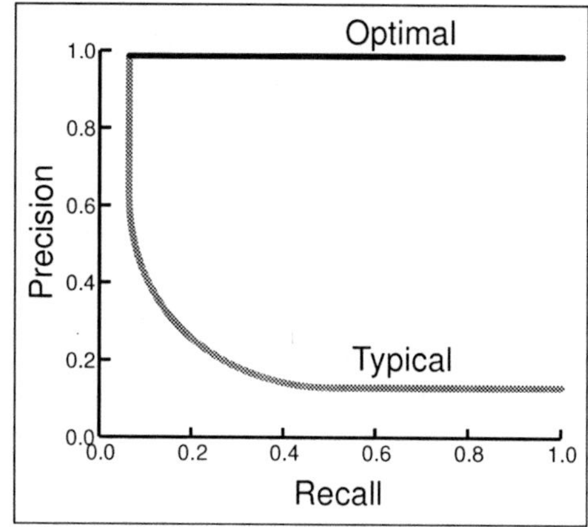

details. A collection of key information retrieval research papers is found in [Sparck Jones and Willett, 1997].

Recent algorithms designed to search large bodies of information are discussed throughout this book. Many research publications describe these algorithms in detail, but they are spread across numerous journals and written in a variety of different styles. Also, they have differing expectations of their reader's background. We provide a relatively brief, but sufficiently detailed overview of the field.

A sophisticated mathematical background is not required. Whenever detailed mathematical constructs are used, we provide a quick refresher of the key points needed to understand the algorithms and detailed examples.

We believe this book is valuable to a variety of readers. Readers familiar with the core of computer science and interested in learning more about information retrieval algorithms should benefit from this text. We provide explanations of the fundamental problems that exist and how people have addressed them in the past.

This book also has value for anyone who currently uses and supports a Relational Database Management System (RDBMS). Chapter 6 gives detailed algorithms that treat text retrieval as an application of a RDBMS. This makes it possible to integrate both structured data and text. We also include a section describing relational database approaches to process semi-structured documents such as those tagged with XML.

To guide the reader through the key issues in ad hoc information retrieval, we partitioned this book into separate but inter-linked processing avenues. In the first section, covered in Chapters 2 and 3, we overview retrieval processing strategies and utilities. All of these strategies and utilities focus on one and only one critical issue, namely, the improvement of retrieval accuracy. In Chapter 2, we describe nine models that were either developed for or adapted to information retrieval specifically for the purpose of enhancing the evaluation or ranking of documents retrieved in response to user queries. Chapter 3 describes utilities that could be applied to enhance any strategy described in Chapter 2.

In Chapter 3, we focus on techniques that are applicable to either all or most of the models. Several of those utilities described are language dependent, e.g., parsing and thesauri, others focus specifically on being language independent, namely, N-gram processing. We note in Chapter 3, that some of the described utilities were proposed as individual processing strategies. In reality, however, it is the combination of these techniques that yields the best improvements. An approach to precisely determine the optimal mix of techniques, the order to execute them, and the underlying models to operate them so as to yield the optimal processing strategy is still unknown.

After describing models and utilities that address accuracy demands, we turn our attention towards processing efficiency. In Chapter 4, we describe various document access schemes. That is, we describe both the constructs and usage of inverted indices as well as other representation schemes such as signature files. Each of these access schemes has advantages and disadvantages. The tradeoffs lie in terms of storage overhead and maintainability versus search and retrieval processing times. After describing the various access methods, we overview several compression schemes.

Chapters 2 and 3 cover the basics of traditional information retrieval models, utilities, and processing strategies. Chapter 4 provides a brief overview of cross-language information retrieval. Chapter 5 describes efficiency issues in Information Retrieval. In Chapters 6, 7, and 8, we focus on special topics in information retrieval. The three topics addressed, namely data integration, parallel, and distributed information retrieval systems, were selected based on where the commercial sector is focusing.

Traditionally, there was a clear separation between structured data, typically stored and accessed via relational database management systems, and semi-structured data such as text, typically stored and accessed via information retrieval systems. Each processing system supported its own data storage files and access methods. Today, the distinction between structured and semi-structured data is quickly vanishing. In fact, we no longer are concerned with just structured and semi-structured data, but also text and often include unstructured data, such as images, in the same storage repository.

To address the integration of structured and unstructured data, commercial vendors such as Oracle, IBM, and Microsoft have integrated information retrieval functionality with their traditional relational database engines. Furthermore, text retrieval vendors such as Convera and Verity have added relational processing components. In all of these cases, however, additional functionality came at the expense of requiring additional, separate, processing units. In Chapter 6, we discuss the issues related to adding processing units and suggest an alternative method that involves implementing information retrieval processing capability as an application of relational databases. Using such an approach, the traditional benefits of relational database processing (i.e., portability, concurrency, recovery, etc.) are made available without requiring additional software development. Since all traditional relational database vendors provide parallel implementations of their database software, implementing an information retrieval system as a relational database application further provides for a parallel instantiation of an information retrieval system.

Having recognized the need for a parallel information retrieval capability, we also describe recent developments in this area. In Chapter 7, we initially describe the earlier parallel processing efforts in information retrieval. These approaches predominantly focus on the use of Single Instruction Multiple Data (SIMD) multiprocessors to efficiently scan the text. However, as the understanding of parallel processing techniques in information retrieval grew, inverted index-based approaches were developed to reduce the unnecessarily high I/O demands commonly associated with text scanning schemes. We discuss several of these approaches and conclude Chapter 7 with recent work in parallel information retrieval focusing on the parallelization of document clustering algorithms.

In the information processing world of today, no treatment of the field is complete without addressing the most frequently used retrieval paradigm, the World Wide Web. Thus, in Chapter 8, we describe the encompassing topic of the Web, namely, distributed information retrieval systems. We overview some of the early theoretical foundations and culminate with a discussion of peer-to-peer information retrieval.

The problem of searching document collections to find relevant documents has been addressed for more than forty years. However, until the advent of the Text REtrieval Conference (TREC) in 1990 (which is hosted by the National Institute of Standards and Technology), there was no standard test bed to judge information retrieval algorithms. Without the existence of a standard test data collection and a standard set of queries, there was no effective mechanism by which to objectively compare the algorithms. Many of these algorithms were run against only a few megabytes of text. It was hoped that the performance of these would scale to larger document collections. A seminal paper showed that some approaches that perform well on small document collections did not perform as well on large collections [Blair and Maron, 1985].

We include a brief description of TREC in Chapter 9 — our final chapter. Given all of the models, utilities, and performance enhancements proposed over the years, clearly measures and procedures to evaluate their effectiveness in terms of accuracy and processing times are needed. Indeed, that was part of the motivation behind the creation of the benchmark data and query sets and evaluation forum called TREC. Today, TREC serves as the de facto forum for comparison across systems and approaches. Unfortunately, only accuracy evaluations are currently supported. Hopefully, in the future, processing efficiency will also be evaluated.

We conclude this book with a discussion of the current limitations of information retrieval systems. We review our successes and project future needs. It is our hope that after reading this text, you the reader, will be interested in furthering the field of information retrieval. In our future editions, we hope to incorporate your contributions.

Chapter 2

RETRIEVAL STRATEGIES

Retrieval strategies assign a measure of similarity between a query and a document. These strategies are based on the common notion that the more often terms are found in both the document and the query, the more "relevant" the document is deemed to be to the query. Some of these strategies employ counter measures to alleviate problems that occur due to the ambiguities inherent in language—the reality that the same concept can often be described with many different terms (e.g., *new york* and *the big apple* can refer to the same concept). Additionally, the same term can have numerous semantic definitions (terms like *bark* and *duck* have very different meanings in their noun and verb forms).

A retrieval strategy is an algorithm that takes a query Q and a set of documents $D_1, D_2, \ldots, D_n$ and identifies the Similarity Coefficient SC(Q,D_i) for each of the documents $1 \leq i \leq n$. (Note: SC is short for Similarity Coefficient, sometimes it is written RSV for Retrieval Status Value).

The retrieval strategies identified are:

- **Vector Space Model**—Both the query and each document are represented as vectors in the term space. A measure of the similarity between the two vectors is computed.

- **Probabilistic Retrieval**—A probability based on the likelihood that a term will appear in a relevant document is computed for each term in the collection. For terms that match between a query and a document, the similarity measure is computed as the combination of the probabilities of each of the matching terms.

- **Language Models**—A language model is built for each document, and the likelihood that the document will *generate* the query is computed.

- **Inference Networks**—A Bayesian network is used to infer the relevance of a document to a query. This is based on the "evidence" in a document that allows an inference to be made about the relevance of the document. The strength of this inference is used as the similarity coefficient.

- **Boolean Indexing**—A score is assigned such that an initial Boolean query results in a ranking. This is done by associating a weight with each query term so that this weight is used to compute the similarity coefficient.

- **Latent Semantic Indexing**—The occurrence of terms in documents is represented with a term-document matrix. The matrix is reduced via Singular Value Decomposition (SVD) to filter out the noise found in a document so that two documents which have the same semantics are located close to one another in a multi-dimensional space.

- **Neural Networks**—A sequence of "neurons," or nodes in a network, that fire when activated by a query triggering links to documents. The strength of each link in the network is transmitted to the document and collected to form a similarity coefficient between the query and the document. Networks are "trained" by adjusting the weights on links in response to predetermined relevant and irrelevant documents.

- **Genetic Algorithms**—An optimal query to find relevant documents can be generated by evolution. An initial query is used with either random or estimated term weights. New queries are generated by modifying these weights. A new query survives by being close to known relevant documents and queries with less "fitness" are removed from subsequent generations.

- **Fuzzy Set Retrieval**—A document is mapped to a fuzzy set (a set that contains not only the elements but a number associated with each element that indicates the strength of membership). Boolean queries are mapped into fuzzy set intersection, union, and complement operations that result in a strength of membership associated with each document that is relevant to the query. This strength is used as a similarity coefficient.

For a given retrieval strategy, many different utilities are employed to improve the results of the retrieval strategy. These are described in Chapter 3. Note that some strategies and utilities are based on very different mathematical constructs. For example, a probabilistic retrieval strategy should theoretically not be used in conjunction with a thesaurus based on the vector space model. However, it might be the case that such a combination could improve effectiveness. We merely note that care should be taken when mixing and matching strategies and utilities that are based on very different mathematical models.

Attempting to refine the query, most of these utilities add or remove terms from the initial query. Others simply refine the focus of the query (using sub-documents or passages instead of whole documents). The key is that each of these utilities (although rarely presented as such) are plug-and-play utilities that should work with an arbitrary retrieval strategy.

Before delving into the details of each strategy, we wish to somewhat caution the reader. In our attempt to present the algorithms in their original form, we intentionally left inconsistencies present. For example, some inventors used $\ln(x)$ while other use $\log(x)$ to achieve a slow growing function. Clearly, we are aware that these functions are strictly a constant multiple of each other, but we felt that presenting the original description was still advantageous although it does introduce some minor confusion. Towards clarity, we tried to use common notation across strategies and provided a running example that uses the same query and documents regardless of each strategy.

2.1 Vector Space Model

The vector space model computes a measure of similarity by defining a vector that represents each document, and a vector that represents the query [Salton et al., 1975]. The model is based on the idea that, in some rough sense, the meaning of a document is conveyed by the words used. If one can represent the words in the document by a vector, it is possible to compare documents with queries to determine how similar their content is. If a query is considered to be like a document, a similarity coefficient (SC) that measures the similarity between a document and a query can be computed. Documents whose content, as measured by the terms in the document, correspond most closely to the content of the query are judged to be the most relevant. Figure 2.1 illustrates the basic notion of the vector space model in which vectors that represent a query and three documents are illustrated.

This model involves constructing a vector that represents the terms in the document and another vector that represents the terms in the query. Next, a method must be chosen to measure the closeness of any document vector to the query vector. One could look at the magnitude of the difference vector between two vectors, but this would tend to make any large document appear to be not relevant to most queries, which typically are short. The traditional method of determining closeness of two vectors is to use the size of the angle between them. This angle is computed by using the inner product (or dot product); however, it is not necessary to use the actual angle. Any monotonic function of the angle suffices. Often the expression "similarity coefficient" is used instead of an angle. Computing this number is done in a variety of ways, but the inner product generally plays a prominent role. Underlying this whole discussion is the idea that a document and a query are similar to the extent that their associated vectors point in the same general direction.

There is one component in these vectors for every distinct term or concept that occurs in the document collection. Consider a document collection with only two distinct terms, α and β. All vectors contain only two components, the first component represents occurrences of α, and the second represents occurrences of β. The simplest means of constructing a vector is to place a one in the corresponding vector component if the term appears, and a zero if the term does not appear. Consider a document, D_1, that contains two occurrences of term α and zero occurrences of term β. The vector $< 1, 0 >$ represents this document using a binary representation. This binary representation can be used to produce a similarity coefficient, but it does not take into account the frequency of a term within a document. By extending the representation to include a count of the number of occurrences of the terms in each component, the frequency of the terms can be considered. In this example, the vector would now appear as $< 2, 0 >$.

A simple example is given in Figure 2.2. A component of each vector is required for each distinct term in the collection. Using the toy example of a language with a two word vocabulary (only *A* and *I* are valid terms), all queries and documents can be represented in two dimensional space. A query and three documents are given along with their corresponding vectors and a graph of these vectors. The similarity coefficient between the query and the documents can be computed as the distance from the query to the two vectors. In this example, it can be seen that document one is represented by the same vector as the query so it will have the highest rank in the result set.

Instead of simply specifying a list of terms in the query, a user is often given the opportunity to indicate that one term is more important than another. This was done initially with manually assigned term weights selected by users. Another approach uses automatically assigned weights — typically based on the frequency of a term as it occurs across the entire document collection. The idea was that a term that occurs infrequently should be given a higher weight than a term that occurs frequently. Similarity coefficients that employed automatically assigned weights were compared to manually assigned weights [Salton, 1969, Salton, 1970b]. It was shown that automatically assigned weights perform at least as well as manually assigned weights [Salton, 1969, Salton, 1970b]. Unfortunately, these results did not include the relative weight of the term across the entire collection.

The value of a collection weight was studied in the 1970's. The conclusion was that relevance rankings improved if collection-wide weights were included. Although relatively small document collections were used to conduct the experiments, the authors still concluded that, "in so far as anything can be called a solid result in information retrieval research, this is one" [Robertson and Sparck Jones, 1976].

Figure 2.1. Vector Space Model

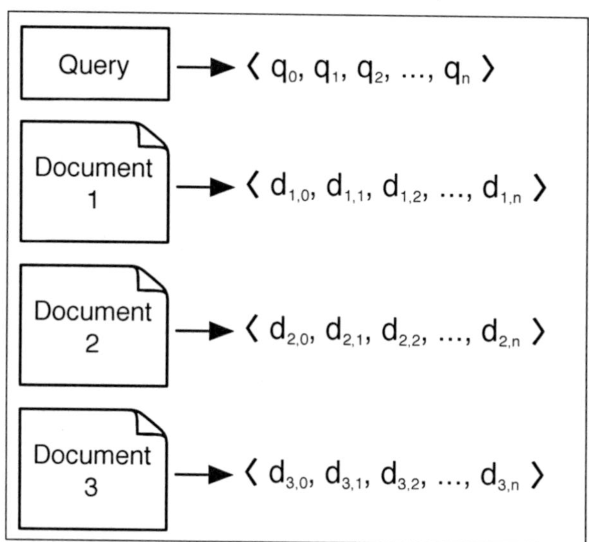

This more formal definition, and slightly larger example, illustrates the use of weights based on the collection frequency. Weight is computed using the *Inverse Document Frequency (IDF)* corresponding to a given term.

To construct a vector that corresponds to each document, consider the following definitions:

t = number of distinct terms in the document collection

tf_{ij}= number of occurrences of term t_j in document D_i. This is referred to as the *term frequency*.

df_j= number of documents which contain t_j. This is the *document frequency*.

idf_j= $\log(\frac{d}{df_j})$ where d is the total number of documents. This is the *inverse document frequency*.

The vector for each document has n components and contains an entry for each distinct term in the entire document collection. The components in the vector are filled with weights computed for each term in the document collection. The terms in each document are automatically assigned weights based

Figure 2.2. Vector Space Model with a Two Term Vocabulary

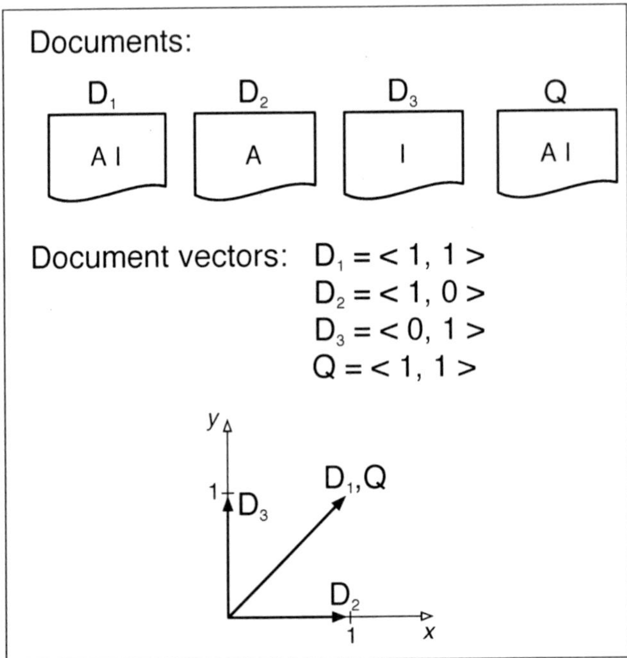

on how frequently they occur in the entire document collection and how often a term appears in a particular document. The weight of a term in a document increases the more often the term appears in one document and decreases the more often it appears in all other documents.

A weight computed for a term in a document vector is non-zero only if the term appears in the document. For a large document collection consisting of numerous small documents, the document vectors are likely to contain mostly zeros. For example, a document collection with 10,000 distinct terms results in a 10,000-dimensional vector for each document. A given document that has only 100 distinct terms will have a document vector that contains 9,900 zero-valued components.

The weighting factor for a term in a document is defined as a combination of term frequency, and inverse document frequency. That is, to compute the value of the jth entry in the vector corresponding to document i, the following equation is used:

$$d_{ij} = tf_{ij} \times idf_j$$

Consider a document collection that contains a document, D_1, with ten occurrences of the term *green* and a document, D_2, with only five occurrences of the term *green.* If *green* is the only term found in the query, then document D_1 is ranked higher than D_2.

When a document retrieval system is used to query a collection of documents with t distinct collection-wide terms, the system computes a vector D $(d_{i1}, d_{i2}, \ldots, d_{it})$ of size t for each document. The vectors are filled with term weights as described above. Similarly, a vector Q $(w_{q1}, w_{q2}, \ldots, w_{qt})$ is constructed for the terms found in the query.

A simple similarity coefficient (SC) between a query Q and a document D_i is defined by the dot product of two vectors. Since a query vector is similar in length to a document vector, this same measure is often used to compute the similarity between two documents. We discuss this application of an SC as it applies to document clustering in Section 3.2.

$$SC(Q, D_i) = \sum_{j=1}^{t} w_{qj} \times d_{ij}$$

2.1.1 Example of Similarity Coefficient

Consider a case insensitive query and document collection with a query Q and a document collection consisting of the following three documents:

Q: "gold silver truck"
D_1: "Shipment of gold damaged in a fire"
D_2: "Delivery of silver arrived in a silver truck"
D_3: "Shipment of gold arrived in a truck"

In this collection, there are three documents, so $d = 3$. If a term appears in only one of the three documents, its *idf* is $\log \frac{d}{df_j} = \log \frac{3}{1} = 0.477$. Similarly, if a term appears in two of the three documents its *idf* is $\log \frac{3}{2} = 0.176$, and a term which appears in all three documents has an *idf* of $\log \frac{3}{3} = 0$.

The idf for the terms in the three documents is given below:

$idf_a = 0$
$idf_{arrived} = 0.176$
$idf_{damaged} = 0.477$
$idf_{delivery} = 0.477$
$idf_{fire} = 0.477$
$idf_{in} = 0$
$idf_{of} = 0$
$idf_{silver} = 0.477$
$idf_{shipment} = 0.176$
$idf_{truck} = 0.176$

$idf_{gold} = 0.176$

Document vectors can now be constructed. Since eleven terms appear in the document collection, an eleven-dimensional document vector is constructed. The alphabetical ordering given above is used to construct the document vector so that t_1 corresponds to term number one which is *a* and t_2 is *arrived*, etc. The weight for term i in vector j is computed as the $idf_i \times tf_{ij}$. The document vectors are shown in Table 2.1.

Table 2.1. Document Vectors

docid	a	arrived	damaged	delivery	fire	gold	in	of	shipment	silver	truck
D_1	0	0	.477	0	.477	.176	0	0	.176	0	0
D_2	0	.176	0	.477	0	0	0	0	0	.954	.176
D_3	0	.176	0	0	0	.176	0	0	.176	0	.176
Q	0	0	0	0	0	.176	0	0	0	.477	.176

$$\begin{aligned} SC(Q, D_1) &= (0)(0) + (0)(0) + (0)(0.477) + (0)(0) \\ &\quad +(0)(0.477) + (0.176)(0.176) + (0)(0) + (0)(0) \\ &\quad +(0)(0.176) + (0.477)(0) + (0.176)(0) \\ &= (0.176)^2 \approx 0.031 \end{aligned}$$

Similarly,

$$SC(Q, D_2) = (0.954)(0.477) + (0.176)^2 \approx 0.486$$

$$SC(Q, D_3) = (0.176)^2 + (0.176)^2 \approx 0.062$$

Hence, the ranking would be D_2, D_3, D_1.

Implementations of the vector space model and other retrieval strategies typically use an inverted index to avoid a lengthy sequential scan through every document to find the terms in the query. Instead, an inverted index is generated prior to the user issuing any queries. Figure 2.3 illustrates the structure of the inverted index. An entry for each of the n terms is stored in a structure called the *index*. For each term, a pointer references a logical linked list called the *posting list*. The posting list contains an entry for each unique document that contains the term. In the figure below, the posting list contains both a document identifier and the term frequency. (In practice, structures more efficient than linked lists are often used, but conceptually they serve the same purpose).

The posting list in the figure indicates that term t_1 appears once in document one and twice in document ten. An entry for an arbitrary term t_i indicates that it occurs tf times in document j. Details of inverted index construction and use are provided in Chapter 5, but it is useful to know that inverted indexes are commonly used to improve run-time performance of various retrieval strategies.

Figure 2.3. Inverted Index

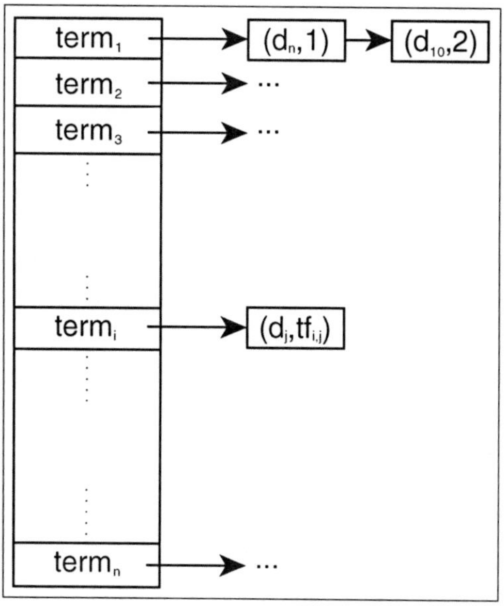

Early work described the vector space model in the late 1960's [Salton and Lesk, 1968]. This model became popular in the mid-1970's [Salton et al., 1975] and is still an extremely popular means of computing a measure of similarity between a query and a document [TREC, 2003]. The measure is important as it is used by a retrieval system to identify which documents are displayed to the user. Typically, the user requests the top n documents, and these are displayed ranked according to the similarity coefficient.

Subsequently, work on term weighting was done to improve on the basic combination of *tf-idf* weights [Salton and Buckley, 1988]. Many variations were studied, and the following weight for term j in document i was identified as a good performer:

$$w_{ij} = \frac{(\log tf_{ij} + 1.0) * idf_j}{\sum_{j=1}^{t}[(\log tf_{ij} + 1.0) * idf_j]^2}$$

The motivation for this weight is that a single matching term with a high term frequency can skew the effect of remaining matches between a query and a given document. To avoid this, the $\log(tf) + 1$ is used reduce the range of term frequencies. A variation on the basic theme is to use weight terms in the query differently than terms in the document.

One term weighting scheme, referred to as *lnc.ltc*, was effective. It uses a document weight of $(1+\log(tf))(idf)$ and query weight of $(1+\log(tf))$. The label *lnc.ltc* is of the form: *qqq.ddd* where *qqq* refers to query weights and *ddd* refers to document weights. The three letters: *qqq* or *ddd* are of the form *xyz*.

The first letter, *x*, is either n, l, or a. n indicates the "natural" term frequency or just tf is used. l indicates that the logarithm is used to scale down the weight so $1 + \log(tf)$ is used. a indicates that an augmented weight was used where the weight is $0.5 + 0.5 \times \frac{tf}{tf_{max}}$.

The second letter, *y*, indicates whether or not the idf was used. A value of n indicates that no idf was used while a value of t indicates that the idf was used.

The third letter, *z*, indicates whether or not document length normalization was used. By normalizing for document length, we are trying to reduce the impact document length might have on retrieval (see Equation 2.1). A value of n indicates no normalization was used, a value of c indicates the standard cosine normalization was used, and a value of u indicates pivoted length normalization was used in [Singhal, 1997].

2.1.2 Similarity Measures

Several different means of comparing a query vector with a document vector have been implemented. These are well documented and are presented here simply as a quick review. The most common of these is the cosine measure where the cosine of the angle between the query and document vector is given:

$$SC(Q, D_i) = \frac{\sum_{j=1}^{t} w_{qj} d_{ij}}{\sqrt{\sum_{j=1}^{t} (d_{ij})^2 \sum_{j=1}^{t} (w_{qj})^2}}$$

Since the $\sqrt{\sum_{j=1}^{t} (w_{qj})^2}$ appears in the computation for every document, the cosine coefficient should give the same relevance results as dividing the inner product by the magnitude of the document vector. Note that the cosine measure "normalizes" the result by considering the length of the document. With the inner product measure, a longer document can result in a higher score simply because it is longer, and thus, has a higher chance of containing terms that match the query—not necessarily because it is relevant.

The Dice coefficient is defined as:

$$SC(Q, D_i) = \frac{2\sum_{j=1}^{t} w_{qj} d_{ij}}{\sum_{j=1}^{t}(d_{ij})^2 \sum_{j=1}^{t}(w_{qj})^2}$$

The Jaccard coefficient is defined as:

$$SC(Q, D_i) = \frac{\sum_{j=1}^{t} w_{qj} d_{ij}}{\sum_{j=1}^{t}(d_{ij})^2 + \sum_{j=1}^{t}(w_{qj})^2 - \sum_{j=1}^{t} w_{qj} d_{ij}}$$

The cosine measure levels the playing field by dividing the computation by the length of the document vector. The assumption used in the cosine measure is that document length has no impact on relevance. Without a normalization factor, longer documents are more likely to be found relevant simply because they have more terms which increases the likelihood of a match. Dividing by the document vector removes the size of the document from consideration.

It turns out that (at least for the TREC data), this basic assumption is not correct. Taking all of the relevant documents found for a set of fifty TREC queries, Singhal found that more documents judged to be relevant actually were found in longer documents [Singhal, 1997]. The reason for this might be that a longer document simply has more opportunity to have some components that are indeed relevant to a given query.

To identify a means of adjusting the normalization factor, Singhal compared the likelihood of relevance with the likelihood of retrieval in a collection where the documents relevant to a set of queries was known. Ideally, if the probability of retrieval and the probability of relevance are both plotted against the length of the document, the two curves should be roughly the same. Since this is not the case (the two curves actually cross), there must be a document length in which the probability of relevance equals the probability of retrieval. Before this point (referred to as the *pivot*), a document is more likely to be retrieved than relevant. After this point, the reverse is true. Once the pivot is found, a "correction factor" can be used to adjust the normalization. The "correction factor" is computed from a linear equation whose value at *pivot* is equal to *pivot* and whose slope is selected to increase the normalization for shorter documents so that their probability of selection is equal to their probability of relevance. Thus, the similarity coefficient is:

$$SC(Q, D_i) = \frac{\sum_{j=1}^{t} w_{qj} d_{ij}}{(1.0 - s)p + (s)\sqrt{\sum_{j=1}^{t}(d_{ij})^2}}$$

This scheme has two variables: s and p for the slope and pivot, respectively. However, it is possible to express the slope as a function of pivot. Singhal selects as pivot the average normalization factor taken over the entire collection prior to any correction and adjusts the slope accordingly. At the same time the normalization factor is divided by $(1.0 - s)p$. The resulting equation for the similarity coefficient:

$$SC(Q, D_i) = \frac{\sum_{j=1}^{t} w_{qj} d_{ij}}{(1.0 - s) + (s)\frac{\sqrt{\sum_{j=1}^{t}(d_{ij})^2}}{avgn}} \tag{2.1}$$

where $avgn$ is the average document normalization factor before any correction is made.

The pivoted scheme works fairly well for short and moderately long documents, but extremely long documents tend to be more favored than those without any normalization. To remedy this, the number of unique terms in a document, $|d_i|$ is proposed as the normalization function prior to any adjustment.

A final adjustment is made to account for extremely high term frequencies that occur in very large documents. First, a weight of $(1 + \log tf)$ is used to scale the frequency. To account for longer documents, an individual term weight is divided by the weight given to the average term frequency.

The new weight, d_{ij}, is computed as—

$$d_{ij} = \frac{1 + \log tf}{1 + \log(atf)}$$

Using this new weight, and dividing it by the correction factor gives the following equation:

$$SC(Q, D_i) = \frac{\sum_{j=1}^{t} w_{qj} d_{ij}}{((1.0 - s)p + (s)(|d_i|))} \tag{2.2}$$

We then compute the average number of unique terms in a document for a given collection and use this as the pivot, p. Once this is done, the collection can be trained for a good slope. Equation 2.2 is referred to as *pivoted unique normalization* and it was shown to provide improved effectiveness over *pivoted cosine normalization* given in Equation 2.1. The modified normalization factor makes it more likely to retrieve longer documents and consistently shows about a ten percent improvement for TREC queries.

It should also be noted that the vector space model assumes terms are independent. One approach to alleviating the question of term independence in the vector space model is to change the basis. Although changing the basis does not totally eliminate the problem, it can reduce it. The idea is to pick a basis vector for each combination of terms that exist in a document (regardless of the number of occurrences of the term). The new basis vectors can be made mutually orthogonal and can be scaled to be unit vectors. The documents and the query can be expressed in terms of the new basis vectors. Using this procedure in conjunction with other (possibly probabilistic) methods avoids independence assumptions, but in practice, it has not been shown to significantly improve effectiveness.

2.2 Probabilistic Retrieval Strategies

The probabilistic model computes the similarity coefficient (SC) between a query and a document as the probability that the document will be relevant to the query. This reduces the relevance ranking problem to an application of probability theory. A survey on probabilistic methods is given in [Fuhr, 1992].

Probability theory can be used to compute a measure of relevance between a query and a document. Two fundamentally different approaches were proposed. The first relies on usage patterns to predict relevance [Maron and Kuhns, 1960], the second uses each term in the query as clues as to whether or not a document is relevant [Robertson and Sparck Jones, 1976].

The original work on the use of probability theory to retrieve documents can be traced to Maron and Kuhns. Their work developed an area of research where the probability that a document will be relevant given a particular term is estimated.

All of the work on probabilistic retrieval stems from the concept of estimating a term's weight based on how often the term appears or does not appear in relevant documents and non-relevant documents, respectively. Section 2.2.1 describes the simple term weight model, a non-binary independence model is discussed in Section 2.2.2, and Sections 2.2.3 and 2.2.4 describe the Poisson and component-based models which have both performed well on the TREC collection. Finally, Section 2.2.5 focuses on two large issues with the model—parameter estimation and independence assumptions.

2.2.1 Simple Term Weights

The use of term weights is based on the Probability Ranking Principle (PRP), which assumes that optimal effectiveness occurs when documents are ranked based on an estimate of the probability of their relevance to a query [Robertson, 1977].

The key is to assign probabilities to components of the query and then use each of these as evidence in computing the final probability that a document is relevant to the query.

The terms in the query are assigned weights which correspond to the probability that a particular term, in a match with a given query, will retrieve a relevant document. The weights for each term in the query are combined to obtain a final measure of relevance.

Most of the papers in this area incorporate probability theory and describe the validity of independence assumptions, so a brief review of probability theory is in order.

Suppose we are trying to predict whether or not a softball team called the Salamanders will win one of its games. We might observe, based on past experience, that they usually win on sunny days when their best shortstop plays. This means that two pieces of evidence, outdoor-conditions and presence of good-shortstop, might be used. For any given game, there is a seventy five percent chance that the team will win if the weather is sunny and a sixty percent chance that the team will win if the shortstop plays. Therefore, we write:

P(win | sunny) = 0.75
P(win | good-shortstop) = 0.6

The conditional probability that the team will win given both situations is written as p(win | sunny, good-shortstop). This is read "the probability that the team will win given that there is a sunny day and the good-shortstop plays." We have two pieces of evidence indicating that the Salamanders will win. Intuition says that together the two pieces should be stronger than either alone. This method of combining them is to "look at the odds." A seventy-five percent chance of winning is a twenty-five percent chance of losing, and a sixty percent chance of winning is a forty percent chance of losing. Let us assume the independence of the pieces of evidence.

P(win | sunny, good-shortstop) = α
P(win | sunny) = β
P(win | good-shortstop) = γ

By Bayes' Theorem:

$$\alpha = \frac{P(win, sunny, good\text{–}shortstop)}{P(sunny, good\text{–}shortstop)} = \frac{P(sunny, good\text{–}shortstop|\mathrm{win})P(win)}{P(sunny, good\text{–}shortstop)}$$

Therefore:

$$\frac{\alpha}{1-\alpha} = \frac{P(sunny, good\text{–}shortstop|\mathrm{win})P(win)}{P(sunny, good\text{–}shortstop|\mathrm{lose})P(\mathrm{lose})}$$

Solving for the first term (because of the independence assumptions):

$$\frac{P(sunny, good\text{–}shortstop|\mathrm{win})}{P(sunny, good\text{–}shortstop|\mathrm{lose})} = \frac{P(sunny|\mathrm{win})P(good\text{–}shortstop|\mathrm{win})}{P(sunny|\mathrm{lose})P(good\text{–}shortstop|\mathrm{lose})}$$

Similarly,

$$\frac{\beta}{1-\beta} = \frac{P(sunny|\text{w}in)P(\text{w}in)}{P(sunny|lose)P(\text{lose})}$$

$$\frac{\gamma}{1-\gamma} = \frac{P(good\text{–}shortstop|\text{w}in)P(\text{w}in)}{P(good\text{–}shortstop|lose)P(\text{lose})}$$

Making all of the appropriate substitutions, we obtain:

$$\frac{\alpha}{1-\alpha} = \left(\frac{\beta}{1-\beta}\right)\left(\frac{P(\text{lose})}{P(\text{w}in)}\right)\left(\frac{\gamma}{1-\gamma}\right)\left(\frac{P(\text{lose})}{P(\text{w}in)}\right)\left(\frac{P(\text{w}in)}{P(\text{lose})}\right)$$

Simplifying:

$$\frac{\alpha}{1-\alpha} = \left(\frac{\beta}{1-\beta}\right)\left(\frac{\gamma}{1-\gamma}\right)\left(\frac{P(\text{lose})}{P(\text{w}in)}\right)$$

Assume the Salamanders are a 0.500 ball club (that is they win as often as they lose) and assume numeric values for β and γ of 0.6 and 0.75, respectively. We then obtain:

$$\frac{\alpha}{1-\alpha} = \left(\frac{0.6}{0.4}\right)\left(\frac{0.75}{0.25}\right)\left(\frac{0.500}{0.500}\right) = (1.5)(3.0)(1.0) = 4.5$$

Solving for α gives a value of $\frac{9}{11} = 0.818$.

Note the combined effect of both sunny weather and the good-shortstop results in a higher probability of success than either individual condition.

The key is the independence assumptions. The likelihood of the weather being nice and the good-shortstop showing up are completely independent. The chance the shortstop will show up is not changed by the weather. Similarly, the weather is not affected by the presence or absence of the good-shortstop. If the independence assumptions are violated : suppose the shortstop prefers sunny weather — special consideration for the dependencies is required. The independence assumptions also require that the weather and the appearance of the good-shortstop are independent given either a win or a loss.

For an information retrieval query, the terms in the query can be viewed as indicators that a given document is relevant. The presence or absence of query term A can be used to predict whether or not a document is relevant. Hence, after a period of observation, it is found that when term A is in both the query and the document, there is an x percent chance the document is relevant. We then assign a probability to term A. Assuming independence of terms, this can be done for each of the terms in the query. Ultimately, the product of all the weights can be used to compute the probability of relevance.

We know that independence assumptions are really not a good model of reality. Some research has investigated why systems with these assumptions have performed reasonably well, despite their theoretical problems [Cooper, 1991]. For example, a relevant document that has the term *apple* in response to a query for *apple pie* probably has a better chance of having the term *pie* than some other randomly selected term. Hence, the key independence assumption is violated.

Most work in the probabilistic model assumes independence of terms because handling dependencies involves substantial computation. It is unclear whether or not effectiveness is improved when dependencies are considered. We note that relatively little work has been done implementing these approaches. They are computationally expensive, but more importantly, they are difficult to estimate. It is necessary to obtain sufficient training data about term cooccurrence in both relevant and non-relevant documents. Typically, it is very difficult to obtain sufficient training data to estimate these parameters.

In figure 2.4, we illustrate the need for training data with most probabilistic models. A query with two terms, q_1 and q_2, is executed. Five documents are returned and an assessment is made that documents two and four are relevant. From this assessment, the probability that a document is relevant (or non-relevant) given that it contains term q_1 is computed. Likewise, the same probabilities are computed for term q_2. Clearly, these probabilities are estimates based on training data. The idea is that sufficient training data can be obtained so that when a user issues a query, a good estimate of which documents are relevant to the query can be obtained.

Consider a document, d_i, consisting of t terms $(w_1, w_2, \ldots, w_t)$, where w_i is the estimate that term i will result in this document being relevant. The weight or "odds" that document d_i is relevant is based on the probability of relevance for each term in the document. For a given term in a document, its contribution to the estimate of relevance for the entire document is computed as:

$$\frac{P(w_i|rel)}{P(w_i|nonrel)}$$

The question is then: How do we combine the odds of relevance for each term into an estimate for the entire document? Given our independence assumptions, we can multiply the odds for each term in a document to obtain the odds that the document is relevant. Taking the log of the product yields:

$$\log\left(\prod_{i=1}^{t} \frac{P(w_i|\ rel)}{P(w_i|\ nonrel)}\right) = \sum_{i=1}^{t} \log\left(\frac{P(w_i|rel)}{P(w_i|nonrel)}\right)$$

We note that these values are computed based on the assumption that terms will occur independently in relevant and non-relevant documents. The assumption is also made that if one term appears in a document, then it has no impact on whether or not another term will appear in the same document.

Figure 2.4. Training Data for Probabilistic Retrieval

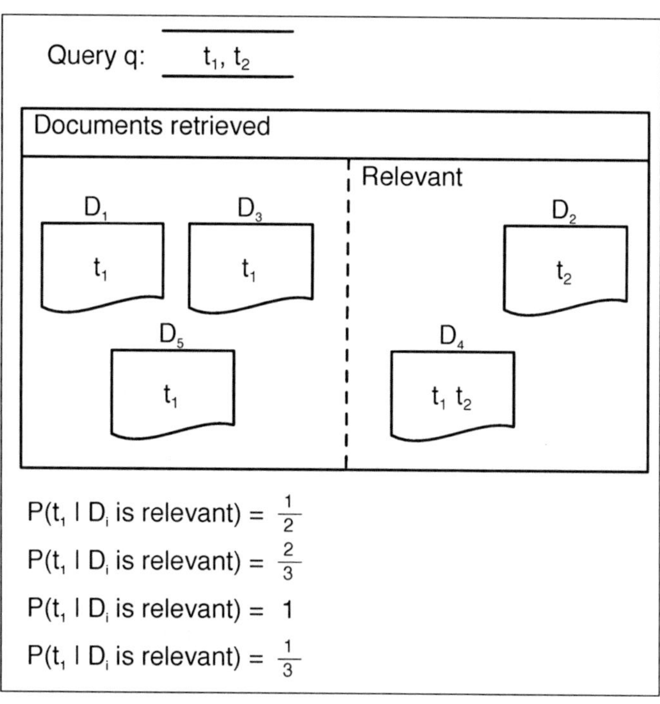

Now that we have described how the individual term estimates can be combined into a total estimate of relevance for the document, it is necessary to describe a means of estimating the individual term weights. Several different means of computing the probability of relevance and non-relevance for a given term were studied since the introduction of the probabilistic retrieval model. In their 1976 paper, Robertson and Sparck Jones considered several methods [Robertson and Sparck Jones, 1976]. They began by presenting two mutually exclusive independence assumptions:

I1: The distribution of terms in relevant documents is independent and their distribution in all documents is independent.

I2: The distribution of terms in relevant documents is independent and their distribution in non-relevant documents is independent.

They also presented two methods, referred to as ordering principles, for presenting the result set:

O1: Probable relevance is based only on the presence of search terms in the documents.

O2: Probable relevance is based on both the presence of search terms in documents and their absence from documents.

I1 indicates that terms occur randomly within a document—that is, the presence of one term in a document in no way impacts the presence of another term in the same document. This is analogous to our example in which the presence of the good-shortstop had no impact on the weather given a win. This also states that the distribution of terms across all documents is independent unconditionally for all documents—that is, the presence of one term in a document in no way impacts the presence of the same term in other documents. This is analogous to saying that the presence of a good-shortstop in one game has no impact on whether or not a good-shortstop will play in any other game. Similarly, the presence of good-shortstop in one game has no impact on the weather for any other game.

I2 indicates that terms in relevant documents are independent—that is, they satisfy I1 and terms in non-relevant documents also satisfy I1. Returning to our example, this is analogous to saying that the independence of a good-shortstop and sunny weather holds regardless of whether the team wins or loses.

O1 indicates that documents should be highly ranked only if they contain matching terms in the query (i.e., the only evidence used is which query terms are actually present in the document). We note that this ordering assumption is not commonly held today because it is also important to consider when query terms are not found in the document. This is inconvenient in practice. Most systems use an inverted index that identifies for each term, all occurrences of that term in a given document. If absence from a document is required, the index would have to identify all terms *not* in a document (for a detailed discussion of inverted indexes see Section 5.1). To avoid the need to track the absence of a term in a document, the estimate makes the zero point correspond to the probability of relevance of a document lacking all the query terms—as opposed to the probability of relevance of a random document. The zero point does not mean that we do not know anything: it simply means that we have some evidence for non-relevance. This has the effect of converting the O2 based weights to presence-only weights.

O2 takes O1 a little further and says that we should consider both the *presence* and the *absence* of search terms in the query. Hence, for a query that asks for term t_1 and term t_2—a document with just one of these terms should be ranked lower than a document with both terms.

Four weights are then derived based on different combinations of these ordering principles and independence assumptions. Given a term, t, consider the following quantities:

$$\begin{aligned} N &= \text{number of documents in the collection} \\ R &= \text{number of relevant documents for a given query } q \\ n &= \text{number of documents that contain term } t \\ r &= \text{number of relevant documents that contain term } t \end{aligned}$$

Choosing I1 and O1 yields the following weight:

$$w_1 = \log\left(\frac{\frac{r}{R}}{\frac{n}{N}}\right)$$

Choosing I2 and O1 yields the following weight:

$$w_2 = \log\left(\frac{\frac{r}{R}}{\frac{n-r}{N-R}}\right)$$

Choosing I1 and O2 yields the following weight:

$$w_3 = \log\left(\frac{\frac{r}{R-r}}{\frac{n}{N-n}}\right)$$

Choosing I2 and O2 yields the following weight:

$$w_4 = \log\left(\frac{\frac{r}{R-r}}{\frac{n-r}{(N-n)-(R-r)}}\right)$$

Robertson and Sparck Jones argue that O2 is correct and that I2 is more likely than I1 to describe what actually occurs. Hence, w_4 is most likely to yield the best results. They then present results that indicate that w_4 and w_3 performed better than w_1 and w_2. Most subsequent work starts with w_4 and extends it to contain other important components such as the within-document frequency of the term and the relative length of a document. We describe these extensions to w_4 in Section 2.2.3.

When incomplete relevance information is available, 0.5 is added to the weights to account for the uncertainty involved in estimating relevance. Robertson and Sparck Jones suggest that, "This procedure may seem somewhat arbitrary, but it does in fact have some statistical justification." The modified weighting function appears as:

$$w = \log\left(\frac{\frac{r+0.5}{(R-r)+0.5}}{\frac{(n-r)+0.5}{(N-n)-(R-r)+0.5}}\right)$$

The claimed advantage to the probabilistic model is that it is entirely based on probability theory. The implication is that other models have a certain arbitrary characteristic. They might perform well experimentally, but they lack a sound theoretical basis because the parameters are not easy to estimate. Either complete training data are required, or an inaccurate estimate must be made.

This debate is similar to one that occurs when comparing a relational to an object-oriented database management system (DBMS). Object-oriented DBMS are sometimes said to model "real world" data, but lack sound theoretical basis. Relational DBMS, on the other hand, have very solid set-theoretic underpinnings, but sometimes have problems modeling real data.

2.2.1.1 Example

Using the same example we used previously with the vector space model, we now show how the four different weights can be used for relevance ranking.

Again, the documents and the query are:

Q : "gold silver truck"
D_1: "Shipment of gold damaged in a fire."
D_2: "Delivery of silver arrived in a silver truck."
D_3: "Shipment of gold arrived in a truck."

Since training data are needed for the probabilistic model, we assume that these three documents are the training data and we deem documents D_2 and D_3 as relevant to the query.

To compute the similarity coefficient, we assign term weights to each term in the query. We then sum the weights of matching terms. There are four quantities we are interested in:

N = number of documents in the collection
n = number of documents indexed by a given term
R = number of relevant documents for the query
r = number of relevant documents indexed by the given term

These values are given in the Table 2.2 for each term in the query. As we stated previously, Robertson and Sparck Jones described the following four different weighting equations to estimate, for a given term, the likelihood that a document which contains the query term is relevant.

Table 2.2. Frequencies for Each Query Term

	gold	*silver*	*truck*
N	3	3	3
n	2	1	2
R	2	2	2
r	1	1	2

$$w_1 = \log \left[\frac{\frac{r}{R}}{\frac{n}{N}} \right]$$

$$w_2 = \log \left[\frac{\frac{r}{R}}{\frac{(n-r)}{(N-R)}} \right]$$

$$w_3 = \log \left[\frac{\frac{r}{(R-r)}}{\frac{n}{(N-n)}} \right]$$

$$w_4 = \log \left[\frac{\frac{r}{(R-r)}}{\frac{(n-r)}{(N-n)-(R-r)}} \right]$$

Note that with our collection, the weight for *silver* is infinite, since $(n-r) = 0$. This is because "silver" only appears in relevant documents. Since we are using this procedure in a predictive manner, Robertson and Sparck Jones recommended adding constants to each quantity [Robertson and Sparck Jones, 1976]. The new weights are:

$$w_1 = \log \left[\frac{\frac{(r+0.5)}{(R+1)}}{\frac{(n+1)}{(N+2)}} \right]$$

$$w_2 = \log \left[\frac{\frac{(r+0.5)}{(R+1)}}{\frac{(n-r+0.5)}{(N-R+1)}} \right]$$

$$w_3 = \log \left[\frac{\frac{(r+0.5)}{(R-r+0.5)}}{\frac{(n+1)}{(N-n+1)}} \right]$$

$$w_4 = \log\left[\frac{\frac{(r+0.5)}{(R-r+0.5)}}{\frac{(n-r+0.5)}{(N-n-(R-r)+0.5}}\right]$$

Using these equations, we derive the following weights:

gold

$$w_1 = \log\left[\frac{\frac{(1+0.5)}{(2+1)}}{\frac{(2+1)}{(3+2)}}\right] = \log\frac{0.5}{0.6} = -0.079$$

silver

$$w_1 = \log\left[\frac{\frac{(1+0.5)}{(2+1)}}{\frac{(1+1)}{(3+2)}}\right] = \log\frac{0.5}{0.4} = 0.097$$

truck

$$w_1 = \log\left[\frac{\frac{(2+0.5)}{(2+1)}}{\frac{(2+1)}{(3+2)}}\right] = \log\frac{0.833}{0.6} = 0.143$$

gold

$$w_2 = \log\left[\frac{\frac{(1+0.5)}{(2+1)}}{\frac{(2-1+0.5)}{(3-2+1)}}\right] = \log\frac{0.5}{0.75} = -0.176$$

silver

$$w_2 = \log\left[\frac{\frac{(1+0.5)}{(2+1)}}{\frac{(1-1+0.5)}{3-2+1}}\right] = \log\frac{0.5}{0.25} = 0.301$$

truck

$$w_2 = \log\left[\frac{\frac{(2+0.5)}{(2+1)}}{\frac{(2-2+0.5)}{3-2+1}}\right] = \log\frac{0.833}{0.25} = 0.523$$

gold

$$w_3 = \log\left[\frac{\frac{(1+0.5)}{(2-1+0.5)}}{\frac{(2+1)}{(3-2+1)}}\right] = \log\frac{1.0}{1.5} = -0.176$$

silver

$$w_3 = \log\left[\frac{\frac{(1+0.5)}{(2-1+0.5)}}{\frac{(1+1)}{(3-1+1)}}\right] = \log\frac{1.0}{0.667} = 0.176$$

truck

$$w_3 = \log\left[\frac{\frac{(2+0.5)}{(2-2+0.5)}}{\frac{(2+1)}{(3-2+1)}}\right] = \log\frac{5}{1.5} = 0.523$$

gold

$$w_4 = \log \left[\frac{\frac{(1+0.5)}{(2-1+0.5)}}{\frac{(2-1+0.5)}{(3-2-2+1+0.5)}} \right] = \log \frac{1}{3} = -0.477$$

silver

$$w_4 = \log \left[\frac{\frac{(1+0.5)}{(2-1+0.5)}}{\frac{(1-1+0.5)}{(3-1-2+1+0.5)}} \right] = \log \frac{1}{0.333} = 0.477$$

truck

$$w_4 = \log \left[\frac{\frac{(2+0.5)}{(2-2+0.5)}}{\frac{(2-2+0.5)}{(3-2-2+2+0.5)}} \right] = \log \left(\frac{5}{0.333} \right) = 1.176$$

The results are summarized in Table 2.3.

Table 2.3. Term Weights

	w_1	w_2	w_3	w_4
gold	-0.079	-0.176	-0.176	-0.477
silver	0.097	0.301	0.176	0.477
truck	0.143	0.523	0.523	1.176

Table 2.4. Document Weights

	w_1	w_2	w_3	w_4
D_1	-0.079	-0.176	-0.176	-0.477
D_2	0.240	0.824	0.699	1.653
D_3	0.064	0.347	0.347	0.699

The similarity coefficient for a given document is obtained by summing the weights of the terms present. Table 2.4 gives the similarity coefficients for each of the four different weighting schemes. For D_1, *gold* is the only term to appear so the weight for D_1 is just the weight for *gold*, which is -0.079. For D_2, *silver* and *truck* appear so the weight for D_2 is the sum of the weights for *silver* and *truck*, which is $0.097 + 0.143 = 0.240$. For D_3, *gold* and *truck* appear so the weight for D_3 is the sum for *gold* and *truck*, which is $-0.079 + 0.143 = 0.064$.

2.2.1.2 Results

Initial tests of the four weights were done on the 1,400 document Cranfield collection. These showed that the third and fourth weights performed somewhat comparably, but were superior to the first and second weights. An additional study against the 27,361 document UKCIS collection measured the difference in the first weight and the fourth weight [Sparck Jones, 1979a]. Again a significant improvement was found in the use of the fourth weight.

Two other baseline tests were run. The first simply ranked documents based on the number of term matches, the second test used inverse document frequency as an estimated weight. Both of these approaches were inferior to any of the four weights, but the use of the idf was better than simply counting term matches. In all cases, the ranking of the documents was D2, D3, D1—the same ranking that was obtained with the vector space model in Section 2.1.

The number of times a term appears in a given document is not used, as the weighting functions are based on whether or not the term appears in lots of relevant documents. Thus, if term t appears 50 times over the span of 10 relevant documents and term u appears only 10 times in the same relevant documents, they are given the same weight.

2.2.1.3 Incorporating Term Frequency

Term frequency was not used in the original probabilistic model. Croft and Harper incorporated term frequency weights in [Croft and Harper, 1979]. Relevance is estimated by including the probability that a term will appear in a given document, rather than the simple presence or absence of a term in a document. The term frequency is used to derive an estimate of how likely it is for the term to appear in a document. This new coefficient is given below.

$$SC(Q, D_j) = C \sum_{i=1}^{t} q_i d_{ij} + \sum_{i=1}^{t} P(d_{ij}) q_i d_{ij} \log \left(\frac{N - n_i}{n_i} \right)$$

The $P(d_{ij})$ indicates the probability that term i appears in document j, and can be estimated simply as the term frequency of term i in document j. Unfortunately, this frequency is not a realistic probability so another estimate, *normalized term frequency* is used. The normalized term frequency is computed as:

$$ntf_{ij} = \frac{tf_{ij}}{max(tf_{1j}, tf_{2j}, \ldots, tf_{tj})}$$

Normalized term frequency is the ratio of the term frequency of a given term to the maximum term frequency of any term in the document. If term i appears ten times in the document, and the highest term frequency of any other term in the document is 100, the ntf_{ij} is 0.1.

Croft and Harper compared the use of the normalized term frequency, the unnormalized term frequency, and a baseline without any use of term frequency for the Cranfield collection and the 11,429 document NPL collection. The results were statistically significant in that the normalized term frequency outperformed the baseline. In many cases, the unnormalized term frequency performed worse than the baseline.

2.2.2 Non-Binary Independence Model

The non-binary independence model developed by Yu, Meng, and Park incorporates term frequency and document length, somewhat naturally, into the calculation of term weights [Yu et al., 1989]. Once the term weights are computed, the vector space model (see Section 2.1) is used to compute an inner product for obtaining a final similarity coefficient.

The simple term weight approach estimates a term's weight based on whether or not the term appears in a relevant document. Instead of estimating the probability that a given term will identify a relevant document, the probability that a *term which appears tf times* will appear in a relevant document is estimated. For example, consider a ten document collection in which document one contains the term *blue* once and document two contains ten occurrences of the term *blue*. Assume both documents one and two are relevant, and the eight other documents are not relevant. With the simple term weight model, we would compute the P(Rel | *blue*) = 0.2 because *blue* occurs in two out of ten relevant documents.

With the non-binary independence model, we calculate a separate probability for each term frequency. Hence, we compute the probability that *blue* will occur one time P(1 | R) = 0.1, because it did occur one time in document one. The probability that *blue* will occur ten times is P(10 | R) = 0.1, because it did occur ten times in one out of ten documents.

To incorporate document length, weights are normalized based on the size of the document. Hence, if document one contains five terms and document two contains ten terms, we recompute the probability that *blue* occurs only once in a relevant document to the probability that *blue* occurs 0.5 times in a relevant document.

The probability that a term will result in a non-relevant document is also used. The final weight is computed as the ratio of the probability that a term will occur *tf* times in relevant documents to the probability that the term will occur *tf* times in non-relevant documents.

More formally:

$$\log \frac{P(d_i|R)}{P(d_i|N)}$$

where P($d_i|R$) is the probability that a relevant document will contain d_i occurrences of the $i^{\underline{th}}$ term, and P($d_i|N$) is the probability that a non-relevant document has d_i occurrences of the $i^{\underline{th}}$ term.

2.2.2.1 Example

Returning to our example, the documents and the query are:

Q : "gold silver truck"
D_1: "Shipment of gold damaged in a fire."
D_2: "Delivery of silver arrived in a silver truck."
D_3: "Shipment of gold arrived in a truck."

Table 2.5. Term to Document Mapping

docid	a	arrived	damaged	delivery	fire	gold	in	of	shipment	silver	truck
D_1	1	0	1	0	1	1	1	1	1	0	0
D_2	1	1	0	1	0	0	1	1	0	2	1
D_3	1	1	0	0	0	1	1	1	1	0	1
Q	0	0	0	0	0	1	0	0	0	1	1

Thus, we have three documents with eleven terms and a single query (see Table 2.5). The training data include both relevant and non-relevant documents. We assume that document two and three are relevant and document one is not relevant (we are free to do this as relevance, after all, is in the eyes of the beholder). Normalizing by document length yields as shown in Table 2.6:

Table 2.6. Normalized Document Length

docid	a	arrived	damaged	delivery	fire	gold	in	of	shipment	silver	truck
D_1	$\frac{1}{7}$	0	$\frac{1}{7}$	0	$\frac{1}{7}$	$\frac{1}{7}$	$\frac{1}{7}$	$\frac{1}{7}$	$\frac{1}{7}$	0	0
D_2	$\frac{1}{8}$	$\frac{1}{8}$	0	$\frac{1}{8}$	0	0	$\frac{1}{8}$	$\frac{1}{8}$	0	$\frac{1}{4}$	$\frac{1}{8}$
D_3	$\frac{1}{7}$	$\frac{1}{7}$	0	0	0	$\frac{1}{7}$	$\frac{1}{7}$	$\frac{1}{7}$	$\frac{1}{7}$	0	$\frac{1}{7}$

We do not normalize the query. The terms present in the query are *gold*, *silver*, and *truck*. For D_1 the weight of *gold* is

$$\log\left[\frac{P(\frac{1}{7}|R)}{P(\frac{1}{7}|N)}\right] = \log\frac{\frac{1}{2}}{1} = -0.3010.$$

Of the two relevant documents, one has a frequency of $\frac{1}{7}$ and one does not, so $P(\frac{1}{7}|R) = \frac{1}{2}$. However, the only non-relevant document has *gold* with a frequency of $\frac{1}{7}$, so $P(\frac{1}{7}|N) = 1$.

For *silver* in D_1 we obtain:

$$\log\left[\frac{P(0|R)}{P(0|N)}\right] = \log\frac{1}{2} = -0.3010.$$

Weights for each term and a given term frequency can be computed in this way for each term in a document. Vectors can then be constructed and a similarity coefficient can be computed between a query and each document.

With our example, there are only a few frequencies to consider, but a normal collection would have a large number of frequencies, especially if document length normalization is used. To alleviate this problem, it is possible to aggregate all of the frequencies into classes. Thus, all of the documents with zero frequency would be in one class, but for terms with positive term frequency, intervals $(0, f_1], (f_1, f_2], \ldots, (f_n, \infty)$ would be selected such that the intervals contain approximately equal numbers of terms. To obtain the weights, $P(d_i|R)$ and $P(d_i|N)$ are replaced by $P(d_i \in I_j|R)$ and $P(d_i \in I_j|N)$, respectively. I_j is the $j^{\underline{th}}$ interval $(f_{j-2}, f_{j-1}]$. The weight becomes:

$$\log\left[\frac{P(d_i \in I_j|R)}{P(d_i \in I_j|N)}\right]$$

2.2.3 Poisson Model

Robertson and Walker developed a probabilistic model which uses a Poisson distribution to estimate probabilities of relevance and incorporate term frequency and document length [Robertson and Walker, 1994]. In the standard probabilistic model, the weighting is given by:

$$w = \log\frac{p(1-q)}{q(1-p)}$$

where p is the probability that the term is present given that a document is relevant, and q is the probability that the term is present given that a document is not relevant.

To incorporate the term frequencies, p_{tf} is used. This indicates the probability that the term is present with frequency tf, given relevance and q_{tf} is the corresponding probability for non-relevance. The subscript 0 denotes the absence of a term. The weighting then becomes:

$$w = \log\frac{(p_{tf})(q_0)}{(q_{tf})(p_0)}$$

The assumption is made that terms randomly occur within the document according to the Poisson distribution.

$$p(tf) = e^{-m}\frac{m^{tf}}{tf!}$$

The parameter m differs according to whether or not the document is *about* the concepts represented by the query terms. This leads to the weighting:

$$w = \log\frac{(p' + (1-p')(\frac{\mu}{\lambda})^{tf}e^{j})(q'e^{(-j)} + (1-q'))}{(q' + (1-q')(\frac{\mu}{\lambda})^{tf}e^{j})(p'e^{(-j)} + (1-p'))}$$

where λ is the Poisson mean for documents which are about the term t,
μ is the Poisson mean for documents which are not about the term t,
j is the difference: $\lambda - \mu$,
p' is the probability that a document is about t given that it is relevant, and
q' is the probability that a document is about t given that it is not relevant.

The difficulty with this weight is in its application; it is unlikely that there will be direct evidence for any of the four parameters: p', q', λ, μ. The shape of the curve is used, and simpler functions are found, based on the more readily observable quantities: term frequency and document length, that have similar shape. To incorporate term frequency, we use the function:

$$w' = w\frac{tf}{k_1 + tf}$$

where w is the standard probabilistic weight, and k_1 is an unknown constant whose value depends on the collection and must be determined experimentally.

Document length is also taken into account. The simplest means to account for document length is to modify the equation given above for w' by substituting:

$$k_1 = \frac{(k_1)(d)}{\Delta}$$

$$d = \text{document length}$$
$$\Delta = \text{average document length}$$

The new equation for w' is:

$$w' = w\left(\frac{tf}{\frac{(k_1)(d)}{\Delta} + tf}\right)$$

The symmetry between documents and queries is used to incorporate the query term frequency in a fashion similar to document frequency. A tuning parameter k_1 is used to scale the effect of document term frequency. Similarly, another parameter k_3 is used to scale the query term frequency (qtf). Finally, a closer match to the 2-Poisson estimate can be attempted with an additional term possessing a scaling factor of k_2. This term is:

$$k_2 \left(|Q| \left(\frac{(\Delta - d)}{(\Delta + d)} \right) \right)$$

where k_2 is a constant that is experimentally determined, and $|Q|$ is the number of query terms. This term enables a high value of k_2 to give additional emphasis to documents that are shorter than average. These modifications result in the following similarity coefficient:

$$SC(Q, D_i) = \sum_{j=1}^{t} \log \left(\frac{\frac{r}{(R-r)}}{\frac{(n-r)}{(N-n)-(R-r)}} \right) \left(\frac{tf_{ij}}{\frac{(k_1 dl_i)}{\Delta} + tf_{ij}} \right) \left(\frac{qtf_j}{k_3 + qtf_j} \right) + \left((k_2)|Q| \left(\frac{(\Delta - dl_i)}{(\Delta + dl_i)} \right) \right)$$

where:

N	=	number of documents in the collection
n	=	number of documents indexed by a given term
R	=	number of relevant documents for the query
r	=	number of relevant documents indexed by the given term
tf_{ij}	=	term frequency of term j in document i
qtf_j	=	term frequency of term j in query Q
dl_i	=	number of terms in document i
$\|Q\|$	=	number of terms in the query
Δ	=	average document length
k_1, k_2, k_3	=	tuning parameters

Small values for k_1 and k_3 have the effect of reducing the impact of term frequency and query term frequency. If either is zero, the effect is to eliminate that quantity. Large values of k_1 and k_3 result in significantly reducing the size of the first term.

Including a factor of $(k_1 + 1)$ and $(k_3 + 1)$ in the numerator does not affect the overall ranking because these factors apply equally to all documents.

However, it does allow for the use of large values of k_1 or k_3 without reducing the magnitude of the first term. Additionally, this normalizes the impact of the tuning parameters. The idea is that when the term frequency is one, there is no need to change the original weights.

To normalize for document length, the similarity measure also includes a denominator of Δ in the first term. This makes good sense if the only reason a document is long is because it is simply giving more detail about the topic. In this case, long documents should not be weighted any more than short documents. However, it could be that a document is long because it is discussing several unrelated topics. In this case, long documents should be penalized. A new tuning parameter, b, allows for tuning a query based on the nature of the document collection. This parameter is incorporated by substituting K for k_1 in the factor involving tf_{ij}, where:

$$K = k_1\left((1-b) + b\left(\frac{dl_i}{\Delta}\right)\right)$$

Incorporating the tuning parameter b and placing $(k_1 + 1)$ and $(k_3 + 1)$ in the numerator yields:

$$\begin{aligned} SC(Q, D_i) &= \sum_{j=1}^{t} \log\left(\frac{\frac{r}{(R-r)}}{\frac{(n-r)}{(N-n)-(R-r)}}\right)\left(\frac{(k_1+1)tf_{ij}}{K+tf_{ij}}\right)\left(\frac{(k_3+1)qtf_j}{k_3+qtf_j}\right) \\ &\quad + \left((k_2)|Q|\frac{\Delta - dl}{\Delta + dl_i}\right) \end{aligned}$$

For the experiments conducted in [Robertson et al., 1995], these values were taken as ($k_1 = 1$, $k_2 = 0$, $k_3 = 8$, $b = 0.6$).

2.2.3.1 Example

Using the same documents and query as before, we previously computed w_4 as:

gold = -0.477
silver = 0.477
truck = 1.176
avgdl = $\frac{22}{3} = 7.33$

Using the same parameters for k_1, k_2, k_3, b, we compute values for dl_i:

$dl_1 = 7$
$dl_2 = 8$
$dl_3 = 7$

For D_1 the only match with the query is "gold" which appears with a $tf = 1$; so, the SC for D_1 is just the value for "gold" (Note the length of dl for D_1 is seven).

$$K = 1\left((1 - 0.6) + \frac{(0.6)(7)}{7.33}\right) = 0.973$$

Now that we have the value of K, it is possible to compute the similarity coefficient for D_1. The coefficient is a summation for all terms, but only one term "gold" will have a non-zero value. We start with the value of $w_4 = -0.477$ which was obtained in Section 2.2.1.1.

$$SC(Q, D_1) = -0.477\left(\frac{(1+1)(1)}{0.973+1}\right)\left(\frac{8+1}{8+1}\right) = -0.477\left(\frac{2}{1.973}\right) = -0.484$$

For D_2 the terms that match the query "silver" and "truck" result in non-zero values in the summation.

$$K = 1\left(0.4 + \frac{(0.6)(8)}{7.33}\right) = 1.055$$

For "silver", tf_{12} = 2:

$$w_4 = 0.477\left(\frac{(1+1)(2)}{1.055+2}\right)\left(\frac{(8+1)(2)}{8+2}\right) = 1.124$$

For "truck", tf_{22} = 1:

$$w_4 = 1.176\left(\frac{(1+1)(1)}{1.055+1}\right)\left(\frac{(8+1)(1)}{8+1}\right) = 1.145$$

$$SC(Q, D_2) = 1.124 + 1.145 = 2.269$$

For D_3, $dl = 7$ so K = 0.973 (as in the case of D_1). We have two terms "gold" and "truck" that both appear once. For "gold", tf_{13} = 1.

$$w_4 = -0.477\left(\frac{(1+1)(1)}{0.973+1}\right)\left(\frac{(8+1)(1)}{8+1}\right) = -0.484$$

For "truck", tf_{23} = 1.

$$w_4 = 1.176\left(\frac{(1+1)(1)}{0.973+1}\right)\left(\frac{(8+1)(1)}{8+1}\right) = 1.192$$

$$SC(Q, D_3) = -0.484 + 1.192 = 0.708$$

Comparing the SC, with the term frequency, to the base SC, without the term frequency we see in Table 2.7 that again, the document ranking is the same: D_2, D_3, D_1.

Table 2.7. Poisson Model: Final Similarity Measure

	No tf	tf
D_1	-0.477	-0.484
D_2	1.653	2.269
D_3	0.699	0.708

2.2.4 Term Components

A variation on the standard probabilistic model is given in [Kwok, 1990]. The premise of the algorithm is to rank documents based on the components of the document. For example, a document can be partitioned into multiple paragraphs, and a similarity coefficient can be computed for each paragraph. Once this is done, a measure is needed to combine the component similarity coefficients to develop a ranking for the entire document. Kwok proposes the use of a geometric mean (for n numbers, the $n^{\underline{th}}$ root of their product) to effectively average the individual components.

The algorithm used to rank a given component certainly can vary, and the size of a component can also vary. If the whole document is used as a component, then we are back at traditional probabilistic information retrieval.

The basic weight for a given component is defined as the ratio of the probability of the component being relevant to the probability that it is not relevant. This is:

$$w_{ak} = \ln\left(\frac{r_{ak}}{(1 - r_{ak})}\right) + \ln\left(\frac{(1 - s_{ak})}{s_{ak}}\right)$$

r_{ak} and s_{ak} are weights that can be estimated in one of three different ways:

- **Initial estimate using self-relevance**. A component which is relevant to itself, results in:

$$r_{ak} = \frac{q_{ak}}{L_a}$$

$$s_{ak} = \frac{F_k}{N_w}$$

where L_a is the number of components in the document, and F_k is the number of occurrences of term k in the collection. N_w is the number of distinct components in the collection.

- **Inverse collection term frequency (ICTF).** The estimate of s above is good because there are probably more non-relevant than relevant documents. Hence, a term that is infrequent in the entire collection has a low value of s_{ik}. Assume the initial estimate of r_{ak} is poor and just use a constant p. Using r_{ak} as a constant results in the whole weight being roughly equivalent to s_{ik}. s_{ik} is estimated by removing the one relevant document, d_{ik} from the estimates that use the whole collection. This is done by using the number of terms, d_{ik}, that match the assumed "relevant document." s_{ik} is then computed as:

$$s_{ik} = \left(\frac{F_k - d_{ik}}{N_w - L_i}\right)$$

Using p in our weight computation yields the following weight which is very close to the *idf*.

$$w_{ik} = \ln\left[\frac{p}{1-p}\right] + \ln\left[\frac{1-s_{ik}}{s_{ik}}\right]$$

- Essentially, weights are computed based on the use of feedback from the user. (Use of relevance feedback will be discussed in more detail in Section 3.1). Once the estimates are obtained, all that remains is to combine the component weights—in either query focused means, a document focused measure, or a combined measure. Using the query as focus, the query is given, and all the weights are computed as related to the query. The geometric mean is then computed for each of the components. This reduces to:

$$\sum_{i=1}^{k}\left(\frac{d_{ik}}{L_i}\right) w_{ak}$$

A document focused measure computes the components of the query and then averages them in relation to a given document. This reduces to:

$$\sum_{i=1}^{k}\left(\frac{q_{ik}}{L_i}\right) w_{ik}$$

The combined measure can then be obtained. This combined measure is simply the sum of the query focused and the document focused measures given as:

$$\sum_{i=1}^{k}\left(\frac{d_{ik}}{L_i}\right) w_{ak} + \sum_{i=1}^{k}\left(\frac{q_{ik}}{L_i}\right) w_{ik}$$

The component theory was shown to be comparable to term-based retrieval, and superior for retrieval in the presence of relevance feedback. The combination of query focused and document focused retrieval was almost always shown to be superior than either query focused or document focused retrieval.

2.2.5 Key Concerns with Probabilistic Models

Typically, probabilistic models must work around two fundamental problems: parameter estimation and independence assumptions. Parameter estimation refers to the problem that accurate probabilistic computations are based on the need to estimate relevance. Without a good training data set, it is often difficult to accurately estimate parameters. The second problem is the use of independence assumptions. It is clear that the presence of the term *new* increases the likelihood of the presence of the term *york* but many probabilistic models require this assumption even though it is not a realistic assumption.

2.2.5.1 Parameter Estimation

The need for good parameter estimation was clearly documented in the 1970's. Initial experiments with simple term weights partitioned the document collection into an *even* and an *odd* component. The even component was used as training data; after relevance information was obtained, it was used to retrieve data in the odd component. For many applications, the *a priori* relevance information is not known. A follow-up paper used reduced relevance information [Sparck Jones, 1979b]. The effect of using only the best one or two most relevant documents as training data, instead of using all relevant documents was measured. For the small Cranfield collection, results from using fewer relevant documents were comparable to using all relevant documents. Unfortunately, when the test was run on the larger UKCIS, the results with only two relevant documents were inferior to results using all relevant documents.

The initial model did not indicate how the process should start. Once relevance information is available (via a training set), it is possible to conduct new searches. In an on-line system where it is not possible to guess which queries will be asked in advance, it is not possible to use the weighting functions given above. They all require values for r and R which can only be obtained by running a query and examining the relevant documents. Certainly, it is possible to use another technique for the initial search, and then ask users for relevance information on the results of the initial search. This information can then be used for subsequent searches. This technique is called *relevance feedback* and is discussed in more detail in Section 3.1.

Using the probabilistic weights as a means of implementing relevance feedback relegates the probabilistic model to an interesting utility that can be applied to an arbitrary retrieval strategy. A cosine measure can be used to identify an initial ranking, and then the probabilistic weights can be used for relevance feedback.

Using the probabilistic model without any *a priori* relevance information creates problems which are addressed in [Croft and Harper, 1979]. In doing so, it becomes clear that the probabilistic model is a retrieval strategy that is capable of ranking documents without any other assistance. The key is that we assume (without any relevance information), the probability that a given term will induce relevance is equal for each term. Thus, the following similarity coefficient is obtained:

$$SC(Q, D_j) = C\sum_{i=1}^{t} q_i d_{ij} + \sum_{i=1}^{t} q_i d_{ij} \log \frac{N - n_i}{n_i}$$

$$\begin{aligned}
N &= \text{number of documents in the collection} \\
n_i &= \text{number of documents indexed by term } i \\
d_{ij} &= 1, \text{ if term } i \text{ appears in document } j \\
d_{ij} &= 0, \text{ if term } i \text{ does not appear in document } j \\
q_i &= 1, \text{ if term } i \text{ appears in the query} \\
q_i &= 0, \text{ if term } i \text{ does not appear in the query}
\end{aligned}$$

C is a constant that can be varied to "tune" the retrieval. The term weight of $\frac{N-n_i}{n_i}$ is very close to the inverse document frequency of $\frac{N}{n_i}$ for large document collections (large values of N). Hence, the whole expression is very close to the *tf-idf* that was used in the vector space model.

The authors tested this SC against the cosine coefficient and a coefficient obtained by simply summing the $idf's$ of each term. The new SC performed slightly better, but it is important to remember that the tests were run on the small Cranfield collection.

Recently, Croft and Harper's work on the problem of computing relevance weights with little or no relevance information was improved [Robertson and Walker, 1997]. They note that the weighting scheme of Croft and Harper can, under some circumstances, lead to negative weights.

In the original model by Robertson and Sparck Jones, two probabilities were used to determine the weighting. The first value, p, estimates for a given term the probability that a document containing the term will be relevant. The probability q estimates the probability that a document containing the term will not be relevant. In previous models, p and q are assumed to be constant, but Robertson and Walker allow p to vary as a function of known evidence of relevance.

Specifically, a weighting function that is developed with no information gives an inverse collection frequency weight (or some slight variation). At the other extreme, with a large amount of relevance information, the weighting function is determined by the relevance information. The equation from Croft and Harper can take on negative weights (when a term appears in over half of the document collection). Robertson and Walker developed new equations that are tunable and that estimate the weights of p and q independently. That is, information about relevance only influences the weight due to p and information about non-relevance only influences the weight due to q.

The new weight is given by:

$$w = \frac{k_5}{k_5 + R}\left(k_4 + \log\frac{N}{N-n}\right) + \frac{R}{k_5 + R}\log\left(\frac{r+0.5}{R-r+0.5}\right)$$
$$-\frac{k_6}{k_6 + S}\log\left(\frac{n}{N-n}\right) - \frac{S}{k_6 + S}\log\left(\frac{(s+0.5)}{(S-s+0.5)}\right)$$

where

R = number of relevant documents

r = number of relevant documents indexed by the given term

S = number of non-relevant documents

s = number of non-relevant documents which contain the term

k_4, k_5, k_6 = tuning constants, where $k_4 \geq 0$

The first two terms give the component of the weight due to relevance information, and the last two terms give the weight due to non-relevance information. (Note that if there is no knowledge (R=S=0), then the equations reduce to $k_4 + \log\frac{N}{n}$). k_4 measures how good the query term should be, while k_5 and k_6 measure the sensitivity to relevance and non-relevance, respectively. A statistically-based argument can be made that, instead of using R and S to scale the terms in the equation, the square roots of R and S should be used.

2.2.5.2 Independence Assumptions

The key assumption that provides for a simple combination of term weights to compute the probability of relevance is the assumption that the terms appear independent of one another. Because this assumption is false, it was suggested that the entire model is derived from a "faulty theory" [Cooper, 1991]. In fact, the inference network strategy and the logistic regression utility are both designed to work around the problem of independence assumptions. These are discussed in Sections 2.4 and 3.5, respectively.

Papers in the late 1970's and early 1980's start to address the failure of the independence assumption [Rijsbergen, 1977, Yu et al., 1983], but they all require co-occurrence information which is very computationally expensive to obtain. Van Rijsbergen suggests that related terms should be grouped together by using simple clustering algorithms and then the dependencies between groups can be obtained [Rijsbergen, 1977].

With increased computational speed, these approaches may soon be more tractable. To our knowledge, none of these modifications have been tried on a large test collection.

2.3 Language Models

A statistical language model is a probabilistic mechanism for "generating" a piece of text. It thus defines a distribution over all the possible word sequences. The simplest language model is the unigram language model, which is essentially a word distribution. More complex language models might use more context information (e.g., word history) in predicting the next word [Charniak, 1993, Rosenfeld, 2000].

Despite more than twenty years of using language models for speech recognition [Hodjat et al., 2003] and language translation, their use for information retrieval started only in 1998 [Ponte and Croft, 1998]. The core idea is that documents can be ranked on their likelihood of *generating* the query. Consider spoken document recognition, if the speaker were to utter the words in a document, what is the likelihood they would then say the words in the query. Formally, the similarity coefficient is simply:

$$SC(Q, D_i) = P(Q|M_{D_i})$$

where M_{D_i} is the language model implicit in document D_i.

There is a need to precisely define what we mean exactly by "generating" a query. That is, we need a probabilistic model for queries. One approach (proposed in [Ponte and Croft, 1998]) is to model the presence or absence of any term as an independent Bernoulli event and view the generation of the whole query as a joint event of observing all the query terms and not observing any terms that are not present in the query. In this case, the probability of the query is calculated as the product of probabilities for both the terms in the query and terms absent. That is,

$$SC(Q, D_i) = \prod_{t_j \in Q} P(t_j|M_{D_i}) \prod_{t_j \notin Q} (1 - P(t_j|M_{D_i}))$$

The model $p(t_j|M_{D_i})$ can be estimated in many different ways. A straightforward method is:

$$p(t_j|M_{D_i}) = p_{ml}(t_j|M_{D_i})$$

where $p_{ml}(t_j|M_{D_i})$ is the maximum likelihood estimate of the term distribution (i.e., the relative term frequency), and is given by:

$$p_{ml}(t_j|M_{D_i}) = \frac{tf(t_j, D_i)}{dl_{D_i}}$$

where dl_{D_i} is the document length of document D_i.

Figure 2.5. Language Model

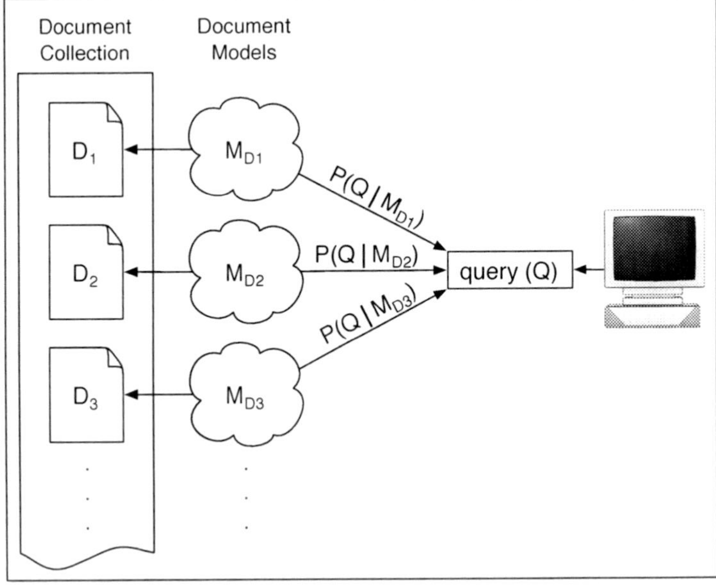

The basic idea is illustrated in Figure 2.5. The similarity measure will work, but it has a big problem. If a term in the query does not occur in a document, the whole similarity measure becomes zero. Consider our small running example of a query and three documents:

Q : "gold silver truck"
D_1: "Shipment of gold damaged in a fire"
D_2: "Delivery of silver arrived in a silver truck"
D_3: "Shipment of gold arrived in a truck"

The term *silver* does not appear in document D_1. Likewise, *silver* does not appear in document D_3 and *gold* does not appear in document D_2. Hence, this would result in a similarity coefficient of zero for all three sample documents and this sample query.

Hence, the maximum likelihood estimate for

$$p_{ml}(silver|M_{D_i}) = \frac{tf(silver, D_i)}{dl_{D_i}} = 0$$

2.3.1 Smoothing

To avoid the problem caused by terms in the query that are not present in a document, various *smoothing* approaches exist which estimate non-zero values for these terms. One approach assumes that the query term could occur in this model, but simply at no higher a rate than the chance of it occurring in any other document. The ratio $\frac{cf_t}{cs}$ was initially proposed where cf_t is the number of occurrences of term *t* in the collection, and *cs* is the number of terms in the entire collection. In our example, the estimate for *silver* would be $\frac{2}{22} = .091$.

An additional adjustment is made to account for the reality that these document models are based solely on individual documents. These are relatively small sample sizes from which to build a model. To use a larger sample (the entire collection) the following estimate is proposed:

$$p_{avg}(t) = \frac{\sum_{d(t \in d)} p_{ml}(t|M_d)}{df_t}$$

where df_t is the document frequency of term *t*, which is also used in computing the idf as discussed in Section 2.1).

To improve the effectiveness of the estimates for term weights it is possible to minimize the risk involved in our estimate. We first define $\bar{f}_t$ as the mean term frequency of term *t* in the document. This can be computed as $\bar{f}_t = p_{avg}(t) \times dl_d$. The risk can be obtained using a geometric distribution as:

$$R_{t,d} = \left(\frac{1.0}{1.0 + \bar{f}_t}\right) \times \left(\frac{\bar{f}_t}{1.0 + \bar{f}_t}\right)^{tf_{t,d}}$$

The first similarity measure described for using language models in information retrieval uses the smoothing ratio $\frac{cf_t}{cs}$ for terms that do not occur in the query and the risk function as a mixing parameter when estimating the values for *w* based on small document models. The term weight is now estimated as:

$$P(t|M_{di}) = \begin{cases} p_{ml}(t,d)^{(1-R(t,d))} \times p_{avg(t)}^{R(t,d)} & \text{if } tf(t,d) > 0 \\ \frac{cf_t}{cs} & \text{otherwise.} \end{cases}$$

2.3.2 Language Model Example

We now illustrate the use of this similarity measure with our running example: There are three documents in our test collection. There are 22 tokens. So, cs=22. The total number of tokens in documents D_1, D_2 and D_3 are 7, 8, and 7, respectively. Table 2.8 contains values for dl_d.

Table 2.8. Term Occurrence

	D_1	D_2	D_3
dl_d	7	8	7

df_t, the document frequency of *t*, is listed in Table 2.9. We use the same term ordering as described in Section 2.1.1.

Table 2.9. Document Frequency

	a	arrived	damaged	delivery	fire	gold	in	of	shipment	silver	truck
df_t	3	2	1	1	1	2	3	3	2	1	2

cf_t, the raw count of token t in the collection is given in Table 2.10.

Table 2.10. Collection Frequency for Each Token

	a	arrived	damaged	delivery	fire	gold	in	of	shipment	silver	truck
cf_t	3	2	1	1	1	2	3	3	2	2	2

$tf_{t,d}$, the raw term frequency of term t in document d is given in Table 2.11. First, we need to calculate $p_{ml}(t|M_d)$, the maximum likelihood estimate of the probability of term t under the term distribution for document d. For each term, t, $P_{ml}(t|M_d) = \frac{tf_{t,d}}{dl_d}$ is given in Table 2.12.

Table 2.11. Raw Term Frequency

	a	arrived	damaged	delivery	fire	gold	in	of	shipment	silver	truck
D_1	1	0	1	0	1	1	1	1	1	0	0
D_2	1	1	0	1	0	0	1	1	0	2	1
D_3	1	1	0	0	0	1	1	1	1	0	1

Table 2.12. Maximum Likelihood for Each Term

$p_{ml}(t\|M_d)$	D_1	D_2	D_3
a	0.143	0.125	0.143
arrived	0	0.125	0.143
damaged	0.143	0	0
delivery	0	0.125	0
fire	0.143	0	0
gold	0.143	0	0.143
in	0.143	0.125	0.143
of	0.143	0.125	0.143
shipment	0.143	0	0.143
silver	0	0.250	0
truck	0	0.125	0.143

Second, we calculate the mean probability of term *t* in documents which contain the term. The equation is:

$$P_{avg}(t) = \frac{\sum_{d(t \in d)} P_{ml}(t|M_d)}{df_t}$$

For the term "arrived", it only appears in D_2 and D_3, so:

$$P_{avg}(arrived) = \frac{P_{ml}(arrived|M_{D_2}) + P_{ml}(arrived|M_{D_3})}{df_{arrived}}$$

Using our previous estimates: we know that $P_{ml}(arrived|M_{D_2}) = 0.125$, $P_{ml}(arrived|M_{D_3}) = 0.143$ and $df_{arrived} = 2$. Thus, $P_{avg}(arrived) = (0.125 + 0.143)/2 = 0.134$. The remaining terms are given in Table 2.13.

Third, we calculate the risk for a term t in a document d. To do that, $\bar{f}_t$, the mean term frequency of term t in a document is computed by the following equation $\bar{f}_t = P_{avg}(t) \times dl_d$. $\bar{f}_t$ of each term t is given in Table 2.14. We then use the following risk function to obtain Equation 2.3.

Table 2.13. Average Probability for Each Term

	a	arrived	damaged	delivery	fire	gold	in	of	shipment	silver	truck
$P_{avg}(t)$	0.137	0.134	0.143	0.125	0.143	0.143	0.137	0.137	0.143	0.250	0.134

Table 2.14. Mean Term Frequency for Each Term

$\bar{f}_t$	a	arrived	damaged	delivery	fire	gold	in	of	shipment	silver	truck
D_1	0.958	0.938	1.000	0.875	1.000	1.000	0.958	0.958	1.000	1.750	0.938
D_2	1.096	1.071	1.143	1.000	1.143	1.143	1.096	1.096	1.143	2.000	1.071
D_3	0.958	0.938	1.000	0.875	1.000	1.000	0.958	0.958	1.000	1.750	0.938

$$R_{t,d} = \left(\frac{1.0}{1.0 + \bar{f}_t}\right) \times \left(\frac{\bar{f}_t}{1.0 + \bar{f}_t}\right)^{tf_{t,d}} \tag{2.3}$$

The risk values per term per document are shown in Table 2.15.

Table 2.15. Risk for Each Term

$R_{t,d}$	D_1	D_2	D_3
a	0.250	0.249	0.250
arrived	0.516	0.250	0.250
damaged	0.250	0.467	0.500
delivery	0.533	0.250	0.533
fire	0.250	0.467	0.500
gold	0.250	0.467	0.250
in	0.250	0.249	0.250
of	0.250	0.249	0.250
shipment	0.250	0.467	0.250
silver	0.364	0.148	0.364
truck	0.516	0.249	0.250

Now, we use the risk value as a mixing parameter to calculate $P(Q|M_d)$, the probability of producing the query for a given document model as mentioned before. It consists of two steps. Initially, we calculate $P(t|M_d)$ as shown in Equation 2.4. The italicized terms in Table 2.16 match a query term. For all other term occurrences the smoothing estimate, $P(t|M_d) = \frac{cf_t}{cs}$, is used.

$$P(t|M_d) = P_{ml}(t|M_d)^{(1.0-R_{t,d})} \times P_{avg}(t)^{R_{t,d}} \tag{2.4}$$

Finally, using the equation 2.5, we compute a final measure of similarity, $P(Q|M_d)$. The actual values are given in Table 2.17.

Table 2.16. Expected Probability for Each Term (with Smoothing)

$P(t\|M_d)$	D_1	D_2	D_3
a	0.141	0.128	0.141
arrived	0.091	0.127	0.141
damaged	0.143	0.045	0.045
delivery	0.045	0.125	0.045
fire	0.143	0.045	0.045
gold	***0.143***	0.091	***0.143***
in	0.141	0.128	0.141
of	0.141	0.128	0.141
shipment	0.143	0.091	0.143
silver	0.091	***0.250***	0.091
truck	0.091	***0.127***	***0.141***

$$P(Q|M_d) = \prod_{t \in Q} P(t|M_d) \times \prod_{t \notin Q} (1.0 - P(t|M_d)) \tag{2.5}$$

Table 2.17. Similarity using Language Models

	D_1	D_2	D_3
$P(Q\|M_d)$	0.000409	0.001211	0.000743

Hence, as with all other strategies that we describe, the final ranking is D_2, D_3 and D_1.

Although other terms in the query match document D_1 (e.g.; *gold*), the similarity measure results in zero for this document simply because one term does not occur. The model we have just presented is based on Ponte and Croft's original model, which models term presence and absence in the query but ignores *query term frequency* or the number of occurrences of a term in the query. Hence it does not matter if the term "silver" occurs once or twice in the query. Other language modeling work, including early work in TREC-7, models the occurrence of every query term with a unigram language model and thus incorporates term frequencies [Miller et al., 1999, Hiemstra and Kraaij, 1998].

Specifically, for a query, $Q = q_1, q_2, \ldots, q_m$, the probability $p(Q|D)$ now incorporates $tf(t, Q)$ to include the query term frequency (as shown in Equation 2.6).

$$p(Q|D) = \prod_{i=1}^{m} p(q_i|M_D) = \prod_{t \in Q} p(t|M_D)^{tf(t,Q)} \quad (2.6)$$

Such a multinomial model is more similar to the language models used in speech recognition. A discussion of this distinction can be found in [McCallum and Nigam, 1998, Song and Croft, 1999]. When using multinomial models, we reduce the retrieval problem to one of language model estimation, i.e., estimating $p(w|M_D)$.

Numerous smoothing functions are used to compute this estimate and detailed surveys are found in [Chen and Goodman, 1998, Manning and Schutze, 1999]. The Good-Turing estimate adjusts raw term frequency scores with the transformation given in equation 2.7:

$$tf^* = (tf + 1)\frac{E(N_{tf+1})}{E(N_{tf})} \quad (2.7)$$

This estimate was used to improve initial language models [Song and Croft, 1999]. Unfortunately, this estimate requires the count of words which have the same frequency in a document. This is a computationally expensive task.

A study of three efficient smoothing methods is given in [Zhai and Lafferty, 2001b]. The three methods were Jelinek-Mercer [Jelinek and Mercer, 1980], Bayesian smoothing using Dirichlet priors [MacKay and Peto, 1995], and Absolute Discounting [Ney et al., 1994]. For long queries, on average, the Jelinek-Mercer smoothing approach is better than the Dirichlet prior and absolute discounting approaches. For title only queries, experimentation demonstrated that Dirichlet prior is superior to absolute discounting and Jelinek-Mercer.

A general description of smoothing methods is to define them in terms of their ability to compute the probability of a term given the presence of a document: $P(t|d)$. Smoothing methods tend to reduce probabilities of terms that are observed in the text and boost the probabilities of terms that are not seen. As a last resort, unseen terms can simply be assigned a probability proportional to their probabilities according to the collection language model $p(t|C)$.

The Jelinek-Mercer method uses a linear interpolation of the maximum likelihood model and the collection model. The parameter λ is used to control the influence of each model. More formally:

$$p_\lambda(t|d) = (1 - \lambda)p_{ml}(t|d) + \lambda P(w|C)$$

Absolute discounting simply lowers the probability of terms that have occurred by subtracting a simple constant from their frequency. More formally:

$$p_\delta(t|d) = \frac{max(tf(t,d) - \delta, 0)}{\sum_t tf(t,d)} + \sigma P(t|C)$$

where $\delta \in [0, 1]$ is a constant and

$$\sigma = \delta \frac{|d|_u}{|d|}$$

where $|d|_u$ is the number of unique terms in document d and $|d|$ is the number of terms in the document.

For long queries, on average, the Jelinek-Mercer smoothing approach is better than the Dirichlet prior and absolute discounting approaches. For title only queries, experimentation demonstrated that Dirichlet prior is superior to absolute discounting and Jelinek-Mercer. In the Bayesian smoothing using Dirichlet priors, the model is given in Equation 2.8.

Returning now to our example, since our sample query contains only three terms, we treat it as a title query. Thus, in the following, we give a brief example illustrating the computation of relevance using the Dirichlet prior smoothing method.

$$p_\mu(t|d) = \frac{tf(t,d) + \mu P(t|C)}{\sum_t tf(t,d) + \mu} \tag{2.8}$$

where $tf(t,d)$ is the number of occurrences of term *t* in document d. $\sum_t tf(t,d)$ is the total count of terms in document d. $P(t|C)$ is the collection language model and is calculated as the number of occurrence of term *t* in the collection C divided by the total number of terms in C, namely, $\frac{\sum_d tf(t,d)}{cs}$.

Smoothing for terms that do not occur in the collection can be done with a Laplace method [Katz, 1987]. Hence, we have $P(t|C) = \frac{1+\sum_d tf(t,d)}{N+cs}$, where N is the number of distinct terms in the collection. In our example, since all query terms appear in the collection, we simply use $\frac{\sum_d tf(t,d)}{cs}$. In general, smoothing of the collection language model has only an insignificant effect as cs is typically quite large.

Finally, μ is an adjustable smoothing parameter. Experimentation has shown that the optimal prior seems to vary from collection to collection. However, it is frequently around 2000. Due to our desire to make the example readable, we will use a value of three in our example (this reduces the number of significant digits needed to present a useful example on this small three document test collection).

First, for each term t, we compute $\sum_d tf(t,d)$. The values are given in Table 2.18. In our sample collection, there are 3 documents. Totally, there are 22 tokens. So, cs = 22. By using $\frac{\sum_d tf(t,d)}{cs}$, we obtain $P(t|C)$, as shown in Table 2.19. Second, the total count of terms in document d is, once again, given in Table 2.20. Third, $tf(t,d)$ is, once again, given in Table 2.21. We now compute the smoothed probabilities by using $p_\mu(t|d) = \frac{tf(t,d)+\mu P(t|C)}{\sum_t tf(t,d)+\mu}$. The new probabilities are shown in Table 2.22. A value of 3 is used for μ to reduce the number of significant digits needed for this example. A new similarity measure is computed as $P(Q|d) = \prod_t p_\mu(t|d)$, and the results are shown in Table 2.23. For example the similarity between document one and the query can now simply be computed as the product of the smoothed probabilities for the three terms in the query. For document one this is $(0.1378)(0.0091)(0.0091) = 0.0000114$.

Table 2.18. $\sum_d tf(t,d)$ for Each Term

	a	arrived	damaged	delivery	fire	gold	in	of	shipment	silver	truck
$\sum_t tf(t,d)$	3	2	1	1	1	2	3	3	2	2	2

Table 2.19. $P(t|C)$ for Each Term

	a	arrived	damaged	delivery	fire	gold	in	of	shipment	silver	truck
P(t|C)	.136	.091	.045	.045	.045	.091	.136	.136	.091	.091	.091

Table 2.20. $\sum_t tf(t,d)$ for Each Document

	D_1	D_2	D_3
$\sum_t tf(t,d)$	7	8	7

Hence, the ranking with this measure is D_3, D_2, and D_1. We now provide a brief description of two additional smoothing methods. The Jelinek-Mercer method is a linear interpolation of the maximum likelihood model with the collection model, using a coefficient λ to control the influence of each model.

$$P_\lambda(t|d) = (1-\lambda)P_{ml}(t|d) + \lambda P(t|C).$$

Table 2.21. $tf(t,d)$ for Each Term

$tf(t,d)$	a	arrived	damaged	delivery	fire	gold	in	of	shipment	silver	truck
D1	1	0	1	0	1	1	1	1	1	0	0
D2	1	1	0	1	0	0	1	1	0	2	1
D3	1	1	0	0	0	1	1	1	1	0	1

Table 2.22. $p_\mu(t|d)$ for Each Term

$p_\mu(t|d)$	a	arrived	damaged	delivery	fire	gold	in	of	shipment	silver	truck
D1	0.141	0.027	0.114	0.014	0.114	0.127	0.141	0.141	0.127	0.027	0.027
D2	0.128	0.116	0.012	0.103	0.012	0.025	0.128	0.128	0.025	0.207	0.116
D3	0.141	0.127	0.014	0.014	0.014	0.127	0.141	0.141	0.127	0.027	0.127

Table 2.23. Final Similarity Measure with Dirichlet Priors

Document	D_1	D_2	D_3
SC(Q, D_i)	0.0000114	0.0002590	0.0001728

P(t|C) is the same as given using Dirichlet priors. For λ, we choose different optimal values for different queries. Experiments have shown that a small value of λ, around 0.1, works well for short queries and a higher value around 0.7 for long queries. The final similarity measure for our example is given in Table 2.24.

Note, as with all our ranking examples, document two is ranked higher than documents three which is ranked higher than document one. The absolute discounting method lowers the probability of seen words by subtracting a constant from their counts. The following equation shows how the discount is incorporated:

$$p_\delta(t|d) = \frac{max((tf(t,d) - \delta), 0)}{\sum_w tf(t,d)} + \sigma P(t|C)$$

where $\delta \in [0, 1]$ and $\sigma = \frac{\delta |d|_u}{|d|}$. $|d|_u$ is the count of unique terms in document d and $|d|$ is the total number of terms in the document. A key difference from the Jelinek-Mercer smoothing is that the optimal value of δ is frequently around 0.7 according to experimental results. This is true for title queries as well as long queries. The final similarity coefficient for our example with absolute discounting is given in Table 2.25.

We briefly described the use of language models as a recent type of search strategy. Although it is an old technique from speech recognition, it was only recently applied to information retrieval. Our discussion is mostly based on Ponte and Croft's pioneering work, which models term presence or absence in the query. We also discussed an alternative multinomial model which treats a query as a sample drawn from a unigram language model (i.e., a multinomial word distribution). In each case, we show how to score a document based on the likelihood of generating the query using a model estimated from the document. The retrieval problem is reduced to the problem of estimating a document language model. A straightforward method of estimating the model using relative frequency has the obvious problem of assigning a zero probability to any word not observed in the document. Smoothing adjusts the estimate to avoid such a situation. This improves the accuracy of the estimated model. Many different smoothing methods are possible. The Dirichlet prior method has thus far performed well.

Table 2.24. Final Similarity Measure with Jelinek-Mercer

	D_1	D_2	D_3
SC(Q, D_i)	0.000314	0.000443	0.000381

Retrieval with these basic language models can be as efficient as retrieval using a traditional model such as the vector space model [Zhai and Lafferty, 2001b], and likewise they were shown to be as effective as, or more effective than, well-tuned traditional models. Perhaps the main advantage of using language models for retrieval lies in the potential for automatic tuning of parameters, which is demonstrated in [Zhai and Lafferty, 2002].

Table 2.25. Final Similarity Measure with Absolute Discounting

	D_1	D_2	D_3
SC(Q, D_i)	0.001215	0.021716	0.005727

Many more complex language models were studied. Some of them attempt to improve the basic language modeling approach (i.e., the query likelihood approach) by going beyond the unigram language models by capturing limited dependencies [Song and Croft, 1999], and by introducing translation models to capture word relatedness [Berger and Lafferty, 1999]. Some others use language models in a different way. For example, in [Lavrenko and Croft, 2001], language models are incorporated into the classic probabilistic information retrieval model, and a novel method is used for estimating the relevance model without relevance judgments.

Recent work focuses on reducing the size of these models [Hiemstra et al., 2004]. Another recent approach builds language models based on clusters (see Section 3.2) of documents instead of the entire document collection [Liu and Croft, 2004].

The basic idea is very similar to pseudorelevance feedback. In other work [Zhai and Lafferty, 2001b, Zhai and Lafferty, 2001a], both a query model and a document model are estimated and a model distance function (i.e., Kullback-Leibler divergence) is used to compute the distance between the two models. This is very similar to the vector space model, except that the representation of documents and the query are based on unigram language models. The main advantage of these alternatives and more sophisticated models is that they can handle relevance feedback (see Section 3.1) more naturally. Most of these alternative models were shown to outperform the simple basic query likelihood scoring method. Development of more accurate and more robust language models remains an active research area.

2.4 Inference Networks

Inference networks use evidential reasoning to estimate the probability that a document will be relevant to a query. They model the probabilistic retrieval strategy discussed in Section 2.2 and enhance that model to include additional evidence that a document may be relevant to a query. In this section, we first give a basic overview of inference networks. We then describe how inference networks are used for relevance ranking.

2.4.1 Background

The essence of an inference network is to take known relationships and use them to "infer" other relationships. This dramatically reduces the computational requirements needed to estimate the probability that an event will occur.

A binary inference network uses events where the event will have either a value of *true* or *false*. A prior probability indicates the likelihood of the event. Assume we know events A, B, C, D and E all occur with respective probabilities $P(A = true) = a$, $P(B = true) = b$, $P(C = true) = c$, $P(D = true) = d$ and $P(E = true) = e$. These events are independent—that is, the probability that all events will still occur is the same regardless of whether or not any of the other events occur. More formally, for all possible combinations of b, c, d and e then $P(A|b, c, d, e) = P(a)$. Assume we know that event F depends on events A, B, C, D and E, and we want to compute the probability that F occurs given the probability that A, B, C, D and E occur. Figure 2.6 illustrates this example inference network.

To do this without an inference network, the computation is exponential and requires consideration of all 2^5 combinations for the events A, B, C, D and

E. Using notation given in [Greiff, 1996], let R be the set of all 2^5 possible subsets of 1, 2, 3, 4, 5. Let p_i indicate the probability that the $i^{\underline{th}}$ event is true—in our example events 1, 2, 3, 4 and 5 correspond to A, B, C, D and E. Let P_i indicate the state value (either true or false) of the ith event—that is P_1 indicates whether or not A is true, P_2 indicates whether or not B is true, etc. Finally, the mere existence of an event or combination of events A, B, C, D or E changes the likelihood that F is true. This probability is called α_R and is defined as:

$$\begin{aligned} \alpha_R &= P(F = \mathtt{true}|P_1, \ldots, P_5) \\ &\quad \mathtt{where}\ i \in R \rightarrow P_i\ \mathtt{is}\ \mathtt{true}, \\ &\quad i \notin R \rightarrow P_i\ \mathtt{is}\ \mathtt{false} \end{aligned}$$

To compute $P(F = true)$, assuming, A, B, C, D and E are independent, the following equation is used:

$$P(F = true) = \sum_{R \subseteq \{1,\ldots,5\}} \alpha_R \prod_{i \in R} p_i \prod_{i \notin R} (1 - p_i) \tag{2.9}$$

For a simple problem with only five values, we end up with a 32-element computation. The exponential nature of this problem is addressed by inference networks with naturally occurring intermediaries. This enables the use of partial inferences to obtain a final inference.

Assume we know that events A, B, and C cause event X, and events D and E cause event Y. We can now use X and Y to infer F. Figure 2.6 illustrates this simple inference network .

Figure 2.6. Simple Inference Network

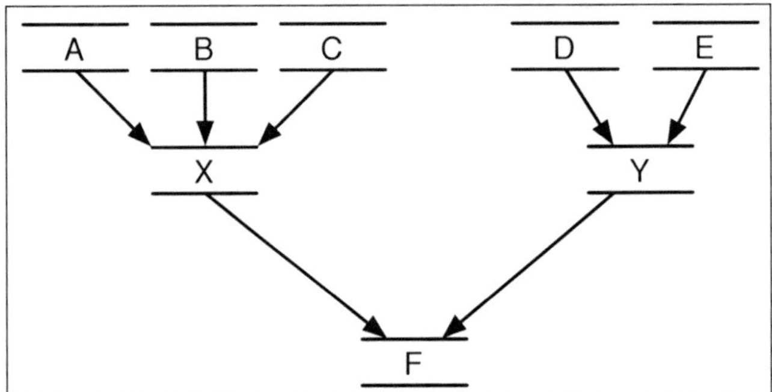

Consider an example where we are trying to predict whether or not the Salamanders will win a softball game. Assume this depends on which coaches are present and which umpires are present. At the top layer of the network might be nodes that correspond to a given coach or umpire being present. The Scott, David, and Catherine nodes (nodes A, B,and C) all correspond to coaches and the Jim and Manny nodes (nodes D and E) correspond to umpires. Now the event "good coach is present" (node X) depends on the Scott, David, and Catherine nodes and the event "good umpire is present" (node Y) depends on the Jim and Manny nodes. The event "Salamanders win" (node F) clearly depends on nodes X and Y.

In our example, the presence of an umpire in no way determines whether or not another umpire attends, but it certainly impacts whether or not the umpires are "friendly" to the Salamanders. Similarly, the presence of a given coach does not impact the presence of other coaches, but it does impact whether or not the whole coaching staff is present. Also, the presence or absence of a coach has no impact on whether or not the umpires will be favorable.

To compute F, equation 2.9 can be used, or we can use an inference network to take advantage of the logical groupings inherent in the events X and Y. First, we compute $P(X = true)$ using the three parents— A, B, and C — this requires 2^3 computations. The impact of the parent nodes on the child node with the variable α and a binary subscript that indicates the likelihood that the child node is true, given various combinations of parent nodes being true. For example, α_{111} indicates the probability that the child node is true given that all three parents are true. Computing $P(X = true)$ we obtain:

$$\begin{aligned} P(X = true) \quad = \quad & \alpha_{111}abc + \alpha_{110}ab(1-c) + \alpha_{101}a(1-b)c + \\ & \alpha_{100}a(1-b)(1-c) + \alpha_{011}(1-a)bc + \\ & \alpha_{010}(1-a)b(1-c) + \alpha_{001}(1-a)(1-b)c + \\ & \alpha_{000}(1-a)(1-b)(1-c) \end{aligned}$$

and now we compute $P(Y = true)$ using the two parents D, E:

$$P(Y = true) = \alpha_{11}de + \alpha_{10}d(1-e) + \alpha_{01}(1-d)e + \alpha_{00}(1-d)(1-e)$$

Once the prior probabilities for X and Y are known, we compute the probability that F is true as:

$$P(F = true) = \alpha_{11}xy + \alpha_{10}x(1-y) + \alpha_{01}y(1-x) + \alpha_{00}(1-x)(1-y)$$

To compute F, it took eight additions for X, four for Y, and finally four for F. Therefore, we now require only sixteen instead of the thirty-two required without the inference network. The key is that F is independent of A, B, C, D and E given X, Y or:

$$P(F = true|a, b, c, d, e, x, y) = P(F = true|x, y)$$

Once the initial values of the top layer of the inference network are assigned (these are referred to as prior probabilities), a node on the network is *instantiated* and all of its links are followed to nodes farther down the network. These nodes are then activated. At this point, the node that is activated is able to compute the *belief* that the node is true or false. The belief is computed based on the belief that all of its parent nodes are true or false. At this point, we have assumed that all parents contributed equally to the belief that a node was present. Link matrices indicate the strength by which parents (either by themselves or in conjunction with other parents) affect children in the inference network.

2.4.2 Link Matrices

Another capability provided by the inference network is the ability to include the dependence of a child on the parents. Suppose we know that a particular umpire, Manny, is much more friendly to the Salamanders than any other umpire. Hence, the contribution of D, E to the value of Y may not be equal.

The link matrix contains an entry for each of the 2^n combinations of parents and (for a binary inference network in which nodes are either true or false) will contain only two rows.

In our example, the link matrix for the node Y that represents the impact of umpires D and E on Y is given as:

	DE	D$\overline{E}$	$\overline{D}E$	$\overline{DE}$
Y true	0.9	0.8	0.2	0.05
Y false	0.1	0.2	0.8	0.95

This matrix indicates that the presence of the friendly umpire Manny (D) coupled with the absence of Jim ($\overline{E}$) results in an eighty percent contribution to the belief that we have friendly umpires for the game. We use the notation $L_i(Y)$ to indicate the value of the ith entry in the link matrix to identify whether or not Y is true and $\overline{L_i(Y)}$ to indicate the value to determine whether or not Y is false.

The link matrix entries are included as an additional element in the computation given above. The new equation to compute the belief that a given node N with n parents using the previously used set R becomes:

$$P(N = true) = \sum_{R \subseteq \{1,\ldots,n\}} L_i(N) \prod_{i \in R} p_i \prod_{i \notin R} (1 - p_i)$$

The link matrix for p parents contains 2^p entries. Again, the link matrix measures the contribution of individual parents to a given inference. The link matrix can be selected such that a closed form computation is possible. The simplest matrix, the L_{AND} for an arbitrary node N is of the form [Turtle, 1991]:

	P_{000}	P_{001}	P_{010}	P_{011}	P_{100}	P_{101}	P_{110}	P_{111}
N true	0	0	0	0	0	0	0	1

The entries are given in binary such that a 1 or 0 is given for each of the possible p parents (p=3 in this case). The computation results in zeros for all combinations of parents except when all p parents exist. The value of P(N=true) will be $(p_1)(p_2)(p_3)$ where p_i indicates the probability that the parent p_i is true. Only a single element must be summed to obtain the final result instead of the worst case of 2^N. Other closed form link matrices exist that essentially average the prior probabilities of parents.

To give an example with our existing inference network, assume there is a seventy percent chance A will attend, and a sixty percent chance B and C will attend (P(A) = 0.7, P(B) = 0.6, P(C) = 0.6). For umpires, assume P(D) = 0.8 and P(E) = 0.4. The links from A, B, C, D and E are followed and the probability that X and Y are true can now be computed. To compute $P(X = true)$, we need the link matrix for X. Let's assume the link matrix results in a closed form average of all parent probabilities

$$\frac{\sum_i^n p_i}{n}$$

$$P(X = true) = \frac{0.7 + 0.6 + 0.6}{3} = 0.633$$

Now to compute the probability for Y, the link matrix given above is used to obtain:

$$\begin{aligned} P(Y = true) &= L_{11}(Y)de + L_{10}(Y)d(1-e) + L_{01}(Y)(1-d)e + \\ &\quad L_{00}(Y)(1-d)(1-e) \end{aligned}$$

$$\begin{aligned} P(Y = true) &= (0.9)(0.8)(0.4) + (0.8)(0.8)(0.6) + (0.2)(0.2)(0.4) + \\ &\quad (0.05)(0.2)(0.6) \end{aligned}$$

$$P(Y = true) = 0.288 + 0.384 + 0.016 + 0.006 = 0.694$$

Now we have the belief that X and Y are true, assume we use the unweighted sum link matrix. This is a closed form link matrix that results in a simple average of the parent probabilities to compute the belief in F. The final value for F is:

$$P(F = true) = \frac{0.694 + 0.633}{2} = 0.6635$$

In this case, we had only three elements to sum to compute X, four to compute Y, and two to compute F. If we did not have a closed form link matrix we would have had 2^3 for X, 2^2 for Y, and 2^2 for F or 16 elements—substantially less than the 2^5 required without an inference network.

2.4.3 Relevance Ranking

Turtle's Ph.D. thesis is the seminal work on the use of inference networks for information retrieval [Turtle, 1991]. The documents are represented as nodes on the inference network , and a link exists from each document to each term in the document. When a document is instantiated, all of the term nodes linked to the document are instantiated. A simple three-layered approach then connects the term nodes directly to query nodes. This three-layered network is illustrated in Figure 2.7. A link exists between a term node and a query node for each term in the query. Note that this is the most simplistic form of inference network for information retrieval. The three-layered approach consists of a document layer, a term layer, and a query layer. Note that the basic algorithm will work if a layer that contains generalizations of terms or *concepts* exists. This layer could sit between the term layer and the query layer. Links from a term to a concept could exist based on semantic processing or the use of a thesaurus (see Sections 3.6 and 3.7). Using a concept layer gives the inference network resilience to the matching problem because terms in the query need not directly match terms in the document; only the *concepts* must match.

An example of an inference network with actual nodes and links is given in Figure 2.8. A query and three documents are given along with the corresponding network. Links exist from the document layer to the term layer for each occurrence of a term in a document.

For our discussion, we focus on a three-layered inference network. Processing begins when a document is instantiated. By doing this, we are indicating that we believe document one (D_1) was observed. This instantiates all term nodes in D_1. We only instantiate the network with a single document at a time. Hence, the closed form for the link matrix for this layer will equal the weight for which a term might exist in a document. Typically, some close variant on $tf - idf$ is used for this weight.

Subsequently, the process continues throughout the network. All links emanate from the term nodes just activated and are instantiated, and a query node is activated. The query node then computes the belief in the query given D_1. This is used as the similarity coefficient for D_1. The process continues until all documents are instantiated.

Figure 2.7. Document-Term-Query Inference Network

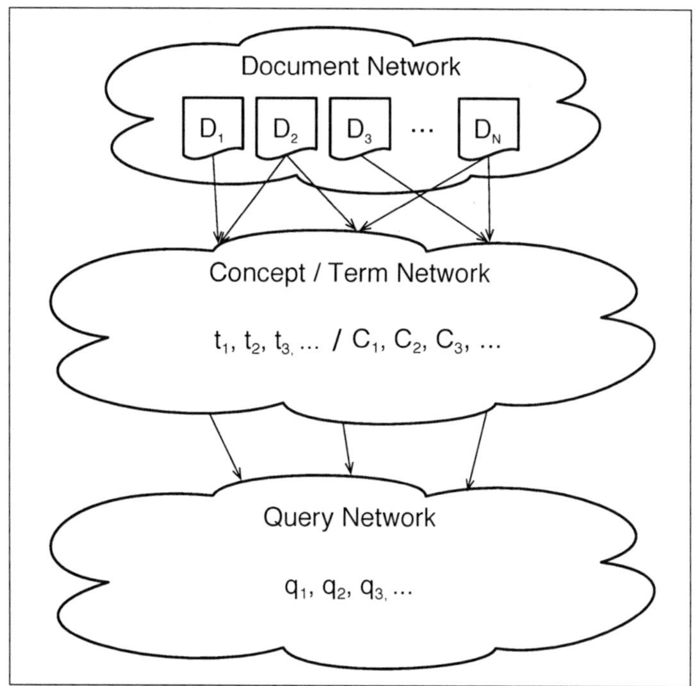

2.4.4 Inference Network Example

We now use an inference network to compute a similarity coefficient for the documents in our example:

Q : "gold silver truck"
D_1: "Shipment of gold damaged in a fire."
D_2: "Delivery of silver arrived in a silver truck."
D_3: "Shipment of gold arrived in a truck."

We need to evaluate our belief in the query given the evidence of a document, D_i. Assuming that our belief is proportional to the frequency within the document and inversely proportional to the frequency within the collection leads us to consider the term frequency, tf, and inverse document frequency, idf. However, both are normalized to the interval [0,1] by dividing tf by the maximum term frequency for the document, and idf by the maximum possible idf (see Table 2.26).

In our three document collection, each term appears 1, 2 or 3 times. The total size of the collection is 3, so for:

Figure 2.8. Inference Network

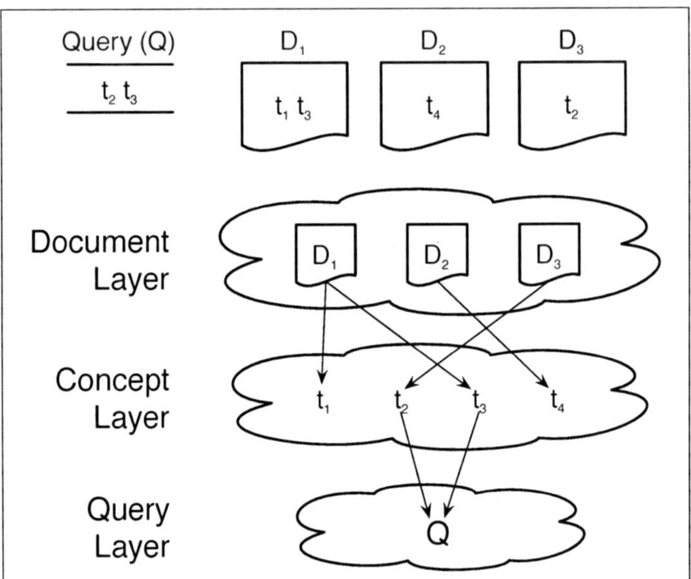

Table 2.26. Initial Values for Example Collection

	a	arrived	damaged	delivery	fire	gold	in	of	shipment	silver	truck
idf	0	0.41	1.10	1.10	1.10	0.41	0	0	0.41	0.41	0.41
nidf	0	0.37	1	1	1	0.37	0	0	0.37	0.37	0.37
D_1	1	0	1	0	1	1	1	1	1	0	0
D_2	0.5	0.5	0	0.5	0	0	0.5	0.5	0	1	0.5
D_3	1	1	0	0	0	1	1	1	1	0	1

$tf = 1$, $idf = \ln \frac{3}{1} = 1.10$

$tf = 2$, $idf = \ln \frac{3}{2} = 0.41$

$tf = 3$, $idf = \ln \frac{3}{3} = 0$

Each term appears in a document either once or not at all, with the single exception of *silver* which appears twice in D_2. For each combination of term and document, we evaluate $P_{ij} = P(r_i = true|d_j = true)$. Turtle used the formula $P_{ij} = 0.5+0.5(ntf_{ij})(nidf_i)$ to compute the belief in a given term for a particular document. Instantiating a document provides equal support for all members of the assigned term nodes. Any node for which there is no support (no documents instantiated) has belief equal to zero.

For each term, a link matrix is constructed that describes the support by its parent nodes. For the concepts in the query, the link matrices are given below:

The link matrix for *gold* is:

	$\overline{D_1 D_3}$	$\overline{D_1} D_3$	$D_1 \overline{D_3}$
False	1	0.315	0.315
True	0	0.685	0.685

The matrix indicates the belief of falsehood (first row) or truth (second row) given the conditions described in the column. When we instantiate a document, it is taken as true. Only one document is instantiated at a time. The number in the table is the value for P_{ij}, or the belief that term i is true given document j has been instantiated.

If D_3 is assigned a value of *true*, the belief is computed as:

$$P_{ij} = 0.5 + 0.5(ntf_{ij})(nidf_i) = 0.5 + 0.5(0.369)(1) = 0.685$$

This is found in the link matrix when D_3 is true. In this case, the link matrix has a closed form. Hence, it need not be stored or computed in advance. The matrix only accounts for three possibilities: both documents are false, D_1 is assigned a value of *true* and not D_3, D_3 is assigned a value of *true* and not D_1. Since *gold* does not appear in document two, there is no need to consider the belief when D_2 is assigned a value of *true* as there is no link from D_2 to the node that represents the term *gold*. Also, since documents are assigned a value of *true* one at a time, there is never a need to consider a case when D_1 and D_3 are true at the same time.

Similarly, the link matrix for *silver* can be constructed. *Silver* only appears in document D_2 so the only case to consider is whether or not D_2 is assigned a value of *true*. The link matrix computes:

$$P_{ij} = 0.5 + 0.5(ntf_{ij})(nidf_i) = 0.5 + 0.5(0.369)(1) = 0.685$$

Similarly, the link matrix for *truck* is constructed. *Truck* has two parents D_2 and D_3.

	$\overline{D_2 D_3}$	$\overline{D_2} D_3$	$D_2 \overline{D_3}$
False	1	0.315	0.408
True	0	0.685	0.592

For D_2 true and D_3 false, we have:

$$P_{ij} = 0.5 + 0.5(ntf_{ij})(nidf_i) = 0.5 + 0.5(0.5)(0.369) = 0.592$$

We have now described all of the link matrices used to compute the belief in a term given the instantiation of a document. Now a link matrix for a query node must be developed.

There is quite a bit of freedom in choosing this matrix. The user interface might allow users to indicate that some terms are more important than others. If that is the case, the link matrix for the query node can be weighted accordingly. One simple matrix is given in Turtle's thesis [Turtle, 1991]. Using g, s, and t to represent the terms *gold*, *silver*, and *truck*, it is of the form:

	$\overline{gst}$	g	s	gs	t	gt	st	gst
False	0.9	0.7	0.7	0.5	0.5	0.3	0.3	0.1
True	0.1	0.3	0.3	0.5	0.5	0.7	0.7	0.9

The rationale for this matrix is that *gold* and *silver* are equal in value and *truck* is more important. Also, even if no terms are present, there is *some* small belief (0.1) that the document is relevant. Similarly, if all terms are present, there is some doubt (0.1). Finally, belief values are included for the presence of multiple terms.

We now instantiate D_1 which means Bel(gold)—the belief that *gold* is true given document D_1—is 0.685, Bel(truck) = 0.5, and Bel(silver) = 0.5. Note "Bel(x)" represents "the belief in x" for this example.

At this point, all term nodes have been instantiated so the query node can now be instantiated.

$$\begin{aligned}\text{Bel}(Q \mid D_1) = {} & 0.1(0.315)(1)(1) + 0.3(0.685)(1)(1) + 0.3(0.315)(0)(1) + \\ & 0.5(0.685)(0)(1) + 0.5(0.315)(1)(0) + 0.7(0.685)(1)(0) + \\ & 0.7(0.315)(0)(0) + 0.9(0.685)(0)(0) = 0.031 + 0.206 = 0.237.\end{aligned}$$

This directly follows from the equation given in our prior examples using the link matrix entries $L_i(Q)$.

Instantiating D_2 gives Bel(gold) = 0, Bel(silver) = 0.685, and Bel(truck) = 0.592. The belief in D_2 is computed as:

$$\begin{aligned}\text{Bel}(Q \mid D_2) = {} & (0.1)(1)(0.315)(0.408) + (0.3)(0)(0.315)(0.408) + \\ & (0.3)(1)(0.685)(0.408) + (0.5)(0)(0.685)(0.408) + \\ & (0.5)(1)(0.315)(0.592) + (0.7)(0)(0.315)(0.592) + \\ & (0.7)(1)(0.685)(0.592) + (0.9)(0)(0.685)(0.592) = \\ & 0.013 + 0.084 + 0.093 + 0.283 = 0.473.\end{aligned}$$

Assigning D_3 a value of *true* gives Bel(gold) = 0.685, Bel(silver) = 0, Bel(truck) = 0.685. The belief in D_3 is computed as:

$$\begin{aligned}\text{Bel}(Q \mid D_3) = {} & (0.1)(0.315)(1)(0.315) + (0.3)(0.685)(1)(0.315) + \\ & (0.3)(0.315)(0)(0.315) + (0.5)(0.685)(0)(0.315) + \\ & (0.5)(0.315)(1)(0.685) + (0.7)(0.685)(1)(0.685) + \\ & (0.7)(0.315)(0)(0.685) + (0.9)(0.685)(0)(0.685) = \\ & 0.01 + 0.065 + 0.108 + 0.328 = 0.511.\end{aligned}$$

In the link matrices throughout this example, we assume that each parent has an equal contribution to the child probability. The assumption is that if two parents exist, regardless of *which parents*, the child probability is greater. Recent work has described the potential to generate closed forms for link matrices in which the presence or absence of each parent is not equal [Greiff et al., 1997]. Only the surface has been scratched with regard to the topology of inference networks for relevance ranking. Potential exists to group common subdocuments in the inference network or to group sets of documents or clusters within the inference network. Also, different representations for the same document can be used. To our knowledge, very little was done in this area.

2.5 Extended Boolean Retrieval

Conventional Boolean retrieval does not lend itself well to relevance ranking because documents either satisfy the Boolean request or do not satisfy the Boolean request. All documents that satisfy the request are retrieved (typically in chronological order), but no estimate as to their relevance to the query is computed.

An approach to extend Boolean retrieval to allow for relevance ranking is given in [Fox, 1983a] and a thorough description of the foundation for this approach is given in [Salton, 1989]. The basic idea is to assign term weights to each of the terms in the query and to the terms in the document. Instead of simply finding a set of terms, the weights of the terms are incorporated into a document ranking. Consider a query that requests (t_1 OR t_2) that is matched with a document that contains t_1 with a weight of w_1 and t_2 with a weight of w_2.

If both w_1 and w_2 are equal to one, a document that contains both of these terms is given the highest possible ranking. A document that contains neither of the terms is given the lowest possible ranking. A simple means of computing a measure of relevance is to compute the Euclidean distance from the point (w_1, w_2) to the origin. Hence, for a document that contains terms t_1 and t_2 with weights w_1 and w_2, the similarity coefficient could be computed as:

$$SC(Q, d_i) = \sqrt{(w_1)^2 + (w_2)^2}$$

For weights of 0.5 and 0.5, the SC would be:

$$SC(Q, d_i) = \sqrt{0.5^2 + 0.5^2} = \sqrt{0.5} = 0.707$$

The highest value of SC occurs when w_1 and w_2 are each equal to one. In this case we obtain $SC(Q, D_i) = \sqrt{2} = 1.414$. If we want the similarity coefficient to scale between 0 and 1, a normalization of $\sqrt{2}$ is added. The SC becomes:

$$SC(Q_{t_1 \bigvee t_2}, d_i) = \frac{\sqrt{(w_1)^2 + (w_2)^2}}{\sqrt{2}}$$

This coefficient assumes we are starting with a query that contains the Boolean OR: $(t_1 \bigvee t_2)$. It is straightforward to extend the computation to include an AND. Instead of measuring the distance to the origin, the distance to the point (1,1) is measured. The closer a query is to the point (1,1) the more likely it will be to satisfy the AND request. More formally:

$$SC(Q_{t_1 \bigwedge t_2}, d_i) = 1 - \frac{\sqrt{(1 - w_1)^2 + (1 - w_2)^2}}{\sqrt{2}}$$

2.5.1 Extensions to Include Query Weights

Consider again the same document that contains query terms t_1 and t_2 with weights w_1 and w_2. Previously, we assumed the query was simply a Boolean request of the form (t_1 OR t_2) or (t_1 AND t_2). We now add the weights q_1 and q_2 to the query. The new similarity coefficient that includes these weights is computed as:

$$SC(Q_{q_1 \bigvee q_2}, d_i) = \frac{\sqrt{q_1^2 w_1^2 + q_2^2 w_2^2}}{\sqrt{q_1^2 + q_2^2}}$$

$$SC(Q_{q_1 \bigwedge q_2}, d_i) = 1 - \left(\frac{\sqrt{q_1^2(1 - w_1)^2 + q_2^2(1 - w_2)^2}}{\sqrt{q_1^2 + q_2^2}} \right)$$

2.5.2 Extending for Arbitrary Numbers of Terms

For Euclidean distances in two-dimensional space, a 2-norm is used. To compute the distance from the origin in multi-dimensional space, an L_p vector norm is used. The parameter, p, allows for variations on the amount of importance the weights hold in evaluating the measure of relevance. The new similarity coefficient for a query Q with terms t_i and t_j with weights q_i and q_j and a document D_i with the same terms having weights of w_i and w_j is defined as:

$$SC(D, Q_{(q_i \bigvee q_j)}) = \left[\frac{q_i^p w_i^p + q_j^p w_j^p}{q_i^p + q_j^p} \right]^{\frac{1}{p}}$$

$$sim(D, Q_{(q_i \bigwedge q_j)}) = 1 - \left[\frac{q_i^p (1 - w_i^p) + q_j^p (1 - w_j^p)}{q_i^p + q_j^p} \right]^{\frac{1}{p}}$$

At p equal to one, this is equivalent to a vector space dot product. At p equal to infinity, this reduces to a normal Boolean system where term weights are not included. Initial tests found some improvement with the extended Boolean indexing over vector space (i.e., p = 2), but these tests were only done for small data collections and were computationally more expensive than the vector space model.

2.5.3 Automatic Insertion of Boolean Logic

Each of the retrieval strategies we have addressed do not require users to identify complex Boolean requests. Hence, with the use of OR, a query consisting only of terms can be used. Weights can be automatically assigned (using something like *tf-idf*) and documents can then be ranked by inserting OR's between each of the terms. The conventional vector space model, implicitly computes a ranking that is essentially an OR of the document terms. Any document that contains at least one of the terms in the query is ranked with a score greater than 0.

Conversely, a more sophisticated algorithm takes a sequence of terms and automatically generates ANDs and ORs to place between the terms [Fox, 1983a]. The algorithm estimates the size of a retrieval set based on a worst-case sum of the document frequencies. If term t_1 appears in 50 documents and term t_2 appears in 100 documents, we estimate that the query will retrieve 150 documents. This will only happen if t_1 and t_2 never co-occur in a document.

Using the worst-case sum, the terms in the query are ranked by document frequency. The term with the highest frequency is placed into a REMOVED set. This is done for the two highest frequency terms. Terms from the REMOVED set are then combined into pairs, and the pair with the lowest estimated retrieval set is added. The process continues until the size of the retrieval set is below the requested threshold.

2.6 Latent Semantic Indexing

Matrix computation is used as a basis for information retrieval in the retrieval strategy called Latent Semantic Indexing [Deerwester et al., 1990]. The premise is that more conventional retrieval strategies (i.e., vector space, probabilistic and extended Boolean) all have problems because they match directly on keywords. Since the same concept can be described using many different keywords, this type of matching is prone to failure. The authors cite a study in which two people used the same word for the same concept only twenty percent of the time.

Searching for something that is closer to representing the underlying semantics of a document is not a new goal. Canonical forms were proposed for natural language processing since the early 1970's [Winograd, 1983, Schank, 1975]. Applied here, the idea is not to find a canonical knowledge representation, but to use matrix computation, in particular Singular Value Decomposition (SVD). This filters out the noise found in a document, such that two documents that have the same semantics (whether or not they have matching terms) will be located close to one another in a multi-dimensional space.

The process is relatively straightforward. A term-document matrix A is constructed such that location (i, j) indicates the number of times term i appears in document j. A SVD of this matrix results in matrices $U \sum V^T$ such that $\sum$ is a diagonal matrix. A is a matrix that represents each term in a row. Each column of A represents documents. The values in $\sum$ are referred to as the singular values. The singular values can then be sorted by magnitude and the top k values are selected as a means of developing a "latent semantic" representation of the A matrix. The remaining singular values are then set to 0. Only the first k columns are kept in U_k; only the first k rows are recorded in V_k^T. After setting the results to 0, a new A' matrix is generated to approximate $A = U \sum V^T$.

Comparison of two terms is done via an inner product of the two corresponding rows in U_k. Comparison of two documents is done as an inner product of two corresponding rows in V_k^T.

A query-document similarity coefficient treats the query as a document and computes the SVD. However, the SVD is computationally expensive; so, it is not recommended that this be done as a solution. Techniques that approximate Σ and avoid the overhead of the SVD exist. For an infrequently updated document collection, it is often pragmatic to periodically compute the SVD.

2.6.1 LSI Example

To demonstrate Latent Semantic Indexing, we once again use our previous query and document example:

Q: "gold silver truck"
D_1 "Shipment of gold damaged in a fire."
D_2: "Delivery of silver arrived in a silver truck."
D_3: "Shipment of gold arrived in a truck."

The A matrix is obtained from the numeric columns in the term-document table given below:

	D_1	D_2	D_3
a	1	1	1
arrived	0	1	1
damaged	1	0	0
delivery	0	1	0
fire	1	0	0
gold	1	0	1
in	1	1	1
of	1	1	1
shipment	1	0	1
silver	0	2	0
truck	0	1	1

This step computes the singular value decompositions (SVD) on A. This results in an expression of A as the product of $U \sum V^T$. In our example, A is equal to the product of:

$$\begin{bmatrix} -0.4201 & 0.0748 & -0.0460 \\ -0.2995 & -0.2001 & 0.4078 \\ -0.1206 & 0.2749 & -0.4538 \\ -0.1576 & -0.3046 & -0.2006 \\ -0.1206 & 0.2749 & -0.4538 \\ -0.2626 & 0.3794 & 0.1547 \\ -0.4201 & 0.0748 & -0.0460 \\ -0.4201 & 0.0748 & -0.0460 \\ -0.2626 & 0.3794 & 0.1547 \\ -0.3151 & -0.6093 & -0.4013 \\ -0.2995 & -0.2001 & 0.4078 \end{bmatrix} \begin{bmatrix} 4.0989 & 0 & 0 \\ 0 & 2.3616 & 0 \\ 0 & 0 & 1.2737 \end{bmatrix} \begin{bmatrix} -0.4945 & -0.6458 & -0.5817 \\ 0.6492 & -0.7194 & -0.2469 \\ -0.5780 & -0.2556 & 0.7750 \end{bmatrix}$$

However, it is not the intent to reproduce A exactly. What is desired, is to find the best rank k approximation of A. We only want the largest k singular values ($k < 3$). The choice of k and the number of singular values in Σ to use is somewhat arbitrary. For our example, we choose $k = 2$. We now have $A_2 = U_2 \sum_2 V_2^T$. Essentially, we take only the first two columns of U and the first two rows of $\sum$ and V^T.

This new product is:

$$\begin{bmatrix} -0.4201 & 0.0748 \\ -0.2995 & -0.2001 \\ -0.1206 & 0.2749 \\ -0.1576 & -0.3046 \\ -0.1206 & 0.2749 \\ -0.2626 & 0.3794 \\ -0.4201 & 0.0748 \\ -0.4201 & 0.0748 \\ -0.2626 & 0.3794 \\ -0.3151 & -0.6093 \\ -0.2995 & -0.2001 \end{bmatrix} \begin{bmatrix} 4.0989 & 0 \\ 0 & 2.3616 \end{bmatrix} \begin{bmatrix} -0.4945 & -0.6458 & -0.5817 \\ 0.6492 & -0.7194 & -0.2469 \end{bmatrix}$$

To obtain a $k \times 1$ dimensional array, we now incorporate the query. The query vector q^T is constructed in the same manner as the original A matrix. The query vector is now mapped into a 2-space by the transformation $q^T U_2 \sum_2^{-1}$.

$$\begin{bmatrix} 0 \\ 0 \\ 0 \\ 0 \\ 0 \\ 1 \\ 0 \\ 0 \\ 0 \\ 1 \\ 1 \end{bmatrix}^T \begin{bmatrix} -0.4201 & 0.0748 \\ -0.2995 & -0.2001 \\ -0.1206 & 0.2749 \\ -0.1576 & -0.3046 \\ -0.1206 & 0.2749 \\ -0.2626 & 0.3794 \\ -0.4201 & 0.0748 \\ -0.4201 & 0.0748 \\ -0.2626 & 0.3794 \\ -0.3151 & -0.6093 \\ -0.2995 & -0.2001 \end{bmatrix} \begin{bmatrix} 0.2440 & 0 \\ 0 & 0.4234 \end{bmatrix} = \begin{bmatrix} -0.2140 & -0.1821 \end{bmatrix}$$

We could use the same transformation to map our document vectors into 2-space, but the rows of V_2 contain the co-ordinates of the documents. Therefore:

D_1 = (-0.4945 -0.0688)
D_2 = (-0.6458 0.9417)
D_3 = (-0.5817 1.2976)

Finally, we are ready to compute our relevance value using the cosine similarity coefficient. This yields the following:

$$D_1 = \frac{(-0.2140)(-0.4945) + (-0.1821)(0.6492)}{\sqrt{(-0.2140)^2 + (-0.1821)^2)}\sqrt{(-0.4945)^2 + (0.6492)^2)}} = -0.0541$$

$$D_2 = \frac{(-0.2140)(-0.6458) + (-0.1821)(-0.7194)}{\sqrt{(-0.2140)^2 + (-0.1821)^2)}\sqrt{(-0.6458)^2 + (-0.7194)^2)}} = 0.9910$$

$$D_3 = \frac{(-0.2140)(-0.5817) + (-0.1821)(-0.2469)}{\sqrt{(-0.2140)^2 + (-0.1821)^2)}\sqrt{(-0.5817)^2 + (-0.2469)^2)}} = 0.9543$$

2.6.2 Choosing a Good Value of k

The value k is the number of columns kept after the SVD, and it is determined via experimentation. Using the MED database of only 1,033 documents and thirty queries, the average precision over nine levels of recall was plotted for different values of k. Starting at twenty, the precision increases dramatically up to values of around 100, and then it starts to level off.

2.6.3 Comparison to Other Retrieval Strategies

A comparison is given between Latent Semantic Indexing (LSI) with a factor of 100 to both the basic *tf-idf* vector space retrieval strategy and the extended Boolean retrieval strategy. For the MED collection, LSI had thirteen percent higher average precision than both strategies. For the CISI collection of scientific abstracts, LSI did not have higher precision. Upon review, the authors found that the term selection for the LSI and *tf-idf* experiments was very different. The LSI approach did not use stemming or stop words. When the same terms were used for both methods, LSI was comparable to *tf-idf*. More work was done with LSI on the TIPSTER collection [Dumais, 1994]. In this work, LSI was shown to perform slightly better than the conventional vector space model, yielding a 0.24 average precision as compared to 0.22 average precision.

2.6.4 Potential Extensions

LSI is relatively straightforward, and few variations are described in the literature. LSI focuses on the need for a semantic representation of documents that is resilient to the fact that many terms in a query can describe a relevant document, but not actually be present in the document.

2.6.5 Run-Time Performance

Run-time performance of the LSI approach is clearly a serious concern. With the vector space or probabilistic retrieval strategy, an inverted index is used to quickly compute the similarity coefficient. Each document in the collection does not need to be examined (unless a term in the query appears in every document). With LSI, an inverted index is not possible as the query is represented as just another document and must, therefore, be compared with all other documents.

Also, the SVD itself is computationally expensive. We note that several parallel algorithms were developed specifically for the computation of the SVD given here [Berry, 1992]. For a document collection with N documents and a singular value matrix $\sum$ of rank k, an $O(N^2k^3)$ algorithm is available. A detailed comparison of several parallel implementations for information retrieval using LSI is given in [Letsche and Berry, 1997].

2.7 Neural Networks

Neural networks consist of nodes and links. Essentially, nodes are composed of output values and input values. The output values, when activated, are then passed along links to other nodes. The links are weighted because the value passed along the link is the product of the sending nodes output and the link weight. An input value of a node is computed as the sum of all incoming weights. Neural networks can be constructed in layers such that all the data the network receives are activated in phases, and where an entire layer sends data to the next layer in a single phase. Algorithms that attempt to learn based on a training set, modify the weights of the links in response to training data. Initial work with neural networks to implement information retrieval was done in [Belew, 1989]. This work used only bibliographic citations, but it illustrates the basic layered approach used by later efforts.

For ad hoc query retrieval, neural nets were used to implement vector space retrieval and probabilistic retrieval. Additionally, relevance feedback can be implemented with neural networks.

Using a neural network to implement vector space retrieval can, at first, appear to be of limited interest. As we have discussed (see Section 2.1), the model can be implemented without the use of neural networks. However, neural networks provide a learning capability in which the network can be changed based on relevance information. In this regard, the network adapts or learns about user preferences during a session with an end-user.

Section 2.7.1 describes a vector space implementation with a neural network. Section 2.7.2 describes implementation of relevance feedback. Section 2.7.3 describes a learning algorithm that can be used with a neural network for information retrieval. Subsequently, we describe a probabilistic implementation in Section 2.7.4. Section 2.7.5 describes how term components can be used within neural networks. Section 2.7.6 uses weights derived from those used for vector space and probabilistic models.

2.7.1 Vector Space

To use a neural network to implement the vector space model, we establish a network of three types of nodes: QUERY, TERM, and DOCUMENT [Crouch et al., 1994]. The links between the nodes are defined as query-term links and document-term links. A link between a query and a term indicates the term appears in the query. The weight of the link is computed as *tf-idf* for the term. Document-term links appear for each term that occurs in a given document. Again, a tf-idf weight can be used.

A feed-forward network works by activating a given node. A node is active when its output exceeds a given threshold. To begin, a query node is activated by setting its output value to one. All of its links are activated and subsequently new input weights for the TERM nodes are obtained. The link sends a value of $(tf)(idf)(1)$ since it transmits the product of the link weight with the value sent by the transmitting node (a one in this case). The weight, *tf-idf* in this case, is received by the term node. A receiving node computes its weight as the sum of all incoming links. For a term node with only one activated query, one link will be activated. The TERM node's output value will be a tf-idf weight. In the next phase, the TERM nodes are activated and all of the links that connect to a document node are activated. The DOCUMENT node contains the sum of all of the weights associated with each term in the document. For a collection with t terms, the DOCUMENT node associated with document j will now have the value:

$$DOC_j = \sum_{i=1}^{t} (tf_{ij})(idf_j)$$

The DOCUMENT node now has a weight associated with it that measures the relevance of the document to a given query. It can easily be seen that this weight is equivalent to a simple dot product similarity coefficient as given in Section 2.1.

2.7.2 Relevance Feedback

To implement relevance feedback, a new set of links are added to the network. The new links connect DOCUMENT nodes back to TERM nodes. The document-term link is activated after the initial retrieval. Figure 2.9 illustrates this process along with a sample query and three documents. Links are fed into a newly defined input site on the TERM node, and their input is added to the value found in the existing query site of the TERM node. Without relevance feedback, the network operates in two phases. The first phase sends information from the QUERY nodes to the TERM nodes. The second phase sends information from the TERM nodes to the DOCUMENT nodes.

If relevance feedback is used, processing continues. The third phase sends information from the DOCUMENT nodes to the TERM nodes for the documents that are deemed relevant. The relevant documents are identified manually, or the top n documents can be deemed relevant. Finally, in the fourth phase, the TERM nodes are activated, if they exceed a threshold parameter. The TERM-DOCUMENT links are used to send the newly defined weights

Figure 2.9. Neural Network with Feedback

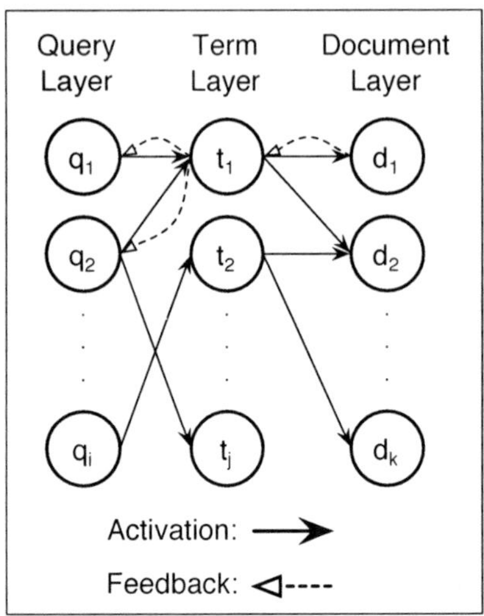

obtained during the relevance feedback phase to the DOCUMENT nodes. At this point, the DOCUMENT nodes are scored with a value that indicates the effect of a single iteration of relevance feedback.

Initial experiments with the MEDLARS and CACM collection found an improvement of up to fifteen percent in average precision for MEDLARS and a degradation of eleven percent for CACM. As mentioned before, these collections are very small. Using a residual evaluation, in which documents found before relevance feedback are no longer considered, the average precision for CACM reached twenty-one percent and MEDLARS was as high as sixty percent.

2.7.3 Learning Modifications

The links between the terms and documents can be modified so that future queries can take advantage of relevance information. Typical vector space relevance feedback uses relevance information to adjust the score of an individual query. A subsequent query is viewed as a brand new event, and no knowledge from any prior relevance assessments is incorporated.

To incorporate relevance information into subsequent queries, the document nodes add a new signal called the learning signal. This is set to one if the user judges the document as relevant, zero if it is not judged, and negative one if it is judged as non-relevant. Term-document links are then adjusted based on the difference between the user assessment and the existing document weight. Documents with high weights that are deemed relevant do not result in much change to the network. A document weighted 0.95 will have a δ of $1 - 0.95 = 0.05$, so each of its term-document links will be increased by only five percent. A document with a low weight that is deemed relevant will result in a much higher adjustment to the network.

Results of incorporating the learning weight were not substantially different than simple relevance feedback, but the potential for using results of feedback sets this approach apart from traditional vector space relevance ranking.

2.7.4 Probabilistic Retrieval

Standard probabilistic retrieval based on neural networks is described in [Crestani, 1994]. The standard term weight given in Sparck Jones and described in more detail in Section 2.2.1 is used. This weight is:

$$\log \frac{r_i(N - n_i - R + r_i)}{(R - r_i)(n_i - r_i)}$$

where:

N = number of documents

R = relevant documents

r_i = number of relevant documents that contain term i

n_i = number of documents (relevant or non-relevant) that contain term i

The weight is a ratio of how often a term appears in relevant documents to the number of times it occurs in the whole collection. A term that is infrequent in the collection, but appears in most of the relevant documents is given a high weight. These weights are used as the weight of the query-term links, the term-document links, and essentially replaces the *tf-idf* weights used in the vector space model. The sum operation to combine links takes place as before, and results in a value that is very similar to the weight computed by the standard probabilistic retrieval model.

The training data are used, and a standard back propagation learning algorithm is used to re-compute the weights. Once training is complete, the top ten terms are computed using the neural network, and the query is modified to include these terms.

Using the Cranfield collection, the neural network-based algorithm performed consistently worse than the *News Retrieval Tool*, an existing probabilistic relevance feedback system [Sanderson and Rijsbergen, 1991]. The authors cite the relative lack of training data as one problem. Also, the authors note that the large number of links in the neural network makes the network cumbersome and consumes a substantial computational resource.

2.7.5 Component Based Probabilistic Retrieval

A component-based retrieval model using neural networks is given in [Kwok, 1989]. A three-layered network is used as before, but the weights are different. Query-term links for query a are assigned a weight of $w_{ka} = \frac{q_{ak}}{L_q}$, where q_{ak} is the frequency of term k in query a. Document term links for document i are assigned $w_{ki} = \frac{d_{ik}}{L_i}$, where d_{ik} indicates the term frequency of term k in document i. L_q is the number of terms in the query and L_i is the number of terms in document i. Term-query links are weighted w_{ak} and document-term links are weighted w_{ik}. The query-focused measure is obtained by activating document nodes and feeding forward to the query. The document–focused measure is obtained by activating the query nodes and feeding forward to the documents.

Kwok extended his initial work with neural networks in [Kwok, 1995]. The basic approach is given along with new learning algorithms that make it possible to modify the weights inside of the neural network based on a training collection. Learning algorithms that added new terms to the query based on relevance feedback were given. Other algorithms did not require any additional query terms and simply modified the weights. The algorithms were tested on a larger corpus using more than three hundred megabytes of the *Wall Street Journal* portion of the TIPSTER collection. Kwok goes on to give learning algorithms based on no training collections, training based on relevance information, and query expansion.

Without a training collection, some initial data estimates can be assigned a constant (see Section 2.2.4). Training with relevance information proceeds using document-term links and term-document links as described in Section 2.7.2.

2.7.6 Combined Weights

A similar input-term-document-output layered neural network was used in [Boughanem and Soule-Depuy, 1997]. To our knowledge, this is the first report of the use of a neural network on a reasonably large document collection.

The key weight, which is used to represent the occurrence of a term in a document, is based on the pivoted document length normalization developed for the vector space model and the document length normalization developed for the probabilistic model (See Section 2.1.2 and Section 2.2.3).

The weight of the link from term t_i to document D_j is:

$$w_{ij} = \frac{(1 + \log(tf_{ij})) * (h_1 + h_2 * \log \frac{N}{df_i}))}{h_3 + h_4 * \frac{d_j}{\Delta}}$$

where:

$$\begin{aligned} tf_{ij} &= \text{weight of term } i \text{ in document } j \\ df_i &= \text{number of documents that contains term } i \\ d_j &= \text{length in terms (not included stop terms) of document } j \\ \Delta &= \text{average document length} \end{aligned}$$

Tuning parameters, h_1, h_2, h_3, and h_4, were obtained by training on the TREC-5 collection. Relevance feedback was also incorporated with the top twelve documents assumed relevant and used to supply additional terms. Documents 500-1000 were assumed non-relevant. An average precision of 0.1772 was observed on the TREC-6 data, placing this effort among the top performers at TREC-6.

2.7.7 Document Clustering

A neural network algorithm for document clustering is given in [Macleod and Robertson, 1991]. The algorithm performs comparably to sequential clustering algorithms that are all hierarchical in nature. On a parallel machine the neural algorithm can perform substantially faster since the hierarchical algorithms are all inherently sequential.

The algorithm works by first associating a node in the network for each cluster. Each node then computes (in parallel) a measure of similarity between the existing document and the centroid that represents the cluster associated with the node. First, a similarity coefficient is computed between the incoming document X and the existing cluster centroids. The input nodes of the neural network correspond to each cluster. If the similarity coefficient, s_1, is higher than a threshold, s_{1avg}, the input node is activated. It then loops back to itself after a small recalculation to participate in a competition to add X to the cluster. Nodes that are not sufficiently close enough to the incoming document are deactivated.

A new pass then occurs for all of the nodes that won the first round, and the similarity coefficient is computed again. The process continues until only one cluster passes the threshold. At this point, a different similarity coefficient is computed, s_2, to ensure the winning cluster is reasonably close to the incoming document. If it is close enough, it is added to the cluster, and the centroid for the cluster is updated. Otherwise, a new cluster is formed with the incoming document.

The algorithm performed comparably to the single linkage, complete linkage, group average, and Ward's method which are described in Section 3.2. Given that this algorithm is non-hierarchical and can be implemented in parallel, it can be more practical than its computationally expensive hierarchical counterparts.

2.8 Genetic Algorithms

Genetic algorithms are based on principles of evolution and heredity. An overview of genetic algorithms used for information retrieval is given in [Chen, 1995]. Chen reviews the following steps for genetic algorithms:

- Initialize Population
- Loop
  - Evaluation
  - Selection
  - Reproduction
  - Crossover
  - Mutation
- Convergence

The initial population consists of possible solutions to the problem, and a fitness function that measures the relative "fitness" of a given solution. Note that the similarity coefficient is a good fitness function for the problem of finding relevant documents to a given query. Some solutions are selected (preferably the ones that are most fit) to survive, and go on to the next generation. The solutions correspond to chromosomes, and each component of a solution is referred to as a gene.

The next generation is formed by selecting the surviving chromosomes. This is done based on the fitness function. A value F is computed as the sum of the individual fitness functions:

$$F = \sum_{i=1}^{population} fitness(V_i)$$

where $population$ is the number of initial solutions. Consider a case where the initial population has a fitness function as given in Table 2.27:
The aggregate sum of the fitness function, F, is 100, and the population size is five. To form the next generation, five values are chosen randomly, with a bias based on their corresponding portion of F.

In Table 2.28, the proportions of the total for each entry in the population are presented. To form a new generation of size five, five random values are selected between zero and one. The selection interval used for each member

Table 2.27. Simple Fitness Function

i	*fitness(i)*
1	5
2	10
3	25
4	50
5	10

of the population is based on its portion of the fitness function. If the random number is 0.50 it falls within the (0.40, 0.90] interval, and member four is selected. The magnitude of the fitness for a given member plays a substantial role in determining whether or not that member survives to the next generation. In our case, member four's fitness function is one half of the fitness function. There is a $1 - (\frac{1}{2})^5 = \frac{31}{32}$ chance of selecting this member into the next round.

Table 2.28. Selection Interval

i	fitness(i)	$\frac{fitness(i)}{F}$	Selection Interval
1	5	0.05	[0,0.05)
2	10	0.10	[0.05,0.15)
3	25	0.25	[0.15,0.40)
4	50	0.50	[0.40,0.90)
5	10	0.10	[0.90,1.0]

Two types of changes can occur to the survivors—a crossover or a mutation. A crossover occurs between two survivors and is obtained by swapping components of the two survivors. Consider a case where the first survivor is represented as 11111 and the second is 00000. A random point is then selected, (e.g., three). After the crossover, the two new children are: 11100 and 00011. This first child is derived from the first three one's from the first parent and the last two zero's of the second parent. The second child is derived from the first three zero's of the second parent with the last two one's of the first parent.

Subsequently, mutations occur by randomly examining each gene of each survivor. The probability of mutation is a parameter to the genetic algorithm. In implementations of genetic algorithms for information retrieval, the genes are represented as bits and a mutation results in a single bit changing its value. In our example, a random mutation in the second bit of the second child results in the second child changing its value from zero to one giving 01011.

The process continues until the fitness function for a new generation or sequence of generations is no better than it was for a preceding generation. This is referred to as *convergence*. Some algorithms do not attain convergence and are stopped after a predetermined number of generations.

2.8.1 Forming Document Representations

An initial foray into the use of genetic algorithms for information retrieval is given in [Gordon, 1988]. The premise being that a key problem in information retrieval is finding a good representation for a document. Hence, the initial population consists of multiple representations for each document in the collection. Each representation is a vector that maps to a term or phrase that is most likely selected by some users. A fixed set of queries is then identified, and a genetic algorithm is used to form the best representation for each document.

The query representation stays fixed, but the document representation is evaluated and modified using the genetic algorithm. The Jaccard similarity coefficient is used to measure the fitness of a given representation. The total fitness for a given representation is computed as the average of the similarity coefficient for each of the training queries against a given document representation. Document representations then "evolve" as described above by crossover transformations and mutations. Overall, the average similarity coefficient of all queries and all document representations should increase. Gordon showed an increase of nearly ten percent after forty generations.

First, a set of queries for which it was known that the documents were relevant were processed. The algorithm was then modified to include processing of queries that were non-relevant. Each generation of the algorithm did two sets of computations. One was done for the relevant queries and another for the non-relevant queries, against each representation. Survivors were then selected based on those that maximized the increase of the average Jaccard score to the relevant queries and maximized a decrease of the average Jaccard score for the non-relevant queries. After forty generations, the average increase was nearly twenty percent and the average decrease was twenty-four percent. Scalability of the approach can not be determined since the queries and the documents came from an eighteen document collection with each document having eighteen different description collections. These results must be viewed as somewhat inconclusive.

It should be noted, however, that although we referred to this as a document indexing algorithm, it is directly applicable to document retrieval. Different automatically generated representations, such as only terms, only phrases, different stemming algorithms, etc., could be used. After some training and evolution, a pattern could emerge that indicates the best means of representing documents. Additionally, we note that this strategy might be more applicable for document routing applications than for ad hoc query processing.

2.8.2 Automatic Generation of Query Weights

A genetic algorithm that derives query weights is given in [Yang and Korfhage, 1994]. It was tested on the small Cranfield collection. Tests using the DOE portion of the TIPSTER collection (and associated modifications that were necessary to scale to a larger collection) are given in [Yang and Korfhage, 1993]. Essentially, the original query is taken without any weights. The initial population is simply composed of randomly generating ten sets of weights for the terms in the original query. In effect, ten queries then exist in the population.

The genetic algorithm subsequently implements each of the queries and identifies a fitness function. First, the distance from the query to each document is computed, and the top x documents are retrieved for the query (x is determined based on a distance threshold used to determine when to stop retrieving documents, with an upper limit of forty documents). The fitness function is based on a relevance assessment of the top x documents retrieved:

$$\text{fitness(i)} = 10R_r - R_n - N_r$$

where:

$$R_r = \text{number of relevant retrieved}$$
$$R_n = \text{number of non-relevant retrieved}$$
$$N_r = \text{number of relevant not retrieved}$$

Basically, a good fitness value is given for finding relevant documents. Since it is difficult to retrieve any relevant documents for larger collections, a constant of ten is used to give extra weight to the identification of relevant documents. Selection is based on choosing only those individuals whose fitness is higher than the average. Subsequently, reproduction takes place using the weighted application of the fitness value such that individuals with a high fitness value are most likely to reproduce. Mutations are then applied with some randomly changed weights. Crossover changes occur in which portions of one query vector are swapped with another. The process continues until all relevant documents are identified. The premise is that the original queries will find some relevant documents and, based on user feedback, other relevant documents will be found.

Tests on the Cranfield collection showed improved average precision, after feedback, to be twenty percent higher than previous relevance feedback approaches. In the follow-up paper using the DOE collection, the authors indicate that the genetic algorithm continues to find new relevant documents in each pass. This is interesting because the only thing that changes in the query are the query weights. No new terms are added or removed from the query.

Yang and Korfhage did use a relatively large collection (the DOE portion of the TIPSTER document collection) but only tested two queries.

2.8.3 Automatic Generation of Weighted Boolean Queries

Genetic algorithms to build queries are given in [Kraft et al., 1994, Petry et al., 1993]. The idea is that the perfect query for a given request can be evolved from a set of single query terms. Given a set of documents known to be relevant to the query, all of the terms in those documents can be used as the initial population for a genetic algorithm. Each term is then a query, and its fitness can be measured with a similarity coefficient (Kraft et al., used the Jaccard coefficient). Mutations of the query terms resulted in weighted Boolean combinations of the query terms. Three different fitness functions were proposed. The first is simple recall:

$$E_1 = \frac{r}{R}$$

where r is the number of relevant retrieved and R is the number of known relevant.

The second combines recall and precision as:

$$E_2 = \alpha(recall) + \beta(precision)$$

where α and β are arbitrary weights.

The results showed that either of E_1 or E_2 fitness functions were able to generate queries that found all of the relevant documents (after fifty generations). Since E_2 incorporated precision, the number of non-relevant documents found decreased from an average of thirty-three (three different runs were implemented for each test) to an average of nine.

This work showed that genetic algorithms could be implemented to generate weighted Boolean queries. Unfortunately, it was only done for two queries on a small document collection (CACM collection with 483 documents), so it is not clear if this algorithm scales to a larger document collection.

2.9 Fuzzy Set Retrieval

Fuzzy sets were first described in [Zadeh, 1965]. Instead of assuming that an element is a member in a set, a membership function is applied to identify the degree of membership in a set. For information retrieval, fuzzy sets are useful because they can describe what a document is "about."

A set of elements where each element describes what the document is about is inherently fuzzy. A document can be about "medicine" with some oblique references to lawsuits, so maybe it is slightly about "medical malpractice." Placing "medical malpractice" as an element of the set is not really accurate, but eliminating it is also inaccurate. A fuzzy set is a membership in which the strength of membership of each element is inherently more accurate. In our example, the set of concepts that describe the document appears as:

$$C = \{(medicine,\ 1.0),\ (malpractice,\ 0.5)\}$$

The set C is a fuzzy set since it has degrees of membership associated with each member. More formally, a fuzzy set including the concepts in $C = \{c_1,\ c_2, \ldots, c_n\}$ is represented as:

$$A = (c_1,\ f_{A(c_1)}),\ (c_2,\ f_{A(c_2)}), \ldots,\ (c_n,\ f_{A(c_n)})$$

where $f_A : C \rightarrow [0, 1]$ is a membership function that indicates the degree of membership of an element in the set.

For finite sets, the fuzzy set A is expressed as:

$$A = \left\{ \frac{f_{A(c_1)}}{c_1}, \frac{f_{A(c_2)}}{c_2}, \ldots, \frac{f_{A(c_n)}}{c_n} \right\}$$

Basic operations of intersection and union on fuzzy sets are given below. Essentially, the intersection uses the minimum of the two membership functions for the same element, and union uses the maximum of the two membership functions for the same element.

The following definitions are used to obtain intersection, union, and complement.

$$f_{A \bigcap B}(c_i) = Min(f_{A(c_i)}, f_{B(c_i)}), \forall c_i \in C.$$

$$f_{A \bigcup B}(c_i) = Max(f_{A(c_i)}, f_{B(c_i)}), \forall c_i \in C.$$

$$f_{A'}(c_i) = 1 - f_{A(c_i)}, \forall c_i \in C.$$

2.9.1 Boolean Retrieval

Fuzzy set extensions to Boolean retrieval were developed in the late 1970's and are summarized in [Salton, 1989]. A Boolean similarity coefficient can be computed by treating the terms in a document as fuzzy because their membership is based on how often they occur in the document.

Consider a set D that consists of all documents in the collection. A fuzzy set D_t can be computed as the set D that describes all documents that contain the term t. This set appears as: $D_t = \{(d_1, 0.8), (d_2, 0.5)\}$. This indicates that d_1 contains element t with a strength of 0.8 and d_2 contains t with a strength of 0.5.

Similarly, a set D_s can be defined as the set of all documents that contain term s. This set might appear as: $D_s = \{(d_1, 0.5), (d_2, 0.4)\}$

Computing $(s \bigvee t)$ requires $D_s \bigcup D_t$ and $(s \bigwedge t)$ $D_s \bigcap D_t$. These can be computed using the maximum value for union and the minimum for intersection. Hence:

$$(s \bigvee t) = D_s \bigcup D_t = \{(d_1, 0.8), (d_2, 0.5)\}$$

$$(s \bigwedge t) = D_s \bigcap D_t = \{(d_1, 0.5), (d_2, 0.4)\}$$

More complex Boolean expressions are constructed by applying the results of these operations to new expressions. Ultimately, a single set that contains the documents and their similarity coefficient is obtained.

One problem with this approach is that the model does not allow for the weight of query terms. This can be incorporated into the model by multiplying the query term weight by the existing membership strength for each element in the set. Another problem is that terms with very low weight dominate the similarity coefficient. Terms that have a very low membership function are ultimately the only factor in the similarity coefficient. Consider a case where document one contains term s with a membership value of 0.0001 and term t with a membership value of 0.5. In a query asking for $s \bigwedge t$, the score for document one will be 0.0001. Should the query have many more terms, this one term dominates the weight of the entire similarity coefficient. A remedy for this is to define a threshold x in which the membership function becomes zero if it falls below x.

2.9.1.1 Fuzzy Set Example

We now apply fuzzy set Boolean retrieval to our example. Our query "gold silver truck" is inadequate as it is designed for a relevance ranking, so we change it to the Boolean request: "gold OR silver OR truck." We take each document as a fuzzy set. To get a strength of membership for each term, we take the ratio of the term frequency within the document to the document length. Hence, our collection of documents becomes a collection of fuzzy sets:

D_1 = {(a, 0.143), (damaged, 0.143), (fire, 0.143), (gold, 0.143), (in, 0.143), (of, 0.143), (shipment, 0.143)}

D_2 = {(a, 0.125), (arrived, 0.125), (delivery, 0.125), (in, 0.125), (of, 0.125), (silver, 0.25), (truck, 0.125)}

D_3 = {(a, 0.143), (arrived, 0.143), (gold, 0.143), (in, 0.143), (of, 0.143), (shipment, 0.143), (truck, 0.143)}

To compute Q(*gold* $\bigvee$ *silver* $\bigvee$ *truck*), we look at the documents which contain each of those terms. *Gold* is in D_1 and D_3 with a strength of membership of 0.143. *Silver* is only in D_2 with a strength of membership of 0.25. Similarly, *truck* is in D_2 with a membership of 0.125 and D_3 with 0.143. Applying the maximum set membership to implement the fuzzy OR, we obtain:

Q(*gold* $\bigvee$ *silver* $\bigvee$ *truck*) = $\{(D_1, 0.143), (D_2, 0.25), (D_3, 0.143)\}$

The documents would then be ranked, D_2, D_1, D_3 based on strength of membership for each document. As another example, consider the query: (*truck* $\bigwedge$ (*gold* $\bigvee$ *silver*)). For this query, we determine D(*truck*) and D(*gold* $\bigvee$ *silver*)—we will refer to these two sets as set A and set B.

A = D(*truck*) = $\{(D_2, 0.125), (D_3, 0.143)\}$

For D(*gold* $\bigvee$ *silver*) we proceed as before, taking the maximum value of each degree of membership for each document in which either term appears. From our previous computation, we determine:

B = D(*gold* $\bigvee$ *silver*) = $\{(D_1, 0.143), (D_2, 0.25), (D_3, 0.143)\}$

Taking the fuzzy intersection of set A with set B we use the minimum strength of membership. This yields:

A $\bigcap$ B = D(*truck* $\bigwedge$ (*gold* $\bigvee$ *silver*)) = $\{(D_2,0.125), (D_3, 0.143)\}$

At this point, we have not incorporated any query weights. We now modify the example to multiply each strength of membership by the *idf* for each query term. We use the following query term weights:

$$\text{gold} = \log \frac{3}{2} = 0.176$$

$$\text{silver} = \log \frac{3}{1} = 0.477$$

$$\text{truck} = \log \frac{3}{2} = 0.176$$

We now compute D(*gold* $\bigvee$ *silver* $\bigvee$ *truck*). D_1 includes only *gold* with a strength of 0.143. *Gold* has a query term weight of 0.176, so D_1 has a weighted strength of membership of (0.143)(0.176) = 0.025. *Silver* and *truck* are found in D_2. *Silver* has a strength of membership of 0.25 and a weight of 0.477; so the weighted strength of (0.25)(0.477) = 0.119. Similarly, for *truck*, the weighted strength is (0.125)(0.176) = 0.022. Since we are taking the union, we take the maximum value so D_2 will have a strength of membership of 0.119.

For D_3, both *gold* and *truck* are present with a strength of 0.143 and both terms are weighted by 0.176. Hence, the weighted strength is (0.143)(0.176) = 0.025. The fuzzy set D(*gold* $\bigvee$ *silver* $\bigvee$ *truck*) = $\{(D_1, 0.025), (D_2, 0.119), (D_3, 0.025)\}$ For the query, D(*truck* $\bigwedge$ (*gold* $\bigvee$ *silver*)) we must again determine D(*gold* $\bigvee$ *silver*) and D(*truck*). Using the weighted strength of membership yields:

A = D(*truck*) = $\{(D_2, 0.022), (D_3, 0.025)\}$
B = D(*gold* $\bigvee$ *silver*) = $\{D_1, 0.025), (D_2, 0.119), (D_3, 0.025)\}$

Again, taking the minimum strength of membership to compute the intersection, we obtain:

A $\bigcap$ B = D(*truck* $\bigwedge$ (*gold* $\bigvee$ *silver*)) = $\{(D_2, 0.022), (D_3, 0.025)\}$

2.9.2 Using a Concept Hierarchy

An approach using fuzzy logical inference with a concept hierarchy was used in the FIRST system (Fuzzy Information Retrieval SysTem) [Lucarella and Morara, 1991].

A concept network is used to represent concepts found in documents and queries and to represent the relationships between these concepts. A concept network is a graph with each vertex representing a concept and a directed edge between two vertices representing the strength of the association of the two concepts. A document can then be represented as a fuzzy set of concepts:

$$d_1 = \{(C_1, w_1), (C_2, w_2), \ldots, (C_3, w_3)\}$$

This indicates that document one contains the concepts (C_1, C_2, C_3) and the strength of each concept is given by (w_1, w_2, w_3). The link relationships are defined as *fuzzy transitive* so that if C_i is linked to C_j, and C_j is linked to C_k, and the strength of C_i to C_k is defined as:

$$F(C_i, C_k) = Min(F(C_i, C_j), F(C_j, C_k))$$

To compute the strength between two concepts, take the minimum value of all edges along the path, then add query Q at the root of the concept hierarchy. For each concept linked to the query, it is possible to obtain the strength of that concept for a given document. To do so, find all paths through the concept graph from the concept to the document and take the minimum of all edges that connect the source concept to the document. Each of these paths results in a single value. An aggregation rule is then applied to compute the strength of the source concept as the maximum of the value returned by each distinct path. A detailed example is given in [Lucarella and Morara, 1991]. Note for queries involving more than one initial concept, the appropriate fuzzy operations are applied to each pair of arguments in a Boolean operator.

A comparison of the vector space model to this approach was done. A 300 document Italian test collection was used with a handbuilt concept graph that contained 175 concepts. Ten queries were chosen, and FIRST had comparable precision to vector space and had higher recall.

2.9.3 Allowing Intervals and Improving Efficiency

In [Chen and Wang, 1995], Lucarella's model was extended through the use of intervals rather than real values as concept weights. Additionally, an efficiency improvement was added in that a concept matrix was developed.

The concept matrix is a C x C matrix that is represented such that M(C_i, C_j) indicates the strength of the relationships between C_i and C_j. The strength is defined as a single value or an interval such that the strength occurs somewhere inside of the interval. The transitive closure T of M is computed via successive matrix multiplications of M. Once the T matrix is computed, an entry $T(C_i, C_j)$ indicates the strength of the relationship of C_i to C_j, where the strength is computed as the maximum of all paths from C_i to C_j.

Although the initial computation of T is expensive for a concept network with a high number of concepts, T efficiently computes a similarity coefficient. First, a new matrix of size $D \times C$ maps all of the documents to concepts. An entry, t_{ij}, in this matrix indicates the strength of the relationship between document i and concept j. Values for t_{ij} are obtained either directly, if the concept appears in the given document, or indirectly, if the concept does not appear in the given document—in this case the T matrix is used to obtain the weight for that concept.

Given a document, D_i, with concepts $(c_{i1}, c_{i2}, \ldots, c_{in})$ and a query Q with concepts $(x_1, x_2, \ldots, x_n)$, a similarity coefficient is computed for all concepts that exist in the query (a concept that does not exist in the query has the value of "-"):

$$SC(Q, D_i) = \sum_{q(j) \neq \text{``}-\text{''} \wedge j=1}^{n} T(t_{ij}, x_j)$$

where T(x,y) = 1 - $|x - y|$.

The function T measures the difference between the strength of the concept found in the document and the user input strength of the concept found in the query. The document strength is computed as the minimum of the strengths found on the path from the document to the concept. A small difference results in a high value of T, and the similarity coefficient simply sums these differences for each concept given in the query.

For intervals, a new function, S, computes the average of the distance between the high and low ends of the interval. For example, an interval of [3, 5] compared with an interval of [2, 6] results in a distance of $\frac{|3-2|+|5-6|}{2} = 1$. These differences are then summed for a similarity coefficient based on intervals.

2.10 Summary

We described nine different strategies used to rank documents in response to a query. The probabilistic model, vector space model, and inference networks all use statistical measures that essentially rely upon matching terms between a query and a document.

The vector space model represents documents and queries as vectors. Similarity among documents, and between documents and queries is defined in terms of the distance between two vectors. For example, one of the common similarity measures is the cosine similarity, which treats the difference between two documents or a document and a query as the cosine of the angle between these two vectors.

The probabilistic model uses basic probability theory with some key assumptions to estimate the probability of relevance. It is often criticized as requiring pre-existing relevance information to perform well. We described various means of circumventing this problem—including Kwok's novel idea of using self-relevance to obtain an initial estimate.

A relatively new strategy, language modeling is an approach that has previously worked well in speech recognition. Numerous papers have been written on this strategy in the last few years and it has now clearly taken its place among the most popular strategies discussed today.

Using *evidence*, inference networks use Bayesian inference to infer the probability that a document is relevant. Since inference networks are capable of modeling both vector space and probabilistic models, they may be seen as a more powerful model. In fact, different inference network topologies have yet to be fully explored.

Latent semantic indexing is the only strategy we presented that directly addresses the problem that relevant documents to a query, at times, contain numerous terms that are identical in meaning to the query but do not share the same syntax. By estimating the "latent semantic" characteristics of a term-term matrix, LSI is able to accurately score a document as relevant to the query even though the term-mismatch problem is present.

Neural networks and genetic algorithms are both used commonly for machine learning applications and have only initially been used in document ranking. Computational resource limitations have prevented their widespread use—but the potential for these strategies to retrieve documents that differ from other strategies makes them intriguing.

The fuzzy set and extended Boolean are older strategies that extend the widespread use of Boolean requests into relevance ranks. Other strategies require users to submit a list of terms—instead of a Boolean request—and a ranking is then obtained. In some applications, users prefer Boolean requests. This is particularly true for those users who have relied on Boolean requests for years.

So, which strategy is best? This is still an area for debate, and therefore, for further investigation. To our knowledge, no head-to-head comparison of all of these strategies has been implemented. TREC (Text REtrieval Conference) activities evaluate complete information retrieval systems, but a system includes a strategy and a set of utilities, as well as, a variety of other implementation details. Thus far, no decisive conclusion can be deduced about the contribution of one strategy given a fixed framework of all other system components. Additional thoughts and comments related to these strategies are described in [Salton, 1989, Kowalski and Maybury, 2000], and some of the original papers describing these efforts were reprinted in [Sparck Jones and Willett, 1997].

2.11 Exercises

1 Show how inference networks can be used to model either the vector space model or the probabilistic model.

2 Download *Alice in Wonderland* from the internet. Write some code to identify the *idf* of each term. Identify how closely this work matches the Zipfian distribution.

3 Devise a new strategy that allows users to implement a Boolean retrieval request. The results should be ranked in order of the similarity to the query. Compare your new strategy with the extended Boolean retrieval strategy.

4 Describe the effect of adding new or changing existing documents to the vector space strategy. Which values must be recomputed? How can the strategy be slightly modified so that it is more resilient to the addition of new documents?

5 Develop a detailed example (as done with our standard query: *gold, silver, truck*) and our standard document collection to compute the similarity between the query and each document using Term Components.

6 Develop a detailed example (as done with our standard query: *gold, silver, truck*) and our standard document collection to compute the similarity between the query and each document using language models with Jelinek-Mercer smoothing.

7 It has been suggested that one or more strategies could be merged to form an improved result set. Give two general heuristics to merge results from two

arbitrary retrieval strategies. Describe the advantages and disadvantages inherent in your approach.

Chapter 3

RETRIEVAL UTILITIES

Many different utilities improve the results of a retrieval strategy. Most utilities add or remove terms from the initial query in an attempt to refine the query. Others simply refine the focus of the query by using subdocuments or passages instead of whole documents. The key is that each of these utilities (although rarely presented as such) are plug-and-play utilities that operate with any arbitrary retrieval strategy.

The utilities identified are:

- **Relevance Feedback**—The top documents found by an initial query are identified as relevant. These documents are then examined. They may be deemed relevant either by manual intervention or by an assumption that the top n documents are relevant. Various techniques are used to rank the terms. The top t terms from these documents are then added back to the original query.

- **Clustering**—Documents or terms are clustered into groups either automatically or manually. The query is only matched against clusters that are deemed to contain relevant information. This limits the search space. The goal is to avoid non-relevant documents before the search even begins.

- **Passage-based Retrieval**—The premise is that most relevant documents have a non-relevant portion, and the relevant passage is somewhat concentrated. Hence, queries are matched to passages (either overlapping or non-overlapping) of documents, and the results for each passage are then combined into a single similarity coefficient. The size of each passage is either fixed or varied based on the passage finding algorithm. Other approaches simply rank each sentence, paragraph, or other naturally occurring subdivision of a document.

- **Parsing** (noun phrase processing, stemming, etc.): Simply matching terms does not always yield good results. The identification and use of phrases is computationally much easier than the use of proximity operators. Parsing rules or lists of known phrases are used to identify valid phrases like "New York." These phrases are then treated as single terms. Other parsing techniques avoid common prefixes or suffixes to allow for matches between query and document terms that share a common root but have different prefixes or suffixes.

- **N-grams**—The query is partitioned into n-grams (overlapping or non-overlapping sequences of n characters). These are used to match queries with the document. The goal is to obtain a "fuzzier" match that would be resilient to misspellings or optical character recognition (OCR) errors. Also, n-grams are language independent.

- **Thesauri**—Thesauri are automatically generated from text or by manual methods. The key is not only to generate the thesaurus, but to use it to expand either queries or documents to improve retrieval.

- **Semantic Networks**—Concept hierarchies exist in which individual concepts are linked to other related concepts. The strength of the relationship is associated with the link. One such network is Wordnet [Beckwith and Miller, 1990], but others exist. Attempts to automatically construct such a network were pursued. The challenge is to use the network to expand queries or documents to contain more terms describing the contents of the query.

- **Regression Analysis**— Statistical techniques are used to identify parameters that describe characteristics of a match to a relevant document. These can then be used with a regression analysis to identify the exact parameters that refine the similarity measure.

3.1 Relevance Feedback

A popular information retrieval utility is relevance feedback. The basic premise is to implement retrieval in multiple passes. The user refines the query in each pass based on results of previous queries. Typically, the user indicates which of the documents presented in response to an initial query are relevant, and new terms are added to the query based on this selection. Additionally, existing terms in the query can be re-weighted based on user feedback. This process is illustrated in Figure 3.1.

An alternative is to avoid asking the user anything at all and to simply assume the top ranked documents are relevant. Using either manual (where the user is asked) or automatic (where it is assumed the top documents are relevant) feedback, the initial query is modified, and the new query is re-executed.

Figure 3.1. Relevance Feedback Process

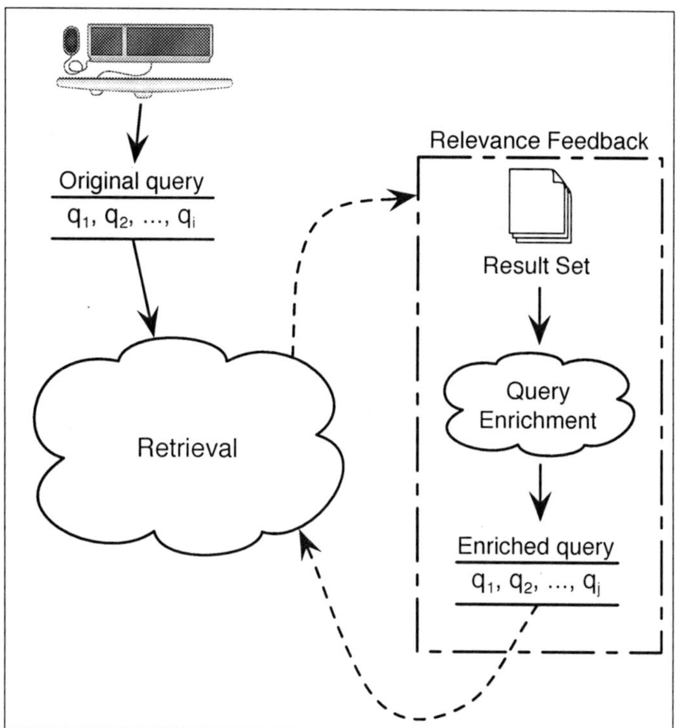

For example, an initial query "find information surrounding the various conspiracy theories about the assassination of John F. Kennedy" has both useful keywords and noise. The most useful keywords are probably *assassination* and *John F. Kennedy.* Like many queries (in terms of retrieval) there is some meaningless information. Terms such as *various* and *information* are probably not stop words (i.e., frequently used words that are typically ignored by an information retrieval system such as *a, an, and, the*), but they are more than likely not going to help retrieve relevant documents. The idea is to use all terms in the initial query and ask the user if the top ranked documents are relevant. The hope is that the terms in the top ranked documents that are said to be relevant will be "good" terms to use in a subsequent query.

Assume a highly ranked document contains the term *Oswald.* It is reasonable to expect that adding the term *Oswald* to the initial query would improve both precision and recall. Similarly, if a top ranked document that is deemed relevant by the user contains many occurrences of the term *assassination*, the weight used in the initial query for this term should be increased.

With the vector space model, the addition of new terms to the original query, the deletion of terms from the query, and the modification of existing term weights has been done. With the probabilistic model, relevance feedback initially was only able to re-weight existing terms, and there was no accepted means of adding terms to the original query. The exact means by which relevance feedback is implemented is fairly dependent on the retrieval strategy being employed. However, the basic concept of relevance feedback (i.e., run a query, gather information from the user, enhance the query, and repeat) can be employed with any arbitrary retrieval strategy.

Section 3.1.1 discusses the initial use of the vector space model to implement relevance feedback. Section 3.1.2 discusses the probabilistic means by which relevance feedback is added.

Relevance feedback has been fertile ground for research, as many tuning parameters are immediately apparent. Most feedback algorithms start with the premise that within the top x ranked documents, the top t terms will be used. Finding correct values for x and t, as well as examining the number of iterations required to obtain good results, has been the subject of a fair amount of research. Recently, a summer workshop was held which focused on identifying good values for x and t [Harman and Buckley, 2004].

3.1.1 Relevance Feedback in the Vector Space Model

Rocchio, in his initial paper, started the discussion of relevance feedback [Rocchio, 1971]. Interestingly, his basic approach has remained fundamentally unchanged.

Rocchio's approach used the vector space model to rank documents. The query is represented by a vector Q, each document is represented by a vector D_i, and a measure of relevance between the query and the document vector is computed as $SC(Q, D_i)$, where SC is the similarity coefficient. As discussed in Section 2.1, the SC is computed as an inner product of the document and query vector or the cosine of the angle between the two vectors. The basic assumption is that the user has issued a query Q and retrieved a set of documents. The user is then asked whether or not the documents are relevant. After the user responds, the set R contains the n_1 relevant document vectors, and the set S contains the n_2 non-relevant document vectors. Rocchio builds the new query Q' from the old query Q using the equation given below:

$$Q' = Q + \frac{1}{n_1}\sum_{i=1}^{n_1} R_i - \frac{1}{n_2}\sum_{i=1}^{n_2} S_i$$

R_i and S_i are individual components of R and S, respectively.

The document vectors from the relevant documents are added to the initial query vector, and the vectors from the non-relevant documents are subtracted. If all documents are relevant, the third term does not appear. To ensure that the new information does not completely override the original query, all vector modifications are normalized by the number of relevant and non-relevant documents. The process can be repeated such that Q_{i+1} is derived from Q_i for as many iterations as desired.

The idea is that the relevant documents have terms matching those in the original query. The weights corresponding to these terms are increased by adding the relevant document vector. Terms in the query that are in the non-relevant documents have their weights decreased. Also, terms that are not in the original query (had an initial component value of zero) are now added to the original query.

In addition to using values n_1 and n_2, it is possible to use arbitrary weights. The equation now becomes:

$$Q' = \alpha Q + \beta \sum_{i=1}^{n_1} \frac{R_i}{n_1} - \gamma \sum_{i=1}^{n_2} \frac{S_i}{n_2}$$

Not all of the relevant or non-relevant documents must be used. Adding thresholds n_a and n_b to indicate the thresholds for relevant and non-relevant vectors results in:

$$Q' = \alpha Q + \beta \sum_{i=1}^{min(n_a, n_1)} \frac{R_i}{n_1} - \gamma \sum_{i=1}^{min(n_b, n_2)} \frac{S_i}{n_2}$$

The weights α, β, and γ are referred to as Rocchio weights and are frequently mentioned in the annual proceedings of TREC. The optimal values were experimentally obtained, but it is considered common today to drop the use of non-relevant documents (assign zero to γ) and only use the relevant documents. This basic theme was used by Ide in follow-up research to Rocchio where the following equation was defined:

$$Q' = \alpha Q + \beta \sum_{i=1}^{n_1} R_i - S_1$$

Only the top ranked non-relevant document is used, instead of the sum of all non-relevant documents. Ide refers to this as the *Dec-Hi* (decrease using highest ranking non-relevant document) approach. Also, a more simplistic weight is described in which the normalization, based on the number of document vectors is removed, and α, β, and γ are set to one [Salton, 1971a]. This new equation is:

$$Q' = Q + \sum_{i=1}^{n_1} R_i - \sum_{i=1}^{n_2} S_i$$

An interesting case occurs when the original query retrieves only non-relevant documents. Kelly addresses this case in [Salton, 1971b]. The approach suggests that an arbitrary weight should be added to the most frequently occurring *concept* in the document collection. This can be generalized to increase the component with the highest weight. The hope is that the term was important, but it was drowned out by all of the surrounding noise. By increasing the weight, the term now rings true and yields some relevant documents. Note that this approach is applied only in manual relevance feedback approaches. It is not applicable to automatic feedback as the top n documents are assumed, by definition, to be relevant.

3.1.2 Relevance Feedback in the Probabilistic Model

We described the basic probabilistic model in Section 2.2. Essentially, the terms in the document are treated as evidence that a document is relevant to a query. Given the assumption of term independence, the probability that a document is relevant is computed as a product of the probabilities of each term in the document matching a term in the query.

The probabilistic model is well suited for relevance feedback because it is necessary to know how many relevant documents exist for a query to compute the term weights. Typically, the native probabilistic model requires some training data for which relevance information is known. Once the term weights are computed, they are applied to another collection.

Relevance feedback does not require training data. Viewed as simply a utility instead of a retrieval strategy, probabilistic relevance feedback "plugs in" to any existing retrieval strategy. The initial query is executed using an arbitrary retrieval strategy and then the relevance information obtained during the feedback stage is incorporated.

For example, the basic weight used in the probabilistic retrieval strategy is:

$$w_i = \log \frac{\frac{r_i}{R-r_i}}{\frac{n_i-r_i}{(N-n_i)-(R-r_i)}}$$

where:

$$
\begin{aligned}
w_i &= \text{weight of term } i \text{ in a particular query} \\
R &= \text{number of documents that are relevant to the query} \\
N &= \text{number of documents in the collection} \\
r_i &= \text{number of relevant documents that contain term } i \\
n_i &= \text{number of documents that contain term } i
\end{aligned}
$$

R and r cannot be known at the time of the initial query unless training data with relevance information is available. Realistically, the presence of domain-independent training data is unlikely. Some other retrieval strategy such as the vector space model could be used for the initial pass, and the top n documents could be observed. At this point, R can be estimated as the total relevant documents found in the top n documents, and r is the number of occurrences in these documents. The problem of requiring training data before the probabilistic retrieval strategy can be used is eradicated with the use of relevance feedback.

3.1.2.1 Initial Estimates

The initial estimates for the use of relevance feedback using the probabilistic model have varied widely. Some approaches simply sum the idf as an initial first estimate. Wu and Salton proposed an interesting extension which requires the use of training data. For a given term t, it is necessary to know how many documents are relevant to term t for other queries. The following equation estimates the value of r_i prior to doing a retrieval:

$$r_i = a + b \log f$$

where *f* is the frequency of the term across the entire document collection.

This equation results in a curve that maps frequency to an estimated number of relevant documents. Frequency is an indicator of the number of relevant documents that will occur because of a given term. After obtaining a few sample points, values for a and b can be obtained by a least squares curve fitting process. Once this is done, the value for r_i can be estimated given a value of f, and using the value of r_i, an estimate for an initial weight (IW) is obtained. The initial weights are then combined to compute a similarity coefficient. In the paper [Wu and Salton, 1981] it was concluded (using very small collections) that idf was far less computationally expensive, and that the IW resulted in slightly worse precision and recall. However, we are unaware of work done with IW on the TREC collection.

3.1.2.2 Computing New Query Weights

Some variations on the basic weighting strategy for use with relevance feedback were proposed in [Robertson and Sparck Jones, 1976]. The potential for using relevance feedback with the probabilistic model was first explored in [Wu and Salton, 1981]. Essentially, Wu and Salton applied Sparck Jones' equation for relevance information [Robertson and Sparck Jones, 1976]. They modified the approach by using the similarity coefficient found in the equation below. Given a vector Q representing the query and a vector D_i representing the documents with a collection of t terms, the following equation computes the similarity coefficient. The components of d_i are assumed to be binary. A one indicates the term is present, and a zero indicates the term is absent, and K is a constant.

$$SC(Q, D_i) = \sum_{i=1}^{t} d_i \log \frac{p_i(1 - u_i)}{u_i(1 - p_i)} + K$$

Using this equation requires estimates for p_i and u_i. The simplest estimate uses $p_i = \frac{r_i+0.5}{R+1}$ and $u_i = \frac{n_i-r_i+0.5}{N-R+1}$. That is, the ratio of the number of relevant documents retrieved that contain term i to the number of relevant documents is a good estimate of the evidence that a term i results in relevance. The 0.5 is simply an adjustment factor. Similarly, the ratio of the number of documents that contain term i that were not retrieved to the number of documents that are not relevant is an estimate of u_i. Substituting these probabilities into the equation yields one of the conventional weights [Robertson and Sparck Jones, 1976], w_2 we described in Section 2.2.1.1:

$$\frac{\frac{r_i+0.5}{R+1}}{\frac{n_i-r_i+0.5}{N-R+1}}$$

Using relevance feedback, a query is initially submitted and some relevant documents might be found in the initial answer set. The top documents are now examined by the user and values for r_i and R can be more accurately estimated (the values for n_i and N are known prior to any retrieval). Once this is done, new weights are computed and the query is executed again. Wu and Salton tested four variations of composing the new query:

1. Generate the new query using weights computed after the first retrieval.

2. Generate the new query, but combine the old weights with the new. Wu suggested that the weights could be combined as:

$$Q' = \frac{1 - \beta}{Q} + (1 - \beta)(T)$$

where Q contains the old weights and T contains the weights computed by using the initial first pass. β is a scaling factor that indicates the importance of the initial weights. The ratio of relevant documents retrieved to relevant documents available collection-wide is used for this value ($\beta = \frac{r_i}{R}$). A query that retrieves many relevant documents should use the new weights more heavily than a query that retrieves only a few relevant documents.

3. Expand the query by combining all the terms in the original query with all the terms found in the relevant documents. The weights for the new query are used as in step one for all of the old terms (those that existed in the original query and in the relevant documents). For terms that occurred in the original query, but not in any documents retrieved in the initial phase, their weights are not changed. This is a fundamental difference from the work done by

Sparck Jones because it allows for expansion as well as reweighting. Before this proposal, work in probabilistic retrieval relied upon the reweighting of old terms, but it did not allow for the addition of new terms.

4. Expand the query using a combination of the initial weight and the new weight. This is similar to variation number two above. Assuming q_1 to q_m are the weights found in the m components of the original query, and $m - n$ new terms are found after the initial pass, we have the following:

$$Q' = \frac{1-\beta}{Q}(q_1, q_2, \ldots, q_m, 0, 0, \ldots, 0) + \beta(q_1, q_2, \ldots, q_m, q_{m+1}, \ldots, q_{m+n})$$

Additionally, a modified estimate for p_i and u_i was computed. These new values are given below:

$$p_i = \frac{r_i + \frac{n_i}{N}}{R+1}$$

$$u_i = \frac{n_i - r_i + \frac{n_i}{N}}{N - R + 1}$$

Here the key element of the idf is used as the adjustment factor instead of the crude 0.5 assumption.

Wu and Salton found the fourth variation, which combines results of reweighting and term expansion, to be the most effective. Relatively little difference was observed with the modified p_i and u_i.

Salton and Buckley give an excellent overview of relevance feedback. Twelve variations on relevance feedback were attempted [Salton and Buckley, 1990]. These included: stemmed Rocchio, Ide, conventional Sparck Jones probabilistic equation (see Section 2.2.1), and the extended probabilistic given in Wu and Salton [Wu and Salton, 1981]. All twelve were tested against six small collections (CACM, CISI, CRAN, INSPEC, MED, and NPL). All of these collections were commonly used by many researchers prior to the development of the larger TIPSTER collection. Different parameters for the variations were tried, such that there were seventy-two different feedback methods in all. Overall Ide Dec-Hi (decrease using the highest ranking elements) performed the best—having a ranking of one in three of the six collections and a ranking of two and six in the others.

3.1.2.3 Partial Query Expansion

The initial work done by Wu and Salton in 1981 either used the original query and reweighted it or added *all* of the terms in the initial result set to the query and computed the weights for them [Wu and Salton, 1981]. The idea of using only a selection of the terms found in the top documents was presented in [Harman, 1988]. In this paper, the top ten documents were retrieved. Some of these documents were manually identified as relevant. The question then arises as to which terms from these documents should be used to expand the initial query. Harman sorted the terms based on six different sort orders and, once the terms were sorted, chose the top twenty terms. The sort order had a large impact on effectiveness. Six different sort orders were tested on the small Cranfield collection.

In many of the sort orders a noise measure, n, is used. This measure, for the $k^{\underline{th}}$ term is computed as:

$$n_k = \sum_{i=1} N \frac{tf_{ik}}{f_k} \log_2 f_k tf_{ik}$$

where:

$$\begin{aligned} tf_{ik} &= \text{number of occurrences of term } i \text{ in document } k \\ f_k &= \text{number of occurrences of term } k \text{ in the collection} \\ N &= \text{number of terms in the collection} \end{aligned}$$

This noise value increases for terms that occur infrequently in many documents, but frequently across the collection. A small value for noise occurs if a term occurs frequently in the collection. It is similar to the idf, but the frequency within individual documents is incorporated.
Additional variables used for sort orders are:

$$\begin{aligned} p_k &= \text{number of documents in the relevant set that contain term } k \\ rtf_k &= \text{number of occurrences of term } k \text{ in the relevant set} \end{aligned}$$

A modified noise measure, rn_k, is defined as the noise within the relevant set. This is computed as:

$$rn_k = \sum_{i=1} p_k \frac{tf_{ik}}{f_k} \log_2 f_k tf_{ik}$$

Various combinations of rn_k, n_k, and p_k were used to sort the top terms. The six sort orders tested were:

- n_k
- p_k
- rn_k
- $n_k \times rtf_k$
- $n_k \times f_k \times p_k$
- $n_k \times f_k$

The sort order: $n_k \times f_k \times p_k$, resulted in the highest improvement in average precision (9.4%). This is very similar to $p_k \times idf$ which is a reasonable measure given that p_k is an intuitively good value to use (i.e., a term that appears frequently in the relevant set is probably a good term to add to the query). However, this will not be the case for noise terms that occur frequently across the collection. This explains why the p_k value did not perform as well as when it was combined with n_k.

Six additional sort orders were tested in a follow-up paper [Harman, 1992]. The sorts tested were:

- $\frac{(RT_j)(df_i)}{N}$ where RT_j is the total number of documents retrieved for query j, df_i is the document frequency or number of documents in the collection that contain term i, and N is the number of documents in the collection. This gives additional weight to terms that appear in multiple documents of the initial answer set.

- $\frac{r_{ij}}{R} - \frac{df_i}{N}$ where r_{ij} is the number of retrieved relevant documents for query j that have term i. R_j is the number of retrieved relevant documents for query j. This gives additional weight to terms that occur in many relevant documents and which occur infrequently across the entire document collection.

- $W_{ij} = \log_2 \frac{p_{ij}(1-q_{ij})}{(1-p_{ij})q_{ij}}$ where W_{ij} is the term weight for term i in query j. This is based on Sparck Jones probabilistic weights given in Section 2.2.1. The probability that term i is assigned within the set of relevant documents to query j is p_{ij}. The probability that term i is assigned within the set of non-relevant documents for query j is q_{ij}. These are computed as:

$$p_{ij} = \frac{r_{ij} + 0.5}{R_j + 1.0} \qquad q_{ij} = \frac{df_i - r_i + 0.5}{N - R_j + 1.0}$$

- $idf_j(p_{ij} - q_{ij})$ where the theoretical foundation is based on the presumption that the term i's importance is computed as the amount that it will increase the difference between the average score of a relevant document and the average score of a nonrelevant document. The means of identifying a term weight are not specified in this work, so for this sort order, idf_j is used. Additional details are given in [Robertson, 1990].

- $W_{ij}(p_{ij} - q_{ij})$ where the term weight is computed as given above.

- $\log(RTF_i + 1)(p_{ij} - q_{ij})$ where RTF_i is the number of occurrences of term i in the retrieved relevant documents.

Essentially, sort three was found to be superior to sorts four, five, and six, but there was little difference in the use of the various sort techniques. Sorts one and two were not as effective.

Once the sort order was identified, the number of terms to add to the new query was studied. A peak at twenty terms was identified. At TREC, similar differences were observed in which some groups engaged in "massive query expansion" in which all terms in the first phase are added to the query, while other groups use only a subset of those terms [Buckley et al., 1994, Salton and Buckley, 1990]. Some groups at TREC have used fifty terms and twenty phrases and obtained good results.

In [Lundquist et al., 1997] additional sort techniques were explored using the TIPSTER collection, and it was found that $p_k \times nidf$ performs well. The variable, $nidf$, is a normalized idf using pivoted document length normalization (see Section 2.1.2). Additionally, it was shown that the use of the top ten items (either terms or phrases) resulted in a thirty-one percent improvement in average precision over the use of the top fifty terms and twenty phrases.

3.1.2.4 Number of Feedback Iterations

The number of iterations
needed for successful relevance feedback was initially tested in 1971 by Salton [Salton, 1971d]. His 1990 work with 72 variations on relevance feedback assumed that only one iteration of relevance feedback was used. Harman investigated the effect of using multiple iterations of relevance feedback in [Harman, 1992].

In her work, the top ten documents were initially retrieved. A count of the number of relevant documents was obtained, and a new set of ten documents was then retrieved. The process continued for six iterations. Searching terminates if no relevant documents are found in a given iteration. Three variations of updating term weights across iterations were used based on whether or not the counting of relevant documents found was static or cumulative. Each iteration used the basic strategy of retrieving the top ten documents, identifying the top 20 terms, and reweighting the terms.

The three variations tested were:

- Cumulative count—counts relevant documents and term frequencies within relevant documents. It accumulates across iterations

- Reset count—resets the number of relevant documents and term frequencies within relevant documents are reset after each iteration

- Reset count, single iteration term—counts are reset and the query is reset such that it only contains terms from the current iteration

In each case, the number of new relevant documents found increased with each iteration. However, most relevant documents were found in the first two iterations. On average, iterations 3, 4, 5, and 6 routinely found less than one new relevant document per query. All three variations of implementing relevance feedback across iterations performed comparably.

3.1.2.5 User Interaction

As earlier stated, the initial work in relevance feedback assumed the user would be asked to determine which documents were relevant to the query. Subsequent work assumes the top n documents are relevant and simply uses these documents. An interesting user study, done by Spink, looked at the question of using the top documents to suggest terms for query expansion, but giving the user the ability to pick and choose which terms to add [Spink, 1994, Spink, 1995]. Users were also studied to determine how much relevance feedback is used to add terms as compared to other sources. The alternative sources for query terms were:

- Original written query
- User interaction—discussions with an expert research user or "intermediary" prior to the search to identify good terms for the query
- Intermediary—suggestion by expert users during the search
- Thesaurus
- Relevance feedback—selection of terms could be selected by either the user or the expert intermediary

Users chose forty-eight terms (eleven percent) of their search terms (over forty queries) from relevance feedback. Of these, the end-user chose fifteen and the expert chose thirty-three. This indicates a more advanced user is more likely to take advantage of the opportunity to use relevance feedback.

Additionally, the study identified which section of documents users found terms for relevance feedback. Some eighty-five percent of the relevance feedback terms came from the title or the descriptor fields in the documents, and only two terms came from the abstract of the document. This study concluded that new systems should focus on using only the title and descriptor elements of documents for sources of terms during the relevance feedback stages.

3.2 Clustering

Document clustering attempts to group documents by content to reduce the search space required to respond to a query. For example, a document collection that contains both medical and legal documents might be clustered such that all medical documents are placed into one cluster, and all legal documents are assigned to a legal cluster (see Figure 3.2). A query over legal material

Figure 3.2. Document Clustering

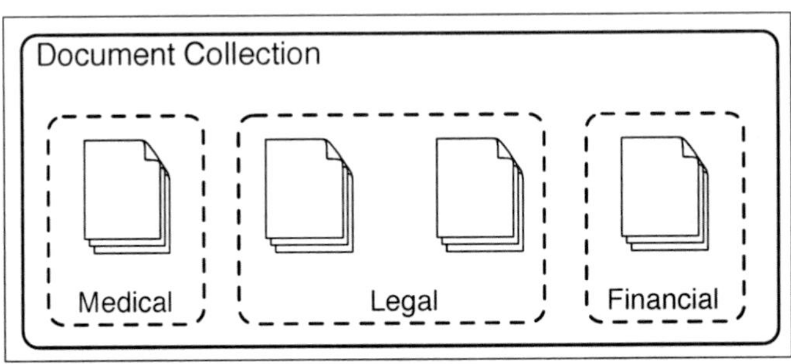

might then be directed (either automatically or manually) to the legal document cluster.

Several clustering algorithms have been proposed. In many cases, the evaluation of clustering algorithms has been challenging because it is difficult to automatically point a query at a document cluster. Viewing document clustering as a utility to assist in ad hoc document retrieval, we now focus on clustering algorithms and examine the potential uses of these algorithms in improving precision and recall of ad hoc and manual query processing.

Another factor that limits the widespread use of clustering algorithms is their computational complexity. Many algorithms begin with a matrix that contains the similarity of each document with every other document. For a 1,000,000 document collection, this matrix has $\frac{1{,}000{,}000^2}{2}$ different elements. Each of these pair-wise similarity calculations is computationally expensive due to the same factors found in the traditional retrieval problem. Namely, when considering each document as a matrix with size corresponding to the number of terms in the lexicon, calculating the similarity between a pair of documents requires comparison across the union of each of their non-zero matrix components. This is complicated by the fact that the document matrices are exceedingly sparse, as many terms appear in only a single document.

This may be an area where clustering will be computationally feasible enough to implement on a large scale. Also, initial work on a Digital Array Processor (DAP) was done to improve run-time performance of clustering algorithms by using parallel processing [Rasmussen and Willett, 1989]. Subsequently, these algorithms were implemented on a parallel machine with a torus interconnection network [Ruocco and Frieder, 1997].

A detailed review of clustering algorithms is given in [Salton, 1989]. Clusters are formed with either a top-down or bottom-up process. In a top-down approach, the entire collection is viewed as a single cluster and is partitioned into smaller and smaller clusters. The bottom-up approach starts with each document being placed into a separate cluster of size one and these clusters are then glued to one another to form larger and larger clusters. The bottom up approach is referred to as hierarchical agglomerative because the result of the clustering is a hierarchy (as clusters are pieced together, a hierarchy emerges).

Other clustering algorithms, such as the popular K-Means algorithm, use an iterative process that begins with random cluster centroids and iteratively adjusts them until some termination condition is met. Some studies have found that hierarchical algorithms, particularly those that use group-average cluster merging schemes, produce better clusters because of their complete document-to-document comparisons [Larsen and Aone, 1999, Willet, 1988, Dubes and Jain, 1988]. More recent work has indicated that this may not be true across all metrics and that some combination of hierarchical and iterative algorithms yields improved effectiveness [Steinbach et al., 2000, Zhao and Karypis, 2002]. As these studies use a variety of different experiments, employ different metrics and (often very small) document collections, it is difficult to conclude which clustering method is definitively superior

3.2.1 Result Set Clustering

Clustering was used as a utility to assist relevance feedback [Lu et al., 1996]. In those cases only the *results* of a query were clustered (a much smaller document set), and in the relevance feedback process, by only new terms from large clusters were selected.

Recently, Web search results were clustered based on significant phrases in the result set [Zeng et al., 2004]. First, documents in a result set are parsed, and two term phrases are identified. Characteristics about these phrases are then used as input to a model built by various learning algorithms (e.g.; linear regression, logistic regression, and support vector regression are used in this work). Once the most significant phrases are identified they are used to build clusters. A cluster is initially identified as the set of documents that contains one of the most significant phrases. For example, if a significant phrase contained the phrase "New York", all documents that contain this phrase would be initially placed into a cluster. Finally, these initial clusters are merged based on document-document similarity.

3.2.2 Hierarchical Agglomerative Clustering

First the N x N document similarity matrix is formed. Each document is placed into its own cluster. The following two steps are repeated until only one cluster exists.

- The two clusters that have the highest similarity are found.
- These two clusters are combined, and the similarity between the newly formed cluster and the remaining clusters recomputed.

As the larger cluster is formed, the clusters that merged together are tracked and form a hierarchy.

Assume documents A, B, C, D, and E exist and a document-document similarity matrix exists. At this point, each document is in a cluster by itself:

{{A} {B} {C} {D} {E}}

We now assume the highest similarity is between document A and document B. So the contents of the clusters become:

{{A,B} {C} {D} {E}}

After repeated iterations of this algorithm, eventually there will only be a single cluster that consists of {A,B,C,D,E}. However, the history of the formation of this cluster will be known. The node {AB} will be a parent of nodes {A} and {B} in the hierarchy that is formed by clustering since both A and B were merged to form the cluster {AB}.

Hierarchical agglomerative algorithms differ based on how {A} is combined with {B} in the first step. Once it is combined, a new similarity measure is computed that indicates the similarity of a document to the newly formed cluster {AB}.

3.2.2.1 Single Link Clustering

The similarity between two clusters is computed as the maximum similarity between any two documents in the two clusters, each initially from a separate cluster. Hence, if eight documents are in cluster A and ten are in cluster B, we compute the similarity of A to B as the maximum similarity between any of the eight documents in A and the ten documents in B.

3.2.2.2 Complete Linkage

Inter-cluster similarity is computed as the minimum of the similarity between any documents in the two clusters such that one document is from each cluster.

3.2.2.3 Group Average

Each cluster member has a greater average similarity to the remaining members of that cluster than to any other cluster. As a node is considered for a cluster its average similarity to all nodes in that cluster is computed. It is placed in the cluster as long as its average similarity is higher than its average similarity for any other cluster.

3.2.2.4 Ward's Method

Clusters are joined so that their merger minimizes the increase in the sum of the distances from each individual document to the centroid of the cluster containing it [El-Hamdouchi and Willett, 1986]. The centroid is defined as the average vector in the vector space. If a vector represents the $i^{\underline{th}}$ document, $D_i =< t_1, t_2, \ldots, t_n >$, the centroid C is written as $C =< c_1, c_2, \ldots, c_n >$. The $j^{\underline{th}}$ element of the centroid vector is computed as the average of all of the $j^{\underline{th}}$ elements of the document vectors:

$$c_j = \frac{\sum_{i=1}^{n} t_{ij}}{n}$$

Hence, if cluster A merged with either cluster B or cluster C, the centroids for the potential cluster AB and AC are computed as well as the maximum distance of any document to the centroid. The cluster with the lowest maximum is used.

3.2.2.5 Analysis of Hierarchical Clustering Algorithms

A paper that describes the implementation of all of these algorithms found that Ward's method typically took the longest to implement, with single link and complete linkage being somewhat similar in run-time [El-Hamdouchi and Willett, 1989].

A summary of several different studies on clustering is given in [Burgin, 1995]. In most studies, clusters found in single link clustering tend to be fairly broad in nature and provide lower effectiveness. Choosing the best cluster as the source of relevant documents resulted in very close effectiveness results for complete link, Ward's, and group average clustering. A consistent drop in effectiveness for single link clustering was noted.

3.2.3 Clustering Without a Precomputed Matrix

Other approaches exist in which the $N \times N$ similarity matrix indicates that the similarity between each document and every other document is not required. These approaches are dependent upon the order in which the input text is received, and do not produce the same result for the same set of input files.

3.2.3.1 One-Pass Clustering

One approach uses a single pass through the document collection. The first document is assumed to be in a cluster of size one. A new document is read as input, and the similarity between the new document and all existing clusters is computed. The similarity is computed as the distance between the new document and the centroid of the existing clusters. The document is then placed into the closest cluster, as long as it exceeds some threshold of closeness. This approach is very dependent on the order of the input. An input sequence of documents $1, 2, \ldots, 10$ can result in very different clusters than any other of the $(10! - 1)$ possible orderings.

Since resulting clusters can be too large, it may be necessary to split them into smaller clusters. Also, clusters that are too small may be merged into larger clusters.

3.2.3.2 Rocchio Clustering

Rocchio developed a clustering algorithm in 1966 [Rocchio, 1966], in which all documents are scanned and defined as either clustered or loose. An unclustered document is tested as a potential center of a cluster by examining the *density* of the document and thereby requiring that n_1 documents have a similarity coefficient of at least p_1 and at least n_2 documents have a correlation of p_2. The similarity coefficient Rocchio most typically used was the cosine coefficient. If this is the case, the new document is viewed as the center of the cluster and the old documents in the cluster are checked to ensure they are close enough to this new center to stay in the cluster. The new document is then marked as *clustered*.

If a document is outside of the threshold, its status may change from *clustered* to *loose*. After processing all documents, some remain loose. These are added to the cluster whose centroid the document is closest to (revert to the single pass approach).

Several parameters for this algorithm were described in 1971 by Grauer and Messier [Grauer and Messier, 1971]. These included:

- Minimum and maximum documents per cluster
- Lower bound on the correlation between an item and a cluster below which an item will not be placed in the cluster. This is a threshold that would be used in the final cleanup phase of unclustered items.
- Density test parameters (n_1, n_2, p_1, p_2)
- Similarity coefficient

3.2.3.3 K-Means

The popular K-means algorithm is a partitioning algorithm that iteratively moves k centroids until a termination condition is met. Typically, these centroids are initially chosen at random. Documents are assigned to the cluster corresponding to the nearest centroid. Each centroid is then recomputed. The algorithm stops when the centroids move so slightly that they fall below a user-defined threshold or a required information gain is achieved for a given iteration [Willett, 1990].

3.2.3.4 Buckshot Clustering

Buckshot clustering is a clustering algorithm designed so that it runs in $O(kn)$ time where k is the number of clusters that are generated and n is the number of documents. For applications where the number of desired clusters is small, the clustering time is close to $O(n)$ which is a clear improvement over the $O(n^2)$ alternatives that require a document-document similarity matrix.

Buckshot clustering works by choosing a random sample of $\sqrt{kn}$ documents. These $\sqrt{kn}$ documents are then clustered by a hierarchical clustering algorithm (any one will do). Using this approach, k clusters can be identified from the cluster hierarchy. The hierarchical clustering algorithms all require a DOC-DOC similarity matrix, so this step will require $O(\sqrt{kn}^2) = O(kn)$ time. Once the k centers are found, the remaining documents are then scanned and assigned to one of the k centers based on the similarity coefficient between the incoming document and each of the k centers. The entire algorithm requires on the order of $O(kn)$ time, as $O(kn)$ is required to obtain the centers and $O(kn)$ is required to scan the document collection and assign each document to one of the centers. Note that buckshot clustering can result in different clusters with each running because a different random set of documents can be chosen to find the initial k centers. Details of the buckshot clustering algorithm and its analysis are given in [Cutting et al., 1992].

3.2.3.5 Non-negative Matrix Factorization

A more recent clustering algorithm uses non-negative matrix factorization (NMF). This provides a latent semantic space (see Section 2.6) where each axis represents the topic of each cluster. Documents are represented as a summation of each axis and are assigned to the cluster associated with the axis for which they have the greatest projection value [Xu et al., 2003].

3.2.4 Querying Hierarchically Clustered Collections

Once the hierarchy is generated, it is necessary to determine which portion of the hierarchy should be searched. A top-down search starts at the root of the tree and compares the query vector to the centroid for each subtree. The subtree with the greatest similarity is then searched. The process continues until a leaf is found or the cluster size is smaller than a predetermined threshold.

A bottom-up search starts with the leaves and moves upwards. Early work showed that starting with leaves, which contained small clusters, was better than starting with large clusters. Subsequently three different bottom-up procedures were studied [Willett, 1988]:

- Assume a relevant document is available, and start with the cluster that contains that document.
- Assume no relevant document is available. Implement a standard vector-space query, and assume the top-ranked document is relevant. Start with the cluster that contains the top-ranked document.
- Start with the bottom level cluster whose centroid is closest to the query.

Once the leaf or bottom-level cluster is identified, all of its parent clusters are added to the answer set until some threshold for the size of the answer set is obtained.

These three bottom-up procedures were compared to a simpler approach in which only the bottom is used. The bottom-level cluster centroids are compared to the query and the answer set is obtained by expanding the top n clusters.

3.2.5 Efficiency Issues

Although the focus of this chapter is on effectiveness, the limited use of clustering algorithms compels us to briefly mention efficiency concerns. Many algorithms begin with a matrix that contains the similarity of each document with every other document. For a 1,000,000 document collection, this matrix has $\frac{1{,}000{,}000^2}{2}$ elements. Algorithms designed to improve the efficiency of clustering are given in [Voorhees, 1986], but at present, no TREC participant has clustered the entire document collection.

3.2.5.1 Parallel Document Clustering

Another means of improving run-time performance of clustering algorithms is to implement them on a parallel processor (see Chapter 7). Initial work on a Digital Array Processor (DAP) was done to improve the run-time of clustering algorithms by using parallel processing [Rasmussen and Willett, 1989]. These algorithms were implemented on a parallel machine with a torus interconnection network [Ruocco and Frieder, 1997]. A parallel version of the Buckshot clustering algorithm (see Section 3.2.3.4) was developed that showed near-linear speedup on a network of sixteen workstations. This enables Buckshot to scale to significantly larger collections and provides a parallel hierarchical agglomerative algorithm [Jensen et al., 2002]. There exists some other work specifically focused on parallel hierarchical clustering [Zhang et al., 1996, Guha et al., 1988], but these algorithms often have large computational overhead or have not been evaluated for document clustering. Some work was done in developing parallel algorithms for hierarchical document clustering [Olson, 1995], however these algorithms were developed for several types of specialized interconnection networks, and it is unclear whether they are applicable to the simple bus connection that is common for many current parallel architectures.

Additional proposals use clustering as a utility to assist relevance feedback [Lu et al., 1996]. Only the *results* of a query are clustered (a much smaller document set), and relevance feedback proceeds by only obtaining new terms from large clusters.

3.2.5.2 Clustering with Truncated Document Vectors

The most expensive step in the clustering process occurs when the distance between the new document and all existing clusters is computed. This is typically done by computing the centroid of each cluster and measuring the cosine of the angle between the new document vector and the centroid of each cluster. Later, it was shown that clustering can be done with vectors that use only a few representative terms from a document [Schutze and Silverstein, 1997].

One means of reducing the size of the document vector is to use Latent Semantic Indexing (see Section 2.6) to identify the most important components. Another means is to simply truncate the vector by removing those terms with a weight below a given threshold. No significant difference in effectiveness was found for a baseline of no truncation, or using latent semantic indexing with twenty, fifty, and one hundred and fifty terms or simple truncation with fifty terms.

3.3 Passage-based Retrieval

Passage-based retrieval [Callan, 1994], is based on the premise that only a small portion of each relevant document (i.e., the relevant passage within the document) contains the information that is relevant to the query. By computing metrics that compare the entire document to the query, the noisy parts of the document (the sections that are nonrelevant) potentially mask the relevant segment of the document.

For instance, consider this book. This section is the only section that contains relevant information in response to a query that searches for *passage-based retrieval.* If the entire book was viewed as a single document, this section might contribute very little to the overall similarity coefficient between the book and the passage.

Since documents often are naturally segmented into chapters, sections, and subsections, it is reasonable to use each of these author-determined boundaries and simply rank the passages to the original query. A similarity coefficient must then merge the passage-based results and obtain a final coefficient.

Consider a document D_1 with sections A, B, C, and D. Further assume section C is the only section that mentions anything about the query. A similarity coefficient $SC(Q, D_1)$ could result in a coefficient that is heavily biased towards nonrelevance because sections A, B, and D have many terms that do not match with terms in the query. The similarity coefficient reflects this and given the length of the document and the relatively small proportion of matching terms, or even terms that are semantically related, the document would have a low similarity coefficient. With passage-based retrieval, four separate coefficients are computed: SC(Q,A), SC(Q,B), SC(Q,C), and SC(Q,D). The four different similarity coefficients would then be merged. Several different techniques for merging these components are presented.

Passage-based research focuses on determining how to delimit a passage and combine each passage into a single similarity coefficient. The following sections discuss each of these problems and demonstrate some initial work in each area.

3.3.1 Marker-based Passages

Marker-based passages use section headers or paragraph indentation and vertical space as a means of partitioning passages. SGML tags found in long Federal Register documents were used in [Zobel et al., 1995].

In similar work, paragraph markers were used. To avoid very long or short paragraphs, long paragraphs were partitioned based on size and short paragraphs were glued together. The passages were bounded such that no passage contained fewer than fifty terms or was larger than 200 terms [Callan, 1994]. In [Zobel et al., 1995] passages were glued together until a size of p was exceeded. In both papers, modest improvement occurred, but results given with the Federal Register should be viewed with care as there are comparatively few relevant documents in this particular collection. The reason given for the limited success of this intuitively appealing approach is that the paragraph markers and section markers are prone to error on the part of the author and may not have resulted in a good semantic partitioning (i.e., one passage might have described numerous concepts).

3.3.2 Dynamic Passage Partitioning

Different approaches have been used to automatically find good partitions. These approaches attempt to partition documents differently based on the particular query [Callan, 1994]. One means of doing this is to find a term that matches the query and then build a passage around this match. If a term matches at position n, passage A will begin at position n and continue until position $n + p$ where p is a variable passage size. The next passage, B, will overlap with A and start at position $n + \frac{p}{2}$. Figure 3.3 illustrates the difference between overlapping and non-overlapping passages. For a term that matches at position ten, a small passage length of fifty results in passages around the terms [10, 60], [35, 85], [60, 110], etc. where [i, j] indicates the passage starts at position i and continues to j. Overlapping passages are intended to avoid splitting sections of relevant text.

Figure 3.3. Overlapping vs Non-Overlapping Passages

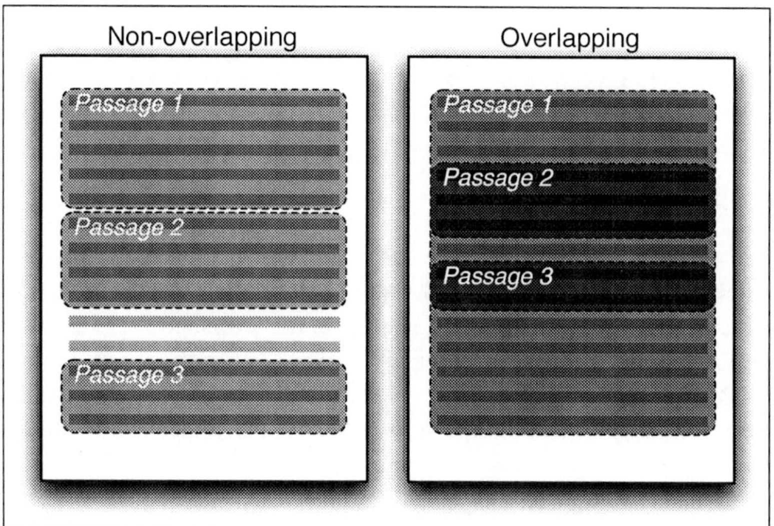

3.3.3 Merging Passage-based Similarity Measures

Passages contribute to the similarity coefficient in a number of different ways. One study tested twenty different methods of merging passage-based contributions [Wilkinson, 1994]. These methods ranged from simply taking the highest ranked passage as the similarity coefficient to combining document level contributions with passage level contributions. The work done in [Callan, 1994] also used a combination score with the document and the passage level evidence to obtain their best results. Similar results also occurred in [Wilkinson, 1994].

3.4 N-grams

Term-based search techniques typically use an inverted index or a scan of the text (details surrounding inverted index construction and search are given in Chapter 5). Additionally, queries that are based on exact matches with terms in a document perform poorly against corrupted documents. This occurs regardless of the source of the errors—either OCR (optical character recognition) errors or those due to misspelling. To provide resilience to noise, n-grams were proposed. The premise is to decompose terms into word fragments of size n, then design matching algorithms that use these fragments to determine whether or not a match exists.

N-grams have also been used for detection and correction of spelling errors [Pollock and Zamora, 1984, Thorelli, 1962, Zamora et al., 1981] and text compression [Yannakoudakis et al., 1982]. A survey of automatic correction techniques is found in [Kukich, 1992]. Additionally, n-grams were used to determine the authorship of documents [Kjell et al., 1994]. Traditional information retrieval algorithms based on n-grams are described in [D'Amore and Mah, 1985, Damashek, 1995, Pearce and Nicholas, 1993, Teuful, 1988, Cavnar and Vayda, 1993].

3.4.1 D'Amore and Mah

Initial information retrieval research focused on n-grams as presented in [D'Amore and Mah, 1985]. The motivation behind their work was the fact that it is difficult to develop mathematical models for terms since the potential for a term that has not been seen before is infinite. With n-grams, only a fixed number of n-grams can exist for a given value of n. A mathematical model was developed to estimate the noise in indexing and to determine appropriate document similarity measures.

D'Amore and Mah's method replaces terms with n-grams in the vector space model. The only remaining issue is computing the weights for each n-gram. Instead of simply using n-gram frequencies, a scaling method is used to normalize the length of the document. D'Amore and Mah's contention was that a large document contains more n-grams than a small document, so it should be scaled based on its length.

To compute the weights for a given n-gram, D'Amore and Mah estimated the number of occurrences of an n-gram in a document. The first simplifying assumption was that n-grams occur with equal likelihood and follow a binomial distribution. Hence, it was no more likely for n-gram "ABC" to occur than "DEF." The Zipfian distribution that is widely accepted for terms is not true for n-grams. D'Amore and Mah noted that n-grams are not equally likely to occur, but the removal of frequently occurring terms from the document collection resulted in n-grams that follow a more binomial distribution than the terms.

D'Amore and Mah computed the expected number of occurrences of an n-gram in a particular document. This is the product of the number of n-grams in the document (the document length) and the probability that the n-gram occurs. The n-gram's probability of occurrence is computed as the ratio of its number of occurrences to the total number of n-grams in the document. D'Amore and Mah continued their application of the binomial distribution to derive an expected variance and, subsequently, a standard deviation for n-gram occurrences. The final weight for n-gram i in document j is:

$$w_{ij} = \frac{f_{ij} - e_{ij}}{\sigma_{ij}}$$

where:

f_{ij} = frequency of an n-gram i in document j
e_{ij} = expected number of occurrences of an n-gram i in document j
σ_{ij} = standard deviation

The n-gram weight designates the number of standard deviations away from the expected value. The goal is to give a high weight to an n-gram that has occurred far more than expected and a low weight to an n-gram that has occurred only as often as expected.

D'Amore and Mah did several experiments to validate that the binomial model was appropriate for n-grams. Unfortunately, they were not able to test their approach against a term-based one on a large standardized corpus.

3.4.2 Damashek

Damashek expanded on D'Amore and Mah's work by implementing a five-gram-based measure of relevance [Damashek, 1995]. Damashek's algorithm relies upon the vector space model, but computes relevance in a different fashion. Instead of using stop words and stemming to normalize the expected occurrence of n-grams, a centroid vector is used to eliminate noise. To compute the similarity between a query and a document, the following cosine measure is used:

$$SC(Q, D) = \frac{\sum_{j=1}^{t}(w_{qj} - \mu_Q)(w_{dj} - \mu_D)}{\sqrt{\sum_{j=1}^{t}(w_{qj} - \mu_q)^2 \sum_{j=1}^{t}(w_{dj} - \mu_D)^2}}$$

Here μ_q and μ_d represent centroid vectors that are used to characterize the query language and the document language. The weights, w_{qj} and w_{dj} indicate the term weight for each component in the query and the document vectors. The centroid value for each n-gram is computed as the ratio of the total number of occurrences of the n-gram to the total number of n-grams. This is the same value used by D'Amore and Mah. It is not used as an expected probability for the n-grams, but merely as a characterization of the n-gram's frequency across the document collection. The weight of a specific n-gram in a document vector is the ratio of the number of occurrences of the n-gram in the document to the total number of all of the n-grams in the document. This "within document frequency" is used to normalize based on the length of a document, and the centroid vectors are used to incorporate the frequency of the n-grams across the entire document collection.

By eliminating the need to remove stop words and to support stemming, (the theory is that the stop words are characterized by the centroid so there was no need to eliminate them), the algorithm simply scans through the document and grabs n-grams without any parsing. This makes the algorithm language independent. Additionally, the use of the centroid vector provides a means of filtering out common n-grams in a document. The remaining n-grams are reverse engineered back into terms and used as automatically assigned keywords to describe a document. A description of this reverse engineering process is given in [Cohen, 1995]. Proof of language independence is given with tests covering English, German, Spanish, Georgian, Russian, and Japanese.

3.4.3 Pearce and Nicholas

An expansion of Damashek's work uses n-grams to generate hypertext links [Pearce and Nicholas, 1993]. The links are obtained by computing similarity measures between a selected body of text and the remainder of the document. After a user selects a body of text, the five-grams are identified, and a vector representing this selected text is constructed. Subsequently, a cosine similarity measure is computed, and the top rated documents are then displayed to the user as dynamically defined hypertext links. The user interface issues surrounding hypertext is the principal enhancement over Damashek's work. The basic idea of constructing a vector and using a centroid to eliminate noise remains intact.

3.4.4 Teufel

Teufel also uses n-grams to compute a measure of similarity using the vector space model [Teuful, 1988]. Stop words and stemming algorithms are used and advocated as a good means of reducing noise in the set of n-grams. However, his work varies from the others in that he used a measure of relevance that is intended to enforce similarity over similar documents. The premise was that if document A is similar to B, and B is similar to C, then A should be roughly similar to C. Typical coefficients, such as inner product, Dice, or Jaccard (see Section 2.1.2), are non-transitive. Teufel uses a new coefficient, H, where:

$$H = X + Y - (XY)$$

and X is a direct similarity coefficient (in this case Dice was used, but Jaccard, cosine, or inner product could also have been used) and Y is an "indirect" measure that enforces transitivity. With the indirect measure, document A is identified as similar to document C. A more detailed description of the indirect similarity measure is given in [Teuful, 1991].

Good precision and recall was reported for the INSPEC document collection. Language independence was claimed in spite of reliance upon stemming and stop words.

3.4.5 Cavnar and Vayda

N-grams were also proposed in [Cavnar, 1993, Cavnar and Vayda, 1993]. Most of this work involves using n-grams to recognize postal addresses. N-grams were used due to their resilience to errors in the address. A simple scanning algorithm that counts the number of n-gram matches that occur between a query and a single line of text in a document was used. No weighting of any kind was used, but, by using a single text line, there is no need to normalize for the length of a document. The premise is that the relevant portion of a document appears in a single line of text.

Cavnar's solution was the only documented approach tested on a large standardized corpus. For the entire TIPSTER document collection, average precision of between 0.06 and 0.15 was reported. It should be noted that for the AP portion of the collection an average precision of 0.35 was obtained. These results on the AP documents caused Cavnar to avoid further tuning. Unfortunately, results on the entire collection exhibited relatively poor performance. Regarding these results, the authors claimed that,"It is unclear why there should be such variation between the retrievability of the AP documents and the other document collections."

3.5 Regression Analysis

Another approach to estimating the probability of relevance is to develop variables that describe the characteristics of a match to a relevant document. Regression analysis is then used to identify the exact parameters that match the training data. For example, if trying to determine an equation that predicts a person's life expectancy given their age:

Age	Life Expectancy
45	72
50	74
70	80

A simple least squares polynomial regression could be implemented, that would identify the correct values of α and β to predict life expectancy (LE) based on age (A):

$$LE = \alpha A + \beta$$

For a given age, it is possible to find the related life expectancy. Now, if we wish to predict the likelihood of a person having heart disease, we might obtain the following data:

Age	Life Expectancy	Heart Disease
45	72	yes
50	74	no
70	80	yes

We now try to fit a line or a curve to the data points such that if a new person shows up and asks for the chance of their having heart disease, the point on the curve that corresponds to their age could be examined. This second example is more analogous to document retrieval because we are trying to identify characteristics in a query-document match that indicate whether or not the document is relevant. The problem is that relevance is typically given a binary (1 or 0) for training data—it is rare that we have human assessments that the document is "kind of" relevant. Note that there is a basic independence assumption that says age will not be related to life expectancy (an assumption we implied was false in our preceding example). Logistic regression is typically used to estimate dichotomous variables—those that only have a small set of values, (i.e., gender, heart disease present, and relevant documents).

Focusing on information retrieval, the problem is to find the set of variables that provide some indication that the document is relevant.

Matching Terms	Size of Query	Size of Document	Relevant?
5	10	30	yes
8	20	45	no

Six variables used in [Fontaine, 1995] are given below:

- The mean of the total number of matching terms in the query.
- The square root of the number of terms in the query.
- The mean of the total number of matching terms in the document.
- The square root of the number of terms in the document.
- The average *idf* of the matching terms.
- The total number of matching terms in the query.

A brief overview of polynomial regression and the initial use of logistic regression is given in [Cooper et al., 1992]. However, the use of logistic regression requires the variables used for the analysis to be independent. Hence, the logistic regression is given in two stages. Composite clues which are composed of independent variables are first estimated. Assume clues 1–3 above are found in one composite clue and 4–6 are in the second composite clue. The two stages proceed as follows:

Stage 1:
A logistic regression is done for each composite clue.

$$\begin{aligned} logO(R|C_1) &= c_0 + c_1X_1 + c_2X_2 + c_3X_3 \\ logO(R|C_2) &= d_0 + d_1X_4 + d_2X_5 + d_3X_6 \end{aligned}$$

At this point the coefficients c_0, c_1, c_2, c_3 are computed to estimate the relevance for the composite clue C_1. Similarly, d_0, d_1, d_2, d_3 estimate the relevance of C_2.

Stage 2:
The second stage of the staged logistic regression attempts to correct for errors induced by the number of composite clues. As the number of composite clues grows, the likelihood of error increases. For N composite clues, the following logistic regression is computed:

$$logO(R|C_1, C_2, \ldots, C_N) = e_0 + e_1Z + e_2N$$

where Z is computed as the sum of the composite clues or:

$$Z = \sum_{i=1}^{N} \log O(R|C_i)$$

The results of the first stage regression are applied to the second stage. It should be noted that further stages are possible.

Once the initial regression is completed, the actual computation of similarity coefficients proceeds quickly. Composite clues are only dependent on the presence or absence of terms in the document and can be precomputed. Computations based on the number of matches found in the query and the document are done at query time, but involve combining the coefficients computed in the logistic regression with the precomputed segments of the query. Further implementation details are found in [Fontaine, 1995].

The question is whether or not the coefficients can be computed in a generic fashion that is resilient to changes in the document collection. The appealing aspects of this approach are that experimentation can be done to identify the best clues, and the basic independence assumptions are avoided. Additionally, the approach corrects for errors incurred by the initial logistic regression.

3.6 Thesauri

One of the most intuitive ideas for enhancing effectiveness of an information retrieval system is to include the use of a thesaurus. Almost from the dawn of the first information retrieval systems in the early 1960's, researchers focused on incorporating a thesaurus to improve precision and recall. The process of using a thesaurus to expand a query is illustrated in Figure 3.4.

Figure 3.4. Using a Thesaurus to Expand a Query

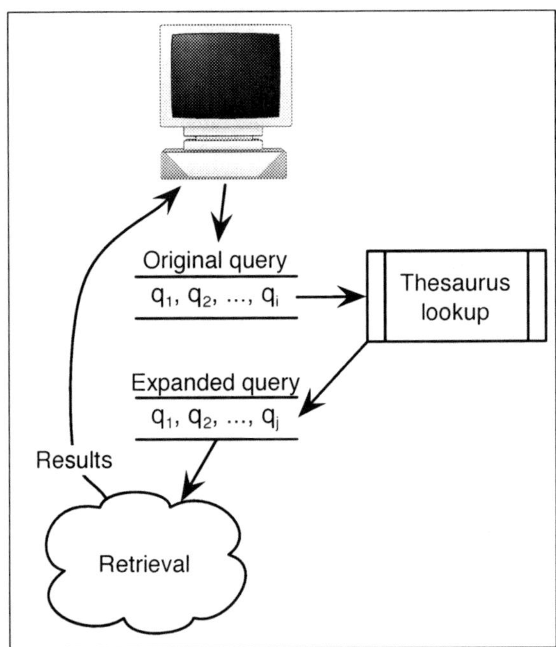

A thesaurus, at first glance, might appear to assist with a key problem—two people very rarely describe the same concepts with the same terms (i.e., one person will say that they went to a *party* while another person might call it a *gathering*). This problem makes statistical measures that rely on the number of matches between a query term and the document terms somewhat brittle when confronted with semantically equivalent terms that happen to be syntactically distinct. A query that asks for information about *dogs* is probably also interested in documents about *canines*.

A document relevant to a query might not match any of the terms in the query. A thesaurus can be used either to assign a common term for all synonyms of a term, or to expand a query to include all synonymous terms. Intuitively this should work fine, but unfortunately, results have not been promising. This section describes the use of hand-built thesauri, a very labor intensive means of building a thesaurus, as well as the quest for a sort of holy grail of information retrieval, an automatically generated thesaurus.

3.6.1 Automatically Constructed Thesauri

A hand-built thesaurus might cover general terms, but it lacks domain-specific terms. A medical document collection has many terms that do not occur in a general purpose thesaurus. To avoid the need for numerous hand-built domain-specific thesauri, automatic construction methods were implemented.

3.6.1.1 Term Co-occurrence

An early discussion of automatic thesaurus generation is found in [Salton, 1971c]. The key to this approach is to represent each term as a vector. The terms are then compared using a similarity coefficient that measures the Euclidean distance, or angle, between the two vectors.

To form a thesaurus for a given term t, related terms for t are all those terms u such that $SC(t, u)$ is above a given threshold. Note, this is an $O(t^2)$ process so it is often common to limit the terms for which a related term list is built. This is done by using only those terms that are not so frequent that they become stop terms, but not so infrequent that there is little chance they have many synonyms.

Consider the following example:
D_1: "a dog will bark at a cat in a tree"
D_2: "ants eat the bark of a tree "

This results in the term-document occurrence matrix found in Table 3.1.
To compute the similarity of term i with term j, a vector of size N, where N is the number of documents, is obtained for each term. The vector corresponds to a row in the following table. A dot product similarity between "bark" and "tree" is computed as:

$$SC(bark, tree) = <1\ 1> \bullet <1\ 1> \ = \ 2$$

The corresponding term-term similarity matrix is given in Table 3.2.

The matrix is symmetric as $SC(t_1, t_2)$ is equivalent to $SC(t_2, t_1)$. The premise is that words are similar or related to the company they keep. Consider "tree" and "bark"; in our example, these terms co-occur twice in two documents. Hence, this pair has the highest similarity coefficient. Other simple extensions to this approach are the use of word stems instead of whole terms (for more on stemming see Section 3.8.1). The use of stemming is important here so that the term *cat* will not differ from *cats*. The *tf-idf* measure can be

Table 3.1. Term-Document Matrix

term	D_1	D_2
a	3	1
ants	0	1
at	1	0
bark	1	1
cat	1	0
dog	1	0
eat	0	1
in	1	0
of	0	1
the	0	1
tree	1	1
will	1	0

Table 3.2. Term-Term Similarity Matrix

term	a	ants	at	bark	cat	dog	eat	in	of	the	tree	will
a	0	1	3	4	3	3	1	3	1	1	4	3
ants	1	0	0	1	0	0	1	0	1	1	1	0
at	3	0	0	1	1	1	0	1	0	0	1	0
bark	4	1	1	0	1	1	1	1	1	1	2	1
cat	3	0	1	1	0	1	0	1	0	0	1	1
dog	3	0	1	1	1	0	0	1	0	1	1	1
eat	1	1	0	1	0	0	0	0	1	0	1	0
in	3	0	1	1	1	1	0	0	0	0	1	1
of	1	1	0	1	0	0	1	0	0	1	1	0
the	1	1	0	1	0	0	1	0	1	0	1	0
tree	4	1	1	2	1	1	1	1	1	1	0	1
will	3	0	1	1	1	1	0	1	0	0	1	0

used in the term-term similarity matrix to give more weight to co-occurrences between relatively infrequent terms.

Early work done with the term-term similarity matrix was given in [Minker et al., 1972]. This paper summarizes much of the work done in the 1960's using term clustering, and provides some additional experiments [Salton, 1971c, Sparck Jones and Jackson, 1968, Sparck Jones and Barber, 1971]. The common theme of these papers is that the term-term similarity matrix can be constructed, and then various clustering algorithms can be used to build clusters of related terms.

Once the clusters are built, they are used to expand the query. Each term in the original query is found in a cluster that was included in some portion or all (depending on a threshold) elements of its cluster. Much of the related work done during this time focused on different clustering algorithms and different thresholds to identify the number of terms added to the cluster. The conclusion was that the augmentation of a query using term clustering did not improve on simple queries that used weighted terms.

Additional work with term-term similarity matrices is presented in [Chen and Ng, 1995]. A domain-specific thesaurus was constructed on information about the *Caenorhabditis elegans* worm in support of molecular biologists [Chen et al., 1995]. A term-term similarity measure was built with phrases and terms. A weight that used *tf-idf* but also included another factor p_i, was used where p_i indicated the number of terms in phrase i. Hence, a two-term phrase was weighted double that of a single term. The new weight was:

$$w_{ij} = tf_{ij} \times \log\left(\frac{N}{df_i} \times p_i\right)$$

Using this new weight, an asymmetric similarity coefficient was also developed. The premise was that the symmetric coefficients are not as useful for ranking because a measurement between t_i, t_j can become very skewed if either t_i or t_j occurs frequently. The asymmetric coefficient allows for a ranking of an arbitrary term t_i, frequent or not, with all other terms. Applying a threshold to the list means that for each term, a list of other related terms is generated—and this can be done for all terms.

The measurement for $SC(t_i, t_j)$ is given as:

$$SC(t_i, t_j) = \left(\frac{\sum_{k=1}^{n} min(tf_{ik}, tf_{jk}) \log\left(\frac{N}{df_{ij}} \times p_j\right)}{\sum_{k=1}^{n} w_{ik}}\right) \times W_j$$

where df_{ij} is the number of co-occurrences of term i with term j. Two additional weights make this measure asymmetric: p_j and W_j. As we have said p_j is a small weight included to measure the size of term j. With all other weights being equal, the measure: *SC(food, apple pie)* > *SC(food, apple)* since phrases are weighted higher than terms. The weighting factor, W_j, gives additional preference to terms that occur infrequently without skewing the relationship between term i and term j. The weight W_j is given as:

$$W_j = \left(\frac{\log\left(\frac{N}{df_j}\right)}{\log N}\right)$$

Consider the term *york* and its relationship to the terms *new* and *castle*. Assume *new* occurs more frequently than *castle*. With all other weights being equal, the new weight, W_j, causes the following to occur:

$$SC(york, castle) > SC(york, new)$$

This is done without regard for the frequency of the term *york*. The key is that we are trying to come up with a thesaurus, or a list of related terms, for a given term (i.e., *york*). When we are deriving the list of terms for *new* we might find that *york* occurs less frequently than *castle* so we would have:

$$SC(new, york) > SC(new, castle)$$

Note that we were able to consider the relative frequencies of *york* and *castle* with this approach. In this case:

$$SC(new, york) = SC(york, new)$$

The high frequency of the term *new* drowns out any real difference between *york* and *castle*—or at least that is the premise of this approach. We note in our example, that *new york* would probably be recognized as a phrase, but that is not really pertinent to this example.

Hence, at this point, we have defined $SC(t_i, t_j)$. Since the coefficient is asymmetric we now give the definition of $SC(t_j, t_i)$:

$$SC(t_j, t_i) = \left(\frac{\sum_{k=1}^{n} min(tf_{ik}, tf_{jk}) \log \left(\frac{N}{df_{ij}} \times p_i \right)}{\sum_{k=1}^{n} w_{jk}} \right) \times W_i$$

A threshold was applied so that only the top one hundred terms were used for a given term. These were presented to a user. For relatively small document collections, users found that the thesaurus assisted their recall. No testing of generic precision and recall for automatic retrieval was measured.

3.6.1.2 Term Context

Instead of relying on term co-occurrence, some work uses the context (surrounding terms) of each term to construct the vectors that represent each term [Gauch and Wang, 1996]. The problem with the vectors given above is that they do not differentiate the senses of the words. A thesaurus relates words to different senses. In the example given below, "bark" has two entirely different senses. A typical thesaurus lists "bark" as:

bark—surface of tree (noun)
bark—dog sound (verb)

Ideally an automatically generated thesaurus would have separate lists of synonyms. The term-term matrix does not specifically identify synonyms, and Gauch and Wang do not attempt this either. Instead, the *relative position* of nearby terms is included in the vector used to represent a term [Gauch and Wang, 1996].

The key to similarity is not that two terms happen to occur in the same document; it is that the two terms appear in the same *context*—that is they have very similar neighboring terms.

Bark, in the sense of a sound emanating from a dog, appears in different contexts than *bark*, in the sense of a tree surface. Consider the following three sentences:

S_1: "The dog yelped at the cat."
S_2: "The dog barked at the cat."
S_3: "The bark fell from the tree to the ground."

In sentences S_1 and S_2, *yelped* is a synonym for *barked*, and the two terms occur in exactly the same context. It is unlikely that another sense of *bark* would appear in the same context. "Bark" as a *surface of tree* more commonly would have articles at one position to the left instead of two positions to the left, etc.

To capture the term's *context*, it is necessary to identify a set of *context terms*. The presence or absence of these terms around a given *target term* will determine the content of the vector for the target term. In [Gauch and Wang, 1996], the authors assume the highest frequency terms are the best context terms, so the 200 most frequent terms (including stop terms) are used as context terms. A window of size seven was used. This window includes the three terms to the left of the target term and the three terms to the right of the target term. The new vector that represents target term i will be of the general form:

$$T_i =< v_{-3}v_{-2}v_{-1}v_1v_2v_3 >$$

where each vector, v_i, and i = -3, -2, -1, 1, 2, and 3 corresponds to a 200 element vector that represents the context of the target term for a given position. The vector v_{-3} contains a component for each of the 200 context terms that occur three terms to the left of the target term. Similarly, the vector v_3 contains a component for each of the 200 context terms that occur three terms to the right of the target.

The v_i vectors are all concatenated to form the entire T_i vector for the term. For a simple example, we build the context vectors for the terms *bark* and *yelp* based on the document collection S_1, S_2, and S_3. To simplify the example, we assume that stemming is done to normalize *bark* and *barked* and that *the* and *at* are the only two context terms occupying components one and two, respectively, of the context vectors. For our test document collection we would obtain:

$$T_{bark} = [< 00 >< 10 >< 10 >< 01 >< 10 >< 10 >]$$

$$T_{yelp} = [< 00 >< 10 >< 00 >< 01 >< 10 >< 00 >]$$

The matching of S_1 and S_2 is the driving force between the two vectors being very similar. The only differences occur because of the additional word sense that occurs in S_3.

This example uses the frequency of occurrence of a context term as the component of the context vectors. In [Gauch and Wang, 1996], the authors use a measure that attempts to place more weight on context terms that occur less frequently than might be expected. The actual component value of the jth component of vector v_i, is a mutual information measure. Let:

$$\begin{aligned} df_{ij} &= \text{frequency of co-occurrence of context term} \\ &\quad\; j \text{ with target term } i \\ tf_i &= \text{total occurrences of context term } i \\ &\quad\; \text{in the collection} \\ tf_j &= \text{the total occurrences of context term } j \\ &\quad\; \text{in the collection} \end{aligned}$$

$$v_{ij} = \log\left(\frac{N df_{ij}}{(tf_i)(tf_j)} + 1\right)$$

This gives a higher weight to a context term that appears more frequently with a given target term than predicted by the overall frequencies of the two terms.

Gauch and Wang use the top 200 terms, with a seven term window size; so each term vector is of size 1200. The vectors are then compared with a standard cosine measure, and all terms with a similarity above a threshold are used. The choice of which target words to choose is difficult, and after some experimentation 4,000 target words were chosen from the frequency list.

Queries were then expanded using only the top n terms that fell above a certain threshold. Unfortunately, average precision for the expanded query was not significantly higher than without the expansion.

Analysis of the repeated failure of automatically generated thesauri built from term-term similarity matrices is given in [Peat and Willett, 1991]. They noted a key problem with using term co-occurrence to generate a thesaurus is that relatively frequent terms co-occur with other frequent terms. The result is a thesaurus in which one relatively general term is found to be related to another general term (e.g., *hairy* might be found to be related to *furry*). Although these terms are related, they do not improve precision and recall because, due to their relatively high frequency, they are not good discriminators.

Interestingly, an early paper showed that randomly selecting terms for expansion was sometimes more effective than using those generated by a term-term similarity matrix [Smeaton and Rijsbergen, 1983]. Given a Zipfian distribution [Zipf, 1949] most terms appear infrequently (over half occur only once), so there is a good chance that the randomly selected terms were low frequency, and hence, did not do as much damage as a high frequency non-discriminating term.

3.6.1.3 Clustering with Singular Value Decomposition

Schutze and Pedersen use term clustering and a singular value decomposition (SVD) to generate a thesaurus [Schutze and Pedersen, 1997]. First a matrix, A, is computed for terms that occur 2000–5000 times. The matrix contains the number of times these terms co-occur with a term window of size k (k is 40 in this work). Subsequently, these terms are clustered into 200 A-classes (group average agglomerative clustering is used—see Section 3.2.2.3). For example, one A-class, g_{A1}, might have terms (t_1, t_2, t_3) and another, g_{A2}, would have (t_4, t_5).

Subsequently, a new matrix, B, is generated for the 20,000 most frequent terms based on their co-occurrence between clusters found in the matrix. For example, if term t_j co-occurs with term t_1 ten times, term t_2 five times, and term t_4 six times, B[1, j] = 15 and B[2, j] = 6. Note the use of clusters has reduced the size of the B matrix and provides substantially more training information. The rows of B correspond to classes in A, and the columns correspond to terms. The B matrix is of size 200 x 20,000. The 20,000 columns are then clustered into 200 B-classes using the buckshot clustering algorithm (see Section 3.2.3.4).

Finally, a matrix, C, is formed for all terms in the collection. An entry $C[i, j]$ indicates the number of times term j co-occurs with the B-classes. Once this is done, the C matrix is decomposed and singular values are computed to represent the matrix. This is similar to the technique used for latent semantic indexing (see Section 2.6). The SVD is more tractable at this point since only 200 columns exist.

A document is represented by a vector that is the sum of the context vectors (vectors that correspond to each column in the SVD). The context vector is used to match a query.

Another technique that uses the context vector matrix, is to cluster the query based on its context vectors. This is referred to as *word factorization.* The queries were partitioned into three separate clusters. A query is then run for each of the word factors and a given document is given the highest rank of the three. This requires a document to be ranked high by all three factors to receive an overall high rank. The premise is that queries are generally *about* two or three concepts and that a relevant document has information relevant to all of the concepts.

Overall, this approach seems very promising. It was run on a reasonably good-sized collection (the Category B portion of TIPSTER using term factorization, average precision improved from 0.27 to 0.32—an 18.5% overall improvement).

3.6.1.4 Using only Document Clustering to Generate a Thesaurus

Another approach to automatically build a thesaurus is described in [Crouch, 1989, Crouch, 1990]. First, a document clustering algorithm is implemented to partition the document collection into related clusters. A document-document similarity coefficient is used. Complete link clustering is used here, but other clustering algorithms could be used (for more details on clustering algorithms see Section 3.2).

The terms found in each cluster are then obtained. Since they occur in different documents within the cluster, different operators are used to obtain the set of terms that correspond to a given cluster. Consider documents with the following terms:

$$\begin{aligned} D_1 &= t_1, t_2, t_3, t_4 \\ D_2 &= t_2, t_4 \\ D_3 &= t_1, t_2 \end{aligned}$$

The cluster can be represented by the union of all the terms $\{t_1, t_2, t_3, t_4\}$, the intersection $\{t_2\}$, or some other operation that considers the number of documents in the cluster that contain the term. Crouch found that simple clustering worked the best. The terms that represented the cluster now appear as a *thesaurus class*, in that they form the automatically generated thesaurus. The class is first reduced to obtain only the *good* terms. This is done by using a term discriminating function that is based on document frequency. (See Section 2.1 for more details on document frequency).

Queries are expanded based on the thesaurus class. Any term that occurs in the query that matches a term in the thesaurus class results in all terms in the class being added to the query. Average precision was shown to improve ten percent for the small ADI collection and fifteen percent for the Medlars collection. Unfortunately, both of these results were for small collections, and the document clustering is computationally expensive, requiring $O(N^2)$ time, where N is the number of documents in the collection.

3.6.2 Use of Manually Generated Thesaurus

Although a manually generated thesaurus is far more time consuming to build, several researchers have explored the use of such a thesaurus to improve precision and recall.

3.6.2.1 Extended Relevance Ranking with Manual Thesaurus

A system developed in 1971 used computers to assist with the manual construction of a thesaurus at the Columbia University School of Library Service. The algorithm was essentially equivalent to a simple thesaurus editor [Hines and Harris, 1971].

Manual thesaurus construction is typically used for domain-specific thesauri. A group of experts is convened, and they are asked to identify the relationship between domain-specific terms. Ghose and Dhawle note that manual generation of these thesauri can be more difficult to build for social sciences than natural sciences given that there is more disagreement about the meaning of domain-specific terms in the social sciences [Ghose and Dhawle, 1977].

A series of handbuilt thesauri (each one was constructed by students) was described in [Wang et al., 1985]. These thesauri were generated by the relationships between two terms—such as *dog* is-a *animal*. Ultimately the thesauri were combined into one that contained seven groups of relations. These groups were:

- Antonyms
- All relations but antonyms
- All relations
- Part-whole and set relations
- Co-location relations
- Taxonomy and synonymy relations
- Paradigmatic relations

The antonym relation identified terms that were opposites of one another (e.g., *night, day*) and is-part-of identifies entities that are involved in a bill-of-materials relationship (e.g., *tire, automobile*). Co-location contains relations between words that frequently co-occur in the same phrase or sentence. Taxonomy and synonym represent synonyms. Paradigmatic relations relate different forms of words that contain the same semantic core such as canine and dog. Experiments in adding each or all of the terms from these relations were done on a small document collection with relevance judgments obtained by the researchers conducting the study. Use of all relations, with the exception of antonyms, delivered the best average precision and recall, but there was little overall improvement.

A study done in 1993 used a thesaurus containing three different relations: equivalence (synonym), hierarchical (is-a), and associative relationships [Kristensen, 1993]. Recall of a fairly large (227,000) document collection composed of Finnish newspaper articles was shown to increase from 47 percent to 100 percent while precision only decreased from 62.5 percent to 51 percent. Fortunately, the work was done on a large collection, however, the thesaurus was hand-built for the test and contained only 1,011 concepts and a total of 1,573 terms. Only thirty queries were used, and the high results are clearly due to "good" terms found in the thesaurus.

Given the nature of the highly specific thesaurus, this result might be very similar in nature to the manual track of the TREC conference where participants are allowed to hand-modify the original query to include more discriminating terms. The synonym, narrower term, and related term searches all showed a 10 to 20% increase in recall from a 50% baseline. The union search (using all values) showed a rather high fifty percent increase in average precision. This work does represent one of the few studies outside of the TIPSTER collection that is run on a sizable collection. It is not clear, however, how applicable the results are to a more general collection that uses a more general thesaurus.

3.6.2.2 Extending Boolean Retrieval With a Hand Built Thesaurus

All work described attempts to improve relevance ranking using a thesaurus. Lee et al., describe the extensions to the extended Boolean retrieval model as a means of including thesaurus information in a Boolean request [Lee et al., 1994]. A description of the extended Boolean model is found in Section 2.5. Values for p were attempted, and a value of six (value suggested for standard extended Boolean retrieval by Salton in [Salton, 1989]) was found to perform the best. Results of this approach showed slightly higher effectiveness.

3.7 Semantic Networks

Semantic networks are based on the idea that knowledge can be represented by *concepts* which are linked together by various relationships. A semantic network is simply a set of nodes and arcs. The arcs are labelled for the type of relationship they represent. Factual information about a given node, such as its individual characteristic (color, size, etc.), are often stored in a data structure called a *frame*. The individual entries in a frame are called *slots* [Minsky, 1975].

A frame for a rose can take the form:

(rose
(*has-color* red)
(*height* 2 feet)
(*is-a* flower)
)

Here the frame *rose* is a single node in a semantic network containing an *is-a* link to the node *flower*. The slots *has-color* and *height* store individual properties of the rose.

Natural language understanding systems have been developed to read human text and build semantic networks representing the knowledge stored in the text [Schank, 1975, Schank and Lehnert, 1977, Gomez and Segami, 1989, Gomez and Segami, 1991]. It turns out that there are many concepts that are not easily represented (the most difficult ones are usually those that involve temporal or spatial reasoning). Storing information in the sentence, "A rose is a flower.", is easy to do as well as to store, "A rose is red", but semantic nets have difficulty with storing this information: "The rose grew three feet last Wednesday and was taller than anything else in the garden." Storing information about the size of the rose on different dates, as well as, the relative location of the rose is often quite difficult in a semantic network. For a detailed discussion see the section on "Representational Thorns" about the large-scale knowledge representation project called *Cyc* (a project in which a large portion of common sense reasoning is being hand-crafted) [Lenat and Guha, 1989].

Despite some of the problems with storing complex knowledge in a semantic network, research was done in which semantic networks were used to improve information retrieval. This work yielded limited results and is highly language specific, however, the potential for improvement still exists.

Semantic networks attempt to resolve the *mismatch* problem in which the terms in a query do not match those found in a document, even though the document is relevant to the query. Instead of matching characters in the query terms with characters in the documents, the *semantic distance* between the terms is measured (by various measures) and incorporated into a semantic network. The premise behind this is that terms which share the same meaning appear relatively close together in a semantic network. *Spreading activation* is one means of identifying the distance between two terms in a semantic network.

There is a close relationship between a thesaurus and a semantic network. From the standpoint of an information retrieval system, a thesaurus attempts to solve the same mismatch problem by expanding a user query with related terms and hoping that the related terms will match the document. A semantic network subsumes a thesaurus by incorporating links that indicate "is-a-synonym-of" or "is-related-to," but a semantic network can represent more complex information such as an is-a hierarchy which is not found in a thesaurus.

One semantic network used as a tool for information retrieval research is WordNet [Beckwith and Miller, 1990]. WordNet is publicly available and contains frames specifically designed for words (some semantic networks might contains frames for more detailed concepts such as *big-and-hairy-person*). WordNet can be found on the Web at: **www.cogsci.princeton.edu/˜wn**.

WordNet contains different entries for the various semantic meanings of a term. Additionally, various term relationships are stored including: *synonyms*, *antonyms* (roughly the opposite of a word), *hyponyms* (lexical relations such as *is-a*), and *meronyms* (is a *part-of*). Most nouns in WordNet are placed in the *is-a* hierarchy while antonyms more commonly relate adjectives.

Interestingly, less commonly known relations of *entailment* and *troponyms* are used to relate verbs. Two verbs are related by entailment when the first verb entails the second verb. For example, to *buy* something entails that you will *pay* for it. Hence, *buy* and *pay* are related by entailment. A troponym relation occurs when the two activities related by entailment must occur at the same time (temporally co-extensive) such as the pair *(limp, walk)*. Software used to search WordNet is further described in [Beckwith and Miller, 1990].

It is reasonable to assume that WordNet would help effectiveness by expanding query terms with synsets found in WordNet. Initial work done by Voorhees [Voorhees, 1993], however, failed to demonstrate an improvement in effectiveness. Even with manual selection of synsets, effectiveness was not improved when queries were expanded. A key obstacle was that terms in queries were not often found in WordNet due to their specificity—terms such as *National Rifle Association* are not in WordNet. Also, the addition of terms that have multiple meanings or word senses significantly degrade effectiveness. More recent work, with improvements to WordNet over time has incorporated carefully selected phrases and showed a small (roughly five percent) improvement [Liu et al., 2004].

Semantic networks were used to augment Boolean retrieval and automatic relevance ranking. We describe these approaches in the remainder of this section.

3.7.1 Distance Measures

To compute the distance between a single node in a semantic network and another node, a spreading activation algorithm is used. A pointer starts at each of the two original nodes and links are followed until an intersection occurs between the two points. The shortest path between the two nodes is used to compute the distance. Note that the simple shortest path algorithm does not apply here because there may be several links that exist between the same two nodes. The distance between nodes a and b is:

Distance(a,b) = minimum number of edges separating a and b

3.7.1.1 R-distance

The problem of measuring the distance between two *sets* of nodes is more complex. Ideally the two sets line up, for example "large rose" and "tall flower" is one such example where "large" can be compared with "tall" and "rose" can be compared with "flower." The problem is that it is difficult to align the concepts such that related concepts will be compared. Hence, the R-distance defined in [Rada et al., 1987] takes all of the individual entries in each set and averages the distance between all the possible combinations of the two sets.

If a document is viewed as a set of terms that are "AND"ed together, and a query is represented as a Boolean expression in disjunctive normal form, then the R-distance identifies a measure of distance between the Boolean query and the document. Also, a NOT applied to a concept yields the distance that is furthest from the concept. Hence, for a query Q for terms ((a AND b AND c) OR (e AND f)) and Document D with terms (t_1 AND t_2), the similarity is computed below.

$$c_1 = \frac{d(a,t_1) + d(a,t_2) + d(b,t_1) + d(b,t_2) + d(c,t_1) + d(c,t_2)}{6}$$

$$c_2 = \frac{d(e,t_1) + d(e,t_2) + d(f,t_1) + d(f,t_2)}{4}$$

SC(Q,D) is computed now as the MIN(c_1, c_2). Essentially, each concept represented in the query is compared to the whole document and the similarity measure is computed as the distance between the document and the closest query concept.

Formally, the R-distance of a disjunctive normal form query Q, and a document D with terms $(t_1, t_2, \ldots, t_n)$ and c_{ij}, indicates the jth term in concept i is defined as:

$$\begin{aligned} SC(Q,D) &= min\,(SC_1(c_1,D), SC_1(c_2,D), \ldots, SC_1(c_m,D)) \\ SC_1(c_i,D) &= \frac{1}{mn}\sum_{i=1}^{n}\sum_{j=1}^{m} d(t_i, c_{ij}) \\ SC(Q,D) &= 0, \texttt{ if } Q = D \end{aligned}$$

3.7.1.2 K-distance

A subsequent distance measure referred to as the K-distance was developed in [Kim and Kim, 1990]. This measure incorporates weighted edges in the semantic network. The distance defined between two nodes is obtained by finding the shortest path between the two nodes (again by using spreading activation) and then summing the edges along the path. More formally the distance between terms t_i and t_j is obtained by:

$$d_{ij} = w_{t_i,x_1} + w_{x_1,x_2} + \ldots + w_{x_n,t_j}$$

where the shortest path from t_i to t_j is: $t_i, x_1, x_2, \ldots, t_j$.

The authors treat NOT as a special case. Details are given in [Kim and Kim, 1990] but the basic idea is to dramatically increase the weights of the arcs that connect the node that is being referenced with a NOT (referred to as separation edges). Once this is done, any paths that include this node are much longer than any other path that includes other terms not referenced by a NOT.

To obtain the distance between two sets, A and B, of nodes with weighted arcs, the K-distance measure computes the minimum of the distances between each node in set A and set B. These minimum distances are then averaged. Since the weights on the arcs may not be equivalent in both directions, the distance measure from A to B is averaged with the distance from B to A. For our same query Q:

((a AND b AND c) OR (e AND f))

Assume document D has only two terms: (t_1 AND t_2), the similarity is computed below.

$$c_1 = \frac{min(d(a,t_1),d(a,t_2)) + min(d(b,t_1),d(b,t_2)) + min(d(c,t_1),d(c,t_2))}{3}$$

$$c_2 = \frac{min(d(e,t_1),d(e,t_2)) + min(d(f,t_1),d(f,t_2))}{2}$$

SC(Q,D) is still the min(c_1, c_2). The value of SC(D,Q) would then be obtained, and the two coefficients are then averaged to obtain the final similarity measure.

The K-distance of a disjunctive normal form query Q and a document D with terms $(t_1, t_2, \ldots, t_n)$ is defined as:

$$SC(Q,D) = \frac{SC_1(Q,D) + SC_1(D,Q)}{2}$$

$$SC_1(Q,D) = min\left(SC_2(c_1,D), SC_2(c_2,D), \ldots, SC_2(c_m,D)\right)$$

$$SC_2(c_i, D) = \frac{1}{n}\left(\sum_{j=1}^{n} min\left(d(c_{ij}, t_j)\right)\right)$$

$$SC(Q, D) = 0, \;\; \texttt{if} \;\; Q = D$$

The R-distance satisfies the triangular inequality such that r-dist(a,c) is less than or equal to r-dist(a,b) + r-dist(b,c). The K-distance does not satisfy this inequality but it does make use of weights along the edges of the semantic network.

3.7.1.3 Incorporating Distance

Lee, et al., incorporated a distance measure using a semantic network into the Extended Boolean Retrieval model and called it—KB-EBM for Knowledge Base—Extended Boolean Model [Lee et al., 1993]. The idea was to take the existing Extended Boolean Retrieval model described in Section 2.5 and modify the weights used to include a distance between two nodes in a semantic network.

The Extended Boolean model uses a function F that indicates the weight of a term in a document. In our earlier description we simply called it w_i, but technically it could be represented as F(d, t_i). Lee, et al., modified this weight by using a semantic network and then used the rest of the Extended Boolean model without any other changes. This cleanly handled the case of NOT.

The primitive distance function, $d(t_i, t_j)$, returns the length of the shortest path between two nodes. This indicates the conceptual closeness of the two terms. What is needed here is the conceptual distance, which is inversely proportional to the primitive distance function. Hence, the new F function uses:

$$distance^{-1}(t_i, t_j) = \frac{\lambda}{\lambda + distance(t_i, t_j)}$$

First, the function F is given for a document with unweighted terms. The new function, F(d, t_i), computes the weight of term t_i in the document as the average distance of t_i to all other nodes in the document. The new function F is then:

$$F(d, t) = \frac{\sum_{i=1}^{n} distance^{-1}(t_i, t)}{1 + \frac{\lambda}{\lambda+1}(n-1)}$$

For existing weights for a term in a document, F is modified to include weights w_i. This is the weight of the ith term in document d.

$$F(d, t) = \frac{\sum_{i=1}^{n} distance^{-1}(t_i, t) w_i}{1 + \frac{\lambda}{\lambda+1}(n-1)}$$

3.7.1.4 Evaluation of Distance Measures

All three distance measures were evaluated on four collections with nine, six, seven, and seven documents, respectively. Precision and recall were not measured, so evaluations were done using comparisons of the rankings produced by each distance. In some cases MESH was used—a medical semantic network—in other cases, the Computing Reviews Classification Scheme (CRCS) was used. Overall, the small size of the test collections and the lack of precision and recall measurements made it difficult to evaluate these measures. They are presented here due to their ability to use semantic networks. Most work done today is not focused on Boolean requests. However, all of these distance measures are applicable if the natural language request is viewed as a Boolean OR of the terms in the query. It would be interesting to test them against a larger collection with a general semantic network such as WordNet.

3.7.2 Developing Query Term Based on "Concepts"

Instead of computing the distance between query terms and document terms in a semantic network and incorporating that distance into the metric, the semantic network can be used as a thesaurus to simply replace terms in the query with "nearby" terms in the semantic network. Vectors of "concepts" can then be generated to represent the query, instead of term-based vectors. This was described in the early 1970's. In 1988, an algorithm was given that described a means of using this approach to improve an existing Boolean retrieval system [Giger, 1988]. Terms in the original Boolean system were replaced with "concepts". These concepts were found in a semantic network that contained links to the original terms. The paper referred to the network as a thesaurus, but the different relationships existing between terms meet our definition of a semantic network.

The system described in [Chen and Lynch, 1992, Chen et al., 1993] used an automatically generated semantic network. The network was developed using two different clustering algorithms. The first was the standard cosine algorithm (see Section 3.2), while the second was developed by the authors and yields asymmetric links between nodes in the semantic net. Users were then able to manually traverse the semantic network to obtain good terms for the query, while the semantic nets were also used to find suitable terms to manually index new documents.

3.7.3 Ranking Based on Constrained Spreading Activation

Two interesting papers appeared in 1987 that are frequently referenced in discussions of knowledge-based information retrieval [Cohen and Kjeldsen, 1987, Kjeldsen and Cohen, 1987]. These papers describe the GRANT system in which potential funding agencies are identified based on areas of research interest. A manually built semantic network with 4,500 nodes and 700 funding agencies was constructed with links that connect agencies and areas of interest based on the topics agencies are interested in.

Given a topic, the links emanating from the topic are activated and spreading activation begins. Activation stops when a funding agency is found. At each step, activation is constrained. After following the first link, three constraints are used. The first is *distance*. If the path exceeds a length of four, it is no longer followed. The second is *fan-out*, if a path reaches a node that has more than four links emanating from it, it is not followed. This is because the node that has been reached is too general to be of much use and it will cause the search to proceed in many directions that are of little use. The third type of constraint is a rule that results in a score for the link. The score is considered an *endorsement*. Ultimately, the results are ranked based on the accumulation of these scores. An example of one such endorsement occurs if a researcher's area of interest is a subtopic or specialization of a general topic funded by the agency it gets a positive endorsement. An agency that funds research on *database systems* will fund research in *temporal database systems*. More formally:

request-funds-for-topic(x) and IS-A(x,y) $\rightarrow$ request-funds-for-topic(y)

A negative endorsement rule exists when the area of research interest is a generalization of a funding agency's areas of research. An agency that funds *database systems* will probably not be interested in funding generic interest in *computer science*.

A best-first search is used such that high-scoring endorsements are followed first. The search ends when a certain *threshold* number of funding agencies are identified. The GRANT system was tested operationally, and found to be superior to a simple keyword matching system that was in use. Searches that previously took hours could be done in minutes. More formal testing was done with a small set of twenty-three queries. However, the semantic network and the document collection were both relatively small so it is difficult to generalize from these results. Overall, the GRANT system is very interesting in that it uses a semantic network, but the network was constrained based on domain-specific rules.

3.8 Parsing

The ability to identify a set of tokens to represent a body of text is an essential feature of every information retrieval system. Simply using every token encountered leaves a system vulnerable to fundamental semantic mismatches between a query and a document. For instance, a query that asks for information about *computer chips* matches documents that describe *potato chips*. Simple single-token approaches, both manual and automatic, are described in

Section 3.8.1. Although these approaches seem crude and ultimately treat text as a bag of words, they generally are easy to implement, efficient, and often result in as good or better effectiveness than many sophisticated approaches measured at the Text REtrieval Conference (TREC). More discussion of TREC is found in Chapter 9).

A step up from single-term approaches is the use of phrases in document retrieval. Phrases capture some of the *meaning* behind the bag of words and result in two-term pairs (or multi-term phrases, in the general case) so that a query that requires information about *New York* will not find information about the *new Duke of York*. Section 3.8.2 describes simple approaches to phrase identification.

More sophisticated approaches to phrase identification are given in Section 3.8.3. These are based on algorithms commonly used for natural language processing (NLP). These include part-of-speech taggers, syntax parsers, and information extraction heuristics. We provide a brief overview of the heuristics that are available and pay particular attention only to those that have been directly incorporated into information retrieval systems. An entire book could be written on this section as the entire field of natural language processing is relevant.

Overall, it should be noted that parsing is critical to the performance of a system. For complex NLP approaches, parsing is discussed in great detail, but to date, these approaches have typically performed with no significant difference in performance than simplistic approaches. A review of some initial work done to integrate NLP into information retrieval systems is given in [Lewis and Sparck Jones, 1996].

3.8.1 Single Terms

The simplest approach to search documents is to require manual intervention and to assign names of terms to each document. The problem is that it is not always easy to assign keywords that distinctly represent a document. Also, when categorizations are employed—such as the Library of Congress subject headings—it is difficult to stay current within a domain. Needless to say, the manual effort used to categorize documents is extremely high. Therefore, it was learned early in the process that manually assigned tokens did not perform significantly better than automatically assigned tokens [Salton, 1971d].

Once scanning was deemed to be a good idea in the early 1960's, the next step was to try to normalize text to avoid simple mismatches due to differing prefixes, suffixes, or capitalization. Today, most information retrieval systems convert all text to a single case so that terms that simply start a sentence do not result in a mismatch with a query simply because they are capitalized.

Stemming refers to the normalization of terms by removing suffixes or prefixes. The idea is that a user who includes the term "throw" in the query might also wish to match on "throwing", "throws", etc. Stemming algorithms have been developed for more than twenty years. The Porter and Lovins algorithms are most commonly used [Porter, 1980, Lovins, 1968]. These algorithms simply remove common suffixes and prefixes. A problem is that two very different terms might have the same stem. A stemmer that removes *-ing* and *-ed* results in a stem of *r* for terms *red* and *ring*. KSTEM uses dictionaries to ensure that any generated stem will be a valid word [Krovetz and Croft, 1989, Krovetz, 1993]. Another approach uses corpus-based statistics (essentially based on term co-occurrence) to identify stems in a language-independent fashion [Croft and Xu, 1994]. These stemmers were shown to result in improved relevance ranking over more traditional stemmers.

Stop words are terms deemed relatively meaningless in terms of document relevance and are not stored in the index. These terms represent approximately forty percent of the document collection [Francis and Kucera, 1982]. Removing these terms reduces index construction, time and storage cost, but may also reduce the ability to respond to some queries. A counterexample to the use of stop word removal occurs when a query requests a phrase that only contains stop words (e.g., "to be or not to be"). Nevertheless, stop word lists are frequently used, and some research was directed solely at determining a good stop word list [Fox, 1990].

Finally, we find that other parsing rules are employed to handle special characters. Questions arise such as what to do with special characters like hyphens, apostrophes, commas, etc. Some initial rules for these questions are given in [Adams, 1991], but the effect on precision and recall is not discussed. Many TREC papers talk about *cleaning up their parser* and the authors confess to having seen their own precision and recall results improved by very simple parsing changes. However, we are unaware of a detailed study on single-term parsing and the treatment of special characters, and its related effect on precision and recall.

3.8.2 Simple Phrases

Many TREC systems identify phrases as any pair of terms that are not separated by a stop term, punctuation mark, or special character. Subsequently, infrequently occurring phrases are not stored. In many TREC systems, phrases occurring fewer than 25 times are removed. This dramatically reduces the number of phrases which decreases memory requirements. [Ballerini et al., 1996].

Once phrases are employed, the question as to how they should be incorporated into the relevance ranking arises. Some systems simply add them to the query, while others do not add them to the query but do not include them in the computation of the document length normalization [Buckley et al., 1995]. The reason for this is that the terms were already being considered. Tests using just phrases or terms were performed on many systems. It was found that phrases should be used to augment, not replace the terms. Hence, a query for *New York* should be modified to search for *new, york*, and *New York*. Phrases used in this fashion are generally accepted to yield about a ten percent improvement in precision and recall over simple terms.

3.8.3 Complex Phrases

The quest to employ NLP to answer a user query was undertaken since the early 1960's. In fact, NLP systems were often seen as diametrically opposed to information retrieval systems because the NLP systems were trying to *understand* a document by building a canonical structure that represents the document. The goal behind the canonical structure is to reduce the inherent ambiguity found in language. A query that asks for information about *walking* should match documents that describe people who *are moving slowly by gradually placing one foot in front of the other*.

A NLP system stores information about *walking* and *moving slowly* with the exact same canonical structure—it does this by first parsing the document syntactically—identifying the key elements of the document (subject, verb, object, etc.) and then building a single structure for the document. Simple primitives that encompass large categories of verbs were proposed [Schank, 1975] such as PTRANS (physically transport), in which *John drove to work* and *John used his car to get to work* both result in the same simple structure *John PTRANS work*.

Progress in NLP has occurred, but the reality is that many problems in knowledge representation make it extremely difficult to actually build the necessary canonical structures. The CYC project has spent the last fifteen years hand-building a knowledge base and has encountered substantial difficulty in identifying the exact means of representing the knowledge found in text [Lenat and Guha, 1989].

A side effect of full-scale NLP systems is that many tools that do not work perfectly for full language understanding are becoming quite usable for information retrieval systems. We may not be able to build a perfect knowledge representation of a document, but by using the same part-of-speech tagger and syntactic parser that might be used by an NLP system, we can develop several algorithms to identify key phrases in documents.

3.8.3.1 Use of POS and Word Sense Tagging

Part-of-speech taggers are based on either statistical or rule-based methods. The goal is to take a section of text and identify the parts of speech for each token. One approach incorporates a pretagged corpus to identify two measures: the frequency a given term is assigned a particular tag and the frequency with which different tag sequences occur [Church, 1988]. For example, *duck* might appear as a noun (creature that swims in ponds) eighty percent of a time and a verb (to get out of the way of a ball thrown at your head) twenty percent of the time. Additionally, "noun noun verb" may occur ten percent of the time while "noun noun noun" may occur thirty percent of the time. Using these two lists (generated based on a pretagged training corpus) a dynamic programming algorithm can be obtained to optimize the assignment of a tag to a token for a given step. DeRose improved on Church's initial tagger in [DeRose, 1988]. Rule-based taggers in which tags are assigned based on the firing of sequences of rules are described in [Brill, 1992].

Part-of-speech taggers can be used to identify phrases. One use is to identify all sequences of nouns such as *Virginia Beach* or sequences of adjectives followed by nouns such as *big red truck* [Allan et al., 1995, Broglio et al., 1994]. Another use of a tagger is to modify processing such that a match of a term in the query only occurs if it matches the same part-of-speech found in the document. In this fashion, *duck* as a verb does not match a reference to *duck* as a noun. Although this seems sensible, it has not been shown to be particularly effective. One reason is that words such as *bark* have many different *senses* within a part of speech. In the sentences *A dog's bark is often stronger than its bite* and *Here is a nice piece of tree bark*, *bark* is a noun in both cases with very different word senses. Some initial development of *word sense taggers* exists [Krovetz, 1993]. This work identifies word senses by using a dictionary-based stemmer. Recent work on sense disambiguation for acronyms is found in [Zahariev, 2004].

3.8.3.2 Syntactic Parsing

As we move along the continuum of increasingly more complex NLP tools, we now discuss syntactic parsing. These tools attempt to identify the key syntactic components of a sentence, such as subject, verb, object, etc. For simple sentences the problem is not so hard. *Whales eat fish* has the simple subject of *Whales*, the verb of *eat*, and the object of *fish*. Typically, parsers work by first invoking a part-of-speech tagger.

Subsequently, a couple of different approaches are employed. One method is to apply a grammar. The first attempt at parsers used augmented transition networks (ATNs) that were essentially non-deterministic finite state automata in which: subject-verb-object would be a sequence of states. The problem is, that for complex sentences, many different paths occur through the automata. Also, some sentences recursively start the whole finite state automata (FSA), in that they contain structures that have all the individual components of a sentence. Relative clauses that occur in sentences such as *Mary, who is a nice girl that plays on the tennis team, likes seafood.* Here, the main structure of *Mary likes seafood* also has a substructure of *Mary plays tennis.* After

ATNs, rule-based approaches that attempt to parse based on firing rules, were attempted.

Other parsing algorithms, such as the Word Usage Parser (WUP) by Gomez, use a dictionary lookup for each word, and each word generates a specialized sequence of states [Gomez, 1988]. In other words, the ATN is dynamically generated based on individual word occurrences. Although this is much faster than an ATN, it requires substantial manual intervention to build the dictionary of word usages. Some parsers such as the Apple Pie Parser, are based on *light* parsing in which rules are followed to quickly scan for key elements of a sentence, but more complex sentences are not fully parsed.

Once the parse is obtained, an information retrieval system makes use of the component structures. A simple use of a parser is to use the various component phrases such as SUBJECT or OBJECT as the only components of a query and match them against the document. Phrases generated in this fashion match many variations found in English. A query with *American President* will match phrases that include *President of America, president who is in charge of America*, etc. One effort that identified head-modifier pairs (e.g., "America+president") was evaluated against a patent collection and demonstrated as much as a sixteen percent improvement in average precision [Osborn et al., 1997]. On the TREC-5 dataset, separate indexes based on stems, simple phrases (essentially adjective-noun pairs or noun-noun pairs), head-modifier pairs, and people name's were all separately indexed [Strzalkowski et al., 1997]. These streams were then combined and a twenty percent improvement in average precision was observed.

To date, this work has not resulted in substantial improvements in effectiveness, although it dramatically increases the run-time performance of the system.

3.8.3.3 Information Extraction

The Message Understanding Conference (MUC) focuses on information extraction—the problem of finding various structured data within an unstructured document. Identification of people's names, places, amounts, etc. is the essential problem found in MUC, and numerous algorithms that attempt to solve this problem exist. Again, these are either rule-based or statistical algorithms. The first step in many of these algorithms is to generate a syntactic parse of the sentence, or at the very least, generate a part-of-speech tag. Details of these algorithms are found in the MUC Proceedings. More recently the Special Interest Group on Natural Language Learning of the Association for Computational Linguistics (CoNLL-2003) held a shared task on Language-Independent Named Entity Recognition. All of the proceedings may be found at **http://cnts.uia.ac.be/signll/conll.html**. In this task, language independent algorithms were used to process standard test collections in English and German. We discuss these in more detail in Section 4.4.5.

Named entity taggers identify people names, organizations, and locations. We present a brief example that we created with a rule-based extractor from BBN Corporation to obtain this new document. This extractor works by using hundreds of hand-crafted rules that use surrounding terms to identify when a term should be extracted. First, we show the pre-extracted text—a paragraph about the guitarist Allen Collins.

<TEXT>
Collins began his rise to success as the lightning-fingered guitarist for the Jacksonville band formed in 1966 by a group of high school students. The band enjoyed national fame in the 1970's with such hits as "Free Bird," "Gimme Three Steps," "Saturday Night Special" and Ronnie Van Zant's feisty "Sweet Home Alabama."
</TEXT>

The following output is generated by the extractor. Tags such as PERSON and LOCATION are now marked.

<TEXT>
<ENAMEX TYPE="PERSON">Collins</ENAMEX> began his rise to success as the lightning-fingered guitarist for the <ENAMEX TYPE="LOCATION">Jacksonville</ENAMEX> band formed in <TIMEX TYPE="DATE">1966</TIMEX> by a group of high school students. The band enjoyed national fame in the <TIMEX TYPE="DATE">1970s </TIMEX> with such hits as "Free <ENAMEX TYPE="PERSON"> Bird </ENAMEX>," "Gimme Three Steps," "Saturday Night Special" and <ENAMEX TYPE="PERSON">Ronnie Van Zant</ENAMEX>'s feisty "Sweet Home <ENAMEX TYPE="LOCATION">Alabama</ENAMEX>."
</TEXT>

In this example, and in many we have hand-checked, the extractor performs well. Many extractors are now performing at much higher levels of precision and recall than those of the early 1990's [Sundheim, 1995]. However, they are not perfect. Notice the label of PERSON being assigned to the term "Bird" in the phrase "Free Bird."

Using extracted data makes it possible for a user to be shown a list of all person names, locations, and organizations that appear in the document collection. These could be used as suggested query terms for a user.

The simplest use of an extractor is to recognize key phrases in the documents. An information retrieval system could incorporate extraction by increasing term weights for extracted terms. Given that extractors are only recently running fast enough to even consider using for large volumes of text, research in the area of using extractors for information retrieval is in its infancy.

3.9 Summary

We described eight utilities, emphasizing that each of these utilities, both independently and in combination with each other can be integrated with any strategy. Most of these utilities address the term-mismatch problem, namely, a document can be highly relevant without having many terms that syntactically match those terms specified in the query. The relevance feedback, thesaurus, and semantic network strategies directly address this problem as they attempt to find related terms that do *match* the document and the query. Parsing and N-grams avoid mismatches by using fragments of terms instead of the actual terms. Fragmentation can avoid mismatches that can occur due to spelling errors or the loss or addition of a common prefix or suffix.

Passages attempt to focus on only the relevant part of a document. Thus, mismatching terms from spurious parts of the document are ignored and do not significantly reduce the similarity coefficient. Clustering algorithms also attempt to focus a user search onto only a relevant cluster of documents, thereby avoiding irrelevant documents.

Regression analysis estimates coefficients for a similarity measure based on a history of relevant documents. Although this does require prior relevance information, it offers an opportunity to fine tune different retrieval strategies.

Which utility is most important? Perhaps a more interesting question is: Which utility or combination of utilities work best with a given strategy? The answer to either of these questions is unclear. Relevance feedback is an accepted part of most systems participating in the TREC activities. Document clustering has exceeded most computational resources, and thus, is not used widely. Thesauri and semantic networks have yet to show dramatic improvements over a baseline comparison. Parsing plays a critical role in all information retrieval systems with much work done on various stemmers. N-grams are not as commonly used because they require substantial growth in an inverted index, but they do offer resilience to spelling errors.

The bottom line is that more testing is needed to identify which utility works best with a given strategy, and which measurements are needed to identify the extent to which a given utility improves effectiveness.

3.10 Exercises

1 Using the text from *Alice in Wonderland*, write some code that will use a trivial strategy for ranking documents. For a query with i matching terms, assign a similarity measure of i for a given document (for simplicity define a document as ten lines of the book). Implement automatic relevance feedback using this strategy to suggest ten new terms for a given query. Use *idf* as your new term sort order.

- Identify a query where five out of the ten terms are "good" in that they directly relate to the query.
- Identify a query where five of the terms are "bad".

2 Develop an example with a retrieval strategy of your choice and show how a modification to the parser will result in fundamentally different results (the document ranking will be different).

3 Implement an automatic thesaurus generation algorithm for the term *teacup* in the book. Give the top three terms most related to this term.

4 Give ten examples where stemming will do what a user would like it to do. Give ten terms where stemming will not do that a user would like.

5 One idea to improve effectiveness of an information retrieval system is to match on both the term and the *sense* of the term. The idea is that for a query of the term *duck* as noun, a document containing "She tried to duck to avoid the ball thrown at her." would not match. Implement five queries with your favorite Web search engine, and for each query identify a document that could have been avoided using this heuristic.

Chapter 4

CROSS-LANGUAGE INFORMATION RETRIEVAL

Cross-Language Information Retrieval (CLIR) is quickly becoming a mature area in the information retrieval world. The goal is to allow a user to issue a query in language L and have that query retrieve documents in language L' (see Figure 4.1). The idea is that the user wants to issue a single query against a document collection that contains documents in a myriad of languages. An implicit assumption is that the user understands results obtained in multiple languages. If this is not the case, it is necessary for the retrieval system to translate the selected foreign language documents into a language that the user can understand. Surveys of cross-language information retrieval techniques and multilingual processing include [Oard and Diekema, 1998, Haddouti, 1999].

4.1 Introduction

The key difference between CLIR and monolingual information retrieval is that the query and the documents cannot be matched directly. In addition to the inherent difficulty in matching the inherent style, tone, word usage, and other features of the query with that of the document, we must now cross the language barrier between the query and the document. Section 4.2 focuses on the core problems involved in crossing the language barrier. Section 4.3 describes cross-language retrieval strategies and Section 4.4 discusses cross-language utilities.

4.1.1 Resources

Numerous resources are needed to implement cross-language retrieval systems. Most approaches use bilingual term lists, term dictionaries, a comparable corpus or a parallel corpus.

A *comparable corpus* is a collection of documents in language L and another collection about the same topic in language L'. The key here is that the documents happen to have been written in different languages, but the documents are not literal translations of each other. A news article in language L by a newspaper in a country which speaks language L and an article in language L' by a newspaper in a country which speaks language L' is an example of comparable documents. The two newspapers wrote their own article; they did not translate an article in one language into another language. Another key with comparable corpora are that they must be *about the same topic*. A book in French on medicine and a book in Spanish on law are not comparable. If both books are about medicine or about law they are comparable. We will discuss CLIR techniques using a comparable corpus in Section 4.3.3.

A *parallel corpus* provides documents in one language L that are then direct translations of language L' or vice versa. The key is that each document is in language L is a direct translation of a corresponding document in language L'. Hence, it is possible to align a parallel corpus at the document level, the paragraph level, the sentence level, the phrase level, or even the individual term level. Legislative documents in countries or organizations that are required to publish their proceedings in at least two languages are a common source of parallel corpora. In general, a parallel corpus will be most useful if it is used to implement cross-language retrieval of documents that are in a similar domain to the parallel corpus. Recent work shows that significant effectiveness can be obtained if the correct domain is selected [Rogati and Yang, 2004]. We discuss parallel corpus CLIR techniques in Section 4.3.2.1.

We also note that even within a single language such as Arabic, there are many different character sets (four are commonly used with Arabic). Language processing resources exist to not only detect a language but also to detect a character set. Cross-language systems often struggle with intricacies involved in working with different character sets within a single language. Unicode (**www.unicode.org**) was developed to map the character representation for numerous scripts into a single character set, but not all electronic documents are currently stored in Unicode.

4.1.2 Evaluation

Different measures are used to evaluate the performance of cross-language information retrieval systems. The most obvious is simply to compute the average precision of the cross-language query.

Another approach is to compute the percentage of monolingual performance. This can occasionally be misleading because the techniques used to achieve a given monolingual performance may be quite different than those used for cross-language performance. Straightforward techniques typically result in 50% of monolingual performance, but the CLIR literature contains results that exceed 100% because of the inherent query expansion that occurs when doing a translation [Levow et al., 2004].

We note that queries with relevance judgements exist in Arabic, Chinese, Dutch, Finnish, French, German, Italian, Japanese, Korean, Swedish and Spanish. These have been used at various evaluations at TREC (Text REtrieval Conference, see **trec.nist.gov**), CLEF (Cross-Language Evaluation Forum see **clef.iei.pi.cnr.it**), and NTCIR (see **research.nii.ac.jp/ntcir**).

4.2 Crossing the Language Barrier

To cross the language barrier, we must answer four core questions [Oard, 2004]:

- What should be translated? Either the queries may be translated, the documents, or both queries and documents may be translated to some internal representation. Query translation is depicted in Figure 4.1). Section 4.2.1 describes query translation approaches. Document translation is shown in Figure 4.2). Section 4.2.2 describes document translation. Finally, we may obtain an internal representation of both the query and the document.

- Which tokens should be used to do a translation (e.g.; stems, words, phrases, etc.)? Phrase translation is described in Section 4.2.3.

- How should we use a translation? In other words, a single term in language L may map to several terms in Language L/. We may use one of these terms, some of these terms, or all of these terms. Additionally, we might weight some terms higher than other terms if we have reason to believe that one translation is more likely than another. Various approaches are described in described in Section 4.2.4.

- How can we remove spurious translations? Typically, there are spurious translations that can lead to poor retrieval. Techniques exist to remove these translations. Pruning translations is described in Section 4.2.5.

We describe several query translation approaches in Section 4.2.1. Translating all of the documents into the language of the query is an arduous task if a complex machine translation system that does full natural language processing is used (lighter translation approaches are certainly viable, but intuitively appear to be less effective).

As with monolingual retrieval, various strategies and utilities exist for cross-language retrieval. As with the monolingual retrieval we organize the chapter according to strategies and utilities. Again, a strategy will take a query in language L and identify a measure of similarity between the query and documents in the target language L'. A utility enhances the work of any strategy. The core

Figure 4.1. Translate the Query

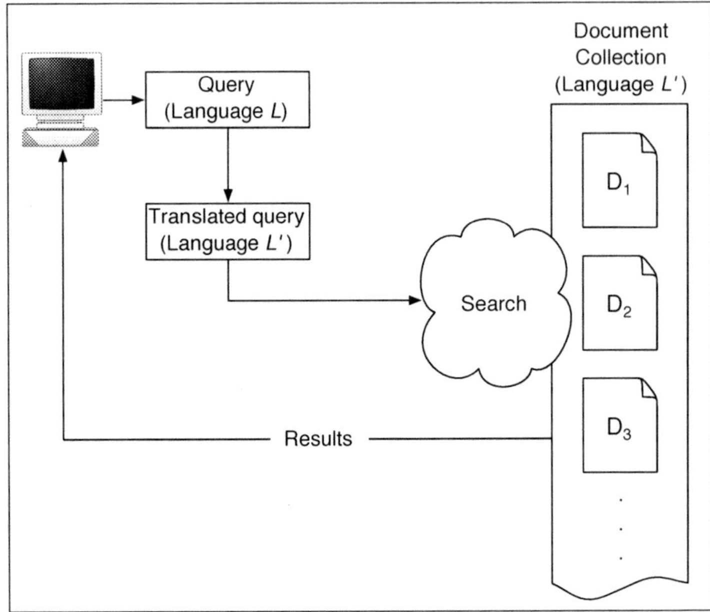

strategies: query translation, document translation, and use of internal representation are the focus of Sections 4.2.1, 4.2.2, and 4.3.2. Utilities such as n-grams, stemming, and entity tagging are described in Section 4.4.

4.2.1 Query Translation

Initial work in query translation was done in the early 1970's where user specified keywords were used to represent documents and a dictionary was used to translate English keywords to German keywords [Salton, 1970a]. Query translation approaches use machine translation, language specific stemmers, dictionaries, thesauri, and automatically generated bilingual term lists to implement the necessary translation of the user query in language L to the target query language L'.

An excellent discussion of dictionary-based query translation techniques is given in [Levow et al., 2004]. In this work, a methodical study of various techniques is presented and effectiveness of specific techniques are measured.

4.2.2 Document Translation

A simple way to "translate" documents is to use any of the query translation approaches that we have already discussed. For example, one or more bilingual

Figure 4.2. Translate the Documents

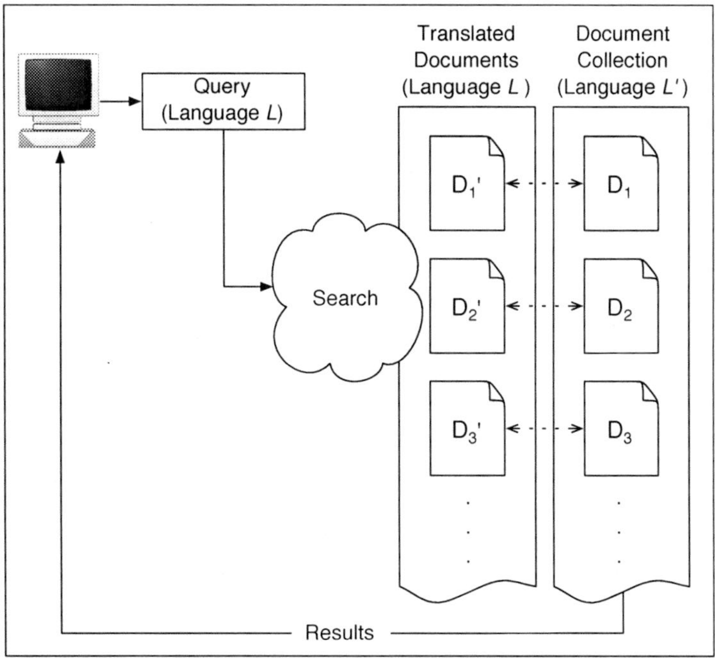

term lists may be used to "translate" a document from language L into language L'.

Since the documents contain natural language text, it is also possible to run machine translation algorithms to translate from language L to language L'. Although machine translation algorithms are not perfect, they have been used as a foundation for CLIR. An advantage of these algorithms is that the use of the full natural language text provides more evidence when selecting a potential translation.

4.2.3 Phrase Translation

Instead of simply using terms for translation, phrase-based approaches were shown to yield substantial improvement. Simply manually translating phrases instead of a term based translation was shown to yield improvement in [Hull and Grefenstette, 1996]. A bilingual phrase list extracted from a parallel text was used in [Davis and Ogden, 1997]. We discuss extraction of bilingual term lists from training texts in Section 4.3.2. Phrase translation using the Collins machine readable dictionary was described in [Ballesteros and Croft, 1997]. A core problem with any phrase translation approach is that there is far more likelihood that a phrase will not be found in a bilingual list used for translation than a single term.

4.2.4 Choosing Translations

Once a bilingual term list or term lists are in place, the next challenge is to choose the appropriate translation. We have discussed dictionary coverage issues associated with query translation. We now focus on the choice of translations and the need to form these translations into a new query for the target language.

There are four different approaches: unbalanced, structured queries, balanced, and the use of a pivot language.

4.2.4.1 Quality of Bilingual Term Lists

Like their monolingual counterparts, most cross-language systems use a variety of techniques to improve accuracy. At the core of these systems are bilingual lexicons. A survey of these approaches is given in [Pirkola et al., 2001]. A lexicon is used to map a source term in language L to a myriad of terms in language L'. Key problems with the lexicon are ambiguities, incomplete coverage of the vocabulary, and the lack of even the existence of a machine-readable source.

Given that word sense disambiguation is very difficult with the short length and lack of context found in a typical query, multiple word senses for a single term result in numerous translations. Consider a query with the term *duck* in English. This term can be translated to many different terms in a target language because there is more than one meaning to the word. Duck can be defined as a *type of bird that floats on lakes* or it can be a command to *move out of the way*. The challenge of cross-language systems is to reduce the ambiguity created by a translated query in the target language that has numerous terms that have nothing to do with the query.

Experiments which focus on measuring the effect of coverage of a dictionary on effectiveness are found in [Demner-Fushman and Oard, 2003]. In this work, a set of 113,000 documents was used with thirty-three queries. Thirty-five different bilingual dictionaries were tested. In each case, the original English query was filtered based on the bilingual dictionary. Only terms found in the dictionary were used. For each dictionary, the average precision was computed based on the ability of that dictionary to filter a query. The idea is that a perfect dictionary would not filter at all. It was discovered that dictionary size linearly increases accuracy when a dictionary contains between 3,000 and 20,000 terms. After that, mean average precision does not increase.

Another key set of experiments on lexicon coverage is given in [McNamee and Mayfield, 2002a]. For a fixed translation resource, they gradually reduce the number of translations found in the resource by randomly eliminating some terms that are translated. This was done for five languages: Dutch, English, French, German, Italian, and Spanish. They find, what one would intuitively expect, performance degrades as lexical coverage degrades. (see Section 4.4.1).

4.2.4.2 Unbalanced

This is the most naive form of using a bilingual term list. For a given word t in language L all terms in language L' that are valid translations of t are used. The problem with this is that a query term that is general may have numerous translations and they are all added to the query. Meanwhile a query term that is very specific may only have one translation and hence it may well be given less weight than the more general term – this is precisely the opposite of what would be preferred – increased weighting of more specific search terms.

4.2.4.3 Balanced Queries

Here, a term t is translated into multiple terms and these terms are assigned a weight that is then averaged across all translations for the term. Hence, a general term with multiple translations will result in all of the translated terms having a lower weight than a very specific translation to only a single term. The weight is a combination of the term frequency (tf), the document frequency (df) and the document length.

More formally, assume we have a weight w_{ij} for a term t_i in document D_j. As usual, the term frequency tf_{ij} of the this term indicates the number of occurrences of term i in document j. Let $|D_j|$ indicate the length of document j. Let df_i equal the number of documents in the collection that contain term i. Our weight w_{ij} will be computed with a function that combines the tf, the df and the size of the document $|D|$. We have discussed both normalized cosine measures (see Section 2.1.2) and probabilistic measures (see Section 2.2). These measures may be thought of as term weighting functions that are increasing in tf_{ij}, decreasing in df_i and decreasing in $|D_j|$.

To compute the weight of query term q_i in language L. Assume we have k translations of term q_i in language L'. For each of these translations t'_i, we can compute the tf'_{ij} and $|D'_i|$ for each document in language L'. Similarly, we can compute the collection frequency, df'_i in language L'. From these we can compute the weight w'_i for each of the translations in language L'. To compute the weight of our initial query term in language L we simply average the corresponding translations as:

$$q_i = \frac{\sum_{i=1}^{k} w'_i}{k}$$

Balanced queries are described in more detail in [Leek et al., 2000, Levow and Oard, 2000].

4.2.4.4 Structured Queries

For structured queries, the overall term frequency for a term in a document is computed as the sum of all of the term frequencies for all of the translations. Similarly, the corresponding document frequencies for all translations of a query term are combined as well. Assume we again have k translations for query term q_i:

$$tf_i = \sum_{i=1}^{k} tf'_{ij} \qquad df_i = \sum_{i=1}^{k} df'i$$

These modified term and document weights are then used to compute w_i. Any translation for a give term contributes to the document frequency of that term. Structured queries are described in more detail in [Pirkola, 1998]. A recent study compared these approaches and found that structured queries significantly outperformed balanced and unbalanced queries [Levow et al., 2004].

4.2.4.5 Pivot Language

There are cases when a translation dictionary from language L to L' is not be available. In these cases, a *pivot language* P can be used to translate from L to P and then from P to L'. This is sometimes referred to as *transitive* translation. An initial discussion with research results is found in [Ballesteros, 2001]. Here, the use of a pivot language was shown to degrade performance by 91% over a direct bilingual translation. This initial degradation was overcome with relevance feedback techniques (see Section 4.4.1).

An approach which uses two different pivot languages is given in [Gollins and Sanderson, 2004]. In this work, translating from German to English is done via two routes. First, translations are obtained by translating from German to Spanish and then to English. Next, these are combined with those from German to Dutch to English. The idea is that translations lost in converting from German to Spanish are improved with those from German to Dutch. Effectiveness was improved when *only* the terms in the target language that were obtained via all translation routes were used.

For example, consider a query with terms t_1 and t_2 and assume that one translation route resulted in translations e_1, e_2, e_3 and another route obtained e_2 and e_4. The only common term, e_2, would be used against the target language. The remaining terms, e_1, e_3, e_4, would be removed as potentially erroneous translations. More recent results with the use of a pivot language are found in [Kishida and Kando, 2003].

4.2.5 Pruning Translations

Once translations are identified, it is often necessary to prune the list of translations for a given phrase. Instead of using all translations, only candidate translations that tend to co-occur are used in [Adriani, 2000].

Recently, work done with bidirectional English-Arabic dictionaries showed that performance improves *only* when translations, t, are used in which a term s is translated to t and then back to s using a bidirectional English-Arabic dictionary [Aljlayl et al., 2002].

The use of HMM's to compute a most likely query translation was shown in [Federico and Bertoldi, 2002]. The most probable translation is used and the result is combined with a more traditional language model (as we just described in Section 4.3.1). The work also used an applied linear smoothing technique as opposed to smoothing approaches described in Section 2.3.2. The authors suggest that their approach is superior to the similarity measure given in Equation 4.1, but we are unaware of any direct comparisons. The authors experimented with using different numbers of query translations. They found, in many cases, a single high quality translation of the query outperformed a variety of translations.

4.3 Cross-Language Retrieval Strategies

Cross-language retrieval strategies develop a similarity measure for a query in language L against documents in Language L/. Section 4.3.1 describes the use of Language Models for CLIR.

4.3.1 Language Models for CLIR

A language modeling (see Section 2.3) approach may be used for cross-language retrieval. To briefly review, a simple monolingual language model will compute the likelihood of generating a query given a document.

$$p(q|D_i \in R) = \prod_{j=1}^{Q} \alpha P(t_j|C) + (1-\alpha)P(t_j|D_i)$$

Given a query $(t_1, t_2, \ldots, t_j, \ldots, t_{|Q|})$ where t_j is a query term; α is estimated using an EM (Expectation Maximization) algorithm [Dempster et al., 1977], and C is the document collection. While formulated as a Hidden Markov Model (HMM), the retrieval method is essentially similar to using the multinomial language model with linear interpolation smoothing (see Section 2.3.2). A good overview on Hidden Markov Models may be found in [Rabbiner, 1989].

The remaining probabilities are computed as:

$$P(t_j|C) = \frac{f_j}{|C|}$$

where f_j is the frequency or number of occurrences of term j in the document collection.

$$P(t_j|D_i) = \frac{tf_{ij}}{|D_i|}$$

where tf_{ij} is the term frequency or number of occurrences of term j in document i. For cross-language retrieval, the model is extended so a document written in language L generates a query in language L' [Xu and Weischedel, 1999]. The notation t_L is used to refer to a term in language L and $t_{L'}$ is used to represent a term in language L'. Similarly, D_{L_i} refers to the document i in language L and $D_{L'_i}$ refers to document i in language L'. Hence, we need to compute:

$$P(q_L|D_{L'_i} \in R) = \prod_{j=1}^{Q} \alpha P(t_{L_j}|C_L) + (1-\alpha) P(t_{L_j}|D_{L'_i}) \qquad (4.1)$$

We now compute the probability that a query in language L will be generated with a document in language L'. All of the probabilities can be computed with no change except for $P(t_{L_j}|D_{L'})$. This probability can be computed with a term dictionary that will enable us to compute a translation probability: $P(t_{L_j}|t_{L'_k})$.

$$P(t_{L_j}|D_{L'_i}) = \sum_{k=1}^{|D_{L'}|} P(t_{L'_k}|D_{L'_i})\ P(t_{L_j}|t_{L'_k}) \qquad (4.2)$$

where the first term is the ratio of our translated query terms to the size of the document retrieved.

$$P(t_{L'_k}|D_{L'_i}) = \frac{tf_{L'_k}}{|D_{L'_i}|}$$

The next term uses the actual translations in the lexicon. The probability $P(t_{L_j}|t_{L'_k})$ is the *translation probability* that given a term in language L' there will be a term in language L. For simplicity, one might assign these probabilities as equally likely so that if a term in language L has five translations in language L' we might assign them each a probability of 0.2. However, this framework allows for the development of other algorithms to estimate the translation probability [Brown et al., 1993]. If a parallel corpus exists (see Section 4.3.2.1) that corpus can be used to estimate the translation probability. A linear combination of three different sources for estimating this probability (e.g; two dictionaries and a bilingual term list generated from a parallel corpus) was used in [Xu et al., 2001].

Table 4.1. Raw Term Frequency for English Collection

$tf_{t,d}$	a	arrived	damaged	delivery	fire	gold	in	of	shipment	silver	truck
D_{e1}	1	0	1	0	1	1	1	1	1	0	0
D_{e2}	1	1	0	1	0	0	1	1	0	2	1
D_{e3}	1	1	0	0	0	1	1	1	1	0	1

Table 4.2. Raw Term Frequency for Spanish Collection

$tf_{t,d}$	camión	$da\tilde{n}\acute{o}$	de	del	el	en	entrega	$env\acute{\imath}o$	fuego	la	$lleg\acute{o}$	oro	plata	un
D_{s1}	0	1	0	1	1	1	0	1	1	0	0	1	0	1
D_{s2}	1	0	2	0	0	1	1	0	0	2	1	0	2	1
D_{s3}	1	0	0	1	1	1	0	1	0	0	1	1	0	1

Table 4.3. $P(t|C_e)$ for All Terms in the English Collection

a	arrived	damaged	delivery	fire	gold	in	of	shipment	silver	truck
$\frac{3}{22}$	$\frac{2}{22}$	$\frac{1}{22}$	$\frac{1}{22}$	$\frac{1}{22}$	$\frac{2}{22}$	$\frac{3}{22}$	$\frac{3}{22}$	$\frac{2}{22}$	$\frac{2}{22}$	$\frac{2}{22}$

4.3.1.1 Example

Returning to our example from Chapter 2, we show how this approach can be used to compute a measure of relevance for our English query: "gold silver truck" and our three test documents in Spanish. All translation probabilities were derived from the use of two online bilingual English-Spanish dictionaries.

Document Collection:

D_{e_1} : "Shipment of gold damaged in a fire."
D_{e_2} : "Delivery of silver arrived in a silver truck."
D_{e_3} : "Shipment of gold arrived in a truck."

D_{s_1} : El $env\acute{\imath}o$ del oro $da\tilde{n}\acute{o}$ en un fuego
D_{s_2} : La entrega de la plata $lleg\acute{o}$ en un $cami\acute{o}n$ de plata
D_{s_3} : El $env\acute{\imath}o$ del oro $lleg\acute{o}$ en un $cami\acute{o}n$

To find the document in the Spanish collection that is most relevant to the English query "gold silver truck", we need to find the translation ratios of "gold",

Table 4.4. $P(t|C_s)$ for All Terms in the Spanish Collection

camión	dañó	de	del	el	en	entrega	envío	fuego	la	llegó	oro	plata	un
$\frac{2}{27}$	$\frac{1}{27}$	$\frac{2}{27}$	$\frac{2}{27}$	$\frac{2}{27}$	$\frac{3}{27}$	$\frac{1}{27}$	$\frac{2}{27}$	$\frac{1}{27}$	$\frac{2}{27}$	$\frac{2}{27}$	$\frac{2}{27}$	$\frac{2}{27}$	$\frac{3}{27}$

Table 4.5. Term Frequency for Spanish Collection

$tf_{t,d}$	camión	dañó	de	del	el	en	entrega	envío	fuego	la	llegó	oro	plata	un
$\frac{tf}{D_{s1}}$	0	$\frac{1}{8}$	0	$\frac{1}{8}$	$\frac{1}{8}$	$\frac{1}{8}$	0	$\frac{1}{8}$	$\frac{1}{8}$	0	0	$\frac{1}{8}$	0	$\frac{1}{8}$
$\frac{tf}{D_{s2}}$	$\frac{1}{11}$	0	$\frac{2}{11}$	0	0	$\frac{1}{11}$	$\frac{1}{11}$	0	0	$\frac{2}{11}$	$\frac{1}{11}$	0	$\frac{2}{11}$	$\frac{1}{11}$
$\frac{tf}{D_{s3}}$	$\frac{1}{8}$	0	0	$\frac{1}{8}$	$\frac{1}{8}$	$\frac{1}{8}$	0	$\frac{1}{8}$	0	0	$\frac{1}{8}$	$\frac{1}{8}$	0	$\frac{1}{8}$

Table 4.6. Translation Probabilities: $P(t_{L_j} \mid t_{L'_k})$

	camión	dañó	de	del	el	en	entrega	envío	fuego	la	llegó	oro	plata	un
gold	$\frac{0}{2}$	0	0	0	0	0	0	0	0	0	0	1	$\frac{0}{1}$	0
silver	$\frac{0}{2}$	0	0	0	0	0	0	0	0	0	0	$\frac{0}{1}$	1	0
truck	$\frac{1}{2}$	0	0	0	0	0	0	0	0	0	0	$\frac{0}{1}$	$\frac{0}{1}$	0

"silver", and "truck". Using Equation 4.2 we obtain the probability of a query term appearing in a document from the Spanish collection.

$$
\begin{aligned}
&P(gold \mid D_{s_1}) = \\
&\quad P(El \mid D_{s_1}) \cdot P(gold \mid El) + P(envío \mid D_{s_1}) \cdot P(gold \mid envío) + \\
&\quad P(del \mid D_{s_1}) \cdot P(gold \mid del) + P(oro \mid D_{s_1}) \cdot P(gold \mid oro) + \\
&\quad P(dañó \mid D_{s_1}) \cdot P(gold \mid dañó) + P(en \mid D_{s_1}) \cdot P(gold \mid en) + \\
&\quad P(un \mid D_{s_1}) \cdot P(gold \mid un) + P(fuego \mid D_{s_1}) \cdot P(gold \mid fuego) \\
&\quad = \frac{1}{8} \cdot \frac{1}{1} = \frac{1}{8}
\end{aligned}
$$

$$
\begin{aligned}
&P(gold \mid D_{s2}) = \\
&\quad P(La \mid D_{s2}) \cdot P(gold \mid La) + P(entrega \mid D_{s2}) \cdot P(gold \mid entrega) + \\
&\quad P(de \mid D_{s2}) \cdot P(gold \mid de) + P(la \mid D_{s2}) \cdot P(gold \mid la) + \\
&\quad P(plata \mid D_{s2}) \cdot P(gold \mid plata) + P(llegó \mid D_{s2}) \cdot P(gold \mid llegó) + \\
&\quad P(en \mid D_{s2}) \cdot P(gold \mid en) + P(un \mid D_{s2}) \cdot P(gold \mid un) + \\
&\quad P(camión \mid D_{s2}) \cdot P(gold \mid camión) \\
&\quad = 0
\end{aligned}
$$

$$
\begin{aligned}
&P(gold \mid D_{s_3}) = \\
&\quad P(El \mid D_{s_3}) \cdot P(gold \mid El) + P(envío \mid D_{s_3}) \cdot P(gold \mid envío) + \\
&\quad P(del \mid D_{s_3}) \cdot P(gold \mid del) + P(oro \mid D_{s_3}) \cdot P(gold \mid oro) + \\
&\quad P(llegó \mid D_{s_3}) \cdot P(gold \mid llegó) + P(en \mid D_{s_3}) \cdot P(gold \mid en) + \\
&\quad P(un \mid D_{s_3}) \cdot P(gold \mid un) + P(camión \mid D_{s_3}) \cdot P(gold \mid camión) \\
&\quad = \tfrac{1}{8} \cdot \tfrac{1}{1} \\
&\quad = \tfrac{1}{8}
\end{aligned}
$$

$$
\begin{aligned}
&P(silver \mid D_{s_1}) = \\
&\quad P(El \mid D_{s_1}) \cdot P(silver \mid El) + P(envío \mid D_{s_1}) \cdot P(silver \mid envío) + \\
&\quad P(del \mid D_{s_1}) \cdot P(silver \mid del) + P(oro \mid D_{s_1}) \cdot P(silver \mid oro) + \\
&\quad P(dañó \mid D_{s_1}) \cdot P(silver \mid dañó) + P(en \mid D_{s_1}) \cdot P(silver \mid en) + \\
&\quad P(un \mid D_{s_1}) \cdot P(silver \mid un) + P(fuego \mid D_{s_1}) \cdot P(silver \mid fuego) \\
&\quad = 0
\end{aligned}
$$

$$
\begin{aligned}
&P(silver \mid D_{s_2}) = \\
&\quad P(La \mid D_{s_2}) \cdot P(silver \mid La) + P(entrega \mid D_{s_2}) \cdot P(silver \mid entrega) + \\
&\quad P(de \mid D_{s_2}) \cdot P(silver \mid de) + P(la \mid D_{s_2}) \cdot P(silver \mid la) + \\
&\quad P(plata \mid D_{s_2}) \cdot P(silver \mid plata) + P(llegó \mid D_{s_2}) \cdot P(silver \mid llegó) + \\
&\quad P(en \mid D_{s_2}) \cdot P(silver \mid en) + P(un \mid D_{s_2}) \cdot P(silver \mid un) + \\
&\quad P(camión \mid D_{s_2}) \cdot P(silver \mid camión) \\
&\quad = \tfrac{2}{11} \cdot \tfrac{1}{1} \\
&\quad = \tfrac{2}{11}
\end{aligned}
$$

$$
\begin{aligned}
&P(silver \mid D_{s_3}) = \\
&\quad P(El \mid D_{s_3}) \cdot P(silver \mid El) + P(envío \mid D_{s_3}) \cdot P(silver \mid envío) + \\
&\quad P(del \mid D_{s_3}) \cdot P(silver \mid del) + P(oro \mid D_{s_3}) \cdot P(silver \mid oro) + \\
&\quad P(llegó \mid D_{s_3}) \cdot P(silver \mid llegó) + P(en \mid D_{s_3}) \cdot P(silver \mid en) + \\
&\quad P(un \mid D_{s_3}) \cdot P(silver \mid un) + P(camión \mid D_{s_3}) \cdot P(silver \mid camión) \\
&\quad = 0
\end{aligned}
$$

$$
\begin{aligned}
&P(truck \mid D_{s_1}) = \\
&\quad P(El \mid D_{s_1}) \cdot P(truck \mid El) + P(envío \mid D_{s_1}) \cdot P(truck \mid envío) + \\
&\quad P(del \mid D_{s_1}) \cdot P(truck \mid del) + P(oro \mid D_{s_1}) \cdot P(truck \mid oro) + \\
&\quad P(dañó \mid D_{s_1}) \cdot P(truck \mid dañó) + P(en \mid D_{s_1}) \cdot P(truck \mid en) + \\
&\quad P(un \mid D_{s_1}) \cdot P(truck \mid un) + P(fuego \mid D_{s_1}) \cdot P(truck \mid fuego) \\
&\quad = 0
\end{aligned}
$$

$$
\begin{aligned}
&P(truck \mid D_{s_2}) = \\
&\quad P(La \mid D_{s_2}) \cdot P(truck \mid La) + P(entrega \mid D_{s_2}) \cdot P(truck \mid entrega) + \\
&\quad P(de \mid D_{s_2}) \cdot P(truck \mid de) + P(la \mid D_{s_2}) \cdot P(truck \mid la) + \\
&\quad P(plata \mid D_{s_2}) \cdot P(truck \mid plata) + P(llegó \mid D_{s_2}) \cdot P(truck \mid llegó) + \\
&\quad P(en \mid D_{s_2}) \cdot P(truck \mid en) + P(un \mid D_{s_2}) \cdot P(truck \mid un) + \\
&\quad P(camión \mid D_{s_2}) \cdot P(truck \mid camión) \\
&\quad = \tfrac{1}{11} \cdot \tfrac{1}{2} \\
&\quad = \tfrac{1}{22}
\end{aligned}
$$

$$
\begin{aligned}
&P(truck \mid D_{s_3}) = \\
&\quad P(El \mid D_{s_3}) \cdot P(truck \mid El) + P(envío \mid D_{s_3}) \cdot P(truck \mid envío) + \\
&\quad P(del \mid D_{s_3}) \cdot P(truck \mid del) + P(oro \mid D_{s_3}) \cdot P(truck \mid oro) + \\
&\quad P(llegó \mid D_{s_3}) \cdot P(truck \mid llegó) + P(en \mid D_{s_3}) \cdot P(truck \mid en) + \\
&\quad P(un \mid D_{s_3}) \cdot P(truck \mid un) + P(camión \mid D_{s_3}) \cdot P(truck \mid camión) \\
&\quad = \tfrac{1}{8} \cdot \tfrac{1}{2} \\
&\quad = \tfrac{1}{16}
\end{aligned}
$$

Now we apply Equation 4.1 to find the probability of the query appearing in each Spanish document. Here $\alpha = 0.3$.

$$
\begin{aligned}
&P(gold, silver, truck \mid D_{s_1}) = \\
&\quad [(0.3)P(gold \mid C_e) + (1 - 0.3)P(gold \mid D_{s_1})] \times \\
&\quad [(0.3)P(silver \mid C_e) + (1 - 0.3)P(silver \mid D_{s_1})] \times \\
&\quad [(0.3)P(truck \mid C_e) + (1 - 0.3)P(truck \mid D_{s_1})] \\
&\quad = (0.3 \cdot \tfrac{2}{22} + 0.7 \cdot \tfrac{1}{8})(0.3 \cdot \tfrac{2}{22} + 0.7 \cdot 0)(0.3 \cdot \tfrac{2}{22} + 0.7 \cdot 0) \\
&\quad = 0.0000854
\end{aligned}
$$

$$
\begin{aligned}
&P(gold, silver, truck \mid D_{s_2}) = \\
&\quad [(0.3)P(gold \mid C_e) + (1 - 0.3)P(gold \mid D_{s_2})] \times \\
&\quad [(0.3)P(silver \mid C_e) + (1 - 0.3)P(silver \mid D_{s_2})] \times \\
&\quad [(0.3)P(truck \mid C_e) + (1 - 0.3)P(truck \mid D_{s_2})] \\
&\quad = (0.3 \cdot \tfrac{2}{22} + 0.7 \cdot 0)(0.3 \cdot \tfrac{2}{22} + 0.7 \cdot \tfrac{2}{11})(0.3 \cdot \tfrac{2}{22} + 0.7 \cdot \tfrac{1}{22}) \\
&\quad = 0.0002491
\end{aligned}
$$

$$
\begin{aligned}
&P(gold, silver, truck \mid D_{s_3}) = \\
&\quad [(0.3)P(gold \mid C_e) + (1 - 0.3)P(gold \mid D_{s_3})] \times \\
&\quad [(0.3)P(silver|C_e) + (1 - 0.3)P(silver \mid D_{s_3})] \times \\
&\quad [(0.3)P(truck|C_e) + (1 - 0.3)P(truck \mid D_{s_3})] \\
&\quad = (0.3 \cdot \tfrac{2}{22} + 0.7 \cdot \tfrac{1}{8})(0.3 \cdot \tfrac{2}{22} + 0.7 \cdot 0)(0.3 \cdot \tfrac{2}{22} + 0.7 \cdot \tfrac{1}{16}) \\
&\quad = 0.0002223
\end{aligned}
$$

D_{s_2} gives the highest probability, therefore, it is most likely to be relevant to the query.

4.3.2 Bilingual Corpus Strategies

Logically, cross-language information retrieval systems should benefit from having *similar* document collections in both language L and L'. It is trivial to find documents in both L and L', but for cross-language information retrieval techniques to work well, it is necessary to find documents that, at the very least, describe the *similar* content. A book translated into both language L and L' is an example of a bilingual corpus of documents. In other cases, we might only have a book in language L and another book on an entirely different topic in L'. Numerous cross-language information retrieval techniques were developed assuming that, at some level, a bilingual corpus exists. Even for obscure languages there are often parallel translations of some texts (e.g.; religious texts) which might be sufficient to build a useful bilingual term list. Additionally, the European Union is legally required to publish decisions regarding patents in multiple languages.

4.3.2.1 Parallel

In the world of machine translation, parallel corpora have been used since the early 1990's to identify potential translations for a given word. The first step is to match up sentences in the two corpora. This is known as *sentence alignment*. One of the first papers that described sentence alignment for parallel corpora to generate translation probabilities is [Brown et al., 1990]. The general idea is to take a document in language L and another document which is a translation of L in language L' and *align* the two texts. The problem is non-trivial as one sentence in L can map to many sentences in L'. The alignment can be at the sentence, paragraph, or document level. Initial approaches for aligning corpora used dynamic programming algorithms based on either the number of words [Brown et al., 1991] in a sentence or the number of characters in the sentence [Gale and Church, 1991].

A bilingual term lexicon can be used to assist in the alignment process (e.g.; if we see a sentence with the word *peace* in English we might align it with the word *shalom* in Hebrew). We note that one use of aligned corpora is to generate a bilingual term lexicon, so in cases of more obscure languages, such a lexicon might not exist.

The problem can be expressed as a means of estimating the translation probability $P(f|e)$ where e is a word in English and f is a word in French. Five models for estimating this probability are given in [Brown et al., 1993]. These are referred to frequently as IBM Model 1, 2, 3, 4, and 5. In model one, word order is not included. Model two uses the word order. Model three includes the length of terms being matched. Models four and five include the probability of a given connection between the English word and the French word.

Later, an approach using HMM's was given in [Vogel et al., 1996]. Software to easily implement these algorithms was not widely available until a workshop was held with the stated purpose of building and disseminating such tools [Al-Onaizan et al., 1999]. At this workshop a program named GIZA was developed and it included IBM Models 1, 2, and 3. Later, a new version GIZA++ was implemented which contained all five IBM models, Vogel's HMM-based model, as well as a variety of other improvements. Today GIZA++ is widely used by CLIR applications that wish to generate a bilingual term list from a parallel corpus of two different languages. Details of GIZA++ as well as comparative results using the different models are given in [Och and Ney, 2000b, Och and Ney, 2000a, Och and Ney, 2003].

An algorithm for using this technique to align English and Norwegian sentences is described in [Hofland, 1996]. A survey of alignment techniques is given in [Somers, 2001, Veronis, 2000]. An approach to building a parallel corpus by starting with a small collection and gradually adding to it with translation models is described in [Callison-Burch and Osborne, 2003].

4.3.2.2 Comparable

Comparable corpora are two collections that are about the same basic content but the documents are not translations of one another. The cross-language information retrieval techniques we discuss in our comparable corpora section assume that document A in language L corresponds to document B in language L'.

4.3.3 Comparable Corpora Strategies

Comparable corpora exist when documents in one language are about the same topic, but are not translations. Many cross-language information retrieval techniques focus on this type of a collection since it is more likely to have a comparable corpus between language pairs than to obtain a parallel corpus.

We note that when the entire document collection exists in language L and a comparable collection exists in L' a simple approach for cross-language information retrieval can be used. The query can be executed in language L and results are obtained. The resulting documents are mapped to their comparable twins in language L'. A document list in language L' is then returned to the user. In most cases, the comparable corpus is simply a subset of training documents which can be used to facilitate cross-language retrieval of larger document collections.

4.3.3.1 Extraction of Bilingual Term Lists

Early work with comparable corpora appeared in [Sheridan and Ballerini, 1996]. In this work, documents are aligned by date and by a language independent descriptor (e.g.; ".mil" indicated that the document was about military issues). In subsequent work, proper nouns in documents were also used to facilitate alignment [Sheridan et al., 1997]. This was done as it was hoped that proper nouns would be somewhat language independent. From this alignment, a bilingual term list was constructed and used as a basis for query translation. A term-term similarity function is then defined, which yields, for a given term, other terms that are similar. This function is used for a query in language L to find terms in language L'.

Ballesteros and Croft also used co-occurrence to reduce ambiguity by using the assumption that good translations should co-occur in target language documents while incorrect translations should not co-occur [Ballesteros and Croft, 1997, Ballesteros and Croft, 1998]. An iterative proportional fitting procedure is used to gradually compute a probability that a given term is a translation of another term. This probability is used to choose among the candidate translations.

Another approach uses a vector to represent a target word [Fung, 1998]. This context vector, T is populated by using the words that surround it. The approach resembles those used to automatically generate a monolingual term list (see Section 3.6). The context words are then translated to source terms using a manually constructed bilingual term list. Let us call the new vector S'. The idea is that at least some of these words will exist in the bilingual term list. Once this is done, context vectors for the source terms are computed based on surrounding terms; we refer to this vector as S. Now, one or more translations are identified simply by using a cosine similarity measure between S and T. This technique was applied in a recent Cross-Language Evaluation Forum (CLEF) submission [Cancedda et al., 2003].

4.3.3.2 Hidden Markov Models

In Section 4.2.5, we described how Hidden Markov Models can be used to incorporate a bilingual term dictionary into cross-language retrieval. With a comparable corpus, this approach can be modified to use a more accurate *translation probability.* Instead of a uniform translation probability, the frequency of occurrence in the comparable corpus can be used. Accuracy was improved in [Federico and Bertoldi, 2002, Bertoldi and Federico, 2003] when probabilities were used in conjunction with the assignment of uniform probabilities based on the bilingual dictionary. The combination protects the system from query words that appear only in the dictionary or only in the parallel corpus.

4.3.3.3 Cross-Language Relevance Models

We described monolingual language models in Section 2.3. Typically, these models differ in how they estimate the likelihood that a given term will appear in a relevant document. To briefly review, this estimate is trivial if there are relevant documents. However, if there are relevant documents from a prior query, there is no need to run the query. Given this inherent *Catch-22*, Section 2.2.1 contained a variety of different estimates for this probability. Estimates can be made by equating the probability of relevance for a given term with the probability of co-occurrence with *every* term in the query. The idea is that if a term appears in a document that contains every query term, it is highly likely to be relevant. More formally:

$$P(w|R_q) \approx P(w|Q) = \frac{P(w, q_1, q_2, \ldots, q_k)}{P(q_1, q_2, \ldots, q_k)}$$

The next step is to compute the probability of an arbitrary term co-occurring with every term in the query. One estimate is:

$$P(w|q_1, q_2, \ldots, q_k) = \sum_{M \in \mu} P(M) \left(P(w|M) \prod_{i=1}^{k} P(q_i|M) \right)$$

where $P(w|M)$ is the probability of finding term w in a model M. The universe of models μ can be all of the documents in the collection. It follows that $P(M) = \frac{1}{\mu}$ if P(M) uses a uniform distribution. Different estimates based on the *tf* and essentially the *idf* can then be used to estimate the $P(w|M)$.

A cross-language version of this model that uses a comparable corpus simply changes the estimate to compute the probability of the term in language L' that co-occurs in a *comparable* document with *all* of the terms in the query language L. Instead of simply computing the probability of co-occurrence, the comparable corpus is used to map the co-occurring document in language L to one in language L'.

More formally:

$$P(w, q_1, \ldots, q_k) = \sum_{M_L, M_{L'} \in \mu} P(M_L, M_{L'}) \left(P(w|M_{L'}) \prod_{i=1}^{k} P(q_i|M_L) \right)$$

To normalize $P(w, q_1, \ldots, q_k)$ it is divided by the summation of $P(w, q_1, \ldots, q_k)$ for every term. Now we use (and this is the big leap that is made when using relevance models) $P(w|Q)$ to estimate $P(w|R_q)$.

For document relevance estimation, the KL divergence relative entropy metrics are used. These metrics compare the $P(w|D)$ distribution from a document to the $P(w|R)$ distribution that was estimated.
Formally:

$$KL(R|D) = \sum_{w} P(w|R) \log \frac{P(w|R)}{P(w|D)}$$

where $P(w|D)$ is estimated by:

$$p(w|D) = \lambda \left(\frac{tf_{w,D}}{\sum_v tf_{v,D}} \right) + (1-\lambda)P(w)$$

where v represents a term in the entire vocabulary of the document collection. $P(w|D)$ has two components. The first denotes the occurrence of the term w in document D. The second includes the occurrence of term w in the document collection. λ may be used to tune the weight of each component.

This model is clearly not scalable because it requires computing probabilities for every term in a language at query time. To speed up computation, only the top documents are retrieved for a query using a more straightforward similarity measure and those documents are then re-ranked with this model. Mean average precision is reported in [Lavrenko et al., 2002].

4.3.3.4 Generalized Vector Space Model

The traditional vector-space model represents documents and queries as vectors in a multi-dimensional term space. Once this is done, a similarity measure can be computed by measuring the distance from a query to a document vector. Another approach is to use a term-document matrix where each row contains the number of occurrences of the term in each document [Wong et al., 1985]. Each column represents a traditional document vector. If we compute $Q' = (A^T)(Q)$, we obtain a new vector representation of the query Q' that has a component for each document in the collection. Each component of Q' is simply an inner product of the query terms with the document that corresponds to this component. A component that represents a document that contains none of the query terms will have a value of zero. A component that represents a document that contains all of the query terms will have a much higher value. For monolingual retrieval, we can simply compute

$$SC(Q, D_i) = \cos\left(Q', A^T D_i\right)$$

where D_i is a document vector.

For cross-language retrieval, using a comparable corpus it is possible to construct the A^T matrix for language L and another matrix B^T for language L' [Carbonell et al., 1997]. To rank document D_i in language L', it is necessary to treat it as we did the query in language L and compute $B^T D_i$. At this point we have a vector with a component for each document in language L and a similar vector for each document in language L'. To compute a cross-language similarity measure, the cosine of the angle between the two vectors is computed. The cross-language similarity measure is given below:

$$SC(Q, D_i) = \cos\left(A^T Q, B^T D_i\right)$$

4.3.3.5 Latent Semantic Indexing

We discussed monolingual Latent Semantic Indexing in Section 2.6. To review, LSI starts with a term document matrix A and uses a singular value decomposition to compute [Dumais, 1994]:

$$A = U\sigma V^T$$

One similarity measure is defined as:

$$SC(Q, D_i) = \cos\left(U^T Q, U^T D_i\right)$$

For cross-language retrieval, the singular value decomposition is applied to the a new term-document matrix that combines the term-document matrix A in language L with the term-document matrix B in language L' [Dumais et al., 1997].

$$\begin{bmatrix} A \\ B \end{bmatrix} = U_2\sigma_2 V_2^T$$

Once this is done the similarity measure can be computed as:

$$SC(Q, D_i) = \cos\left(U_2^T Q, U_2^T D_i\right)$$

We note that different head to head comparisons of LSI and GVSM for cross-language retrieval were reported in [Carbonell et al., 1997, Littman and Jiang, 1998]. Furthermore, VSM, LSI, and GVSM were shown to be variations of a common algorithm that projects documents and queries into a vector space using singular vectors. The algorithms then differ on how they weight the components of the vectors.

A monolingual comparison of VSM, LSI, and GVSM on the small Cranfield collection and the substantially larger TREC collection is given in [Littman and Jiang, 1998]. For monolingual retrieval, LSI had the best performance on the Cranfield collection, but VSM had the highest effectiveness on the TREC collection.

For cross-language retrieval using TREC French and German documents, LSI outperformed GVSM. An improvement over LSI is obtained by using a new algorithm called ADE (Approximate Dimension Equalization) which is roughly a weighted combination of LSI and GVSM.

GVSM Example:

We now give a brief GVSM example using the same English and Spanish documents used in our example in Section 4.3.1. First we compute a vector for the original query. This is computed by multiplying the query vector by the document matrix.

$$Q\prime = A^T Q = \begin{bmatrix} 1 & 1 & 1 \\ 0 & 1 & 1 \\ 1 & 0 & 0 \\ 0 & 1 & 0 \\ 1 & 0 & 0 \\ 1 & 0 & 1 \\ 1 & 1 & 1 \\ 1 & 1 & 1 \\ 1 & 0 & 1 \\ 0 & 2 & 0 \\ 0 & 1 & 1 \end{bmatrix}^T \times \begin{bmatrix} 0 \\ 0 \\ 0 \\ 0 \\ 0 \\ 1 \\ 0 \\ 0 \\ 0 \\ 1 \\ 1 \end{bmatrix} = \begin{bmatrix} 1 & 3 & 2 \end{bmatrix} \tag{4.3}$$

Next, we obtain vectors for the Spanish Collection. The vectors will represent Q' but will be computed using the Spanish document matrix and the Spanish document collection vectors. We then compute one vector for each document in the collection.

$$Q' = B^T D_{s_1} = \begin{bmatrix} 0 & 1 & 1 \\ 1 & 0 & 0 \\ 0 & 2 & 0 \\ 1 & 0 & 1 \\ 1 & 0 & 1 \\ 1 & 1 & 1 \\ 0 & 1 & 0 \\ 1 & 0 & 1 \\ 1 & 0 & 0 \\ 0 & 2 & 0 \\ 0 & 1 & 1 \\ 1 & 0 & 1 \\ 0 & 2 & 0 \\ 1 & 1 & 1 \end{bmatrix}^T \times \begin{bmatrix} 0 \\ 1 \\ 0 \\ 1 \\ 1 \\ 1 \\ 0 \\ 1 \\ 1 \\ 0 \\ 0 \\ 1 \\ 0 \\ 1 \end{bmatrix} = \begin{bmatrix} 8 & 2 & 6 \end{bmatrix} \tag{4.4}$$

$$Q' = B^T D_{s2} = \begin{bmatrix} 0 & 1 & 1 \\ 1 & 0 & 0 \\ 0 & 2 & 0 \\ 1 & 0 & 1 \\ 1 & 0 & 1 \\ 1 & 1 & 1 \\ 0 & 1 & 0 \\ 1 & 0 & 1 \\ 1 & 0 & 0 \\ 0 & 2 & 0 \\ 0 & 1 & 1 \\ 1 & 0 & 1 \\ 0 & 2 & 0 \\ 1 & 1 & 1 \end{bmatrix}^T \times \begin{bmatrix} 1 \\ 0 \\ 2 \\ 0 \\ 0 \\ 1 \\ 1 \\ 0 \\ 0 \\ 2 \\ 1 \\ 0 \\ 2 \\ 1 \end{bmatrix} = \begin{bmatrix} 2 & 17 & 4 \end{bmatrix} \quad (4.5)$$

$$Q' = B^T D_{s3} = \begin{bmatrix} 0 & 1 & 1 \\ 1 & 0 & 0 \\ 0 & 2 & 0 \\ 1 & 0 & 1 \\ 1 & 0 & 1 \\ 1 & 1 & 1 \\ 0 & 1 & 0 \\ 1 & 0 & 1 \\ 1 & 0 & 0 \\ 0 & 2 & 0 \\ 0 & 1 & 1 \\ 1 & 0 & 1 \\ 0 & 2 & 0 \\ 1 & 1 & 1 \end{bmatrix}^T \times \begin{bmatrix} 1 \\ 0 \\ 0 \\ 1 \\ 1 \\ 1 \\ 0 \\ 1 \\ 0 \\ 0 \\ 1 \\ 1 \\ 0 \\ 1 \end{bmatrix} = \begin{bmatrix} 6 & 4 & 8 \end{bmatrix} \quad (4.6)$$

Finally, we compute the similarity between the English query vector and each Spanish document vector.

$$SC(Gold, Silver, Truck, D_{s_1}) = cos(< 1, 3, 2 >, < 8, 2, 6 >) = 0.6814$$
$$SC(Gold, Silver, Truck, D_{s_2}) = cos(< 1, 3, 2 >, < 2, 17, 14 >) = 0.9274$$
$$SC(Gold, Silver, Truck, D_{s_3}) = cos(< 1, 3, 2 >, < 6, 4, 8 >) = 0.8437$$

4.4 Cross Language Utilities

As we described monolingual utilities in Chapter 3, we now describe cross-language utilities. The idea is that a utility should be impervious to a given strategy.

4.4.1 Cross Language Relevance Feedback

Given that we are taking a query in language L, translating it to language L' and then submitting the query, there are two different opportunities to apply relevance feedback (see Section 3.1). Expansion is possible both before the query is translated and after the query is translated. Ballesteros and Croft were the first to describe this in [Ballesteros and Croft, 1997]; they showed improvements in English-Spanish accuracy from both pre and post translation query expansion.

The process was repeated for English-Arabic in [Larkey et al., 2002b]. For pre-translation, using English queries, the top ten documents for each query were obtained. Terms from these documents were ranked based on their weight across the ten documents. The top five terms were added to the query but were only weighted half as important as the original query terms. For post-translation Arabic terms, the top ten documents were retrieved, and the top fifty terms were added to the query.

Another form of query expansion was described in [Adriani, 2000]. Here, it was assumed that the real problem was with the query translation so only post-translation query expansion was used. The top 20 passages from the initial result set were obtained, and a term-term co-occurrence matrix was built for these results. Next, the sum of the similarity of these terms and each post-translation query term was computed. The top ten terms from these passages were then added to the query. A direct application of Rocchio relevance feedback [Rocchio, 1971] (see Section 3.1.1) for post-translation processing was described in [Ruiz, 2003].

Work on query expansion is given in [McNamee and Mayfield, 2002a]. In this work, the authors cite different studies that showed very different results (e.g.; expansion works, expansion does not work). The authors implemented new studies on a sufficiently large dataset. They found that a combination of pre and post translation query expansion provided a fifteen percent effectiveness improvement. They further showed that pre and post translation expansion improved effectiveness even when translation resources were degraded. In these experiments they were testing the impact of limited translation resources. Their key conclusion is that pre-translation expansion does not result in much improvement if translation resources have substantial lexical coverage. This expansion provides significant improvement if lexical coverage is poor.

Relevance feedback in conjunction with logistic regression was recently used for a multilingual retrieval over Chinese, Japanese, and Korean. It was shown to result in as much as a 66 percent improvement in effectiveness [Chen and Gey, 2003].

Interestingly, a more recent result has shown that pre-translation query expansion does improve effectiveness when querying a French document collection with an English query, but it actually degrades performance when querying a Mandarin Chinese collection [Levow et al., 2004].

4.4.2 Stemming

We discussed stemming for English in Section 3.8. For cross-language retrieval, stemming can have a significant impact in a variety of architectural components. First, the source query processor must identify terms. Next, the precise bilingual term list used for translation might dictate the type of stemming needed. A bilingual term list that was built with the Porter stemmer [Porter, 1980] might not be very effective when used with query terms obtained with the Lovins stemmer [Lovins, 1968].

Stemmers for a variety of languages are available and many of them are freely available on the Internet. Broadly speaking, European language stemmers tend to follow the general patterns of the Porter and Lovins stemmers, removing common prefixes and suffixes. We note that with some languages like German, extremely long terms can be difficult to stem as they correspond to several terms in English. A method of *decompounding* long German terms is given in [Kamps et al., 2003].

4.4.2.1 Backoff Translation

When using blingual term lists or lexicons for document or query translation with stemmers, it can be useful to gradually try to match the query term with the term the translation lexicon. A term "jumping" might not match anything in the lexicon, but the root form "jump" might match. When matching an unstemmed or *surface* form of the term with a stem, four combinations exist. In our examples below we use stem(t) to indicate the stem of term t.

- Surface form of query or document term may match with surface form of term in lexicon (e.g.; *jumping* matches with *jumping*).

- Stem form of query or document term may match with surface form of term in lexicon (e.g.; stem(*jumping*) matches with *jump*).

- Surface form of query or document term may match with stem form of term in lexicon (e.g.; *jump* matches with stem(*jumping*)).

- Stem form of query or document term may match with stem form of term in lexicon (e.g.; stem(*jumping*) with stem(*jumped*)).

These matches can be done in succession. Using this progression in which we gradually relax the constraints needed to match a query or document term with a term in a translation lexicon is referred to as *backoff translation*. This technique has been shown to improve effectiveness and was used on the CLEF data in [Oard et al., 2000].

The concern is that there are hundreds of languages and some of them are not popular enough to justify allocating resources to build a language dependent stemmer. Additionally work was done on automatic generation of stemmers (often referred to as *statistical stemming*).

4.4.2.2 Automatically Building a Stemmer

Initial work in Spanish showed that a stemmer could be produced by identifying lexicographically similar words to find common suffixes [Buckley et al., 1994]. Automatically building a stemmer is related to work done in the *Linguistica* software package which is a program that automatically learns the structure of words in any human language solely by examining raw text. The idea is that the software can take an English text and identify that there is a category of terms with suffixes *ing, ed, s.* With only 500,000 terms candidate suffixes can be reasonably identified. A full description of Linguistica may be found in [Goldsmith, 2001]. First basic candidate suffixes are found using weighted mutual information. Regular signatures for each class of words are identified and then a minimum description length (MDL) is used to correct errors. The MDL ensures that breakpoints should find a common stem with a common suffix. The only problem with this for CLIR is that some unusual terms may not be found. Hence, additional work was done to augment the Linguistica set of stems with rule induction. This work grouped stems by frequency for all terms with more than three characters. All two, three, and four character stems were sorted by frequency (after removing stems that were overlapped by a longer stem). Essentially, the most frequent suffixes are used to stem input terms. More details are found in [Oard et al., 2000].

The core idea is that a stemmer is simply a tool that identifies a good *split point* for a term in that the start of the term is the stem, and the rest of the term is the portion that does not need to be stemmed. Results that combined statistical stemming and backoff translation were significantly more effective than an unstemmed collection [Oard et al., 2000]. Interestingly, the stemming based on rule-induction was found to slightly outperform stemming based on Linguistica.

Recently, hidden Markov models were designed to build stemmers [Nunzio et al., 2003]. This approach did not remove prefixes, but started with initial states that ultimately transition to suffix states of size one, two, three, or four characters (at present, this approach is focused on European languages). By simply submitting a list of terms from a new language to the Markov model, it is possible to identify which terms are stems of one another because of their frequency. Once, the model is trained, a term can be processed and the model will output the most likely stem for a given term.

The motivation for this approach is that a training language can have many more instances of *jump* than *jumping*, and the model will learn that there is a high probability of generating the term *jump* when *jumping* is input. A set of experiments comparing the Markov model-based automatically generated stemmer to the Porter stemmer in Dutch, French, German, Italian, and Spanish found that the automatically derived Markov model stemmer achieved only slightly lower (less than five percent) effectiveness than the manually derived Porter stemmer.

4.4.2.3 Arabic Stemmers

Middle Eastern languages have also been studied at length. The first work on Arabic information retrieval is given in [Al-Kharashi and Evens, 1994]. This work used a hand-crafted stemmer in which a lexicon was used to map each vocabulary term to its corresponding stem or root. Khoja removed common prefixes and suffixes and tried to identify the *root* of a given term [Khoja and Garside, 1999]. Enhancements to this stemmer are given in [Larkey and Connell, 2000]. The problem with this approach is that the root of a term is often very broad. For example, the Arabic word for *office* and *book* both have the same root. Subsequently, work that simply removed plurals and other less harmful stems demonstrated substantial improvement. These Arabic stemmers are referred to as *light* stemmers. Light stemmers for Arabic are described in [Larkey et al., 2002b, Darwish and Oard, 2003, Aljlayl et al., 2002, Aljlayl and Frieder, 2002]. A head-to-head comparison of an early light stemmer named *Al-Stem*, the light stemmer described in [Larkey et al., 2002b] and a modified *Al-Stem* is given in [Darwish and Oard, 2003]. Additional, slight improvements are given in [Chen and Gey, 2002]. We note that these stemmers would be useful for monolingual Arabic retrieval, but they are clearly useful for CLIR as well as they support queries from a query in language L to then be translated into Arabic, the newly translated query may then be run against the Arabic collection, and Arabic documents will be retrieved.

4.4.2.4 Asian Languages

Chinese and other Asian languages pose the interesting problem that white space is not used to denote a word boundary. A statistical approach using staged logistic regression to identify Chinese word boundaries from a trained set of 300 sentences is given in [Dai et al., 1999]. In this work, the relative frequency of individual characters and two character pairs called *bigrams* was used with the document frequency, the weighted document frequency, the local frequency, contextual information (frequency of surrounding characters), and positional information. A combined approach is given in [Xue and Converse, 2002] – this combines frequency based algorithms and dictionary-based algorithms which simply look for the longest matching set of characters in a machine-readable dictionary. Interestingly, it has been shown that the segmentation problem can be ignored for Chinese and Japanese CLIR and reasonable results can be obtained simply by using overlapping n-grams (see Section 4.4.3).

4.4.3 N-grams

A language-independent approach uses sequences of characters called *n-grams* [Damashek, 1995]. We described n-grams for use in English in Section 3.4. For European languages, n-grams of size $n = 4$ or $n = 5$ showed good effectiveness. Interestingly, n-grams were compared to stemming. An approach that used the least common n-gram to represent a term, resulted in a slight improvement over a Porter stemmer [Mayfield and McNamee, 2003]. The idea is that a single carefully chosen n-gram for each word might serve as an adequate stem substitute.

The problem of segmentation for Asian languages was avoided when n-grams were used by in [McNamee, 2001]. Interestingly, results were comparable to more sophisticated segmentation algorithms. Additional cross-language experiments with 6-grams are described in [Qu et al., 2003b].

4.4.4 Transliteration

Recent work focused on using forms of transliteration to assist with the cross-language name matching problem. Pirkola et al use transformation rules to identify how a name in language L should be transliterated into a name in language L' [Pirkola et al., 2003]. The core motivation is that these technical terms and names are not found in machine readable bilingual term lists typically used to translate query or document terms. In this effort, transformation rules are learned by using paired lists of terms in a source and target language. First, terms are identified that are within some reasonable threshold of closeness as defined by their edit distance. The Levenshtein edit distance is computed as the minimum number of substitutions, insertions, and deletions needed to modify the source term into the target term [Levenshtein, 1966]. For example the edit distance between *fuzzy* and *fuzy* is one.

Once the candidate sets of terms are found, all transformations that resulted in the minimum edit distance were considered. An error value was assigned for each character by character transformation. The assignments included error values of zero for no change, and one for less substantial changes such as consonant replaces consonant, vowel replaces vowel, or insert or delete of one character. A value of two is assigned for more substantial changes (e.g.; a consonant replaces vowel or vowel replaces consonant). The transformation with the least error values are then identified. Once this is done, a threshold is used to ensure that a given transformation occurs frequently. These transformations are then used for source to target translation. The confidence of a given rule can be varied such that more rules with higher recall can be generated or fewer rules with higher precision. Test results showed that for several languages, there was significant improvement when using these transformation in conjunction with n-grams [Pirkola et al., 2003].

4.4.4.1 Phonetic Approach

For English-Japanese retrieval, transliteration using a phonetic approach was studied in [Qu et al., 2003a]. For English-Japanese the general approach is to use the phonetic sounds of the term. Transliteration is done:

English word → English phonetic → Japanese phonetic → Japanese word

English phonetic representations are found for a given English term. The first phonetic representation for a term in the CMU Speech Pronunciation Dictionary is used. The dictionary contains 39 different phonemes. Once the Japanese phonemes are identified a standard mapping converts from Japanese phoneme to the target *katakana* character set.

For Japanese-English the problem is harder because of the lack of word boundaries in Japanese. First, a word segmentation algorithm which essentially matches the longest match word in a dictionary is used. The EDICT Japanese-English dictionary is used. Using the same phonetic process as used for English-Japanese, Japanese-English phonetic transliterations are obtained. These transliterations can be thought of as simply additions to the EDICT dictionary. Checking the transliteration is required because it is possible to have dramatic word segmentation failures. An example of the term *Venice* which has no entry in EDICT is transliterated into *bunny* and *cheer* because of the subparts of the Japanese word that did match EDICT. Hence, transliterations are checked to see if they co-occur with a reasonable mutual information in the target corpus as they occur in the source corpus. Dramatic improvements in query effectiveness were found for queries that contained terms that did not occur in EDICT.

4.4.5 Entity Tagging

Identifying entities in English was described in Section 3.8. An obvious extension to this is to identify people, places, and locations in documents written in other languages. If we are able to identify these entities it may well open the door to improved transliteration and phonetic techniques specific to these entities for CLIR (see Section 4.4.4 and 4.4.4.1). Also, if we know an item is a person name, perhaps we could suppress incorrect translations by avoiding a lookup in a common translation dictionary.

Machine learning techniques were shown to work well for this problem as a training set of named entities can be identified and learning algorithms can be used to identify them [Carreras et al., 2002]. Earlier work used a language independent bootstrapping algorithm based on iterative learning and re-estimation of contextual and morphological patterns [Cucerzan and Yarowsky, 1999]. This algorithm learns from un-annotated text and achieves good performance when trained on a very short labelled name list with no other required language specific information.

For each entity class to be recognized and tagged, it is assumed that the user can provide a short list (around one hundred) unambiguous examples (seeds). Additionally, some specifics of the language should be known (e.g.; presence of capitalization and the use of word separators). This algorithm relies on both internal and contextual clues as independent evidence. Internal clues refer to the morphological structure of the word. These clues use the presence of prefixes and suffixes as indicators for certain entities. For example, knowing that *Maria, Marinela, and Maricica* are feminine first names in Romanian, the same classification can be a good guess for *Mariana* because of the common prefix: *Mari*. Suffixes are typically even more informative, for example: *-escu* is an almost perfect indicator of a last name in Romanian – the same applies to *-wski* in Polish *-ovic* and *-ivic* in Serbo-Croatian and *-son* in English. Such morphological information is learned during bootstrapping. The algorithm was used to mark named entities in named entities in English, Greek, Hindi, Rumanian and Turkish.

A language dependent Arabic entity tagger that relies on specific patterns to do morphological analysis is described in [Maloney and Niv, 1998]. An Arabic entity tagger without language dependent resources is described in [McNamee and Mayfield, 2002b]. These use algorithms similar to those used in English entity taggers.

It was shown that bilingual term lists frequently lack coverage of entities. For some cross-language tasks (typically using English and European languages), it is possible to recognize an entity and hope that it simply will be spelled the same in both languages. Recent experiments showed that when proper names were removed from a bilingual lexicon, performance was reduced by over fifty percent.

The Conference on Computational Natural Language Learning (CoNLL-2003) focused on language independent named entity recognition. Results for both English and German were obtained and the effectiveness of the top ranked systems were well above eighty-five percent for both precision and recall. In German, the accuracy was between eighty and eighty-five percent [Sang and Meulder, 2003]. The top three results in English and the top two in German used Maximum Entropy Models [Guiasu and Shenitzer, 1985].

Overall, entity tagging in foreign languages and exploiting these entities for cross-language retrieval is a topic of future research.

4.4.6 Fusion

Fusion of different retrieval strategies for monolingual retrieval is discussed at length in Section 8.3. Simply merging results from different strategies (e.g., vector space model, language models, LSI, etc.) has not been shown to improve accuracy, but merging results from different representations (e.g.; title only queries, title+description, etc.) was shown to help. Fusing different query representations for Arabic cross-language retrieval is described in [Larkey et al., 2002a]. The reality is that a user can issue a query to multiple document collections, and each collection can be written in a different language. This can be viewed as multilingual information retrieval (MLIR). For multilingual retrieval, two architectures exists: centralized and distributed. A distributed architecture indexes documents in each language separately. A centralized collection combines all of the documents in a single index.

To rank documents for an MLIR, three approaches were tested recently:

- Translate the query into each language and build a separate index with each language. Normalize all relevance scores and present a single ranked list of documents. This is a distributed approach.
- Translate the query into each language and build a separate index with each language, but instead of merging by score, merge by the relative position in the result list. This is a distributed approach.
- Translate the query into each language and concatenate all terms into one big query. Index all of the documents in each language into one large index. Run the single query against the single index. This is a centralized approach.

The centralized approach performed better than the previous two. It can be that the presence of proper nouns and the ability to track their distribution over the entire document collection is the reason for this success [Martinez et al., 2003]. Fusion can also be done by weighting a document collection based on its predicted retrieval effectiveness. With this approach, a source collection might receive a low weight if a poor-quality translation dictionary exists.

Additionally, the number of ambiguous words in a query for a given collection can be used to weight a collection. It was shown that this approach results in a slight improvement in accuracy [Lin and Chen, 2003].

4.5 Summary

In some cases, cross-language retrieval systems actually exceed monolingual retrieval. Hence, some have deemed cross-language retrieval a *solved* problem. However, much work remains to be done in terms of user interaction of these systems and more study as to why they are not in widespread use.

Directions for the future of cross-language retrieval are described in [Oard, 2003].

Numerous commercial search engines focus on monolingual search. However, CLIR systems have not been widely adopted. A key question is: How many users truly wish to query documents using a language they know and return results in a language that they do not know? More studies need to be done on how many projects exist with this requirement and such work should gather precise reasons as to why these systems have not deployed existing CLIR algorithms.

4.6 Exercises

1 Consider a system in which documents are obtained in multiple languages. Describe what factors would you use to determine if the documents should be translated prior to indexing or if you should simply translate incoming queries.

2 Give a detailed example of how a CLIR result might exceed 100 percent of its monolingual counterpart.

3 Consider two documents collections in languages A and B. Documents in language A all have a corresponding document in Language B. Describe CLIR algorithms that could be used to take advantage of this comparable corpus.

Chapter 5

EFFICIENCY

Thus far, we have discussed algorithms used to improve the effectiveness of query processing in terms of precision and recall. Retrieval strategies and utilities all focus on finding the relevant documents for a query. They are not concerned with how long it takes to find them.

However, users of production systems clearly are concerned with run-time performance. A system that takes too long to find relevant documents is not as useful as one that finds relevant documents quickly. The bulk of information retrieval research has focused on improvements to precision and recall since the hope has been that machines would continue to speed up. Also, there is valid concern that there is little merit in speeding up a heuristic if it is not retrieving relevant documents.

Sequential information retrieval algorithms are difficult to analyze in detail as their performance is often based on the selectivity of an information retrieval query. Most algorithms are on the order of $O(q(tf_{max}))$ where q is the number of terms in the query and tf_{max} is the maximum selectivity of any of the query terms. This is, in fact, a high estimate for query response time as many terms appear infrequently (about half are *hapax legomena*, or those that occur once according to Zipf's law [Zipf, 1949]).

We are not aware of a standard analytical model that effectively can be used to estimate query performance. Given this, sequential information retrieval algorithms are all measured empirically with experiments that require large volumes of data and are somewhat time consuming.

The good news is that given larger and larger document collections, more work is appearing on improvements to run-time performance. We describe that work in this chapter. Additional research was done to speed up information retrieval algorithms by employing multiple processors. That work is covered in Chapter 7. However, in any study of parallel algorithms, it is important that work be compared with the best sequential algorithm. Hence, this chapter describes the best sequential algorithms that we are aware of for information retrieval.

We also note that most algorithms described in this chapter are directed at the vector space model. These algorithms are also directly applicable to the probabilistic model. Clearly, similar work is needed to improve performance for other retrieval strategies and utilities.

Early information retrieval systems simply scanned very small document collections. Subsequently, inverted indexes were used to speed query processing at the expense of storage and time to build the index. Signature files were also proposed. These are typically smaller and faster, but support less retrieval functionality than an inverted index.

Compression of inverted indexes is often used to speed up query processing. Additionally, partial document rankings that are much faster than full rankings can be done at relatively low cost. In some cases precision and recall are comparable to doing a full ranking [Lee and Ren, 1996].

In Section 5.1, we first survey inverted indexing and then describe methods used to compress an inverted index. In Section 5.2, we describe algorithms that improve run-time of query processing, and in Section 5.3, we review signature files.

5.1 Inverted Index

Since many document collections are reasonably static, it is feasible to build an inverted index to quickly find terms in the document collection. Inverted indexes were used in both early information retrieval and database management systems in the 1960's [Bleir, 1967]. Instead of scanning the entire collection, the text is preprocessed and all unique terms are identified. This list of unique terms is referred to as the *index*. For each term, a list of documents that contain the term is also stored. This list is referred to as a *posting list*. Figure 5.1 illustrates an inverted index.

An entry in the list of documents can also contain the location of the term in the document (e.g., word, sentence, paragraph) to facilitate proximity searching. Additionally, an entry can contain a manually or automatically assigned weight for the term in the document. This weight is frequently used in computations that generate a measure of relevance to the query. Once this measure is computed, the document retrieval algorithm identifies all the documents that are "relevant" to the query by sorting the coefficient and presenting a ranked list to the user.

Indexing requires additional overhead since the entire collection is scanned and substantial I/O is required to generate an efficiently represented inverted index for use in secondary storage. Indexing was shown to dramatically reduce the amount of I/O required to satisfy an ad hoc query [Stone, 1987]. Upon

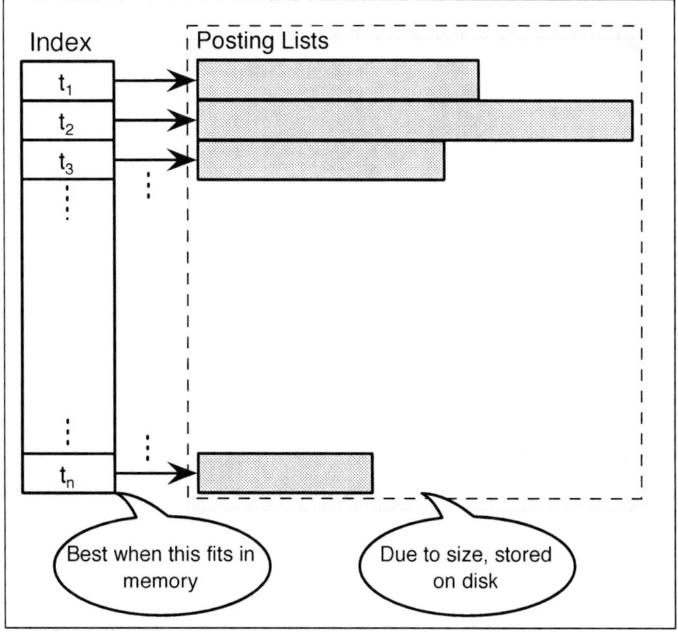

Figure 5.1. Inverted Index

receiving a query, the index is consulted, the corresponding posting lists are retrieved, and the algorithm ranks the documents based on the contents of the posting lists.

The size of the index is another concern. Many indexes can be equal to the size of the original text. This means that storage requirements are doubled due to the index. However, compression of the index typically results in a space requirement of less than ten percent of the original text [Witten et al., 1999]. The terms or phrases stored in the index depend on the parsing algorithms that are employed (see Section 3.8).

The size of posting lists in the inverted index can be approximated by the Zipfian distribution—Zipf proposed that the term frequency distribution in a natural language is such that if all terms were ordered and assigned a rank, the product of their frequency and their rank would be constant [Zipf, 1949]. Table 5.1 illustrates the Zipfian distribution when this constant is equal to one.

Using $\frac{C}{r}$, where r is the rank and C is the value of the constant, an estimate can be made for the number of occurrences of a given term. The constant, C, is domain-specific and equals the number of occurrences of the most frequent term.

Table 5.1. Top Five Terms in Zipfian Distribution

Rank	Frequency	Constant
1	1.00	1
2	0.50	1
3	0.33	1
4	0.25	1
5	0.20	1

5.1.1 Building an Inverted Index

An inverted index consists of two components, a list of each distinct term referred to as the *index* and a set of lists referred to as *posting lists.* To compute relevance ranking, the term frequency or weight must be maintained. Thus, a posting list contains a set of tuples for each distinct term in the collection. The set of tuples is of the form <*doc_id, tf*> for each distinct term in the collection. A typical uncompressed index spends four bytes on the document identifier and two bytes on the term frequency since a long document can have a term that appears more than 255 times.

Consider a document collection in which document one contains two occurrences of *sales* and one occurrence of *vehicle.* Document two contains one occurrence of *vehicle.* The index would contain the entries *vehicle* and *sales.* The posting list is simply a linked list that is associated with each of these terms. For this example, we would have:

$$sales \rightarrow (1, 2)$$
$$vehicle \rightarrow (1, 1)\ (2, 1)$$

The entries in the posting lists are stored in ascending order by document number. Clearly, the construction of this inverted index is expensive, but once built, queries can be efficiently implemented. The algorithms underlying the implementation of the query processing and the construction of the inverted index are now described.

A possible approach to index creation is as follows: An inverted index is constructed by stepping through the entire document collection, one term at a time. The output of the index construction algorithm is a set of files written to disk. These files are:

- **Index file**. Contains the actual posting list for each distinct term in the collection. A term, t that occurs in i different documents will have a posting list of the form:

$$t \rightarrow (d_1, tf_{1j}), (d_2, tf_{2j}), \ldots, (d_i, tf_{ij})$$

where d_i indicates the document identifier of document i and tf_{ij} indicates the number of times term j occurs in document i.

- **Document file**. Contains information about each distinct document—document identifier, long document name, date published, etc.
- **Weight file**. Contains the weight for each document. This is the denominator for the cosine coefficient—defined as the cosine of the angle between the query and document vector (see Section 2.1).

The construction of the inverted index is implemented by scanning the entire collection, one term at a time. When a term is encountered, a check is made to see if this term is a stop word (if stop word removal is used) or if it is a previously identified term. A hash function is used to quickly locate the term in an array. Collisions caused by the hash function are resolved via a linear linked list. Different hashing functions and their relative performance are given in [McKenzie et al., 1990]. Once the posting list corresponding to this term is identified, the first entry of the list is checked to see if its document identifier matches the current document. If it does, the term frequency is merely incremented. Otherwise, this is the first occurrence of this term in the document, so a new posting list entry is added to the start of the list.

The posting list is stored entirely in memory. Memory is allocated dynamically for each new posting list entry. With each memory allocation, a check is made to determine if the memory reserved for indexing has been exceeded. If it has, processing halts while all posting lists resident in memory are written to disk. Once processing continues, new posting lists are written. With each output to disk, posting list entries for the same term are chained together.

Processing is completed when all of the terms are processed. At this point, the inverse document frequency for each term is computed by scanning the entire list of unique terms. Once the inverse document frequency is computed, it is possible to compute the document weight (the denominator for the cosine coefficient). This is done by scanning the entire posting list for each term.

5.1.2 Compressing an Inverted Index

A key objective in the development of inverted index files is to develop algorithms that reduce I/O bandwidth and storage overhead. The size of the index file determines the storage overhead imposed. Furthermore, since large index files demand greater I/O bandwidth to read them, the size also directly affects the processing times.

Although compression of text was extensively studied [Bell et al., 1990, Gutmann and Bell, 1994, Gupte and Frieder, 1995, Trotman, 2003], relatively little work was done in the area of inverted index compression. However, in work by Moffat and Zobel, an index was generated that was relatively easy to decompress. It comprised less than ten percent of the original document collection, and, more impressively, *included stop terms*.

Two primary areas in which an inverted index might be compressed are the term dictionary and the posting lists. Given relatively inexpensive memory costs, we do not focus on compression of indexes, although some work is described in [Witten et al., 1999]. The King James Bible (about five megabytes) contains 9,020 distinct terms and the traditional TREC collection (slightly over two gigabytes) contains 538,244 distinct terms [Witten et al., 1999]. The number of new terms always slightly increases as new domains are encountered, but it is reasonable to expect that it will stabilize at around one or two million terms. With an average term length of six, a four byte document frequency counter, and a four byte pointer to the first entry in the posting list, fourteen bytes are required for each term. For the conservative estimate of two million terms, the uncompressed index is likely to fit comfortably within 32 MB. Even if we are off by an order of magnitude, the amount of memory needed to store the index is conservatively under a gigabyte.

Given the relatively small size of an index and the ease with which it should fit in memory, we do not describe a detailed discussion of techniques used to compress the index. We note that stemming reduces this requirement and Huffman encoding can be used in a relatively straightforward fashion [Witten et al., 1999]. Also, the use of phrases improves precision and recall (see Section 3.8.2). Storage of phrases in the index may well require compression. This depends upon how phrases are identified and restricted. Most systems eliminate phrases that occur infrequently.

To introduce index compression algorithms, we first describe a relatively straightforward one that is referred to as the Byte Aligned (BA) index compression [Grossman, 1995]. BA compression is done within byte boundaries to improve runtime at a slight cost to the compression ratio. This algorithm is easy to implement and provides good compression (about fifteen percent of the size of an uncompressed inverted index when stop words are used). Variable length encoding is described in [Witten et al., 1999]. Although such efforts yield better compression, they do so at the expense of increased implementation complexity.

5.1.2.1 Fixed Length Index Compression

As discussed in the previous section, the entries in a posting list are in ascending order by document identifier. An exception to this document ordering occurs when a pruned inverted index approach is used (see Section 5.1.5). Hence, run-length encoding is applicable for document identifiers. For any document identifier, only the offset between the current identifier and the iden-

Table 5.2. Storage Requirements Based on Integer Size

Length	**Number of Bytes Required**
$0 \leq x < 64$	1
$64 \leq x < 16,384$	2
$16,384 \leq x < 4,194,304$	3
$4,194,304 \leq x < 1,073,741,824$	4

tifier immediately preceding it are computed. For the case in which no other document identifier exists, a compressed version of the document identifier is stored. Using this technique, a high proportion of relatively low numerical values is assured.

This scheme effectively reduces the domain of the identifiers, allowing them to be stored in a more concise format. Subsequently, the following method is applied to compress the data. For a given input value, the two left-most bits are reserved to store a count for the number of bytes that are used in storing the value. There are four possible combinations of two bit representations; thus, a two bit length indicator is used for all document identifiers. Integers are stored in either 6, 14, 22, or 30 bits. Optimally, a reduction of each individual data record size by a factor of four is obtained by this method since, in the best case, all values are less than $2^6 = 64$ and can be stored in a single byte. Without compression, four bytes are used for all document identifiers.

For each value to be compressed, the minimum number of bytes required to store this value is computed. (Note: this statement is not exactly accurate. Since there is no need for zero displacement, it is possible to store a displacement of one less than is actually needed. Since such a storage approach always requires an additional increment operation, and it only favors borderline conditions, it is seldom used.) Table 5.2 indicates the range of values that can be stored, as well as the length indicator for one, two, three, and four bytes. For document collections exceeding 2^{30} documents, this scheme can be extended to include a three bit length indicator which extends the range to $2^{61} - 1$.

For term frequencies, there is no concept of using an offset between the successive values as each frequency is independent of the preceding value. However, the same encoding scheme can be used. Since we do not expect a document to contain a term more than $2^{15} = 32,768$ times, either one or two bytes are used to store the value with one bit serving as the length indicator.

Table 5.3. Byte-Aligned Compression

Value	Compressed Bit String
1	00 000001
2	00 000010
4	00 000100
63	00 111111
180	01 000000 10110100

Table 5.4. Baseline: No Compression

Value	Uncompressed Bit String
1	00000000 00000000 00000000 00000001
3	00000000 00000000 00000000 00000011
7	00000000 00000000 00000000 00000111
70	00000000 00000000 00000000 01000110
250	00000000 00000000 00000000 11111010

5.1.2.2 Example: Fixed Length Compression

Consider an entry for an arbitrary term, t_1, which indicates that t_1 occurs in documents 1, 3, 7, 70, and 250. Byte-aligned (BA) compression uses the leading two high order bits to indicate the number of bytes required to represent the value. For the first four values, only one byte is required; for the final value, 180, two bytes are required. Note that only the differences between entries in the posting list must be computed. The difference of $250 - 70 = 180$ is all that must be computed for this final value. The values and their corresponding compressed bit strings are shown in Table 5.3.

Using no compression, the five entries in the posting list require four bytes each for a total of twenty bytes. The values and their corresponding compressed bit strings are shown in Table 5.4.

In this example, uncompressed data requires 160 bits, while BA compression requires only 48 bits.

5.1.3 Variable Length Index Compression

Moffat and Zobel also use the differences in the posting list. They capitalize on the fact that for most long posting lists, the difference between two

Table 5.5. Gamma Encoding: First Eight Integers

x	γ
1	0
2	10 0
3	10 1
4	110 00
5	110 01
6	110 10
7	110 11
8	1110 000

entries is relatively small. They first mention that patterns can be seen in these differences and that Huffman encoding provides the best compression. In this method, the frequency distribution of all of the offsets is obtained through an initial pass over the text, a compression scheme is developed based on the frequency distribution, and a second pass uses the new compression scheme. For example, if it was found that an offset of one has the highest frequency throughout the entire index, the scheme would use a single bit to represent the offset of one.

Moffat and Zobel use a family of universal codes described in [Elias, 1975]. This code represents an integer x with $2\lfloor log_2 x\rfloor + 1$ bits. The first $\lfloor log_2 x\rfloor$ bits are the unary representation of $\lfloor log_2 x\rfloor$. (Unary representation is a base one representation of integers using only the digit one. The number 5_{10} is represented as 11111_1.) After the leading unary representation, the next bit is a single stop bit of zero. At this point, the highest power of two that does not exceed x has been represented. The next $\lfloor log_2 x\rfloor$ bits represent the remainder of $x - 2^{\lfloor \log_2 x\rfloor}$ in binary.

As an example, consider the compression of the decimal 14. First, $\lfloor log_2 x\rfloor = 3$ is represented in unary as 111. Next, the stop bit is used. Subsequently, the remainder of $x - 2^{\lfloor \log_2 x\rfloor} = 14 - 8 = 6$ is stored in binary using $\lfloor \log_2 14\rfloor = 3$ bits as 110. Hence, the compressed code for 14_{10} is 1110110.
Decompression requires only one pass, because it is known that for a number with n bits prior to the stop bit, there will be n bits after the stop bit. The first eight integers using the Elias γ encoding are given in Table 5.5:

Table 5.6. Gamma Compression

Value	Compressed Bit String
1	0
2	10 0
4	110 00
63	111110 11111
180	11111110 0110100

5.1.3.1 Example: Variable Length Compression

For our same example, the differences of 1, 2, 4, 63, and 180 are given in Table 5.6. This requires only 35 bits, thirteen less than the simple BA compression. Also, our example contained an even distribution of relatively large offsets to small ones. The real gain can be seen in that very small offsets require only a 1 or a 0. Moffat and Zobel use the γ code to compress the term frequency in a posting list, but use a more complex coding scheme for the posting list entries.

5.1.4 Varying Compression Based on Posting List Size

The $gamma$ scheme can be generalized as a coding paradigm based on the vector V with positive integers i where $\sum v_i \geq N$. To code integer $x \geq 1$ relative to V, find k such that:

$$\sum_{j=1}^{k-1} v_j < x \leq \sum_{j=1}^{k} v_j$$

In other words, find the first component of V such that the sum of all preceding components is greater than or equal to the value, x, to be encoded. For our example of 7, using a vector V of <1, 2, 4, 8, 16, 32> we find the first three components that are needed (1, 2, 4) to equal or exceed 7, so k is equal to three. Now k can be encoded in some representation (unary is typically used) followed by the difference:

$$d = x - \sum_{j=1}^{k-1} v_j - 1$$

Using this sum we have: $d = 7 - (1 + 2) - 1 = 3$ which is now coded in $\lceil \log_2 v_k \rceil = \lceil \log_2 4 \rceil = 2$ binary bits. With this generalization, the γ scheme

Table 5.7. Variable Compression based on Posting List Size

Value	Compressed Bit String
1	0 00
2	0 01
4	0 11
63	11110 000010
180	111110 0110111

can be seen as using the vector V composed of powers of 2 <1, 2, 4, 8, ..., > and coding k in binary.

Clearly, V can be changed to give different compression characteristics. Low values in v optimize compression for low numbers, while higher values in v provide more resilience for high numbers. A clever solution given by [Zobel et al., 1992] was to vary V for each posting list such that V = $< b, 2b, 4b, 8b, 16b, 32b, 64b, \ldots, >$ where b is the median offset given in the posting list.

5.1.4.1 Example: Using the Posting List Size

Using our example of 1, 2, 4, 63, 180, the median, b, has four results in the vector V = < 4, 8, 16, 32, 64, 128, 256>. Table 5.7 contains an example for the five posting lists using this scheme.

This requires thirty-three bits as well and we can see that, for this example, the use of the median was not such a good choice as there was wide skew in the numbers. A more typical posting list in which numbers were uniformly closer to the median could result in better compression.

5.1.4.2 Throughput-optimized Compression

Anh and Moffat developed an index compression scheme that yields good compression ratios while maintaining fast decompression time for efficient query processing [Anh and Moffat, 2004]. They developed a variable-length encoding that takes advantage of the distribution of the document identifier offsets for each posting list. This is a hybrid of bit-aligned and byte-aligned compression; each 32-bit word contains encodings for a variable number of integers, but each integer within the word is encoded using an equal number of bits. Words are divided into bits used for a "selector" field and bits used for storing data.

The selector field contains an index into a table of inter-word partitioning strategies based on the number of bits available for storing data, ensuring that each integer encoded in the word uses the same number of bits. The appropriate partitioning strategy is chosen based on the largest document identifier offset in the posting list. Anh and Moffat propose three variants based on this strategy, differing primarily in how the bits in a word are partitioned:

- Simple-9: Uses 28 bits for data and 4 bits for the selector field; the selection table has nine rows, as there are nine different ways to split 28 bits equally.
- Relative-10: Similar to Simple-9, but uses only two bits for the selector field, leaving 30 data bits with 10 partitions. The key difference is that, with only 2 selector bits, each word can only chose from 4 of the 10 available partitions – these are chosen relative to the selector value of the previous word. This algorithm obtains slight improvements over Simple-9.
- Carryover-12: This is a variant of Relative-10 where some of the wasted space due to partitioning is reclaimed by using the leftover bits to store the selector value for the next word, allowing that word to use all of its bits for data storage. This obtains the best compression of the three, but it is the most complex, requiring more decompression time.

5.1.4.3 Example: Simple-9

To continue our example using the differences of 1, 2, 4, 63, and 180, we show the selection table in Table 5.8. To find the appropriate coding scheme, we examine each row in the table. We cannot use row a because there is a value in the first 28 offsets greater than 2^1. We can not use row b because there is a value in the first 14 offsets greater than 2^2. Continuing down the list, we find that we also can not use row e because there is a value in the first five offsets greater than 2^5. We must use row f, since the highest value in the first four offsets (63) is less than $2^7 = 128$. This yields four 7-bit codes for the first four offsets (see Table 5.9), along with row f encoded in four bits (e.g., 0101).

The final offset in our example, 180, will not fit within the first 32-bit word; therefore, a second 32-bit word is needed to encode it. Thus, 64 total bits are required to compress our example using Simple-9. This example illustrates that these compression schemes are most effective with longer posting lists. Additionally, it should be clear that these schemes allow for very fast decompression time, as each value is encoded at a fixed length within each word.

5.1.4.4 Block-addressing compressed indexes

Another method of reducing index size is to build an index that addresses blocks of text with fixed sizes which may contain more than one document. Specific term counts can then be obtained by linearly scanning these blocks.

Table 5.8. Nine Different Ways of Partitioning 28 Data Bits (for Simple-9)

Selector	Codes	Length (bits)	Number of Unused bits
a	28	1	0
b	14	2	0
c	9	3	1
d	7	4	0
e	5	5	3
f	4	7	0
g	3	9	1
h	2	14	0
i	1	28	0

Table 5.9. Example of Simple-9 Compression

Value	Compressed Bit String
1	0000000
2	0000001
4	0000011
63	0111110

This allows for an adjustable balance between the time to create the index and the storage used for the index and query processing speed [Navarro et al., 2000].

5.1.5 Index Pruning

To this point, we have discussed lossless approaches for inverted index compression. A lossy approach is called static index pruning. The basic idea was described in [Carmel et al., 2001]. Essentially, posting list entries may be removed or pruned without significantly degrading precision. Experiments were done with both term specific pruning and uniform pruning. With term specific pruning, different levels of pruning are done for each term. Static pruning simply eliminates posting list entries in a uniform fashion – regardless of the term. It was shown that pruning at levels of nearly seventy percent of the full inverted index did not significantly affect average precision. A hardware implementation of this basic approach is described in [Agun and Frieder, 2003].

5.1.6 Reordering Documents Prior to Indexing

Index compression efficiency can also be improved if we use an algorithm to reorder documents prior to compressing the inverted index [Blandford and Blelloch, 2002, Silvestri et al., 2004]. Since the compression effectiveness of many encoding schemes is largely dependent upon the *gap* between document identifiers, the idea is that if we can feed documents to the algorithm correctly, we could reduce the average gap, thereby maximizing compression. Consider documents d_1, d_{99}, and d_{1000}, all which contain the same term t. For these documents we obtain a posting list entry for t of $t \rightarrow d_1, d_{51}, d_{101}$.

The document gap between each posting list entry is 50. If however, we arranged the documents prior to submitting them to the index, we could submit these documents as d_1, d_2, and d_3 which completely eliminates this gap. We note that for D documents there are 2^D possible orderings, so any attempt to order documents will be faced with significant scalability concerns.

The algorithms compare documents to other documents prior to submitting them for indexing. The idea is that similar documents will contain similar terms and document gaps are reduced if we order documents based on their similarity to one another. Each algorithm uses the Jaccard similarity coefficient (see Section 2.1.2) to obtain a measure of document similarity. Two basic approaches have been proposed: top-down (starting from the collection as a whole) or bottom-up (starting from each individual document).

5.1.6.1 Top-Down

Generally, the two top-down algorithms consist of four main phases. In the first phase, called *center selection*, two groups of documents are selected from the collection and used as partitions in subsequent phases. In the *redistribution* phase, all remaining documents are divided among the selected centers according to their similarity. In the *recursion* phase, the previous phases are repeated recursively over the two resulting partitions until each one becomes a singleton. Finally, in the *merging* phase, the partitions formed from each recursive call are merged bottom-up, creating an ordering.

The first of the two proposed top-down algorithms is called *transactional B & B*, as it is an implementation of the Blelloch and Blandford algorithm described in [Blandford and Blelloch, 2002]. This reordering algorithm obtains the best compression ratios of the four, however it is not scalable.

The second top-down algorithm is called *Bisecting*, so named because its *center selection* phase consists of choosing two random documents as centers, thereby dramatically reducing the cost of this phase. Since its center selection is so simple, the *Bisecting* algorithm obtains less effective compression but it is more efficient.

5.1.6.2 Bottom-Up

The bottom-up algorithms begin by considering each document in the collection separately and they progressively group documents based on their similarity. The first bottom-up algorithms is inspired by the popular *k-means* approach to document clustering (see Section 3.2.3.3). The second uses *k-scan*; an algorithm that is a simplified version of k-means which is based on a centroid-search algorithm.

The *k-means* algorithm initially chooses k documents as cluster representatives, and assigns all remaining documents to those clusters based on a measure of similarity. At the end of the first pass, the cluster centroids are recomputed and the documents are reassigned according to their similarity to the new centroids. This iteration continues until the cluster centroids stabilize. The single-pass version of this algorithm only performs the first pass of this algorithm, and the authors select the k initial centers using the *Buckshot* clustering technique (see Section 3.2.3.4).

The *k-scan* algorithm is a simplified version of single-pass k-means, requiring only k steps to complete. It forms clusters in place at each step, by first selecting a document to serve as the centroid for a cluster, and then assigning a portion of unassigned documents that have the highest similarity to that cluster.

5.2 Query Processing

Recent work has focused on improving query run-time. Moffat and Zobel have shown that query performance can be improved by modifying the inverted index to support fast scanning of a posting list [Moffat and Zobel, 1996, Moffat and Zobel, 1994]. Other work has shown that reasonable precision and recall can be obtained by retrieving fewer terms in the query [Grossman et al., 1997]. Computation can be reduced even further by eliminating some of the complexity found in the vector space model [Lee and Ren, 1996].

5.2.1 Inverted Index Modifications

Moffat and Zobel show how an inverted index can be segmented to allow for a quick search of a posting list to locate a particular document [Witten et al., 1999]. The typical ranking algorithm scans the entire posting list for each term in the query. An array of document scores is updated for each entry in the posting list. Moffat and Zobel suggest that the least frequent terms should be processed first.

The premise is that less frequent terms carry the most meaning and probably have the most significant contribution to a high-ranking documents. The entire posting lists for these terms are processed. Some algorithms suggest that processing should stop after d documents are assigned a non-zero score. The premise is that at this point, the high-frequency terms in the query will simply be generating scores for documents that will not end up in the final top t documents, where t is the number of documents that are displayed to the user.

A suggested improvement is to continue processing all the terms in the query, but only update the weights found in the d documents. In other words, after some threshold of d scores has been reached, the remaining query terms become part of an AND (they only increment documents who contain another term in the query) instead of the usual vector space OR. At this point, it is cheaper to reverse the order of the nested loop that is used to increment scores. Prior to reaching d scores, the basic algorithm is:

```
For each term t in the query Q
        Obtain the posting list entries for t
        For each posting list entry that indicates t is in doc i
            Update score for document i
```

For query terms with small posting lists, the inner loop is small; however, when terms that are very frequent are examined, extremely long posting lists are prevalent. Also, after d documents are accessed, there is no need to update the score for every document, it is only necessary to update the score for those documents that have a non-zero score.

To avoid scanning very long posting lists, the algorithm is modified to be:

```
For each term t in the query Q
        Obtain posting list, p, for documents that contain t
        For each document x in the reversed list of d documents
            Scan posting list p for x
            if x exists
                update score for document x
```

The key here is that the inverted index must be changed to allow quick access to a posting list entry. It is assumed that the entries in the posting list are sorted by a document identifier. As a new document is encountered, its entry can be appended to the existing posting list. Moffat and Zobel propose to change the posting list by partitioning it and adding pointers to each partition. The posting list can quickly be scanned by checking the first partition pointer (which contains the document identifier of the highest document in the partition and a pointer to the next partition). This check indicates whether or not a jump should be made to the next partition or if the current partition should be scanned. The process continues until the partition is found, and the document we are looking for is matched against the elements of the partition. A small size, d, of about 1,000 resulted in the best CPU time for a set of TREC queries against the TREC data [Moffat and Zobel, 1996].

5.2.2 Partial Result Set Retrieval

Another way to improve run-time performance is to stop processing after some threshold of computational resources is expended. One approach counts disk I/O operations and stops after a threshold of disk I/O operations is reached [Yee et al., 1993]. The key to this approach is to sort the terms in the query based on some indicator of term *goodness* and process the terms in this order. By doing this, query processing stops after the important terms have been processed. Sorting the terms is analogous to sorting their posting lists. Three measures used to characterize a posting list are now described.

5.2.2.1 Cutoff Based on Document Frequency

The simplest measure of term quality is to rely on document frequency. This was described in [Grossman et al., 1997, Grossman et al., 1994] which showed that using between twenty-five to seventy-five percent of the query terms after they were sorted by document frequency resulted in almost no degradation in precision and recall for the TREC-4 document collection. In some cases, precision and recall improves with fewer terms because lower ranked terms are sometimes noise terms such as *good, nice, useful, etc.* These terms have long posting lists that result in scoring thousands of documents and do little to improve the quality of the result. Using term frequency is a means of implementing a dynamic stop word list in which high-frequency terms are eliminated without using a static set of stop words.

5.2.2.2 Cutoff Based on Maximum Estimated Weight

Two other measures of sorting the query terms are described in [Yee et al., 1993]. The first computes the maximum term frequency of a given query term as tf_{max} and uses the following as a means of sorting the query.

$$tf_{max} \times idf$$

The idea is that a term that appears frequently in all the documents in which it appears, is probably of more importance than a term that appears infrequently in the documents that it appears in. The assumption is that the maximum value is a good indicator of how often the term appears in a document.

5.2.2.3 Cutoff Based on the Weight of a Disk Page in the Posting List

The cutoffs based on term weights can be used to characterize posting lists and choose which posting list to process first. The problem is that a posting list can be quite long and might have substantial skew. To avoid this problem, a new measure sorts disk pages within a posting list instead of the entire posting list. At index creation time, the posting lists are sorted in decreasing order by term frequency and instead of just a pointer that points to the first entry in the posting list, the index contains an entry for each page of the posting list. The entry indicates the maximum term frequency on a given page. The posting list pages are then sorted by:

$$tf_{max} \times idf \times f(I)$$

where $f(I)$ is a function that indicates the number of entries on a page. This is necessary since some pages will not be full and a normalization is needed such that they are not sorted in exactly the same way as a full page. One value that is used for $f(I)$ is i^e where $0 < e < 1$.

Unfortunately, this measure requires an entry in the index for each page in the posting list. However, results show (for a variety of query sizes) that only about forty percent of the disk pages need to be retrieved to obtain eighty percent of the documents that would be found if all one hundred percent of the pages were accessed. All of these tests were performed using small document collections.

5.2.3 Vector Space Simplifications

Recent work has shown, in many cases, that simplifications to the vector space model can be made with only limited degradation in precision and recall [Lee et al., 1997]. In this work, five variations to the basic cosine measure (see Section 2.1) were tested on five small collections and 10,000 articles from the *Wall Street Journal* portion of the TREC collection. To review, the baseline cosine coefficient is:

$$SC(Q, D_i) = \frac{\sum_{j=1}^{t} w_{qj} d_{ij}}{\sqrt{\sum_{j=1}^{t}(d_{ij})^2 \sum_{j=1}^{t}(w_{qj})^2}}$$

The first variation was to replace the document length normalization that is based on weight with the square root of the number of terms in D_i. The second variation was to simply remove the document length normalization (simple dot product coefficient) given by:

$$SC(Q, D_i) = \sum_{j=1}^{t} w_{qj} d_{ij}$$

The third measure drops the idf. This eliminates one entry in the index for each term.

$$SC(Q, D_i) = \sum_{j=1}^{t} tf_{qj} tf_{ij}$$

The fourth measure drops the tf but retains the idf. This eliminates the need to store the tf in each entry of the posting list. This significantly reduces both computational, storage, and I/O costs.

$$SC(Q, D_i) = \sum_{j=1}^{t} w_{qj} w_{ij}$$

The weight, w_{qj}, is one if term j is in the query and zero if otherwise. The weight, w_{ij} is equal to idf_j if term j is in the document and zero otherwise.

The fifth and final method simply counts matches between the query and the terms. That is:

$$SC(Q, D_i) = \sum_{j=1}^{t} w_{qj} w_{ij}$$

where w_{qj} is one if term j is in the query and zero otherwise, and w_{ij} is equal to one if term j is in the document and zero otherwise.

For the TREC subset, two tests were done. The first was with the TREC narratives (long queries) and the second was with the TREC concepts (short queries). With the narratives, the baseline cosine measure performed the best with the square root document length normalization doing slightly better. The concept queries had the interesting result that the fourth and fifth (no idf and simple match counting) methods had a higher precision than the baseline. The only explanation for this somewhat surprising result is that the concept queries are very specific in nature so the effect of additional weights did not have much impact.

5.3 Signature Files

The use of signature files lies between a sequential scan of the original text and the construction of an inverted index. A signature is an encoding of a document. The idea is to encode all documents as relatively small signatures (often the goal is to represent a signature in only a few bits). Once this is done, the signatures can be scanned instead of the entire documents. Typically, signatures do not uniquely represent a document (i.e., a signature represents multiple documents), so it is usually necessary to implement a retrieval in two phases. The first phase scans all of the signatures and identifies possible hits, and the second phase scans the original text of the documents in the possible hit list to ensure that they are correct matches. Hence, signature files are combined with pattern matching. Figure **??** illustrates the mapping of documents onto the signatures.

Construction of a signature is often done with different hashing functions. One or more hashing functions are applied to each word in the document. Of-

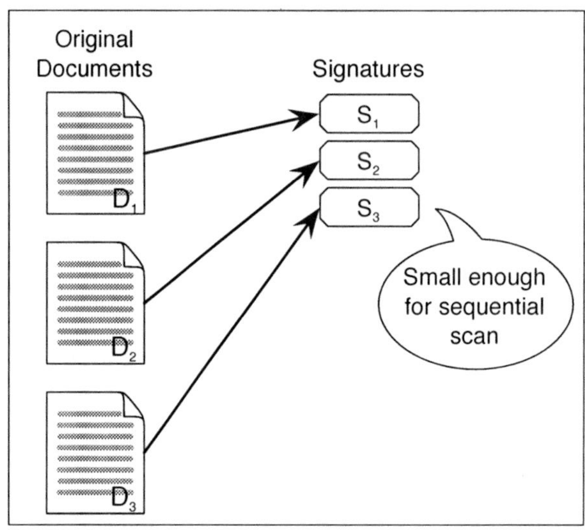

Table 5.10. Building a Signature

term	*h(term)*
t_1	0101
t_2	1010
t_3	0011

ten, the hashing function is used to set a bit in the signature. For example, if the terms *information* and *retrieval* were in a document and *h(information)* and *h(retrieval)* corresponded to bits one and four respectively, a four bit binary signature for this document would appear as 1001.

A false match occurs when a word that is not in the list of w signatures has the same bitmap as one of these signatures. For example, consider a term t_1 that sets bits one and three in the signature and another term t_2 that sets bits two and four in the signature. A third term t_3 might correspond to bits one and two and thereby be deemed a *match* with the signature, even though it is not equal to t_1 or t_2. Table 5.10 gives the three terms just discussed and their corresponding hash values.

Consider document d_1 that contains t_1, document d_2 contains t_1 and t_3 and document d_3 contains t_1 and t_2. Table 5.11 has the signatures for these three documents.

Table 5.11. Document Signatures

Document	Signature
d_1	0101
d_2	0111
d_3	1111

Hence, a query that is searching for term t_3 will obtain a false match on document d_3 even though it does not contain t_3.

By lengthening the signature to 1,024 bits and keeping the number of words stored in a signature small, the chance of a false match can be shown to be less than three percent [Stanfill and Thau, 1991].

To implement document retrieval, a signature is constructed for the query. A Boolean AND is executed between the query signature and each document signature. If the AND returns TRUE, the document is added to the possible hit list. Similarly, a Boolean OR can be executed if it is only necessary for any word in the query to be in the document. To minimize false positives, multiple hashing functions are applied to the same word [Stanfill and Kahle, 1986].

A Boolean signature cannot store proximity information or information about the weight of a term as it appears in a document. Most measures of relevance determine that a document that contains a query term multiple times will be ranked higher than a document that contains the same term only once. With Boolean signatures, it is not possible to represent the number of times a term appears in a document; therefore, these measures of relevance cannot be implemented.

Signatures are useful if they can fit into memory. Also, it is easier to add or delete documents in a signature file than to an inverted index, and the order of an entry in the signature file does not matter. This somewhat orderless processing is amenable to parallel processing (see Section 7.1.2). However, there is always a need to check for false matches, and the basic definition does not support ranked queries. A modification to allow support for document ranking is to partition a signature into groups where each term frequency is associated with a group [Lee and Ren, 1996].

5.3.1 Scanning to Remove False Positives

Once a signature has found a match, scanning algorithms are employed to verify whether or not the match is a false positive due to collisions. We do not cover these in detail as a lengthy survey surrounding the implementation of many text scanning algorithms is given in [Lecroq, 1994]. Signature algorithms can be employed without scanning for false drops (if a long enough signature is used) and no significant degradation in precision and recall occurs [Lee and Ren, 1996]. However, for completeness, we do provide a brief summary of text scanning algorithms.

Pattern matching algorithms are related to the use of scanning in information retrieval since they strive to find a pattern in a string of text characters. Typically, pattern matching is defined as finding all positions in the input text that contain the start of a given pattern. If the pattern is of size p and the text is of size s, the naive nested loop pattern match requires $O(ps)$ comparisons.

Aho and Corasick's algorithms implement deterministic finite state automata to identify matches in the text [Aho and Corasick, 1975]. Knuth, Morris, and Pratt (KMP) also describe an algorithm that runs in $O(s)$ time that scans forward along the text, but uses preprocessing of the pattern to determine appropriate skips in the string that can be safely taken [Knuth et al., 1977].

The Boyer-Moore algorithm is another approach that preprocesses the pattern, but starts at the last character of the pattern and works backwards towards the beginning of the string. Two preprocessed functions of the pattern are developed to skip parts of the pattern when repetition in the pattern occurs and to skip text that simply cannot match the pattern. These functions use knowledge gleaned from the present search point [Boyer and Moore, 1977]. The algorithm was improved to run in linear time even when multiple occurrences of the pattern are present [Galil, 1979].

Later, in the 1980's, a pattern matching algorithm that works by applying a hash function to the pattern and the next p characters in the text was given in [Karp and Rabin, 1987]. If a match in the hash function occurs (i.e., a collision between *h(pattern)* and *h(text)*), the contents of the pattern and text are examined. The goal is to reduce false collisions. By using large prime numbers, collisions occur extremely rarely, if at all. Another pattern matching algorithm is presented in [Frakes and Baeza-Yates, 1993]. This algorithm uses a set of bit strings which represent Boolean states that are constantly updated as the pattern is streamed through the text.

The best of these algorithms runs in a linear time αs where α is some constant $0 \leq \alpha \leq 1.0$ and s is the size of the string. The goal is to lower the constant. In the worst case, s comparisons must be done, but the average case for these algorithms is often sublinear. An effort is made in these algorithms to avoid having to look backward in the text. The scan continues to move forward with each comparison to facilitate a physically contiguous scan of a disk. The KMP algorithm builds a finite state automata for many patterns so it is directly applicable. An algorithm by Uratani and Takeda combines the FSA approach by Aho and Corasick with the Boyer-Moore idea of avoiding much of the search space. Essentially, the FSA is built by using some of the search space reductions given by Boyer-Moore. The FSA scans text from right to left, as done in Boyer-Moore. Note this is done for a query that contains multiple terms [Uratani and Takeda, 1993]. In a direct comparison with repeated use of the Boyer-Moore algorithm, the Uratani and Takeda algorithm is shown to execute ten times fewer probes for a query of 100 patterns. For only two patterns, the average probe ratio (the ratio of the number of references in the text and the length of the text) of Boyer-Moore is 0.236 while Uratani-Takeda is 0.178.

5.4 Duplicate Document Detection

A method to improve both efficiency and effectiveness of an information retrieval system is to remove duplicates or near duplicates. Duplicates can be removed either at the time documents are added to an inverted index or upon retrieving the results of a query. The difficulty is that we do not simply wish to remove exact duplicates, we may well be interested in removing *near* duplicates as well. However, we do not wish our threshold for *nearness* to be so broad that documents are deemed duplicate when, in fact, they are sufficiently different that the user would have preferred to see each of them as individual documents.

For Web search, the duplicate document problem is particularly acute. A search for the term *apache* might yield numerous copies of Web pages about the Web server product and numerous duplicates about the Indian tribe. The user should only be shown two hyperlinks, but instead is shown thousands. Additionally, these redundant pages can affect term and document weighting schemes. Additionally, they can increase indexing time and reduce search efficiency [Chowdhury et al., 2002, Cho et al., 1999].

5.4.1 Finding Exact Duplicates

Duplicate detection is often implemented by calculating a unique hash value for each document. Each document is then examined for duplication by looking up the value (hash) in either an in-memory hash or persistent lookup system. Several common hash functions used are MD2, MD5, or SHA [SHA1, 1995]. These functions are used because they have three desirable properties, namely: they can be calculated on arbitrary document lengths, they are easy to compute, and they have very low probabilities of collisions.

While this approach is both fast and easy to implement, the problem is that it will find only *exact* duplicates. The slightest change (e.g.; one extra white space) results in two similar documents being deemed unique. For example, a Web page that displays the number of visitors along with the content of the page will continually produce different signatures even though the document is the same. The only difference is the counter, and it will be enough to generate a different hash value for each document.

5.4.2 Finding Similar Duplicates

While it is not possible to define precisely at which point a document is no longer a duplicate of another, researchers have examined several metrics for determining the similarity of a document to another. The first is *resemblance* [Broder et al., 1997]. This work suggests that if a document contains roughly the same semantic content, it is a duplicate whether or not it is a precise syntactic match.

$$r(D_i, D_j) = \frac{|S(D_i) \bigcap S(D_j)|}{|S(D_i) \bigcup S(D_j)|} \tag{5.1}$$

The resemblance r of document D_i and document D_j, as defined in Equation 5.1, is the intersection of features over the union of features from two documents. This metric can be used to calculate a fuzzy similarity between two documents. For example, assume D_i and D_j share fifty percent of their terms and each document has 10 terms. Their resemblance would be $\frac{5}{15} = 0.33$. Many researchers have explored using resemblance to provide a threshold t to find duplicate documents [Brin et al., 1995, Garcia-Molina et al., 1996, Shivakumar and Garcia-Molina, 1996, Broder et al., 1997, Shivakumar and Garcia-Molina, 1998, Fetterly et al., 2003] where if t was exceeded the documents would be considered duplicate.

Two general issues were explored when using resemblance. The first is what features and threshold t should be used. The second is efficiency issues that come into play with large collections and the optimizations that can be applied [Broder, 1998]. The cosine measure (see Section 2.1.2) is commonly used to identify the similarity between two documents.

For duplicate detection a binary feature representation produces a similarity of two documents similar to term-based resemblance. Thus, as the distance of two documents approaches 1.0, they become more similar in relation to the features being compared.

5.4.2.1 Shingles

The first near-duplicate algorithm we discuss is the use of shingles. A shingle is simply a set of contiguous terms in a document. Shingling techniques, such as COPS [Brin et al., 1995], KOALA [Heintze, 1996], and DSC [Broder, 1998], essentially all compare the number of matching shingles.

The comparison of document subsets allows the algorithms to calculate a percentage of overlap between two documents using resemblance as given in Equation 5.1. This relies on hash values for each document subsection/feature set and filters those hash values to reduce the number of comparisons the algorithm must perform. This filtration of features, therefore, improves the runtime performance. Note that the simplest filter is strictly a syntactic filter based on simple syntactic rules, and the trivial subset is the entire collection. In the shingling approaches, rather than comparing documents, subdocuments are compared, and thus, each document can produce many potential duplicates. Returning many potential matches requires vast user involvement to sort out potential duplicates, diluting the potential usefulness of these types of approaches. To combat the inherent efficiency issues, several optimization techniques were proposed to reduce the number of comparisons made.

The DSC algorithm reduces the number of shingles used. Frequently occurring shingles are removed in [Heintze, 1996]. Every $25^{\underline{th}}$ shingle is saved in [Broder et al., 1997]. This reduction, however, hinders effectiveness. Worse still, even when relatively infrequent shingles are removed (only those that occur in over 1000 documents) and keeping only every $25^{\underline{th}}$ shingle, the implementation of the DSC algorithm took 10 CPU days to process 30 million documents [Broder, 1998].

The DSC algorithm has a more efficient alternative, DSC-SS, which uses super shingles. This algorithm takes several shingles and combines them into a super shingle. The result is a document with a few super shingles instead of many shingles. Resemblance is defined as matching a single super shingle in two documents. This is much more efficient because it no longer requires a full counting of all overlaps. The authors, however, noted that DSC-SS does "not work well for short documents" so no runtime results were reported [Broder, 1998]. This makes sense because super shingles tend to be somewhat large and will, in all likelihood, completely encompass a short document.

5.4.2.2 Duplicate Detection via Similarity

Another approach is to simply compute the similarity coefficient between two documents. If the document similarity exceeds a threshold, the documents can be deemed duplicates of each other [Sanderson, 1997, Buckley et al., 2000, Hoad and Zobel, 2002]. These approaches are similar to work done in document clustering (see Section 3.2). Unfortunately, they require all pairs of documents to be compared, i.e., each document is compared to every other document and a similarity weight is calculated. A document to document similarity comparison approach is thus computationally prohibitive given the theoretical $O(d^2)$ runtime, where d is the number of documents. In reality, these approaches only evaluate documents with an overlap of terms. Thus, the actual runtime is data dependent and difficult to accurately predict.

5.4.2.3 Treating the Document as a Query

Another approach treats each result document as a new query and looks for other documents that match this document. This approach is not computationally feasible for large collections or dynamic collections since each document must be queried against the entire collection. Sanderson and Cooper used a variation on this where the terms are selected using Rocchio relevance feedback (see Section 3.1.1 [Sanderson, 1997, Cooper et al., 2002]). For large collections, where a common term can occur in millions of documents, this is not scalable. For term selection approaches this cost is significantly less, but still requires at least the same number of I/O operations as the number of terms selected via the relevance feedback algorithm. Kolcz et. al. proposed an optimization to the more typical cosine similarity measure. In this work, it was assumed that terms that occurred in more than five percent of the collection actually occurred in each document. This optimization produced results within ninety percent of the full cosine similarity measure, but executed an order of magnitude faster [Kolcz et al., 2004].

5.4.2.4 I-Match

I-Match uses a hashing scheme that uses only *some* terms in a document. The decision of which terms to use is key to the success of the algorithm. I-Match is a hash of the document that uses collection statistics, for example, idf, to identify which terms should be used as the basis for comparison. The use of collection statistics allows one to determine the usefulness of terms for duplicate document detection. Previously, it was shown that terms with high collection frequencies often do not add to the semantic content of the document [Grossman et al., 1995, Smeaton et al., 1997]. I-Match assumes that that removal of very infrequent terms or very common terms results in good document representations for identifying duplicates. Pseudo-code for the algorithm is as follows.

- Get document
- Parse document into a token steam, removing format tags.
- Using term thresholds (idf), retain only significant tokens.
- Insert relevant tokens into unicode ascending ordered tree of unique tokens.
- Loop through token tree adding each unique token to the SHA1 [4] digest. Upon completion of loop, a (doc_id, SHA1 digest) tuple is defined.
- The tuple (doc_id, SHA1 digest) is inserted into the storage data structure using the key.
- If there is a collision of digest values then the documents are similar.

The overall runtime of the I-Match approach is $(O(d \log d))$ in the worst case where all documents are duplicates of each other and $(O(d))$ otherwise, where d is the number of documents in the collection. All similar documents must be grouped together. That is, the corresponding document identifiers must be stored as a group. In the most extreme case, all of the hash values are the same (all the documents are similar to each other). In such a case, to store all the document identifiers together in a data structure (tree) requires $(O(d \log d))$ time. Typically, however, the processing time of the I-Match approach is $O(d)$ time. The calculation of idf values can be approached with either of two methods. The first is with the use of a training collection to produce a set of terms idf tuples before the de-duplication work occurs. It was shown that term idf weights change slightly as collection sizes grow so this is an acceptable solution [Frieder et al., 2000a].

A second approach is to run two passes over the documents, where the first pass calculates the idf weights of the terms, and the second pass finds duplicates with the I-Match algorithm. This approach increases the actual run time of the algorithm, but the theoretical complexity would remain unchanged. Conrad et. al. examined these approaches when using a dynamic collection and only using high idf terms and found the approach not stable if a dynamic vocabulary is used [Conrad et al., 2003]. Recently, they developed a new test collection for inexact duplicate document detection [Conrad and Schriber, 2004]. This suggests that the first approach may be the more applicable for this problem.

The I-Match time complexity is comparable to the DSC-SS algorithm, which generates a single super shingle if the super shingle size is large enough to encompass the whole document. Otherwise, it generates k super shingles while I-Match only generates one. Since k is a constant in the DSC-SS analysis, the two algorithms are equivalent.

I-Match, is more efficient in practice. However, the real benefit of I-Match over DSC-SS is that small documents are not ignored. With DSC-SS, it is quite likely that for sufficiently small documents, no shingles are identified for duplicate detection. Hence, those short documents are not considered even though they may be duplicated. While I-Match is efficient it suffers from the same brittleness that the original hashing techniques suffered from, when some slight variation in that hash is made. One recent enhancement to I-Match has been the use of random lexicon variations of the feature *idf* range. These variations are then used to produce multiple signatures of a document. All of the hashes can be considered a valid signature, this modification to I-Match reduces the brittleness of I-Match. Kolcz et. al. showed that this randomization approach improved the recall effectiveness of I-Match by 40-60 percent without hurting precision, when using 10 random lexicons [Kolcz et al., 2004].

5.5 Summary

Performance evaluation considerations of information retrieval systems involve both effectiveness (accuracy) and efficiency (run-time and storage overhead) measures. In this chapter, we focused on the efficiency considerations.

Initially, we described the concept of and motivation for the use of an inverted index. An inverted index is a many-to-many mapping of terms onto documents. Using an inverted index, only documents that contain the specified query terms are accessed, thus significantly reducing the I/O requirements as compared to other search processing structures. Having described the concept of an inverted index, we continued by illustrating a method to implement an inverted index and a pruned variation. We also outlined various techniques for compressing the index. Two compression techniques were reviewed. The first, fixed length compression, has the advantage of simplicity and slightly more efficient query processing times as compared to the second, variable length compression. Variable length compression, however, does result in a slightly better compression ratio.

We concluded the chapter with an overview of signature files. Signature files contain a set of document signatures, one signature per document. A document signature is an encoding of each document. Key terms contained in the document are hashed onto a vector; the existence of a term j in the document i is denoted by a one in the $j^{\underline{th}}$ bit of document signature i. To determine which documents are relevant to a particular query, only the signature file must be examined. Since term hashing can result in false positive indications, a two pass search strategy is necessary. In the first pass, involving the examination of the signature file, all potential candidates are determined. In the second phase, a full text scan of the potential candidates determined in the first pass is performed.

Although greater attention has traditionally been placed on the effectiveness of information retrieval systems, efficiency issues are critical. Failure to optimize the efficiency of an information retrieval system can result in a highly accurate system that suffers prohibitive execution or storage performance. As storage technology continues to improve and decrease in cost, storage constraints are becoming less critical. However, with the continued exponential growth of online data, storage constraints are still a concern and run-time performance considerations are of paramount importance. Parallel processing techniques used to improve the overall run-time performance are described in Chapter 7.

5.6 Exercises

1 Write a utility called *index* that builds an inverted index of *Alice in Wonderland.* Assume ten lines of input is a separate document. Assume you have enough memory to store all of the posting lists in memory while you are building the inverted index. Identify how much space your index requires and how long it takes to build it. Store the *idf* for each term in the index. Each posting list entry should contain the term frequency in the document. Use the 100 most frequent terms as stop terms. Test your index by computing a vector space *tf-idf* similarity measure for the following five queries.

- *rabbit watch*
- *looking glass*
- *tea party*
- *cheshire cat*
- *queen of hearts*

2 Now modify the code you just wrote to use an inverted index compression technique. Pick one in this chapter. Measure query performance for the same five queries, storage overhead, and the time to build the index. Repeat this, an now use a pruned index.

3 Pick a query that contains ten terms. Execute it and retrieve the top documents choosing ten that are relevant. Now, sort the query terms by their term frequency across the collection. Re-execute the query with one term—the least frequently occurring term in the collection. Identify the number of relevant documents found with just this term. Repeat this process, adding a single term to the query each time. Are all ten terms needed to find the relevant documents you found with the original query? Talk about what you have learned with this exercise and how this technique could be used to improve run-time without a corresponding loss in accuracy.

4 Develop a signature-based index where you build a signature for each "document" in the book. Use a 24-bit signature for each document. Now implement the ten queries used in the previous exercises as a simple Boolean OR. Compare run-time performance of the use of signatures to the inverted index. Describe the loss in functionality inherent in the use of signatures. Identify a heuristic in which signatures could be used as a "first-pass filter" for a very large collection and then describe how an inverted index could be used for detailed analysis.

Chapter 6

INTEGRATING STRUCTURED DATA AND TEXT

Essential problems associated with searching and retrieving relevant documents were discussed in the preceding chapters. However, simply searching massive quantities of unstructured data is not sufficient.

Terabytes of structured data currently exist. NCR recently demonstrated the use of its database system on a 300 terabyte database [Holmes, 2004]. It is reasonable to expect databases to soon grow into the petabyte range. The study of database management systems (DBMS) focuses on the algorithms necessary to support thousands of concurrent users adding, deleting, updating, and retrieving structured data.

It is difficult to formally characterize *structured data.* Structured data are data that have a certain repetitive nature—data that fit within an easily recognizable datatype. Examples of structured data include *name, address, phone number, and salary.* Each occurrence of a structured data item is recognizable, sometimes it is possible to list only a few valid values for a structured data element (i.e., gender has only two valid values—*male* or *female*).

Airline reservation systems, automated teller machines, and credit card validation devices are all systems that pervade everyday life. Each is replete with structured data. One large production structured database has 300 terabytes and uses 1,1016 processors [Holmes, 2004].

There is clearly a need to integrate both structured data and text. Most production systems implemented with a relational database management system (RDBMS) have some text—such as a *comment* field—which allows users to enter a free text comment about a particular order. Commercial database systems allow users to store these unstructured fields in Binary Large OBject (BLOB) or Character Large OBjects (CLOB) datatypes unstructured data to be stored in a relation. The problem is that these unstructured fields cannot be accessed efficiently. Access methods such as inverted indexes found in information retrieval systems are lacking, and when they do exist, they are implemented in a non-standard fashion.

Similarly, information retrieval systems typically have large quantities of structured information, (i.e., author of a document, publication date, etc.) and usually have the ability to store data in *zoned* fields. These fields have a particular start and stop delimiter that identifies a *zone* in a document. The problem is that these structured fields cannot be accessed efficiently. Access methods for structured data (e.g., B-trees) and query optimization techniques that determine the best access method to the data are not usually found in information retrieval systems.

A database management system (DBMS) and an information retrieval system are analogous to a martial artist who is trained to fight others who are trained in the same art. A Tai Kwon Do master is capable of defending against other Tai Kwon Do masters. An information retrieval system is capable of efficiently handling unstructured data. A Judo master is capable of defending against other Judo masters. A database management system is capable of efficiently handling structured data. The problem arises when the Tai Kwon Do master faces a Judo master. This is analogous to accessing unstructured data in a structured database system.

The approach described in the remainder of this chapter is to build some unstructured data handling techniques on top of an existing relational database management system. This is analogous to teaching the Judo master some Tai Kwon Do techniques, but doing so in a way that still relies upon Judo.

It is possible to start with a database system and extend it to handle unstructured data or to start with an unstructured system and extend it to handle structured data. The approach taken in this chapter is to extend the database system. Information retrieval is then treated as an application of the database system (see Figure 6). The reason for this is that relational database systems, over the years, have developed substantially more infrastructure than information retrieval systems. Hence, to solve the integration problem, a straightforward approach is to start with an existing database system and add the necessary information retrieval functionality. In addition to providing integration, two additional benefits are obtained: parallel processing and dynamic updates.
Parallel processing takes advantage of multiple processors to improve run-time performance.

In Chapter 7, several parallel information retrieval algorithms are described. Although these algorithms do improve performance, none of them have shown particularly good speedup, that is, when additional processors are added they are not fully used. However, most major database vendors (i.e., IBM, Sybase, Oracle, Microsoft) all have parallel solutions. Some database vendors specialize in special-purpose parallel hardware that implements a proprietary database

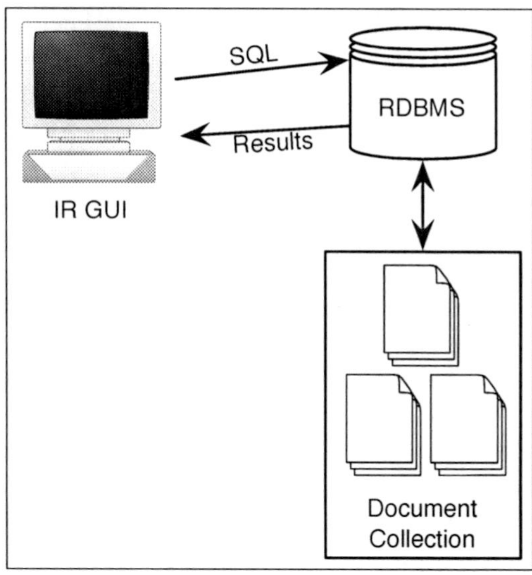

Figure 6.1. IR as an Application of a RDBMS

system (the NCR Teradata). Relational, set-theoretic operators are intrinsically unordered, and it is this lack of order that makes it easier to implement parallel operations. Treating information retrieval as a database application is intrinsically a parallel information retrieval algorithm because the underlying DBMS can be parallelized.

A second advantage of treating information retrieval as an application of a relational database management system (RDBMS) is that document data can be easily updated. Most information retrieval systems have a lengthy preprocessing phase in which the inverted index is constructed. To add, modify, or delete an existing document usually requires a process in which the inverted index is modified. Most information retrieval systems do not support on-line modifications to a document. A RDBMS has substantial infrastructure (concurrency control and recovery management) to ensure that updates may be done in real-time, and if an error occurs in the middle of an update, pieces of the update are not partially stored in the database systems.

A key question remains: Which database model should we use and how should the information retrieval functionality be added? Database system models include the inverted list, hierarchical, network, relational, and object-oriented models [Date, 1994]. Most current commercial systems rely upon the relational model. Although it is interesting to contemplate whether or not another model would be better suited for unstructured data, pragmatism dictates the use of the relational model. Sales of RDBMS software reached $7.1 billion in the past year. Using a different data model to obtain integration would mean that countless sites would have to convert their existing DBMS to a new model. The cost for this would be astronomical.

To gauge how long relational systems will dominate the market, it is useful to look at their predecessors. IMS, a hierarchical system, and IDMS, a network system, dominated the market in the 1970's. By 1980, both were well established. At that time, Oracle, the first relational vendor, was founded. Relational systems had been advocated heavily in the research community during the mid-1970's with substantial work having been done with a full-fledged prototype named System R.

IBM introduced its first commercial relational system, SQL/DS, in 1984 and its successor, DB2, in 1986. Relational systems did not gain significant market share until the early 1990's, a full ten years after Oracle was founded. We first use the relational model, and we later discuss the use of more recently developed multi-dimensional database systems.

The final question is: How should we use the relational model? Two choices exist: extend the relational engine or treat information retrieval as an application of an RDBMS.

Section 6.2 reviews prior attempts to extend the relational model. The main problem with these attempts is that they are all non-standard. Portability is lost because each relational extension is somewhat different, and users are not able to move applications from one system to another. Other problems are that query optimization must be modified to support any additions to the engine. Additionally, adding new functionality to the engine makes an already complex engine even more complex. Some additions allow users to add functions to the engine. This makes integrity an issue as a malicious or negligent user can intentionally or unintentionally introduce bugs into the database engine. Finally, parallel algorithms must be developed for each addition.

By treating information retrieval as an application of a RDBMS, these problems are eliminated. The key concern is to develop efficient unchanged Structured Query Language (SQL) algorithms that adhere to the ANSI SQL-2003 standard [SQL, 2003] for each type of information retrieval functionality. This chapter describes relational approaches for the following information retrieval functionality:

- Boolean keyword search
- Proximity search
- Relevance ranking with terms
- Relevance feedback

Relevance ranking with Spanish, phrases, passages, n-grams, and relevance feedback have all been implemented as an application of a relational DBMS with standard, unchanged SQL by using straightforward modifications to the approaches described in this chapter. Details are found in [Lundquist et al., 1997, Grossman et al., 1997].

In Section 6.1, we briefly review the relational model and SQL. A historical progression of integrating database technology with information retrieval functionality is provided in Section 6.2. In Section 6.3, we describe the algorithms used to treat the previously described information retrieval strategies and utilities together as an application of a relational system. Only standard SQL is used.

Next, in Section 6.4, we describe a method to support semi-structured data search. Here, we provide a description of how a fully featured XML retrieval engine can be built, once again, as an application of a relational database system. Thus, as a whole, we demonstrate the integration, all via standard relational database techniques, of structured, semi-structured, and text data.

Continuing with Section 6.5, we describe the use of a multi-dimensional data model to support the integration of hierarchically structured data and text. Using this approach, naturally occurring hierarchies can be supported directly by the integrating fabric.

Finally, in the section on mediators, Section 6.6, we review a method to integrate disparate data stored geographically across multiple domains that supports a question-answer paradigm. As always, a summary and our future projections conclude this chapter.

6.1 Review of the Relational Model

The relational model was initially described by Codd [Codd, 1970]. Prior data models were navigational, in that application developers had to indicate the means by which the database should be traversed. They specifically described how to find the data. The relational model stores data in relations and enables the developer to simply describe *what* data are required, not *how* to obtain the data. During the early 1970's, relational systems were not developed as they incur additional computational and storage overhead. Over the years, algorithms were developed to improve query optimization. These algorithms reduce the amount of overhead expended when using a relational system.

Over time, the benefits of the relational model have outmatched the costs, and the relational model is now the centerpiece of most production database systems. For some extremely high-performance applications, navigational systems are used, but relational systems have prevailed.

Table 6.1. Employee (EMP)

emp_no	*emp_name*	*age*	*salary*
100	Hank	35	$10,000
200	Fred	40	$20,000
300	Mary	25	$30,000
400	Sue	23	$40,000
500	Mike	30	$50,000

6.1.1 Relational Database, Primitives and Nomenclature

A relational database system stores data in set-theoretic relations. An attribute within a relation is any symbol from a finite set $\mathcal{L} = \{A_0, A_1, A_2, \ldots, A_n\}$. A relation $\mathcal{R}$ on the set $\mathcal{L}$ is a subset of the Cartesian product dom(A_0)$\times$ dom(A_1) $\times$ dom(A_2) $\times$ ... dom(A_n) where dom(A_i) is the domain of A_i. R[$A_0 A_1 A_2 \ldots A_n$] represents $\mathcal{R}$ on the set $\{A_0, A_1, A_2, \ldots, A_n\}$ and is referred to as the schema of $\mathcal{R}$. In R[$A_0 A_1 A_2 \ldots A_n$], each column A_i is called an *attribute* of R, and is denoted as $R.A_i$.

Simply stated, each attribute contains values, preferably a singular value, chosen from a given domain of values. An attribute *color* can have a domain of *red, green, black, etc.* A relation is then a collection of attributes. A row, or *tuple*, in the relation has a value for each attribute such that the value comes from the domain for that attribute.

Each tuple of R is designated by $< a_0, a_1, a_2, \ldots, a_n >$, where $a_i \in$ dom(A_i). The value of attribute A_i of tuple $x \in R$ is denoted as x[A_i]. Similarly, if tuple $x \in R$, then x[W] is the value of the attributes of attribute set W in tuple x.

Table 6.2. Employee-Project (EMP_PROJ)

emp_no	*project*
100	A
100	B
100	C
200	B
300	A
300	C
400	A

Consider the relations EMP and EMP-PROJ (see Tables 6.1 and 6.2). Relation EMP has four attributes (*emp_no, emp_name, age, salary*) while the EMP-PROJ relation has two attributes (*emp_no, project*). The EMP relation contains a tuple for each employee in the organization indicating the employee's unique identification number, name, age, and salary. An employee can also be assigned to an arbitrary number of projects. Simply adding a *project* attribute to the EMP relation would not work since it would only hold a single value. Another solution—adding *project1, project2, project3* attributes is also inadequate because an employee may have worked on more than three projects. In this case, there would be no place to store the 4th to n^{th} project.

Data models primarily differ in how they handle this type of *multi-valued relationship.* This is referred to as a MANY-MANY relationship in that one employee can be assigned to many projects while a project can be assigned to many employees. In a navigational model, a pointer points from the EMP master record with all single-valued occurrences to a list that contains the multi-valued occurrences. A user who wishes to see which projects an employee is assigned to issues a request to traverse the link from the master record to the multi-valued list.

Additional relations are developed for the relational solution. In our case, a single relation EMP-PROJ can be added to store the multi-valued information. Notice that EMP-PROJ has an attribute *emp_no* that matches values in the EMP relation. Hence, employee number 100 works on projects A, B, and C. The key point is that no *a priori* link between EMP and EMP_PROJ exists. At query time, a user may request that all tuples having matching values in the two relations be obtained. In this fashion, the user has only specified *what* is required not *how* to obtain the data.

This is important since requests for data may occur on an ad hoc basis long after the database has been created and populated with data. The relational model is well-suited to ad hoc requests because work is not required to redefine relationships between the data. Additionally, data independence is intended to reduce application development time because developers are not forced to learn all of the intricacies of retrieving data from multi-valued relationships. The database optimizer makes decisions and chooses the best access path to the data.

A problem exists if it is necessary to track single-valued information about a project such as the delivery date for the completed project or the budget for the project. If the EMP-PROJ relation is modified to include these additional attributes, needless repetition occurs (see Table 6.3).

Notice the attributes *delivery_date* and *budget* are single-valued descriptors of a project (all dates are assumed to be represented as Julian dates, and hence, are single-valued descriptors). These are repeated for each employee who is working on a project. Employees 100, 300, and 400 all work on Project A, and the *delivery_date* and *budget* are replicated for each of these tuples. If an update was required (i.e., the budget increased), it would be necessary to update each occurrence. To avoid these problems, a third relation is typically used to store the single-valued data for PROJECT. It would appear as given (see Table 6.4).

Table 6.3. Employee-Project (EMP_PROJ)

emp_no	*project*	*delivery_date*	*budget*
100	A	06/30/1997	$90,000,000
100	B	09/15/1997	$25,000,000
100	C	03/31/1998	$60,000,000
200	B	09/15/1997	$25,000,000
300	A	06/30/1997	$90,000,000
300	C	03/31/1998	$60,000,000
400	A	06/30/1997	$90,000,000

Table 6.4. Project

project	*delivery_date*	Budget
A	06/30/1997	$90,000,000
B	09/15/1997	$25,000,000
C	03/31/1998	$60,000,000

At this point three relations exist, one to represent the EMP entity, one to represent the PROJECT entity, and one to represent the relation EMP_PROJ that exists between the two relations. It should be clear that an update to single-valued information about a project only involves a single tuple.

Peter Chen, in a seminal paper, described the entity-relationship (ER) diagram in which entities and relationships are defined first, and the actual underlying relations are subsequently defined [Chen, 1976]. Typically, for large relational systems, an ER diagram is developed to ensure the developers understand all of the relationships between the data. Once complete, a normalized database design is implemented.

Normalization is the process of ensuring the database design satisfies very specific rules developed to reinforce the consistency and integrity of the data. First Normal Form (1NF) simply indicates that data are stored in single-valued attributes. Our example relation, EMP, is clearly in 1NF. However, if the *name* attribute were expanded to allow the employee's full first and last name in the same attribute, this entity would no longer be in 1NF because the *name* attribute would permit the values for both the first and last names to coexist in a single data element.

A relation is in second normal form (2NF) if all attributes are fully dependent on the primary key of the relation. Our example of the modified EMP_PROJ relation is not in 2NF because the attributes of the relation *delivery_date* and *budget* are not fully dependent on the composite primary key of *emp_number* and *project*. Instead, *delivery_date* and *budget* are dependent solely on the *project* attribute. An entity is in third normal form (3NF) if all attributes of the entity are dependent on the primary key of the relation and are not also dependent on another key. The *primary key* is one or more attributes that uniquely identifies a tuple in a relation. A database should satisfy at least 3NF.

It should be clear that no *a priori* linkages exist between any of the relationships, and any linking of relations is done at query processing time rather than data definition time.

Since the relations are based on set theory, all typical set-theoretic operations: Cartesian product, union, intersection, and set difference are implemented in the relational model. Additional operations include:

Select—The selection on R[XYZ], denoted as $\sigma_{A=a}(R)$, is defined by:

$$\sigma_{A=a}(R) = \{x|x[A] = a, x \in R\}$$

where A is an attribute of R.

Project— The projection on R[XYZ], denoted as $\pi_A(R)$, is defined by:

$$\pi_A(R) = \{x[A]|x \in R\}$$

where A is a set of attributes of R.

Join— The join of two relations R[XYZ] and S[VWX] (sharing the common attribute X) is denoted as:

$$\text{R[XYZ]} \bowtie \text{S[VWX]} = \{x|\ \text{x[VWX]} \in \text{S and x[XYZ]} \in \text{R}\}$$

where V, W, X, Y, and Z are a disjoint set of attributes. If no common attribute exists, the join of R and S is the Cartesian product of R and S.

When the relational model was first proposed nearly thirty-five years ago, relational algebra and calculus were used to compute data manipulation. The select, project, and join operators form a part of relational algebra. Since this was not very user friendly, two different query languages QUEL and SQL (originally derived from SEQUEL) were developed. SQL became popular with IBM's adoption in its commercial database system, SQL/DS, in 1982 and with ANSI's adoption of the first SQL standard in 1985. Today, SQL is one of the few standards that is agreed upon by industry, academia, and various international standards committees. SQL-2003 was recently adopted [SQL, 2003].

A good overview of SQL can be found in [Date, 1994]. A SQL query has the structure:

```
SELECT <list of attributes>
   FROM <list of relations>
[ WHERE <list of conditions> ]
[ ORDER BY <list of attributes> ]
[ GROUP BY <list of attributes> ]
[ HAVING <list of conditions> ]
```

A list of attributes is specified after the SELECT keyword. The FROM clause indicates the relations that are used. The WHERE clause describes conditions that must be satisfied for a tuple to be returned. Hence, the entire query is actually a *specification of a result*. The following query indicates that only the employee numbers from the EMP table should be retrieved. It does not, in any form, indicate how the employee numbers should be retrieved. Another form includes the addition of a WHERE clause.

```
SELECT emp_no
   FROM EMP
```

The following query indicates that only tuples with an *emp_no* of 400 are to be retrieved. Nothing is indicated as to how to find this tuple. If the system has a B-tree index on the *emp_no* attribute, an $O(\log n)$ algorithm traverses the tree and finds all such tuples, otherwise, a linear scan is used. In any event, the author of the query does not specify the algorithm to use to retrieve these data.

```
SELECT emp_no
   FROM EMP
   WHERE emp_no = 400
```

GROUP BY is used to partition the result set into groups and apply an aggregate function to the group. Aggregate functions in the SQL standard include COUNT (size of the partition), SUM (the total of an attribute in the partition), MIN (the smallest value in the partition), MAX (highest value in the partition), and AVG (average of all values in the partition). If a GROUP BY is not present, these operators work on the entire result set.

Consider a request to develop a report that contains each employee's number and the total number of projects to which they have been assigned. The following query obtains this information:

```
SELECT emp_no, COUNT(*)
   FROM EMP_PROJ
   GROUP BY emp_no
```

Grouping by the employee number partitions the EMP_PROJ relation into a partition for each employee. COUNT returns zero if no tuples are found. If a WHERE clause existed it would specify that the partitions should consider only the tuples identified by the WHERE clause.

HAVING restricts groups, typically based on an aggregate. The following query finds all employees who worked on at least 4 projects:

```
SELECT emp_no, COUNT(*)
   FROM EMP_PROJ
   GROUP BY emp_no
   HAVING COUNT(*) > 3
```

ORDER BY is used to sort the tuples in the order of the attributes specified in the ORDER BY clause. Since sets do not have any inherent ordering, the result set of a query may be obtained in an arbitrary order unless the ORDER BY clause is used. Executing this query results in a list comprising all employee numbers in ascending order (the DESC option must be used to obtain descending order).

```
SELECT emp_no
   FROM EMP_PROJ
   ORDER BY emp_no
```

A JOIN is implemented by first specifying multiple relations in the FROM clause and then adding the JOIN condition in the WHERE clause. The following query implements a join to find the age of all employees who worked on project A.

```
SELECT a.emp_no, a.age
   FROM EMP a, EMP_PROJ b
   WHERE a.emp_no = b.emp_no AND
            b.project = 'A'
```

This query joins the two relations. Again nothing is said about the join order or the order in which the WHERE clause is executed.

6.2 A Historical Progression

Previous work can be partitioned into systems that combine information retrieval and DBMS together, or systems that extend relational DBMS to include information retrieval functionality. We now describe each of these approaches in detail.

6.2.1 Combining Separate Systems

Several researchers proposed integrated solutions which consist of writing a central layer of software to send requests to underlying DBMS and information retrieval systems [Schek and Pistor, 1982]. Queries are parsed and the structured portions are submitted as a query to the DBMS, while text search portions of the query are submitted to an information retrieval system. The results are combined and presented to the user. It does not take long to build this software, and since information retrieval systems and DBMS are readily available, this is often seen as an attractive solution.

The key advantage of this approach is that the DBMS and information retrieval system are commercial products that are continuously improved upon by vendors. Additionally, software development costs are minimized. The disadvantages include poor data integrity, portability, and run-time performance.

6.2.1.1 Data Integrity

Data integrity is sacrificed because the DBMS transaction log and the information retrieval transaction log are not coordinated. If a failure occurs in the middle of an update transaction, the DBMS will end in a state where the entire transaction is either completed or it is entirely undone. It is not possible to complete half of an update.

The information retrieval log (if present) would not know about the DBMS log. Hence, the umbrella application that coordinates work between the two systems must handle all recovery. Recovery done within an application is typically error prone and, in many cases, applications simply ignore this coding. Hence, if a failure should occur in the information retrieval system, the DBMS will not know about it. An update that must take place in both systems can succeed in the DBMS, but fail in the information retrieval system. A partial update is clearly possible, but is logically flawed.

6.2.1.2 Portability

Portability is sacrificed because the query language is not standard. Presently, a standard information retrieval query language does not exist. However, some work is being done to develop standard information retrieval query languages. If one existed, it would require many years for widespread commercial acceptance to occur. The problem is that developers must be retrained each time a new DBMS and information retrieval system is brought in. Additionally, system administration is far more difficult with multiple systems.

6.2.1.3 Performance

Run-time performance suffers because of the lack of parallel processing and query optimization. Although most commercial DBMS have parallel implementations, most information retrieval systems do not.

Query optimization exists in every relational DBMS. The optimizer's goal is to choose the appropriate access path to the data. A rule-based optimizer uses pre-defined rules, while a cost-based optimizer estimates the cost of using different access paths and chooses the cheapest one. In either case, no rules exist for the unstructured portion of the query and no cost estimates could be obtained because the optimizer would be unaware of the access paths that may be chosen by the information retrieval system. Thus, any optimization that included both structured and unstructured data would have to be done by the umbrella application. This would be a complex process. The difficulties with such optimization were discussed by the authors who suggested this approach [Lynch and Stonebraker, 1988]. Hence, run-time performance would suffer due to a lack of parallel algorithms and limited global query optimization.

6.2.1.4 Extensions to SQL

Blair, in an unpublished paper in 1974, proposed that SQL (actually a precursor named SEQUEL) could be modified to support text [Blair, 1974]. Subsequently, a series of papers between 1978 and 1981 were written that described several extensions to SQL [Macleod, 1978, Macleod, 1979, Crawford, 1981]. The SMART information retrieval prototype initially developed in the 1980's used the INGRES relational database system to store its data [Fox, 1983b].

These papers described extensions to support relevance ranking as well as Boolean searches. The authors focused on the problem of efficiently searching text in a RDBMS. They went on to indicate that the RDBMS would store the inverted index in another table thereby making it possible to easily view the contents of the index. An information retrieval system typically hides the inverted index as simply an access structure that is used to obtain data. By storing the index as a relation, the authors pointed out that users could easily view the contents of the index and make changes if necessary. The authors mentioned extensions, such as RELEVANCE(*), that would compute the relevance of a document to a query using some pre-defined relevance function.

More recently, a language called SQLX was used to access documents in a multimedia database [Ozkarahan, 1995]. SQLX assumes that an initial cluster-based search has been performed based on keywords (see Section 3.2 for a description of document clustering). SQLX extensions allow for a search of the results with special connector attributes that obviate the need to explicitly specify joins.

6.2.2 User-defined Operators

User-defined operators that allow users to modify SQL by adding their own functions to the DBMS engine were described as early as [Stonebraker et al., 1983]. Commercialization of this idea has given rise to several products including the Teradata Multimedia Object Manager, Oracle Cartridges, IBM DB2 Text Extender, as well as features in Microsoft SQL Server [Connell et al., 1996, Loney, 1997]. An example query that uses the user-defined area function is given below. Area must be defined as a function that accepts a single argument. The datatype of the argument is given as rectangle. Hence, this example uses both a user-defined function and a user-defined datatype.

Ex: 1
```
SELECT MAX(AREA(Rectangle))
  FROM SHAPE
```

In the information retrieval domain, an operator such as *proximity()* could be defined to compute the result set for a proximity search. In this fashion the "spartan simplicity of SQL" is preserved, but users may add whatever functionality is needed. A few years later user-defined operators were defined to implement information retrieval [Lynch and Stonebraker, 1988].
The following query obtains all documents that contain the terms *term1*, *term2*, and *term3*:

Ex: 2
```
SELECT Doc_Id
  FROM DOC
 WHERE SEARCH-TERM(Text, Term1, Term2, Term3)
```

This query can take advantage of an inverted index to rapidly identify the terms. To do this, the optimizer would need to be made aware of the new access method. Hence, user-defined functions also may require user-defined access methods.

The following query uses the proximity function to ensure that the three query terms are found within a window of five terms.

Ex: 3
```
SELECT Doc_Id
  FROM DOC
 WHERE PROXIMITY(Text, 5, Term1, Term2, Term3)
```

The advantages of user-defined operators are that they not only solve the problem for text, but also solve it for spatial data, image processing, etc. Users may add whatever functionality is required. The key problems with user-defined operators again are integrity, portability, and run-time performance.

6.2.2.1 Integrity

User-defined operators allow application developers to add functionality to the DBMS rather than the application that uses the DBMS. This unfortunately opens the door for application developers to circumvent the integrity of the DBMS. For user-defined operators to be efficient, they must be linked into the same module as the entire DBMS, giving them access to the entire address space of the DBMS. Data that reside in memory or on disk files that are currently opened, can be accessed by the user-defined operator. It is possible that the user-defined operator could corrupt these data.

To protect the DBMS from a faulty user-defined operator, a remote procedure call (RPC) can be used to invoke the user-defined operator. This ensures the operator has access only to its address space, not the entire DBMS address space. Unfortunately, the RPC incurs substantial overhead, so this is not a solution for applications that require high performance.

6.2.2.2 Portability

A user-defined operator implemented at SITE A may not be present at SITE B. Worse, the operator may appear to exist, but it may perform an entirely different function. Without user-defined operators, anyone with an RDBMS may write an application and expect it to run at any site that runs that RDBMS. With user-defined operators, this perspective changes as the application is limited to only those sites with the user-defined operator.

6.2.2.3 Performance

Query optimization, by default, does not know much about the specific user-defined operators. Optimization is often based on substantial information about the query. A query with an EQUAL operator can be expected to retrieve fewer rows than a LESS THAN operator. This knowledge assists the optimizer in choosing an access path.

Without knowing the semantics of a user-defined operator, the optimizer is unable to efficiently use it. Some user-defined operators might require a completely different access structure like an inverted index. Unless the optimizer knows that an inverted index is present and should be included in path selection, this path is not chosen.

Lynch's work discussed information that must be stored with each user-defined operator to assist with query optimization. For user-defined operators to gain widespread acceptance, some means of providing information about them to the optimizer is needed.

Additionally, parallel processing of a user-defined operator would be something that must be defined inside of the user-defined operator. The remainder of the DBMS would have no knowledge of the user-defined operator, and as such, would not know how to parallelize the operator.

6.2.3 Non-first Normal Form Approaches

Non-first normal form (NFN) approaches have also been proposed [Desai et al., 1987, Schek and Pistor, 1982, Niemi and Jarvelin, 1995]. The idea is that many-many relationships are stored in a cumbersome fashion when 3NF (third normal form) is used. Typically, two relations are used to store the entities that share the relationship, and a separate relation is used to store the relationship between the two entities.

For an inverted index, a many-many relationship exists between documents and terms. One term may appear in many documents, while one document may have many terms. This, as will be shown later, may be modelled with a DOC relation to store data about documents, a TERM relation to store data about individual terms, and an INDEX relation to track an occurrence of a term in a document.

Instead of three relations, a single NFN relation could store information about a document, and a nested relation would indicate which terms appeared in that document.

Although this is clearly advantageous from a run-time performance standpoint, portability is a key issue. No standards currently exist for NFN collections. Additionally, NFN makes it more difficult to implement ad hoc queries.

Since both user-defined operators and NFN approaches have deficiencies, we describe an approach using the unchanged, standard relational model to implement a variety of information retrieval functionality. This approach was shown to support integrity and portability while still yielding acceptable run-time performance [Grossman et al., 1997].

Some applications, such as image processing or CAD/CAM may require user-defined operators, as their processing is fundamentally not set-oriented and is difficult to implement with standard SQL.

6.2.4 Bibliographic Search with Unchanged SQL

Blair explored the potential of relational systems to provide typical information retrieval functionality [Blair, 1988]. Blair's work included queries using structured data (e.g., affiliation of an author) with unstructured data (e.g., text found in the title of a document). The following relations model the document collection.

- DIRECTORY(*name*, *institution*)—identifies the author's name and the institution the author is affiliated with.
- AUTHOR(*name, DocId*)—indicates who wrote a particular document.
- INDEX(*term, DocId*)—identifies terms used to index a particular document

The following query ranks institutions based on the number of publications that contain *input_term* in the document.

Ex: 4
```
SELECT UNIQUE institution, COUNT(UNIQUE name)
   FROM DIRECTORY
   WHERE name IN
      (SELECT name
         FROM AUTHOR
         WHERE DocId IN
            SELECT DocId
               FROM INDEX
            WHERE term = input_term
            ORDER BY 2 DESCENDING)
```

Blair cites several benefits for using the relational model as a foundation for document retrieval. These benefits are the basis for providing typical information retrieval functionality in the relational model, so we will list some of them here.

- Recovery routines
- Performance measurement facilities
- Database reorganization routines
- Data migration routines
- Concurrency control
- Elaborate authorization mechanisms
- Logical and physical data independence
- Data compression and encoding routines
- Automatic enforcement of integrity constraints
- Flexible definition of transaction boundaries (e.g., commit and rollback)
- Ability to embed the query language in a sequential applications language

6.3 Information Retrieval as a Relational Application

Work with extensions to SQL started first in an unpublished paper [Blair, 1974] and continued with several papers by Macleod and Crawford between 1978 and 1981 [Macleod, 1978, Crawford, 1981].

Initial extensions described by Macleod are based on the use of a QUERY (*term*) relation that stores the terms in the query, and an INDEX (*DocId, term*) relation that indicates which terms appear in which documents. The following query lists all the identifiers of documents that contain at least one term in QUERY:

Ex: 5
```
SELECT DISTINCT(i.DocId)
  FROM INDEX i, QUERY q
 WHERE i.term = q.term
```

Frequently used terms or stop terms are typically eliminated from the document collection. Therefore, a STOP_TERM relation may be used to store the frequently used terms. The STOP_TERM relation contains a single attribute (*term*). A query to identify documents that contain any of the terms in the query except those in the STOP_TERM relation is given below:

Ex: 6
```
SELECT DISTINCT(i.DocId)
  FROM INDEX i, QUERY q, STOP_TERM s
 WHERE i.term = q.term AND
       i.term ≠ s.term
```

Finally, to implement a logical AND of the terms *InputTerm1*, *InputTerm2*, and *InputTerm3*, Macleod and Crawford proposed the following query:

Ex: 7
```
SELECT DocId
  FROM INDEX
 WHERE term = InputTerm1
INTERSECT
 SELECT DocId
  FROM INDEX
 WHERE term = InputTerm2
INTERSECT
 SELECT DocId
  FROM INDEX
 WHERE term = InputTerm3
```

The query consists of three components. Each component results in a set of documents that contain a single term in the query. The INTERSECT keyword is used to find the intersection of the three sets. After processing, an AND is implemented.

Macleod and Crawford went on to present extensions for relevance ranking. The key extension was a *corr()* function—a built-in function to determine the similarity of a document to a query.

The SEQUEL (a precursor to SQL) example that was given was:

Ex: 8
```
SELECT DocId
   FROM INDEX i, QUERY q
  WHERE i.term = q.term
GROUP BY DocId
HAVING CORR() > 60
```

Other extensions, such as the ability to obtain the first n tuples in the answer set, were given. Macleod and Crawford gave detailed design examples as to how a document retrieval system should be treated as a database application.

We now describe work that relies on the unchanged relational model to implement information retrieval functionality with standard SQL [Grossman et al., 1997]. First, a discussion of preprocessing text into files for loading into a relational DBMS is required.

6.3.1 Preprocessing

Input text is originally stored in source files either at remote sites or locally on CD-ROM. For purposes of this discussion, it is assumed that the data files are in ASCII or can be easily converted to ASCII with SGML markers. SGML markers are a standard means by which different portions of the document are marked [Goldfarb, 1990]. The markers in the working example are found in the TIPSTER collection which was in previous years as the standard dataset for TREC. These markers begin with a < and end with a > (e.g., <TAG>).

A preprocessor that reads the input file and outputs separate flat files is used. Each term is read and checked against a list of SGML markers. The main algorithm for the preprocessor simply parses terms and then applies a hash function to hash them into a small hash table. If the term has not occurred for this document, a new entry is added to the hash table. Collisions are handled by a single linked list associated with the hash table. If the term already exists, its term frequency is updated. When an end-of-document marker is encountered, the hash table is scanned. For each entry in the hash table a record is generated. The record contains the document identifier for the current document, the term, and its term frequency. Once the hash table is output, the contents are set to NULL and the process repeats for the next document. A variety of experiments designed to identify the most efficient means of implementing the preprocessor are given in [Pulley, 1994].

After processing, two output files are stored on disk. The output files are then bulk-loaded into a relational database. Each file corresponds to a relation. The first relation, DOC, contains information about each document.

The second relation, INDEX, models the inverted index and indicates which term appears in which document and how often the term has appeared.

The relations are:

INDEX(*DocId, Term, TermFrequency*)

DOC(*DocId, DocName, PubDate, Dateline*).

These two relations are built by the preprocessor. A third TERM relation tracks statistics for each term based on its number of occurrences across the document collection. At a minimum, this relation contains the document frequency (df) and the inverse document frequency (idf). These were described in Section 2.1. The term relation is of the form: TERM(*Term, Idf*).

It is possible to use an application programming interface (API) so that the preprocessor stores data directly into the database. However, for some applications, the INDEX relation has one hundred million tuples or more. This requires one hundred million separate calls to the DBMS INSERT function. With each insert, a transaction log is updated. All relational DBMS provide some type of bulk-load facility in which a large flat file may be quickly migrated to a relation without significant overhead. Logging is often turned off (something not typically possible via an on-line API) and most vendors provide efficient load implementations. For parallel implementations, flat files are loaded using multiple processors. This is much faster than anything that can be done with the API.

For all examples in this chapter, assume the relations were initially populated via an execution of the preprocessor, followed by a bulk load. Notice that the DOC and INDEX tables are output by the preprocessor. The TERM relation is not output. In the initial testing of the preprocessor, it was found that this table was easier to build using the DBMS than within the preprocessor. To compute the TERM relation once the INDEX relation is created, the following SQL statement is used:

Ex: 9

```
INSERT INTO TERM
    SELECT Term, log(N / COUNT(*))
     FROM INDEX
    GROUP BY Term
```

N is the total number of documents in the collection, and it is usually known prior to executing this query. However, if it is not known then SELECT COUNT(*) FROM DOC will obtain this value. This statement partitions the INDEX relation by each term, and COUNT(*) obtains the number of documents represented in each partition (i.e., the document frequency). The *idf* is computed by dividing N by the document frequency.

Consider the following working example. Input text is provided, and the preprocessor creates two files which are then loaded into the relational DBMS to form DOC and INDEX. Subsequently, SQL is used to populate the TERM relation.

6.3.2 A Working Example

Throughout this chapter, the following working example is used. Two documents are taken from the TIPSTER collection and modelled using relations. The documents contain both structured and unstructured data and are given below.

```
<DOC>
<DOCNO> WSJ870323-0180 </DOCNO>
<HL> Italy's Commercial Vehicle Sales </HL>
<DD> 03/23/87 </DD>
<DATELINE> TURIN, Italy </DATELINE>
<TEXT>
Commercial-vehicle sales in Italy rose 11.4% in February from a year earlier,
to 8,848 units, according to provisional figures from the Italian Association of Auto Makers.
</TEXT>
</DOC>
```

```
<DOC>
<DOCNO> WSJ870323-0161 </DOCNO>
<HL> Who's News: Du Pont Co. </HL>
<DD> 03/23/87 </DD>
<DATELINE> Du Pont Company, Wilmington, DE </DATELINE>
<TEXT>
John A. Krol was named group vice president, Agriculture Products department,
of this diversified chemicals company, succeeding Dale E. Wolf, who will retire
May 1. Mr. Krol was formerly vice president in the Agricultural Products department.
</TEXT>
</DOC>
```

The preprocessor accepts these two documents as input and creates the two files that are then loaded into the relational DBMS. The corresponding DOC and INDEX relations are given in Tables 6.5 and 6.6.

Table 6.5. DOC

DocId	**DocName**	**PubDate**	**Dateline**
1	WSJ870323-0180	3/23/87	TURIN, Italy
2	WSJ870323-0161	3/23/87	Du Pont Company, Wilmington, DE

Table 6.6. INDEX

DocId	**Term**	**TermFrequency**
1	commercial	1
1	vehicle	1
1	sales	1
1	italy	1
1	february	1
1	year	1
1	according	1
...	...	...
2	krol	2
2	president	2
2	diversified	1
2	company	1
2	succeeding	1
2	dale	1
2	products	2
...	...	...

INDEX models an inverted index by storing the occurrences of a term in a document. Without this relation, it is not possible to obtain high performance text search within the relational model. Simply storing the entire document in a Binary Large OBject (BLOB) removes the storage problem, but most searching operations on BLOB's are limited, in that BLOB's typically cannot be indexed. Hence, any search of a BLOB involves a linear scan, which is significantly slower than the $O(log\ n)$ nature of an inverted index.

In a typical information retrieval system, a lengthy preprocessing phase occurs in which parsing is done and all stored terms are identified. A posting list that indicates, for each term, which documents contain that term is identified (see Section 5.1 for a brief overview of inverted indexes). A pointer from the term to the posting list is implemented. In this fashion, a hashing function can be used to quickly jump to the term, and the pointer can be followed to the posting list. This inverted file technique is so effective that it was used in some of the earliest structured systems in the mid-1960's such as TDBMS [Bleir, 1967].

The fact that one term can appear in many documents and one document contains many terms indicates that a many-many relationship exists between terms and documents. To model this, *document* and *term* may be thought of as entities (analogous to *employee* and *project*), and a linking relation that describes the relationship EMP_PROJ must be modeled. The INDEX relation described below models the relationship. A tuple in the INDEX relation is equivalent to an assertion that a given term appears in a given document.

Note that the term frequency (*tf*) or number of occurrences of a term within a document, is a specific characteristic of the APPEARS-IN relationship; thus, it is stored in this table. The primary key for this relation is (*DocId,Term*), hence, term frequency is entirely dependent upon this key.

For proximity searches such as "Find all documents in which the phrase *vice president* exists," an additional *offset* attribute is required. Without this, the INDEX relation indicates that *vice* and *president* co-occur in the same document, but no information as to their location is given. To indicate that *vice* is adjacent to *president*, the offset attribute identifies the current term offset in the document. The first term is given an offset of zero, the second an offset of one, and, in general, the $n^{\underline{th}}$ is given an offset of $n-1$. The INDEX_PROX relation given in Table 6.7 contains the necessary *offset* attribute required to implement proximity searches.

Several observations about the INDEX_PROX relation should be noted. Since stop words are not included, offsets are not contiguously numbered. An offset is required for each occurrence of a term. Thus, terms are listed multiple times instead of only once, as was the case in the original INDEX relation.

Table 6.7. INDEX_PROX

DocId	**Term**	**Offset**
1	commercial	0
1	vehicle	1
1	sales	2
1	italy	4
1	rose	5
1	february	8
1	year	11
...	...	...
1	makers	26
...	...	...
2	krol	2
...	...	...

To obtain the INDEX relation from INDEX_PROX, the following statement can be used:

Ex: 10
```
INSERT INTO INDEX
    SELECT DocId, Term, COUNT(*)
      FROM INDEX_PROX
    GROUP BY DocId, Term
```

Finally, single-valued information about terms is required. The TERM relation (see Table 6.8) contains the *idf* for a given term. To review, a term that occurs frequently has a low *idf* and is assumed to be relatively unimportant. A term that occurs infrequently is assumed very important. Since each term has only one *idf*, this is a single-valued relationship which is stored in a collection-wide single TERM relation.

Table 6.8. TERM

Term	**Idf**
according	0.9031
commercial	1.3802
company	0.6021
dale	2.3856
diversified	2.5798
february	1.4472
italy	1.9231
krol	4.2768
president	0.6990
products	0.9542
...	...
...	...
sales	1.0000
succeeding	2.6107
vehicle	1.8808
year	0.4771
...	...

To maintain a syntactically fixed set of SQL queries for information retrieval processing, and to reduce the syntactic complexities of the queries themselves, a QUERY relation is used. The QUERY relation (see Table 6.9) contains a single tuple for each query term. Queries are simplified because the QUERY relation can be joined to INDEX to see if any of the terms in QUERY are found in INDEX. Without QUERY, a lengthy WHERE clause is required to specifically request each term in the query.

Finally, STOP_TERM (see Table 6.10) is used to indicate all of the terms that are omitted during the parsing phase. This relation is not used in this chapter, but illustrates that the relational model can store internal structures that are used during data definition and population.

Table 6.9. QUERY

Term	**tf**
vehicle	1
sales	1

Table 6.10. STOP_TERM

Term
a
an
and
...
the
...

The following query illustrates the potential of this approach. The SQL satisfies the request to "Find all documents that describe *vehicles* and *sales* written on 3/23/87." The keyword search covers unstructured data, while the publication date is an element of structured data.

This example is given to quickly show how to integrate both structured data and text. Most information retrieval systems support this kind of search by making DATE a "zoned field"—a portion of text that is marked and always occurs in a particular section or *zone* of a document. These fields can then be parsed and stored in a relational structure. Example 6.1.1 illustrates a sequence of queries that use much more complicated unstructured data, which could not easily be queried with an information retrieval system.

Ex: 11
```
SELECT d.DocId
  FROM DOC d, INDEX i
 WHERE i.Term IN ("vehicle","sales") AND
       d.PubDate = "3/23/87" AND
       d.DocId = i.DocId
```

6.3.3 Boolean Retrieval

A Boolean query is given with the usual operators—AND, OR, and NOT. The result set must contain all documents that satisfy the Boolean condition.

For small bibliographic systems (e.g., card catalog systems), Boolean queries are useful. They quickly allow users to specify their information need and return all matches. For large document collections, they are less useful because the result set is unordered, and a query can result in thousands of matches. The user is then forced to tune the Boolean conditions and retry the query until the result is obtained. Relevance ranking avoids this problem by ranking documents based on a measure of relevance between the documents and the query. The user then looks at the top-ranked documents and determines whether or not they fill the information need.

We start with the use of SQL to implement Boolean retrieval. We then show how a proximity search can be implemented with unchanged SQL, and finally, a relevance ranking implementation with SQL is described.

The following SQL query returns all documents that contain an arbitrary term, *InputTerm*.

Ex: 12
```
SELECT DISTINCT(i.DocId)
  FROM INDEX i
 WHERE i.Term = InputTerm
```

Obtaining the actual text of the document can now be performed in an application specific fashion. The text is found in a single large attribute that contains a BLOB or CLOB (binary or character large object), possibly divided into separate components (i.e., paragraphs, lines, sentences, phrases, etc.). If the text is found in a single large attribute (in this example we call it *Text*), the query can be extended to execute a subquery to obtain the document identifiers. Then the identifiers can be used to find the appropriate text in DOC.

Ex: 13
```
SELECT d.Text
  FROM DOC d
 WHERE d.DocId IN
        (SELECT DISTINCT(i.DocId)
           FROM INDEX i
          WHERE i.Term = InputTerm)
```

For the remainder of the section, we are only concerned with obtaining the document identifiers found in the answer set. Either a separate query may be executed using the document identifiers in an application specific fashion or the queries can be extended in the form given in Example 13.

It is natural to attempt to extend the query in Example 12 to allow for n terms. If the Boolean request is an OR, the extension is straightforward and does not increase the number of joins found in the query.

Ex: 14
```
SELECT DISTINCT(i.DocId)
  FROM INDEX i
 WHERE i.Term = InputTerm1 OR
       i.Term = InputTerm2 OR
       i.Term = InputTerm3 OR
       ...
       i.Term = InputTermN
```

Unfortunately, a Boolean AND results in a dramatically more complex query. For a query containing n input terms, the INDEX relation must be joined n times. This results in the following query.

Ex: 15
```
SELECT a.DocId
  FROM INDEX a, INDEX b, INDEX c, ... INDEX n − 1, INDEX n
 WHERE a.Term = InputTerm_1 AND
       b.Term = InputTerm_2 AND
       c.Term = InputTerm_3 AND
       ...
       n.Term = InputTerm_n AND
       a.DocId = b.DocId AND
       b.DocId = c.DocId AND
       ...
       n − 1.DocId = n.DocId
```

Multiple joins are expensive. The order that the joins are computed affects performance, so a cost-based optimizer will compute costs for many of the orderings [Elmasri and Navathe, 1994]. Pruning the list is discussed in [Selinger, 1979], but it is still expensive.

In addition to performance concerns, the reality is that commercial systems are unable to implement more than a fixed number of joins. Although it is theoretically possible to execute a join of n terms, most implementions impose limits on the number of joins (around sixteen is common) [White and Date, 1989, McNally, 1997]. It is the complexity of this simple Boolean AND that has led many researchers to develop extensions to SQL or user-defined operators to allow for a more simplistic SQL query.

An approach that requires a fixed number of joins regardless of the number of terms found in the input query is given in [Grossman et al., 1997]. This reduces the number of conditions found in the query. However, an additional sort is needed (due to a GROUP BY) in the query where one previously did not exist.

The following query computes a Boolean AND using standard syntactically fixed SQL:

Ex: 16
```
SELECT i.DocId
  FROM INDEX i, QUERY q
 WHERE i.Term = q.Term
 GROUP BY i.DocId
 HAVING COUNT(i.Term) =
        (SELECT COUNT(*) FROM QUERY)
```

The WHERE clause ensures that only the terms in the query relation that match those in INDEX are included in the result set. The GROUP BY specifies that the result set is partitioned into groups of terms for each document. The HAVING ensures that the only groups in the result set will be those whose cardinality is equivalent to that of the query relation.

For a query with k terms $(t_1, t_2, \ldots, t_k)$, the tuples as given in Table 6.11 are generated for document d_i containing all k terms.

Table 6.11. Result Set

DocId	*term*
d_i	t_1
d_i	t_2
...	...
d_i	t_k

The GROUP BY clause causes the cardinality, k, of this document to be computed. At this point, the HAVING clause determines if the k terms in this group matches the number of terms in the query. If so, a tuple d_i appears in the final result set.

Until this point, we assumed that the INDEX relation contains only one occurrence of a given term for each document. This is consistent with our example where a term frequency is used to record the number of occurrences of a term within a document. In proximity searches, a term is stored multiple times in the INDEX relation for a single document. Hence, the query must be modified because a single term in a document might occur k times which results in d_i being placed in the final result set, even when it does not contain the remaining $k-1$ terms.

The following query uses the DISTINCT keyword to ensure that only the distinct terms in the document are considered. This query is used on INDEX relations in which term repetition in a document results in term repetition in the INDEX relation.

Ex: 17
```
SELECT i.DocId
  FROM INDEX i, QUERY q
WHERE i.Term = q.Term
GROUP BY i.DocId
HAVING COUNT(DISTINCT(i.Term))
        = (SELECT COUNT(*) FROM QUERY)
```

This query executes whether or not duplicates are present, but if it is known that duplicate terms within a document do not occur, this query is somewhat less efficient than its predecessor. The DISTINCT keyword typically requires a sort.

Using a set-oriented approach to Boolean keyword searches results in the fortunate side-effect that a Threshold AND (TAND) is easily implemented. A partial AND is one in which the condition is true if k subconditions are true. All of the subconditions are not required. The following query returns all documents that have k or more terms matching those found in the query.

Ex: 18
```
SELECT i.DocId
  FROM INDEX i,QUERY q
WHERE i.Term = q.Term
GROUP BY i.DocId
HAVING COUNT(DISTINCT(i.Term)) ≥ k
```

6.3.4 Proximity Searches

To briefly review, proximity searches are used in information retrieval systems to ensure that the terms in the query are found in a particular sequence or at least within a particular window of the document. Most users searching for a query of "vice president" do not wish to retrieve documents that contain the sentence, "His primary vice was yearning to be president of the company."

To implement proximity searches, the INDEX_PROX given in our working example is used. The *offset* attribute indicates the relative position of each term in the document.

The following query, albeit a little complicated at first glance, uses unchanged SQL to identify all documents that contain all of the terms in QUERY within a term window of *width* terms. For the query given in our working example, "vice" and "president" occur in positions seven and eight, respectively. Document two would be retrieved if a window of two or larger was used.

Ex: 19
```
SELECT a.DocId
  FROM INDEX_PROX a, INDEX_PROX b
 WHERE a.Term IN (SELECT q.Term FROM QUERY q) AND
   b.Term IN (SELECT q.Term FROM QUERY q) AND
   a.DocId = b.DocId AND
   (b.Offset - a.Offset) BETWEEN 0 AND (width - 1)
 GROUP BY a.DocId, a.Term, a.Offset
 HAVING COUNT(DISTINCT(b.Term)) =
 (SELECT COUNT(*) FROM QUERY)
```

The INDEX_PROX table must be joined to itself since the distance between each term and every other term in the document must be evaluated. For a document d_i that contains k terms $(t_1, t_2, \ldots, t_k)$ in the corresponding term offsets of $(o_1, o_2, \ldots, o_k)$, the first two conditions ensure that we are only examining offsets for terms in the document that match those in the query. The third condition ensures that the offsets we are comparing do not span across documents. The following tuples make the first three conditions evaluate to TRUE.

In Table 6.12, we illustrate the logic of the query. Drawing out the first step of the join of INDEX_PROX to itself for an arbitrary document d_i yields tuples in which each term in INDEX_TERM is matched with all other terms. This table shows only those terms within document d_i that matched with other terms in document d_i. This is because only these tuples evaluate to TRUE when the condition "a.DocId = b.DocId" is applied. We also assume that the terms in the table below match those found in the query, thereby satisfying the condition "b.term IN (SELECT q.term FROM QUERY)."

Table 6.12. Result of Self-Join of INDEX_PROX

a.DocId	*a.Term*	*a.Offset*	*b.DocId*	*b.Term*	*b.Offset*
d_i	t_1	o_1	d_i	t_1	o_1
d_i	t_1	o_1	d_i	t_2	o_2
d_i	t_1	o_1	d_i	t_k	o_k
d_i	t_2	o_2	d_i	t_1	o_1
d_i	t_2	o_2	d_i	t_2	o_2
d_i	t_2	o_2	d_i	t_k	o_k
d_i	t_k	o_k	d_i	t_1	o_1
d_i	t_k	o_k	d_i	t_2	o_2
d_i	t_k	o_k	d_i	t_k	o_k

The fourth condition examines the offsets and returns TRUE only if the terms exist within the specified window. The GROUP BY clause partitions each particular offset within a document. The HAVING clause ensures that the size of this partition is equal to the size of the query. If this is the case, the document has all of terms in QUERY within a window of size *offset*. Thus, document d_i is included in the final result set.

For an example query with "vehicle" and "sales" within a two term window, all four conditions of the WHERE clause evaluate to TRUE for the following tuples. The first three have eliminated those terms that were not in the query, and the fourth eliminated those terms that were outside of the term window. The GROUP BY clause results in a partition in which "vehicle", at offset one, is in one partition and "sales", at offset two, is in the other partition. The first partition has two terms which match the size of the query, so document one is included in the final result set (see Table 6.13).

Table 6.13. Result After All Four Conditions of the WHERE Clause

a.DocId	*a.Term*	*a.Offset*	*b.DocId*	*b.Term*	*b.Offset*
1	vehicle	1	1	vehicle	1
1	vehicle	1	1	sales	2
1	sales	2	1	sales	2

6.3.5 Computing Relevance Using Unchanged SQL

Relevance ranking is critical for large document collections as a Boolean query frequently returns many thousands of documents. Recent World Wide Web search engines such as *Google* and *Yahoo!*, as well as commercial information retrieval systems such as Convera's *RetrievalWare* and Verity's *Topic*, all implement relevance ranking. Numerous algorithms exist to compute a measure of similarity between a query and a document. We have discussed many of these variations in Chapter 2.

As we previously mentioned in Section 2.1, the vector-space model is commonly used. Systems based on this model have repeatedly performed well at the Text REtrieval Conference (TREC). Recall, that in the vector space model, documents and queries are represented by a vector of size t, where t is the number of distinct terms in the document collection (see Section 2.1). The distance between the query vector Q and the document vector D_i is used to rank documents. The following dot product measure computes this distance:

$$SC(Q, D_i) = \sum_{j=1}^{t} w_{qj} \times d_{ij}$$

where w_{qj} is weight of the $j^{\underline{th}}$ term in the query q, and d_{ij} is the weight of the $j^{\underline{th}}$ term in the $i^{\underline{th}}$ document.

In the simplest case, each component of the vector is assigned a weight of zero or one (one indicates that the term corresponding to this component exists). Numerous weighting schemes exist, an example of which is *tf-idf*.

Here, the term frequency is combined with the inverse document frequency (see Section 2.2.1). The following SQL implements a dot product query with the *tf-idf* weight.

Ex: 20
```
SELECT i.DocId, SUM(q.tf * t.idf * i.tf * t.idf)
  FROM QUERY q, INDEX i, TERM t
 WHERE q.Term = t.Term AND
       i.Term = t.Term
 GROUP BY i.DocId
 ORDER BY 2 DESC
```

The WHERE clause ensures that only terms found in QUERY are included in the computation. Since all terms not found in the query are given a zero weight in the query vector, they do not contribute to the summation. The *idf* is obtained from the TERM relation and is used to compute the *tf-idf* weight in the select-list. The ORDER BY clause ensures that the result is sorted by the similarity coefficient.

At this point, we have used a simple similarity coefficient. Many variations of this coefficient are found in the literature [Salton, 1989]. Unchanged SQL can be used to implement these coefficients as well. Typically, the cosine coefficient or its variants is commonly used. The cosine coefficient is defined as:

$$SC(Q, D_i) = \frac{\sum_{j=1}^{t} w_{qj} d_{ij}}{\sqrt{\sum_{j=1}^{t}(d_{ij})^2 \sum_{j=1}^{t}(w_{qj})^2}}$$

The numerator is the same as the dot product, but the denominator requires a normalization which uses the size of the document vector and the size of the query vector. Each of these normalization factors could be computed at query time, but the syntax of the query becomes overly complex. To simplify the SQL, two separate relations are created: DOC_WT (*DocId, Weight*) and QUERY_WT (*Weight*). DOC_WT stores the size of the document vector for each document and QUERY_WT contains a single tuple that indicates the size of the query vector.

These relations may be populated with the following SQL:

Ex: 21
```
INSERT INTO DOC_WT
  SELECT DocId, SQRT(SUM(i.tf * t.idf * i.tf * t.idf))
    FROM INDEX i, TERM t
  WHERE i.Term = t.Term
  GROUP BY DocId
```

EX: 22
```
INSERT INTO QRY_WT
    SELECT SQRT(SUM(q.tf * t.idf * q.tf * t.idf))
        FROM QUERY q, TERM t
    WHERE q.Term = t.Term
```

For each of these INSERT-SELECT statements, the weights for the vector are computed, squared, and then summed to obtain a total vector weight. The following query computes the cosine.

EX: 23
```
SELECT i.DocId, SUM(q.tf * t.idf * i.tf * t.idf) /
                      (dw.Weight * qw.Weight)
  FROM QUERY q, INDEX i, TERM t, DOC_WT dw, QRY_WT qw
WHERE q.Term = t.Term AND
        i.Term = t.Term AND
        i.DocId = dw.DocId
GROUP BY i.DocId, dw.Weight, qw.Weight
ORDER BY 2 DESC
```

The inner product is modified to use the normalized weights by joining the two new relations, DOC_WT and QRY_WT. An additional condition is added to the WHERE clause in order to obtain the weight for each document.

To implement this coefficient, it is necessary to use the built-in square root function which is often present in many SQL implementations. We note that these queries can all be implemented without the non-standard square root function simply by squaring the entire coefficient. This modification does not affect the document ranking as $a \leq b \Rightarrow a^2 \leq b^2$ for $a, b \geq 0$. For simplicity of presentation, we used a built-in *sqrt* function (which is present in many commercial SQL implementations) to compute the square root of an argument.

Modifications to the SUM() element permit implementation of other similarity measures. For instance, with the additional computation and storage of some document statistics, (log of the average term frequency), some collection statistics (average document length and the number of documents) and term statistics (document frequency), pivoted normalization and a probabilistic measure can be implemented.

SQL for the pivoted normalization measure described in Section 2.1.2 and for the probabilistic measure described in Section 2.2.3 is given in [McCabe et al., 1999]. Essentially, the only change is that the SUM operator is modified to contain new weights. The result is that fusion of multiple similarity measures can be easily implemented in SQL. We will describe the use of a combination of similarity measures in more detail in Section 8.3.

6.3.6 Relevance Feedback in the Relational Model

Relevance feedback can be supported using the relational model [Lundquist et al., 1997]. Recall, relevance feedback is the process of adding new terms to a query based on documents presumed to be relevant in an initial running of the query (see Section 3.1). In this work, separate SQL statements were used for each of the following steps:

Step 1: Run the initial query. This is done using the SQL we have just described.

Step 2: Obtain the terms in the top n documents. A query of the INDEX relation given a list of document identifiers (these could be stored in a temporary relation generated by Step 1) will result in a distinct list of terms in the top n documents. This query will run significantly faster if the DBMS has the ability to limit the number of tuples returned by a single query (many commercial systems have this capability). An INSERT-SELECT can be used to insert the terms obtained in this query into the QUERY relation.

Step 3: Run the modified query. The SQL remains the same as used in Step 1.

6.3.7 A Relational Information Retrieval System

The need to integrate structured and unstructured data led to the development of a scalable, standard SQL-based information retrieval prototype engine called SIRE [Frieder et al., 2000b, Frieder et al., 2003]. The SIRE approach, initial built for the National Institutes of Health National Center for Complementary and Alternative Medicine, leverages the investment of the commercial relational database industry by running as an application of the Oracle DBMS. It also includes all the capabilities of the more traditional customized information retrieval approach. Furthermore, additional functionality common in the relational database world, such as concurrency control, recovery, security, portability, scalability, and robustness, are provided without additional effort. Such functionality is not common in the traditional information retrieval market. Also, since database vendors continuously improve these features and likewise incorporate advances made in hardware and software, a SIRE-based solution keeps up with the technology curve with less investment on the part of the user as compared to a more traditional (custom) information retrieval system solution.

To demonstrate the applicability and versatility of SIRE, key information retrieval strategies and utilities such as leading similarity measures, proximity searching, n-grams, passages, phrase indexing, and relevance feedback were all implemented using standard SQL. By implementing SIRE on a host of relational database platforms including NCR DBC-1012, Microsoft SQL Server, Sybase, Oracle, IBM DB2 and SQL/DS, and even mySQL, system portability was demonstrated. Efficiency was enhanced using several optimization approaches including some described earlier (see Chapter 5) and some specific to relational database technology. These included the use of a pruned index and query thresholds as well as clustered indexes. All of these optimizations reduced the I/O volume, hence significantly reduced query execution time. Additional implementation details, including a query-processing framework that supported query and result caching, are found in [Frieder et al., 2000b].

More recent related efforts have focused on scaling the SIRE-based approach using parallel technology and incorporating efficient document updating into the paradigm. With the constant changes to text available particularly in Web environments, updating of the documents is becoming a necessity. Traditionally, information retrieval was a "read only" environment. Early parallel processing efforts used an NCR machine configured with 24 processors and achieved a speedup of 22-fold on [Lundquist et al., 1999]. A later effort at the University of Tokyo [Goda et al., 2001] demonstrated further scalability using the SIRE approach on a 100+ node PC cluster. At ETH-Zurich, researchers showed that the SIRE approach can be used to improve throughput for document insertion and update as well as simple retrieval [Grabs et al., 2001].

6.4 Semi-Structured Search using a Relational Schema

Numerous proprietary approaches exist for searching eXtensible Markup Language (XML) documents, but these lack the ability to integrate with other structured or unstructured data. Relational systems have been used to support XML by building a separate relational schema to map to a particular XML schema or DTD (Document-type Definitions) [Schmidt et al., 2000, Shanmugasundaram et al., 1999]. An approach which uses a static relational schema was described in [Florescu and Kossman, 1999] and additional support for a full implementation of an XML query language XML-QL is also described [Deutsch et al., 1999]. More recently, algorithms that translate XQuery expressions to SQL were presented [DeHaan et al., 2003].

6.4.1 Background

XML has become the standard for platform-independent data exchange [Buneman et al., 1996, Goldman et al., 1999]. There were a variety of methods proposed for storing XML data and accessing them efficiently [Abiteboul, 1997].

One approach is a customized tree file structure, but this lacks portability and does not leverage existing database technology [Kanne and Moerkotte, 2000]. Other approaches include building a database system specifically tailored to storing semi-structured data from the ground up [McHugh et al., 1997, Quass et al., 1996] or using a full inverted index [Shin, 1998].

There are several popular XML query languages [Luk et al., 2002, Deutsch et al., 1999, Bonifati and Ceri, 2000]. In August 1997, initial work on XPath, touted as a basic path-based query language, was submitted to the W3C (World Wide Web Consortium). In 1998, XML-QL, a query language developed at AT&T [Deutsch et al., 1999], was designed to meet the requirements of a full-featured XML query language set out by the W3C. The specification describing XPath as it is known today was released in 1999. In December 2001, XPath 2.0 was released. One of the newest semi-structured query languages, XQuery, is also among the most powerful. It borrows many ideas from prior work on other semi-structured query languages such as XML-QL and XPath, as well as from relational query languages like SQL. The first public draft of the XQuery 1.0 specification was released in June 2001 and has a current update as of May 2003. [Boag et al., 2003].

6.4.2 Static Relational Schema to support XML-QL

We now briefly describe a static relational schema that supports arbitrary XML schemas. This was first proposed in [Florescu and Kossman, 1999] to provide support for XML query processing. Later, in the IIT Information Retrieval Laboratory (**www.ir.iit.edu**), it was shown that a full XML-QL query language could be built using this basic structure. This is done by translating semi-structured XML-QL to SQL. The use of a static schema accommodates data of any XML schema without the need for document-type definitions or XSchemas.

The static relational storage schema stores each unique XML path and its value from each document as a separate row in a relation. This is similar to the edge table described in [Florescu and Kossman, 1999], named for the fact that each row corresponds to an edge in the XML graph representation. This static relational schema is capable of storing an arbitrary XML document.

The hierarchy of XML documents is kept in tact such that any document indexed into the database can be reconstructed using only the information in the tables. The relations used are:

TAG_NAME (*TagId, tag*) ATTRIBUTE (*AttributeId, attribute*)
TAG_PATH (*TagId, path*) DOCUMENT (*DocId, fileName*)
INDEX (*Id, parent, path, type, tagId, attrId, pos, value*)

For the remainder of this section, consider once again our sample text.

```
<DOC>
<DOCNO> WSJ870323-0180 </DOCNO>
<HL> Italy's Commercial Vehicle Sales </HL>
<DD> 03/23/87 </DD>
<DATELINE> TURIN, Italy </DATELINE>
<TEXT>
Commercial-vehicle sales in Italy rose 11.4% in February from a year earlier,
to 8,848 units, according to provisional figures from the Italian Association of Auto Makers.
</TEXT>
</DOC>

<DOC>
<DOCNO> WSJ870323-0161 </DOCNO>
<HL> Who's News: Du Pont Co. </HL>
<DD> 03/23/87 </DD>
<DATELINE> Du Pont Company, Wilmington, DE </DATELINE>
<TEXT>
John A. Krol was named group vice president, Agriculture Products department,
of this diversified chemicals company, succeeding Dale E. Wolf, who will retire
May 1. Mr. Krol was formerly vice president in the Agricultural Products department.
</TEXT>
</DOC>
```


6.4.3 Storing XML Metadata

These tables store the metadata (data about the data) of the XML files. TAG_NAME (see Table 6.14) and TAG_PATH (see Table 6.15) together store the information about tags and paths within the XML file. TAG_NAME stores the name of each unique tag in the XML collection. TAG_PATH stores the unique paths found in the XML documents. The ATTRIBUTE (see Table 6.16) relation stores the names of all the attributes. In our example, we have added an attribute called LANGUAGE which is an attribute of the tag TEXT. In the TAG_NAME and TAG_PATH relations, the *tagId* is a unique key assigned by the preprocessing stage. Similarly, *attributeId* is uniquely assigned as well. As with our examples earlier in the chapter, these tables are populated each time a new XML file is indexed. This process consists of parsing the XML file and extracting all of this information and storing it into these tables.

6.4.4 Tracking XML Documents

Since XML-QL allows users to specify what file(s) they wish to query, many times we do not want to look at each record in the database but only at a subset of records that correspond to that file. Each time a new file is indexed, it

Table 6.14. TAG_NAME

tagId	**tag**
10	DOC
11	DOCNO
12	HL
13	DD
14	DATELINE
15	TEXT

Table 6.15. TAG_PATH

tagId	**path**
10	[DOC]
11	[DOC, DOCNO]
12	[DOC, HL]
13	[DOC, DD]
14	[DOC,DATELINE]
15	[DOC,TEXT]

Table 6.16. ATTRIBUTE

AttributeId	**attribute**
7	LANGUAGE

receives a unique identifier that is known as the *pin* value. This value corresponds to a single XML file. The DOCUMENT relation contains a tuple for each XML document. For our example, we only store the actual file name that contains this document. An example of this relation is shown in Table 6.17. Other relevant attributes might include the length of the document – or the normalized length [Kamps et al., 2004].

Table 6.17. DOCUMENT

docId	**fileName**
2	doc_0.xml
3	doc_1.xml

6.4.5 INDEX

The INDEX table (see Table 6.18) models an XML index. It contains the mapping of each tag, attribute or value to each document that contains this value. Also, since the order of attributes and tags is important in XML (e.g.; there is a notion of the first occurrence, the second occurrence, etc.), the *position* or order of the tags is also stored.

The *id* column is a unique integer assigned to each element and attribute in a document. The *parent* attribute indicates the *id* of the tag that is the parent of the current tag. This is needed to preserve the inherently hierarchical nature of XML documents.

The *path* corresponds to the primary key value in the *TagPath*. The *type* indicates whether the path terminates with an element or an attribute (E or A). The *TagId* and *AttrId* is a foreign key to the *TagId* in the TagName and *Attribute* tables. The *DocId* attribute indicates the XML document for a given row. The *pos* tracks the order of a given tag and is used for queries that use the index expression feature of XML-QL and indicates the position of this element relative to others under the same parent (starting at zero). This column stores the original ordering of the input XML for explicit usage in users' queries. Finally, *value* contains the atomic unit in XML – the value inside the lowest level tags. Once we have reached the point of *value*, all of the prior means of using relations to model an inverted index for these values apply.

Table 6.18. INDEX

id	**parent**	**path**	**type**	**tagId**	**AttrId**	**docId**	**pos**	**value**
41	0	10	E	10	1	6	0	NULL
42	41	11	E	11	1	6	0	WSJ870323-0180
43	41	12	E	12	1	6	0	Italy's Commercial...
44	41	13	E	13	1	6	0	03/23/87
45	41	14	E	14	1	6	0	TURIN, Italy
46	41	15	E	15	1	6	0	Commercial-vehicle ...
47	46	15	A	15	7	6	0	English
48	0	10	E	10	1	7	0	NULL
49	48	11	E	11	1	7	0	WSJ870323-0161
50	48	12	E	12	1	7	0	Who's News...
51	48	13	E	13	1	7	0	03/23/87
52	48	14	E	14	1	7	0	Du Pont Co...DE
53	48	15	E	15	1	7	0	John A. Krol ...
54	53	15	A	15	7	7	0	English

6.5 Multi-dimensional Data Model

In the preceding two sections, we described methods to use the relational model as the core storage and retrieval components for an information retrieval system or an XML-IR system. It is also possible to use a multi-dimensional data model to provide similar functionality. Such a model inherently supports hierarchical dimensions and is well suited for natural hierarchies that occur in some documents. A DOCUMENT dimension might include the hierarchy of a document (e.g.; document, chapter, section, paragraph, sentence). Two additional dimensions are LOCATION and TIME. The location of a document and the publication date of a document are both common in information retrieval applications. The corresponding hierarchies of LOCATION (e.g.; country, region, state, city) and TIME (e.g.; year, month, day) are well suited to multi-dimensional modeling.

Processing of data in a multi-dimensional data model is referred to as OLAP (On-Line Analytical Processing). ROLAP (Relational OLAP) refers to a multi-dimensional model that is implemented with a relational database system. MOLAP refers to a multi-dimensional model that is implemented with a multi-dimensional database system. For our discussion it is not important whether or not ROLAP or MOLAP is used. The key is that we are now able to more easily represent hierarchical dimensions that naturally occur in text.

Typically, a star schema is used for OLAP applications. Our dimensions: DOCUMENT, TIME, and LOCATION are arranged in a star around a single *fact* table. The fact table is analogous to the INDEX relation we described in Section 6.3. This table maps a given term to its corresponding dimensions of DOCUMENT, TIME, and LOCATION.

Once data are represented with a star schema, it can then be migrated to a ROLAP or MOLAP system. These multi-dimensional systems offer the added advantage that they more naturally represent hierarchical data often found in a document collection. Relevance ranking using a MOLAP system is described in [McCabe et al., 2000].

6.6 Mediators

At this point, we have described a means of integrating structured data, semi-structured data and text via the relational model. This approach is able to harness the power of existing relational systems and provides a means by which data can be easily integrated when it is practical to store it in a centralized repository.

The reality is that some applications require the storage of data in disparate locations. For text collections in the multi-terabyte range that already have search engines that access them, it is not realistic to expect that a redundant copy of these collections will be made in a relational system. Instead, a *me-*

diator that resides between a user and the data determines which data sources are most relevant to query, submits the query to those engines that search the determined relevant sources, and then consolidate the results. If all the sources are text, this becomes a relatively straightforward metasearch. Metasearch is simply a search of a set of search engines. If some sources are text, others are XML, and still others are relational, then a mediator is needed to run on top of these sources and mediate between the different sources and the user.

In spite of much research, a recent survey of data integration agreed that integration of structured, semi-structured, and unstructured data remains a key research problem [Raghavan and Garcia-Molina, 2002]. All of the work done on mediators is directly focused on this problem. Two types of mediators exist: Internet mediators and intranet mediators.

6.6.1 Internet Mediators

Internet mediators respond to user queries by issuing a plurality of queries to search engines on remote Internet sites, consolidate the results returned from the remote search engines and present these results to the user. For example, a user might have a query about books for sale on the Internet and choose to query both *Waldenbooks* and *Daltonbooks*. The Internet mediator would send a request to both sites and come up with a consolidated answer. In the trivial case, all the sites follow a common schema, but an Internet mediator addresses the more challenging problem of reconciling disparate schemas at the time of the query.

At present, there are a small number of existing mediator research projects in the academic world. All of these focus on different areas of the data mediation problem. The MIX project, from the University of California at San Diego, concentrates on schema integration [Baru et al., 1998]. Large data collections are viewed as one large distributed database, wherein all data are represented as XML documents for which there is a well-formed schema. These data are queried using XML query languages. A key disadvantage to this approach is that any legacy data must be made to conform to this schema. This may be reasonable for some small applications, but for multi-terabyte applications, this is not a viable process. The Tukwila Data Integration system under development at the University of Washington adopts a similar approach [Ives et al., 1999], but it too focuses on schema integration *only*; their primary goal is not to provide an answer to a user's question. Stanford's TSIMMIS project concentrates on being able to interface with large volumes of data and search them in a typical Web-search manner [Garcia-Molina et al., 1997].

A mediation infrastructure for digital libraries is described by Melnik, et. al [Melnik et al., 2000]. This infrastructure allows users to develop wrappers around various sources and to query all the sources using a common language. A high-level, query language SDLIP (Simple Digital Library Interoperability

Protocol) is used to query the sources. This requires the user to identify how to identify the correct sources for a given query.

The mediation infrastructure described by Melinik, et. al avoids many of the details of numerous unstructured sources. The query language assumes that users are querying a single document collection; nothing in the query language facilitates queries over structured or semi-structured data. In many respects, this mediation infrastructure is similar to the InfoBus in which CORBA was used to hide details of various unstructured services on the Web [Paepcke et al., 2000]. In each of these efforts, the core focus is on multiple site result integration solely. The problem of source selection, a key challenge for a mediator that must sit on top of numerous sources, is neglected.

Overall, it is difficult for an Internet mediator to accomplish schema reconciliation prior to query execution time. If one source lacks an attribute like *publisher_date* and another has this attribute, it is a non-trivial effort to identify this at the time of the query. Since these sources are completely outside the control of the mediator, it is not feasible to identify sufficient metadata prior to the query. With an intranet mediator, the situation is very different. Metadata can be defined well in advance of the query and schema reconciliation can be accomplished as well.

6.6.2 Intranet Mediator

The key to the architecture of an intranet mediator is that all of the schemas for the data sources are available long before the time of the query. A high-level sample mediator architecture is given in Figure 6.2.

Essentially, the sample mediator consists of the following key components: *Query Processor:* The query processor takes the natural language query and parses it into key grammatical constructs such as *subject, verb,* and *objects*. Additionally, the query parser performs a part-of-speech tagging operation on the query to identify the most likely part of speech for each term in the query. Finally, an entity tagger is used to identify top-level semantic concepts, such as *location, person, place, organization, etc.* in the query. These tools are often used in various question/answering systems, but they lack the efficiency required to work on enormous document collections. Hence, the mediator only uses these tools to parse the *query*. We make the assumption that time exists to do complex natural language processing on the query, but not the document collection.

Level 0 Rules: The first set of rules is referred to as 'level 0'. These rules take the syntactic elements in the query and existing metadata lists and identify higher-level semantic concepts in the query. Consider a course number like "*CS 522*". This might be recognized by the two character prefix "*CS*", and then the three digit sequence.

A level 0 rule might be of the form:

If *subject or object = [list of course prefixes]* [3 digits]
then *subject or object = [COURSE_NUMBER].*

Level 1 Rules: 'Level 1' rules take output from the query processor and semantic concepts identified by level 0 rules and map to one or more *retrieval functions* which are then used to obtain the actual data that comprise the answer to the query.

Retrieval Functions: These are small functions, key to the mediator, which contain the code needed to actually retrieve data from a source. These speak to the source in the language of the source. For example, a relational source will communicate using an SQL script, and an XML source might be sent XML-QL or some other XML query language. This flexibility is a key feature, as it allows the mediator to easily connect to virtually *any* type of data source. Simply stated, if a source can be queried, then the mediator can access it via a retrieval function. One might note that the whole game of retrieval from multiple heterogeneous sources is simply one of taking the English query and, from it, choosing the right retrieval functions. The idea is that the combined efforts of the rules framework (both level 0 and level 1 rules) enable the selection of the correct retrieval functions.

Dispatchers: The various source-type dispatchers handle the task of asynchronously invoking the appropriate retrieval functions for the sources that are deemed appropriate to the query.

Results Manager: The results manager combines the results from the various sources with some sources weighted higher than others.

Metadata Analyzers: The mediator also contains analyzers that examine new input sources and identify key aspects of the source. The analyzers assume that a source is the actual data. Analyzers exist for structured, unstructured, and semi-structured data.

6.7 Summary

We discussed several approaches focused on the integration of structured and text data. To aid the reader, we initially provided a limited review of the relational database model and continued with a historical progression of the data integration field. We discussed the key concerns involved in data integration—namely data integrity, portability, and performance—and noted that maintaining and coordinating two separate systems was difficult and expensive to do.

Having motivated the integration of traditional relational database management features with traditional information retrieval functionality, we described

Figure 6.2. Intranet Mediator Architecture

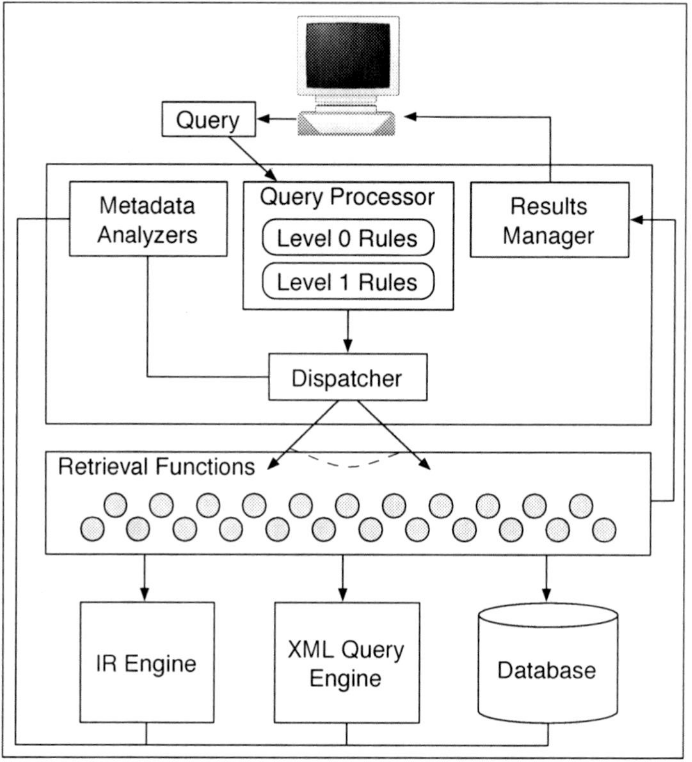

early efforts that extended relational database management systems with user-defined operators. These extensions provided information retrieval functionality, but also potentially incurred performance and portability penalties. We then provided a detailed illustration of the integration of both information retrieval and relation database functionality using standard, unchanged SQL. Next, we described an actual implementation, SIRE, of this approach. Subsequently, the ability to treat XML retrieval as an application of the relational model was explored. The chapter concluded with a brief discussion of data integration using multi-dimensional data models and mediators.

6.8 Exercises

1 Using *Alice in Wonderland* develop a utility to output a file that is suitable for populating the INDEX relation described in this chapter.

2 Load the output obtained in the preceding exercise into the relational DBMS of your choice.

3 Implement a simple dot product SQL query to query the data you have just loaded. Implement ten different queries.

4 Notice that the term *Alice* is replicated numerous times. Implement a Huffman encoding compression algorithm to reduce the space stored for each term. Reload the INDEX relation and compute the amount of storage overhead.

5 Show how the probabilistic approach developed by Robertson and Sparck Jones described in Section 2.2.1 can be implemented as an application of a relational database system. Repeat this exercise for the approach developed by Kwok described in section 2.2.4.

Chapter 7

PARALLEL INFORMATION RETRIEVAL

Parallel architectures are often described based on the number of instruction and data streams, namely single and multiple data and instruction streams. A complete taxonomy of different combinations of instruction streams and data was given in [Flynn, 1972]. To evaluate the performance delivered by these architectures on a given computation, *speedup* is defined as $\frac{T_s}{T_p}$, where T_s is the time taken by the *best* sequential algorithm, and T_p is the time taken by the parallel algorithm under consideration. The higher the speedup, the better the performance. The motivation for measuring speedup is that it indicates whether or not an algorithm scales. An algorithm that has near linear speedup on sixteen processors may not exhibit similar speedup on hundreds of processors. However, an algorithm that delivers very little or no speedup on only two processors will certainly not scale to large numbers of processors.

Multiple Instruction Multiple Data (MIMD) implies that each processing element is potentially executing a different instruction stream. This is the case in most of the modern parallel engines. Synchronization is more difficult with this approach, as compared to a Single Instruction Multiple Data (SIMD) system, because one processor can still be running some code while another is waiting for a message.

In SIMD architectures, all processors execute the same instruction concurrently. A controlling master processor sends an instruction to a collection of slave processors, and they all execute it at the same time on different sequences of data. SIMD systems are effective when all processors work on different pieces of data with the same instruction. In such cases, large speedups using SIMD engines are possible. Some image processing applications, where each pixel or set of pixels is assigned to a processor, are solved efficiently by SIMD solutions.

In this chapter, we include only algorithms written for a parallel processor. We distinguish these algorithms from distributed algorithms since they are fundamentally different. A distributed information retrieval algorithm is designed to satisfy the need to store data in many physically disparate locations. The most known example of a distributed information retrieval system is the World Wide Web (WWW). We discuss this and other distributed information retrieval systems in Chapter 8. However, with parallel systems, the processing elements are close to one another—often on the same circuit board.

7.1 Parallel Text Scanning

In parallel pattern match, the text collection consisting of n documents is partitioned into p partitions (p is typically the number of available processors) [Evans and Ghanemi, 1988]. Each available processor receives a partition of the text and a copy of the query. A sequential algorithm executes on each $\lceil \frac{n}{p} \rceil$ sized portion of text. Once this is done, all of the hits are returned to the controlling processor. Since it is possible for a pattern to span across two or more partitions, an additional step is required to check for matches that span partitions. This extra checking results in additional overhead for the parallel algorithm.

Parallel string matching is a simpler case of parallel text scanning, in that string matching assumes that the text to be searched is completely memory resident. A survey of parallel string matching algorithms is found in [Breslauer and Galil, 1991]. This survey describes several different parallel algorithms that search a text string of size l for a pattern of size k.

The parallel pattern matching algorithm has a key flaw in that patterns which span partitions result in considerable overhead. For some cases, the parallel algorithm yields no speedup at all. The parallel signature file approach yields linear speedup over the sequential file, but run time for this algorithm is not better than the time required to implement a sequential indexing algorithm. This fact was pointed out by Salton when he implemented this algorithm on a Connection Machine and a SUN3 [Salton, 1988]. Additionally, Stone used an analytical model to compute that a sequential machine will outperform a parallel machine with 32K processors. This occurs if an inverted index is used for the sequential matching and the file scan is used on the 32K processor machine [Stone, 1987]. Another repetition of the theme that information retrieval does not require enough processing to enable good parallel processing algorithms is given in [Cockshott, 1989].

Generally, parallel algorithms start with the best sequential algorithm. Comparing a parallel scanner to a sequential scanner is not an accurate measure of speedup, as it is well known that the best sequential algorithms use an inverted index.

7.1.1 Scanning Hardware

Numerous special purpose hardware machines were built to scan text. A survey of these is found in [Hurson et al., 1990]. We briefly review two of these as they serve to illustrate the need for this portion of our taxonomy.

7.1.1.1 Utah Retrieval System

The Utah Retrieval System (URS) is implemented as a non-deterministic Finite State Automata (FSA) with a series of special purpose comparators [Hollaar and Haskins, 1984, Hollaar and Haskins, 1991]. The FSA is constructed so that many non-deterministic paths are explored at the same time; therefore, it never requires a backward look. The URS is essentially a smart disk controller, as the hardware is placed close to the disk controller so that only data that match the retrieval criteria are returned to the calling processor. As always, the motivation behind the special purpose algorithm is run-time performance. While proximity searching can be done, it is not clear that the URS can be used to store weights of terms in a document. Hence, this approach has some of the same problems as a signature-based approach.

Subsequent work with the URS employed an index and a simplified posting list. This posting list does not contain proximity information so the index is used simply to identify which documents should be scanned. The FSA is used to scan the documents to obtain the required response to the query. This scanning step is needed to determine the locations of terms within the document.

7.1.1.2 A Data Parallel Pattern Matching Approach

To avoid precomputation of a FSA and to search large blocks of text simultaneously a data parallel pattern matching (DPPM) algorithm was developed [Mak et al., 1991]. In the DPPM algorithm, a block of data is compared against a sequential serial portion of the pattern. Sequentially characters of the search pattern are compared individually against an entire block of text. Given the high degree of mismatch between the pattern and the block of text an "early-out" mismatch detection scheme flushes the entire block of text. This occurs once a match with the pattern is no longer possible. This early mismatch detection mechanism greatly reduces the total search processing time as redundant comparisons are avoided.

An architecture that relied on multiple individual DPPM search engines to identify document offsets where the pattern matches were found was outlined. Based on simple computations and the predetermined offsets, the required information retrieval operators proposed for the Utah Retrieval System were supported. A VLSI realization of the DPPM engine, and a corresponding analysis of the global architecture, was presented. The analysis demonstrated a potential search rate of one gigabyte of text per second.

Bailey et al. examined parallel search on the PADRE system, a distributed in-memory pattern matching system, and explored the issues of scaling it to one terabyte [Bailey and Hawking, 1996]. Additionally, their scaling approach partitioned data to many CPUs of a virtual machine – an approach that has since been shown to not always be reasonable [Chowdhury and Pass, 2003].

7.1.2 Parallel Signature Files

Several approaches have been used to parallelize the scanning of signature files. Since a signature file can be scanned in an arbitrary order, this structure is inherently parallelizable.

7.1.2.1 Connection Machine

An early algorithm developed for the Connection Machine used signature files to represent documents [Stanfill and Kahle, 1986]. Details of sequential algorithms that use text signatures are described in Section 5.3.

Several signatures are stored in each processing element. Each processing element is assigned signatures only for a single document. The reason for this is that it was assumed that a document would not expand beyond a single processing element. A query is processed by generating the bitmap for a term in the query and broadcasting it to all processors. Each processor checks the bitmap against the list of signatures. When a match occurs, the mailbox in the processing element that corresponds to the document is updated with the weight of the query term. Document weights due to repetition within a document are lost because the signature does not capture the number of occurrences of a word in a document. However, a global weight across the document collection is used.

Once all the signatures are scanned, the documents are ranked by doing a global maximum of all mailboxes. The processors whose mailboxes contain the global maximum are then zeroed, and the global maximum is repeated. This continues until the number of documents that should be retrieved is obtained.

The commercial implementation of this algorithm contained several refinements [Sherman, 1994]. The actual values for the signatures for the CM were:

$$
\begin{aligned}
w &= \text{30 words per signature} \\
s &= \text{1024 bits in a signature} \\
i &= \text{10 hash functions used to code a word}
\end{aligned}
$$

Fifty-five signatures were placed in a single processing element. The assumption that one processing element maps to a corresponding signature is removed. Additionally, weights are not done by document. They are computed for signature pairs. The idea being that a sixty word radius is a better document segment to rank than an entire document. Hence, a weight is maintained for each signature.

To resolve a query, the top one hundred query weights were used. The bitmap for the query was generated as before, and rapid microcode was used to quickly check the corresponding i bits in the signature. Whenever a query term appeared to match a signature, the corresponding weight was updated appropriately. Once the signature match was complete, the signature pairs were then combined using a proprietary scoring algorithm that averaged the weights of the two signatures. The use of signature pairs made it possible to incorporate proximity information into the relevance ranking. Some interprocessor communication occurs to obtain the single signature part that crosses a document boundary (both above and below the processing element). However, the overhead for these two processor "sends" is low because it occurs only between adjacent processors.

The algorithm was completely memory resident, as the application queried a news wire service in which only the most recent news articles were used in retrieval. As documents aged, they were exported from the CM to make room for new documents. Several million documents could then be stored in memory and run-time performance was routinely within one to three seconds.

7.1.2.2 Digital Array Processor (DAP)

Signatures were used initially in the Digital Array Processor (DAP) by using a two-phased search. Many of the parallel algorithms are based on a bit serial implementation of the sequential algorithms given in [Mohan and Willett, 1985]. In this algorithm, signatures are assigned by using a term dictionary and setting a single bit in the signature for each term. The 1024 bit-long signatures are distributed to each processor (4096 processors). Hence, 4096 documents are searched in parallel. The query is broadcast to each processor. Since only one bit is set per term, the number of matching bits is used as a measure of relevance. This uses the assumption that a bit match with the query indicates a match with the term. Since several terms can map to the same bit in the signature, this is not always true.

To verify that a match really occurs, a second phase begins. In this phase, a pattern matching algorithm is implemented, and the document is examined to compute the number of terms that really match. This is done sequentially and only for the documents that ranked highly during the first phase. Performance of the algorithm is claimed to be "good," but no specific results are presented [Pogue and Willett, 1987].

7.1.2.3 HYTERM

Another approach by Lee, HYbrid TExt Retrieval Machine (HYTERM), uses a hybrid approach between special-purpose search hardware and partitioned signature files, which can be done via hardware or software [Lee, 1995]. This architecture employs a signature file using superimposed signatures to identify possible matches to a Boolean request. Once this is done, the false hits are removed either by a software scan or a special-purpose pattern match device.

Signatures are partitioned such that each partition has a certain key or portion of the signatures. This saves memory as the signatures in a given partition need not store the partition key. The key is checked quickly to determine whether or not the entire partition must be searched. The partitions are stored in memory, and are spread across the processors or, as Lee calls them signature modules, as they are filled. Initially, only one signature module is used. Once it is full, a single-bit key is used, and the signatures are partitioned across two processors. The process continues until all free processors are full, then new ones can be added and the process can continue indefinitely.

The actual text is stored across numerous small texts. Once the signature modules have identified candidate documents to be checked for false drops, the text processing modules retrieve the document from a disk. It is noted that by spreading the documents across numerous disks, the resilience to failure improves. When a disk is down, it only means a few documents will be inaccessible. The overall query will still work, it will just have lower precision and recall than if the disk had been working. Documents are uniformly distributed to the disks, either by hashing or round-robin allocation.

7.1.2.4 Transputers

Two algorithms were developed with transputers in the early 1990's [Cringean et al., 1990, Cringean et al., 1991]. The first was a term-based algorithm in which only full terms were encoded in a signature, the second algorithm uses trigrams (overlapping three character sequences—see Section 3.4) to respond to wildcard searches.

Another signature-based algorithm was implemented on a transputer network. Transputers essentially serve as building blocks to an arbitrary parallel interconnection network, and are often distributed as a chip in which *links* are present that can be connected to other transputers. For this approach, different interconnection networks were tested, but ultimately a *triple chain* network was used in which a master processor sends messages to three separate linear arrays. Using only a single linear array, data transmission requires on the order of p steps, where p is the number of processors.

A two-phased algorithm is again used. In this first phase, a master processor sequentially scans signatures for each document. The documents that correspond to signature matches are then distributed to the p processors, and a sequential string matching algorithm is implemented on each of the p processors. In this work, a modified Boyer-Moore algorithm by Horspool is used for sequential string matching [Horspool, 1983].

During one performance test, the signatures were eliminated and only string matching was done. For this test with fifteen processors, a speedup of 12.6 was obtained. Additional tests with varying signature lengths were conducted. For larger signatures, fewer false hits occur. Thus, less string matching in parallel is needed. With 512 bit signatures, fifteen processors only obtained a speedup of 1.4 because only thirteen percent of the original document collection were searched.

Additional tests were done with signatures based on trigrams instead of terms. Each trigram was hashed to a single bit. The pattern-matching algorithm implemented on each processor was modified to search for wildcards. These searches include symbols that indicate one or more characters will satisfy the search (e.g., a search for "st*" will find all strings with a prefix of "st"). Initial speedups for trigram-based signatures were only 2.1 for fifteen processors. This poor speedup was caused by the sequential signature match in the first phase of the algorithm. To alleviate this, additional transputer components were added so that two and then four processors were used to scan the signature file in parallel. With four transputers for the parallel signature match, speedup improved to 4.5 for twelve processors.

Another term-based transputer algorithm is found in [Walden and Sere, 1988]. In this work, a master processor sends the query to each of the processors where all "relevant" documents are identified and returned to the master for final ranking. "Relevant" is defined as having matched one of the terms in the query. Document signatures are used to save storage, but no work is done to avoid false hits. The interesting aspect of this work is that three different interconnection networks were investigated: ring, linear array, and tree. Speedups for a 10 megabyte document collection with a ring interconnection network were almost linear for up to fifteen processing elements, but fell to only 6.14 for sixty-three processing elements. Essentially, the test collection was too small to exploit the work of the processing elements. In a tree structure, sixty-three processing elements yielded a speedup of 7.33.

7.2 Parallel Indexing

Yet another approach is to parallelize the inverted index. The idea is to partition the index such that portions of the index are processed by different processors. Figure 7.1 illustrates an inverted index that was partitioned between two processors. This is intrinsically more difficult, in that simply partitioning the index and sending an equal number of terms to each of the p processors does not always result in equal amounts of work. Skew in posting list size poses a difficult problem. Nevertheless, parallel index algorithms were developed for the Connection Machine, the DAP, and some others. We discuss these algorithms in this section.

Figure 7.1. Partitioning an Inverted Index

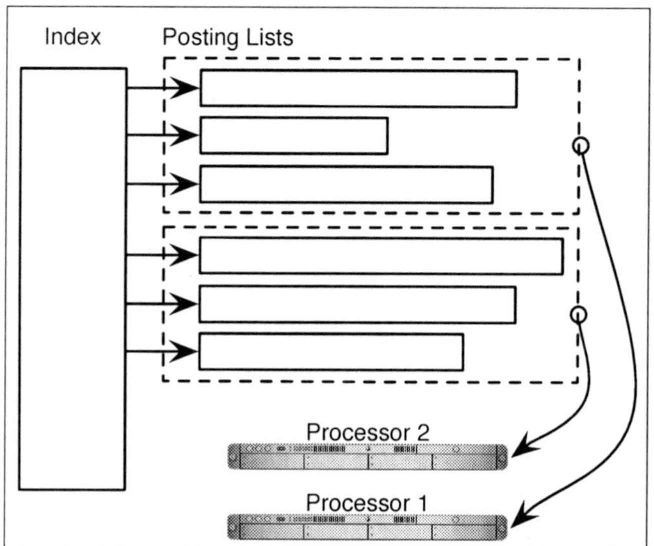

7.2.1 Parallel Indexing on a Connection Machine

The signature-based algorithm did not improve on the *best* sequential algorithm, so a new approach based on an inverted index was developed. Both an entirely memory resident index and a disk-based index were constructed [Stanfill et al., 1989]. The posting lists were sequences of document identifiers that were placed in a two dimensional array. Mapping between posting list entries, and placement within a two dimensional array was defined. The entries of the posting were allocated one at a time, starting with the first row and moving to the second row only after the first row was full. This has had the effect of allocating data to the different processors (since each column is processed by an individual processor) in a round-robin fashion.

Consider a posting list with terms t_1, t_2, and t_3. Assume t_1 occurs in documents d_1 and d_2. The posting list for this term will be stored in the first two positions of row zero, in an array stored in memory. Assume t_2 occurs in documents d_1 and d_3, and t_3 occurs in documents d_1, d_2, and d_3. For these three terms, the 2×4 dimensional array shown in Table 7.1 is populated.

Table 7.1. Parallel Storage of Posting Lists

1	2	1	3
1	2	3	

Using this approach a row of 1024 postings can be processed in a single step if all processors are used. A full row is referred to as a *stripe*. Since the terms have been scattered across the array, it is necessary to track which entries map to a given posting list. A second array is used for this purpose. It holds an entry for the term followed by a start row, a start column, and a length for the posting list. The start row and column indicate the first location in the posting list that corresponds to the term. Continuing our example, the index table for the terms 0, 1, and 2 is given in Table 7.2.

The first row of this entry indicates that term t_1 contains a posting list that starts at position [0,0] and continues to position [0,1] of the two dimensional posting list array given in Table 7.2. This can be inferred because the row-at-a-time allocation scheme is used.

A query of n terms is processed in n steps. Essentially, the algorithm is:

```
do i = 1 to n
    curr_row = index(i)
    for j = 1 to row_length do in parallel
        curr_doc_id = doc_id(curr_row)
        score(curr_doc_id) = score(curr_doc_id) + weight(curr_row)
    end
end
```

This is only a sketch of the algorithm. Extra work must be done to deactivate processors when an entire row is not required (a bit mask can be used to deactivate a processor). Additionally, for long posting lists, or posting lists that start at the end of a stripe, more than one row must be processed during a single iteration of the inner loop.

Table 7.2. Mapping of Index Terms to Posting List Entries

Term	Start Row	Start Column	Length
t_1	0	0	2
t_2	0	2	2
t_3	1	0	3

For each query term, a lookup in the index is done to determine which stripe of the posting list is to be processed. Each processor looks at its entry for the stripe in the *doc_id*. It is this *doc_id* whose score must be updated, as the entry in the posting list implies that the term in the query is matched by a term in this document. A one-dimensional score array (referred to as a "mailbox" in the original algorithm) is updated. This one-dimensional array is distributed as one element to each processor, so each processor corresponds to a document. For a document collection with more documents than processors a "virtual processor" must be used. (Note: There will never be more than one update to the score element as the posting list only contains one entry for each term-doc appearance). The final ranking is done with a global maximum to find the highest-ranked element of the score array and to successively mask that element. This can be repeated until all documents have been retrieved.

This algorithm obtains good speedup when a posting list uses an entire stripe. The problem is that often a stripe is only being used for one or two entries. A posting list containing one entry results in 1023 processors doing nothing while one processor issues the update to the score array. The posting table can be partitioned by node [Stanfill, 1990, Stanfill and Thau, 1991] to accommodate clusters of processors (or nodes). This facilitates the movement of data from disk into the posting array.

One node consists of thirty-two processors. The problem is that if the posting list entries are arbitrarily assigned to nodes based on a document range (i.e., node one receives postings for documents zero and two, while node two receives postings for documents one and three) it is conceivable that one node can have substantially more postings than another. To avoid this problem, the nodes are partitioned such that each partition contains a range of term identifiers. Occasionally, empty space occurs in a partition as there may be no data for a given range of terms in a particular range of documents. It can be shown that for typical document collections, eighty to ninety percent of the storage is used. This partitioned posting list yields improved speedup as the number of idle processors is reduced.

7.2.2 Inverted Index on the Connection Machine

The previous algorithm processed one query term at a time. Parallel processing was done to update the ranking, but even with optimal processor utilization (fully used stripes), the time taken for a query of t terms is on the order of $O(t)$. An approach that allows logarithmic time is given in [Asokan et al., 1990]. The algorithm consists of the following steps:

Step 1: Partition the set of processors into clusters. Each cluster works on a single query term.

Step 2: Each cluster simultaneously references the index to determine the posting list that corresponds to its own cluster. Hence, cluster 1 obtains the posting list for term 1, cluster 2 obtains the posting list for term 2, etc.

Step 3: Use all p processors to merge the $\lceil \frac{n}{p} \rceil$ posting lists, where n is the number of documents. This effectively produces a sorted list of all documents that are referenced by the terms in the query. Since the posting list contains the weight, a document weight appears as well. Hence, a merged posting list might appear as:

$$< D1, 0.5 >< D1, 0.3 >< D2, 0.5 >< D2, 0.9 >.$$

This posting list occurs if document one contains two query terms with weights of 0.5 and 0.3, respectively, and document two contains two terms with weights of 0.5 and 0.9 respectively.

Step 4: Use all processors to eliminate duplicates from this list and generate a total score. After this step, our posting list appears as:

$$< D1, 0.8 >< D2, 1.4 >$$

Step 5: Sort the posting list again based on the score assigned to each document. Our posting list will now appear as:

$$< D2, 1.4 >< D1, 0.8 >$$

A modified bitonic sort can be done to merge the lists so the complexity of the algorithm is $O(\log_2 t)$ time. This appears superior to the O(t) time, but it should be noted that the algorithm requires $O(\lceil \frac{n}{p} \rceil)$ processors assigned to a cluster to process a single posting list for a given term. If too many terms exist, it may be necessary to overlay some of the operations.

7.2.3 Parallel Indexing on a Digital Array Processor (DAP)

As with the Connection Machine, an earlier scanning algorithm that uses term signatures on the DAP, was replaced with an indexing algorithm [Reddaway, 1991, Bond and Reddaway, 1993].

The key difference between the DAP algorithm and the CM algorithm is that a compressed posting list is used. Additionally, the algorithm running on the DAP is claimed to be more efficient as the DAP uses a simpler interconnection network (a mesh instead of a hypercube) and the global operations such as global maximum are substantially faster. Since no really remote "send" operations are done, the authors of the DAP approach claim that it is not necessary to have a hypercube.

The compression scheme is based on the observation that large hit lists often have the same leading bits. Consider a hit list that contains documents 8, 9, 10,

11, 12, 13, 14, and 15. The binary values all have a leading bit of 1 (1000, 1001, 1010, 1011, 1100, 1101, 1110, and 1111). By allocating one bit as a *block indicator*, the hits within the block can be stored in three bits. Hence, block 1 would contain the references (000, 001, 010, 011, 100, 101, 110, and 111). The total bits for the representation changes from $(8)(4) = 32$ to $1 + (8)(3) = 25$. Clearly, the key to this representation is the number of hits within a block. For the DAP, a 24-bit code (no compression) is used for rare terms (those that occur only once in every 50,000 documents). For terms that appear more frequently, an 8-bit block code with a 16-bit offset within the block (the block holds up to 64K) references entries in the posting list. Finally, for the most frequent terms, a 64K document block is treated as 256 separate sub-blocks. A key difference in the parallel algorithm for the DAP is that the expansion of the posting list into an uncompressed form is done in parallel. Performance of the DAP-based system is claimed to be 200 times faster than the previous sequential work. Other experiments using 4096 processors indicate the DAP 610 yields a significant (over one hundred times faster) improvement over a VAX 6000 [Manning, 1989, Reddaway, 1991].

7.2.4 Partitioning a Parallel Index

An analytical model for determining the best means of partitioning an inverted index in a shared nothing environment is given in [Tomasic and Garcia-Molina, 1993]. Three approaches were studied. The first, referred to as the *system* approach, partitioned the index based on terms. The entire posting list for term *a* was placed on disk 1, the posting list for term *b* was placed on disk 2, etc. The posting lists were assigned to disks in a round-robin fashion.

Partitioning based on documents was referred to as the *disk* strategy. In this approach, all posting list entries corresponding to document 1 are placed on disk 1, document 2 on disk 2, etc. Documents were assigned to disks in a round-robin fashion. Hence, to retrieve an entire posting list for term *a*, it is necessary to retrieve the partial posting lists from each disk for term *a* and merge them. Although the merge takes more time than the system entry, the retrieval can take place in parallel.

The *host* strategy partitioned posting list entries for each document and placed them on separate processors. Hence, document 1 is sent to processor 1, document 2 to processor 2, etc.

An analytical model was also developed by fitting a frequency distribution to some text (a more realistic approach than blindly following Zipf's Law). The results of the analytical simulation were that the *host* and *disk* strategy perform comparably, but the *system* strategy does not perform as well. This is because the *system* strategy requires sequential reading of potentially long posting lists and transmission of those lists. The *system* strategy becomes competitive when the communication costs were dramatically reduced.

7.2.5 A Parallel Inverted Index Algorithm on the CM-5

Another algorithm on the CM-5 is described in [Masand and Stanfill, 1994]. In this work, the documents were distributed to sixty-four different processors where a compressed inverted index was built for each of the processors. Construction of the inverted index was extremely fast. In twenty minutes, a 2.1 gigabyte document collection was indexed, and the size of the index file was only twenty-four percent of the size of the raw text.

Queries were processed by sending the query to each of the processors and obtaining a relevance ranking for each processor. Once obtained, a global maximum was computed to determine the highest ranked document among all the processors. This document was ranked first. The global maximum computation was repeated until the number of documents that were to be retrieved was reached.

7.2.6 Computing Boolean Operations on Posting Lists

Another area in which parallel processing is used in conjunction with an inverted index is the computation of Boolean operations on two posting lists, A and B [Bataineh et al., 1989, Bataineh et al., 1991]. The posting lists are partitioned so that the total number of elements in each partition is of equal size. The Boolean computation is obtained by computing the Boolean result for each partition. There is no need to compare values located in one partition with another because the partitions are constructed such that each partition contains values within a specific range and no other partition contains values that overlap within that range. This partitioning process can be done in parallel.

Once the partitions are identified, each one is sent to a separate processing element. Subsequently, each processing element individually computes the Boolean result for its values. Finally, the results are obtained and stored on disk. The algorithm was originally implemented on the NCUBE/4 and the Intel iPSC/2. For posting lists corresponding to term *human* and *English* of 520,316 and 115,831 postings, respectively (the MEDLINE database was used), speedups of five for an eight processor NCUBE were observed and a speedup of seven for a sixteen processor IPSC were obtained. It was noted that the parallel algorithm began to degrade as the number of processors increased. As this happens, the amount of work per processor is reduced and communication overhead is increased.

7.2.7 Parallel Retrieval as an Application of an RDBMS

One of the motivating factors behind the development of an information retrieval engine as an application of the relational database model (see Chapter 6) was the availability of commercial parallel database implementations. Executing the SQL scripts that implement the information retrieval application on a parallel relational database engine results in a parallel implementation of an information retrieval system.

In [Grossman et al., 1997], the feasibility of implementing a parallel information retrieval application as a parallel relational database application was demonstrated. From these findings, it was hypothesized that it was possible to develop a scalable, parallel information retrieval system using parallel relational database technology.

To validate this hypothesis, scaling experiments were conducted using a twenty-four processor database engine [Lundquist et al., 1999]. The initial findings were, however, disappointing. Using the same relational table definitions described in [Grossman et al., 1997], only a forty percent processor efficiency was achieved.

The parallel hardware used (the NCR DBC/1012) for the experiments supports automatic load balancing. The hashing scheme used to implement the load balancing is based on the index structure in the defined relational schema. In the DBC/1012 architecture used to evenly distribute the load, a uniformly distributed set of attributes must be the input to the hashing function. In the initial implementation, the hashing function was based on terms, and thus, was nonuniform. Modifying the input to the hashing function to include document identifiers, as well as terms, resulted in a uniform distribution of load to the processors. In later experimentation, a balanced processor utilization of greater than 92% was demonstrated, and a speedup of roughly twenty-two using twenty-four nodes, as compared to a comparable uniprocessor implementation, was achieved.

7.2.8 Summary of Parallel Indexing

Parallel processing within information retrieval is becoming more applicable as the cost of parallel I/O is reduced. Previous algorithms had problems with memory limitations and expensive communication between processors. Signature files were popular, but have not been used recently due to their unnecessarily high I/O demand and their inability to compute more sophisticated measures of relevance. Parallel inverted index algorithms are becoming more popular, and with improved compression techniques, they are becoming substantially more economical.

7.3 Clustering and Classification

Parallel clustering and classification implementations were developed for the Intel Paragon [Ruocco and Frieder, 1997]. Using a production machine, the authors developed a parallel implementation for the single-pass clustering and single-link classification algorithms (see Section 3.2). Using the *Wall Street*

Journal portion of the TREC document collection, the authors evaluated the efficiency of their approach and noted near-linear scalability for sixteen nodes.

More recently, the popular and effective Buckshot clustering algorithm [Cutting et al., 1992] was also parallelized [Jensen et al., 2002]. This parallel algorithm was developed for use on a low-cost cluster of PC's, and uses MPI for communication. No specialized parallel hardware is needed. The authors tested this algorithm using larger, more modern TREC document collections and demonstrated near-linear scalability in terms of number of nodes and collection size.

To accurately compare the efficiency of the developed approaches, the results derived from both the parallel and serial implementations must be identical. Otherwise, an improvement in the efficiency of the algorithm (via parallelism) could come at the expense of accuracy.

The single-pass clustering algorithm is data, presentation, and order dependent. Namely, the order in which the data are presented as input directly affects the output produced. Thus, it was necessary to provide mechanisms in the parallel implementation that mimicked the order of the presentation of the documents as input to the algorithm. Guaranteeing the identical order of document presentation resulted in the formation of identical clusters in both the serial and parallel implementations. The authors noted that the size of the clusters varied dramatically and suggested measures to reduce the cluster size disparity. Since the size disparity is a consequence of the single-pass algorithm, no modification was made.

7.4 Large Parallel Systems

There has been some work towards developing large, general-purpose parallel IR systems. This section details efforts for some of the most prominent ones. An overview of some work on parallel information retrieval systems can be found in [MacFarlane et al., 1997].

7.4.1 PADRE - A Parallel Document Retrieval Engine

The PADRE system for parallel document retrieval was initially developed for text retrieval on the Fujitsu AP1000 system. Over the years, it has been developed into a modern search system, and currently forms the core of CSIRO's Panoptic Enterprise search engine. At its core, PADRE is a distributed, in-memory pattern-matching system that also supports relevance ranking. The architecture has evolved over the years, first being developed for the AP1000 system as outlined in [Hawking, 1991, Hawking, 1994b, Hawking, 1994a, Bailey and Hawking, 1996], and later being applied to tasks as esoteric as XML retrieval in the recent INEX competition [Hawking et al., 2000, Craswell et al., 2002, Vercoustre et al., 2002].

Bailey et al. examined parallel search on the PADRE system and explored the issues of scaling it to one terabyte [Bailey and Hawking, 1996]. Additionally, their scaling approach partitioned data to many CPUs of a virtual machine – an approach that has since been shown to not always be reasonable [Chowdhury and Pass, 2003].

7.4.2 Frameworks for Parallel IR

Some work has been done investigating what frameworks would be most suitable to performing Parallel IR on Symmetrical Multiprocessors[Lu et al., 1997]. A mutithreaded, multitasking search engine was built to investigate the most efficient way to execute parallel queries. In addition, a simulator supports the varying of system parameters such as number of CPUs, threads, and disks, and compared the results of the simulator to those of their implementation. Using this approach, bottleneck points were identified. At this points, no additional resources such as threads, CPUs, and disks do not provide any further scalability. Generally, scalable retrieval performance was found for a variety of system configurations.

7.4.3 PLIERS - Portable Parallel IR using MPI

Researchers at Microsoft Research Cambridge have also developed a parallel information retrieval system called PLIERS [MacFarlane et al., 1999]. This system makes use of the MPI parallel application framework to create a portable parallel IR system [Gropp and Lusk, 1998]. The PLIERS system contains parallelized versions of the Indexing, Document Search, Document Update, and Information Filtering modules of the Okapi uniprocessor IR system [Robertson, 1997], made parallel via the use of standard MPI communication procedures. In addition, the system supported several modes of search, including Boolean and Proximity search, passage retrieval, and relevance-based search. Also, several different MPI implementations found that there were some implementation-specific differences, but nothing that impeded portability. Eventually, the system was ported to many different architectures such as a Network of Workstations (NOW), the Fujitsu AP1000 and AP3000 parallel machines, a cluster of PC's, and an Alpha farm. The authors conclude that there is a performance gain to be had by parallel IR systems designed in this way, and in particular they found that MPI collective operations improve query transactions for IR and term selection in information filtering.

7.5 Summary

As volumes of data available on-line continued to grow, information retrieval solutions needed to be developed that could cope with ever expanding collections. Towards addressing this data growth explosion, parallel solutions were investigated. Initially, parallel information retrieval solutions focused on hardware-based full-text filtering. Eventually, these hardware solutions gave way to software implementations that roughly mirrored the hardware approaches. Recent parallel efforts are mostly algorithmic and architecturally independent.

We began our review by describing parallel text scanning techniques. We described two hardware solutions for full-text scanning, the Utah Retrieval System and the data parallel data matching system. Both systems supported hardware-level filtering to reduce the retrieved document sets. Although they did demonstrate significant improvements as compared to software full-text scanning, in general, full-text scanning introduces excessive I/O demands as all documents must be scanned. Later efforts using the Utah Retrieval System relied on indexing. However, most recent architectures use general purpose processors since they are able to more quickly incorporate enhancements. This has reduced the popularity of special purpose solutions.

Later efforts developed software supported text scanning. To reduce the I/O demands associated with full-text scanning, most efforts focused on signature analysis. Early studies relied on SIMD architectures, namely the DAP architecture and the Connection Machine. Results demonstrated limited scalability in terms of performance. Later signature analysis efforts were evaluated on MIMD systems such as the Inmos Transputers with somewhat better results.

The prohibitive I/O demands of text scanning approaches, both full-text and signature analysis, resulted in the development of parallel indexing approaches. The need for index-based approaches was clearly demonstrated in [Stone, 1987] where it was shown that serial computers using indexing techniques sustained faster retrieval speeds than parallel engines using a signature analysis approach. Parallel indexing approaches on both SIMD and MIMD architectures were developed, with some efforts resulting in near linear speedup.

We then described parallelizations of both clustering and classification algorithms. The approaches described were implemented on an Intel Paragon that was in production use. For all the algorithms studied, near linear speedup was noted.

We concluded this chapter with a brief discussion of Parallel Search Systems. Parallel information retrieval continues to be a relatively unexplored area. Parallel, scalable algorithms that efficiently support the strategies discussed in Chapter 2 and the utilities listed in Chapter 3 need to be developed. Currently, very few such algorithms are known, and even fewer, have been implemented and evaluated in a production environment.

A different approach to developing parallel information retrieval systems was addressed in [Lundquist et al., 1999]. In these efforts, a mapping from information retrieval operators onto parallel databases primitives was defined. Parallelism was achieved without requiring new parallel algorithms to be developed. Roughly a 22-fold speedup using twenty-four nodes was achieved. Such speedup is encouraging, and especially so, since it was unnecessary to implement new software.

Given the diversity of the commercially available parallel systems and the vast types of applications that constitute the realm of information retrieval, all that is clear is that it is still an open question of how best to support the domain of parallel information retrieval.

7.6 Exercises

1 Develop an average-case algorithmic analysis for a sequential inverted index for a *tf-idf* vector space query with t terms. Compare this to a parallel linear scan of a document collection with p processors.

2 Develop an algorithm to search an inverted index in parallel with a MIMD machine that will perform as well as or better than the sequential algorithm. Analyze your algorithm and clearly describe your analysis.

3 Design a simple parallel document clustering algorithm and analyze its performance. Compare this to a sequential document clustering algorithm.

Chapter 8

DISTRIBUTED INFORMATION RETRIEVAL

Until now, we focused strictly on the use of a single machine to provide an information retrieval service. In Chapter 7, we discussed the use of a single machine with multiple processors to improve performance. Although efficient performance is critical for user acceptance of the system, today, document collections are often scattered across many different geographical areas. Thus, the ability to process the data where they are located is arguably even more important than the ability to efficiently process them. Possible constraints prohibiting the centralization of the data include data security, their sheer volume prohibiting their physical transfer, their rate of change, political and legal constraints, as well as other proprietary motivations. For a comprehensive discussion from a data engineering perspective on the engineering of data processing systems in a distributed environment, see [Shuey et al., 1997].

One of the latest popular processing infrastructures is the "Grid" [Foster et al., 2001, Foster, 2002, Alliance, 2004]. The grid is named after the global electrical power grid. In the power grid, appliances (systems in our domain) simply "plug in" and immediately operate and become readily available for use or access by the global community. A similar notion in modern search world is the use of Distributed Information Retrieval Systems (DIRS). DIRS provides access to data located in many different geographical areas on many different machines (see Figure 8.1).

In the early 1980's, it was already clear that distributed information retrieval systems would become a necessity. Initially, a theoretical model was developed that described some of the key components of a distributed information retrieval system. We describe this model in Section 8.1.

In Section 8.2, we also briefly discuss Web search engines. We note that a Web search engine is really just an implementation, albeit a very popular one, of some of the algorithms and efficiency techniques already discussed in this

Figure 8.1. Distributed Document Retrieval

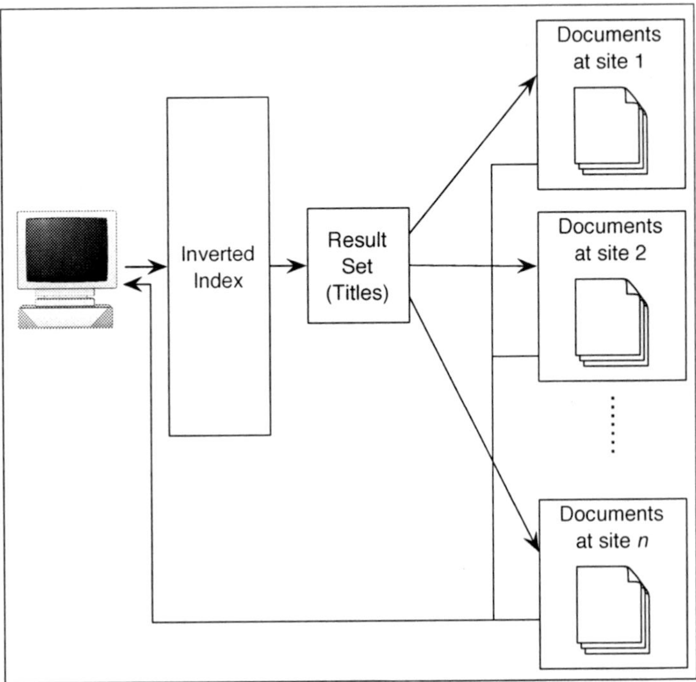

book. We do not include the specifics of any particular engine as such details are not only often proprietary but are constantly changing. Had we chosen to provide such details, they would be obsolete by the time our book appeared in press. Furthermore, by including such details we would turn this chapter into an endorsement of a particular engine, and that would be inappropriate and outside of the scope of this book. We do note, however, that a thorough listing of search engines is available at **www.searchenginewatch.com**. Several popular Web engines include *Google*, *Yahoo!*, *MSN Search*, and *AOL Search*.

Finally, Section 8.4 concludes this chapter with a brief description of Peer-to-Peer (P2P) efforts. Such efforts are currently only in their relative infancy. In future editions of this book, we hope to better describe the advancement in this now fledgling specialty.

8.1 A Theoretical Model of Distributed Retrieval

We first define a model for a centralized information retrieval system and then expand that model to include a distributed information retrieval system.

8.1.1 Centralized Information Retrieval System Model

Formally, an information retrieval system is defined as a triple, I = (D, R, δ) where D is a document collection, R is the set of queries, and $\delta_j : R_j \rightarrow 2^{D_j}$ is a mapping assigning the $j^{\underline{th}}$ query to a set of relevant documents.

Many information retrieval systems rely upon a thesaurus, in which a user query is expanded, to include synonyms of the keywords to match synonyms in a document. Hence, a query that contains the term *curtain* will also include documents containing the term *drapery*.

To include the thesaurus in the model, it was proposed in [Turski, 1971] that the triple be expanded to a quadruple as:

$$I = (T, D, R, \delta)$$

where T is a set of distinct terms and the relation $\rho \subset T \times T$ such that $\rho(t_1, t_2)$ implies that t_1 is a synonym of t_2. Using the synonym relation, it is possible to represent documents as a set of *descriptors* and a set of *ascriptors*. Consider a document D_1, the set of descriptors d consists of all terms in D_1 such that:

- Each descriptor is unique
- No descriptor is a synonym of another descriptor

An ascriptor is defined as a term that is a synonym of a descriptor. Each ascriptor must be synonymous with only one descriptor. Hence, the descriptors represent a minimal description of the document.

In addition to the thesaurus, a generalization relation over the sets of descriptors is defined as $\gamma \subset d \times d$ where $\gamma(t_1, t_2)$ implies that t_1 is a more general term than t_2. Hence, $\gamma(animal, dog)$ is an example of a valid generalization.

The generalization relation assumes that it is possible to construct a hierarchical knowledge base of all pairs of descriptors. Construction of such knowledge bases was attempted both automatically and manually [Lenat and Guha, 1989], but many terms are difficult to define. Relationships pertaining to spatial and temporal substances, ideas, beliefs, etc. tend to be difficult to represent in this fashion. However, this model does not discuss how to construct such a knowledge base, only some interesting properties that occur if one could be constructed.

The motivation behind the use of a thesaurus is to simplify the description of a document to only those terms that are not synonymous with one another. The idea being that additional synonyms do not add to the semantic value of the document. The generalization relation is used to allow for the processing of a query that states "List all animals" to return documents that include information about dogs, cats, etc. even though the term *dog* or *cat* does not appear in the document.

The generalization can then be used to define a partial ordering of documents. Let the partial ordering be denoted by $\preceq$ and let $t(d_i)$ indicate the list of descriptors for document d_i. Partial ordering, $\preceq$, is defined as:

$$t(d_1) \preceq t(d_2) \Leftrightarrow (\forall t' \in t(d_1))(\exists t'' \in t(d_2))(\gamma(t', t''))$$

Hence, a document d_1 whose descriptors are all generalizations of the descriptors found in d_2 will have the ordering $d_1 \preceq d_2$. For example, a document with the terms *animal* and *person* will precede a document with terms *dog* and *John*. Note that this is a partial ordering because two documents with terms that have no relationship between any pairs of terms will be unordered.

To be *inclusive*, the documents that correspond to a general query q_1 must include (be a superset of) all documents that correspond to the documents that correspond to a more specific query q_2, where $q_1 \preceq q_2$. Formally:

$$(q_1, q_2 \in Q) \wedge (q_1 \preceq q_2) \rightarrow (\delta(q_1) \supset \delta(q_2))$$

The model described here was proven to be inclusive in [Turski, 1971]. This means that if two queries, q_1 and q_2, are presented to a system such that q_1 is more general than q_2, it is not necessary to retrieve from the entire document collection for each query. It is only necessary to obtain the answer set for q_1, $\delta(q_1)$, and then iteratively search $\delta(q_1)$ to obtain the $\delta(q_2)$.

8.1.2 Distributed Information Retrieval System Model

The centralized information retrieval system can be partitioned into n local information retrieval systems $S_1, S_2, \ldots, S_n$ [Mazur, 1984]. Each system S_j is of the form: $S_j = (T_j, D_j, R_j, \delta_j)$, where T_j is the thesaurus; D_j is the document collection; R_j the set of queries; and $\delta_j : R_j \rightarrow 2^{D_j}$ maps the queries to documents.

By taking the union of the local sites, it is possible to define the distributed information retrieval system as:

$$S = (T, D, R, \delta)$$

where:

$$T = \bigcup_{j=1}^{n} T_j$$

$$s_j = s \bigcap (T_j \times T_j), R_j = R \bigcap (d_j \times d_j)$$

This states that the global thesaurus can be reconstructed from the local thesauri, and the queries at the sites j will only include descriptors at site j. This is done so that the terms found in the query that are not descriptors will not retrieve any documents.

$$D = \bigcup_{j=1}^{n} D_j$$

The document collection, D, can be constructed by combining the document collection at each site.

$$R \supset \bigcup_{j=1}^{n} R_j, \preceq_j = \preceq \bigcap (R_j \times R_j)$$

The queries can be obtained by combining the queries at each local site. The partial ordering defined at site j will only pertain to queries at site j.

$$(\forall r \in R)(\delta(r) = d : d \in D \wedge r \preceq t(d))$$

For each query in the system, the document collection for that query contains documents in the collection where the documents are at least as specific as the query.

The hierarchy represented by γ is partitioned among the different sites. A query sent to the originating site would be sent to each local site and a local query would be performed. The local responses are sent to the originating site where they are combined into a final result set. The model allows for this methodology if the local sites satisfy the criteria of being a *subsystem* of the information retrieval system.

$S_1 = (T_1, D_1, R_1, \delta_1)$ is a subsystem of $S_2 = (T_2, D_2, R_2, \delta_2)$ if:

$$(T_1 \supset T_2) \wedge (R_1 = R_2) \bigcap (d_1 \times d_2) \wedge (s_1 = s_2) \bigcap (T_1 \times T_2)$$

The thesaurus of T_1 is a superset of T_2.

$$D_1 \supset D_2$$

The document collection at site S_1 contains the collection D_2.

$$R_1 \in R_2 \wedge \preceq_1 = \preceq_2 \bigcap (R_1 \times R_2)$$

The queries at site S_1 contain those found in S_2.

$$\delta_1(r) = \delta_2(r) \bigcap D_1 for \;\; r \in R$$

The document collection returned by queries in S_1 will include all documents returned by queries in S_2. The following example illustrates that an arbitrary partition of a hierarchy may not yield valid subsystems.

Consider the people hierarchy:

γ(people, Harold), γ(people, Herbert), γ(people, Mary)

and the second animal hierarchy:

γ(animal, cat), γ(animal, dog), γ(cat, black-cat),
γ(cat, cheshire), γ(dog, doberman),
γ(dog, poodle)

Assume that the hierarchy is split into sites S_1 and S_2. The hierarchy at S_1 is:

γ(people, Harold), γ(people, Mary)
γ(animal, cat), γ(animal, dog), γ(dog, doberman), γ(dog, poodle)

The hierarchy at S_2 is:

γ(people, Herbert), γ(people, Harold)
γ(animal, cat), γ(animal, doberman), γ(cat, cheshire), γ(cat, black-cat)

Consider a set of documents with the following descriptors:

D_1 = (Mary, Harold, Herbert)
D_2 = (Herbert, dog)
D_3 = (people, dog)
D_4 = (Mary, cheshire)
D_5 = (Mary, dog)
D_6 = (Herbert, black-cat, doberman)
D_7 = (Herbert, doberman)

A query of the most general terms (people, animal) should return all documents 2 through 7 (document 1 contains no animals, and the query is effectively a Boolean AND). However, the hierarchy given above as S_1 will only retrieve documents D_3 and D_5, and S_2 will only retrieve documents D_6 and D_7. Hence, documents D_2 and D_4 are missing from the final result if the local results sets are simply concatenated. Since, the document collections cannot simply be concatenated, the information retrieval systems at sites S_1 and S_2 fail to meet the necessary criterion to establish a subsystem.

In practical applications, there is another problem with the use of a generalization hierarchy. Not only are they hard to construct, but also it is non-trivial to partition them. This distributed model was expanded to include weighted keywords for use with relevance [Mazur, 1988].

8.2 Web Search

No chapter on distributed information retrieval would be complete without some mention of Web search engines. Search tools that access Web pages via the Internet are prime examples of the implementation of many of the algorithms and heuristics discussed in this book. These systems are, by nature, distributed in that they access data stored on Web servers around the world. Most of these systems have a centralized index, but all of them store pointers in the form of hypertext links to various Web servers.

These systems service tens of millions of user queries a day, and all of them index several Terabytes of Web pages. We do not describe each search engine in vast detail because search engines change very frequently (some vendors produce new releases or publish fixes in a week). We note that sixteen different Web search engines are listed at **www.searchenginewatch.com** while **www.searchengineguide.com** lists over 2,500 specialized search engines.

8.2.1 Evaluation of Web Search Engines

As will be discussed in Section 9, in traditional information retrieval environments, individual systems are evaluated using standard queries and data. In the Web environment, such evaluation conditions are unavailable. Furthermore, manual evaluations on any grand scale are virtually impossible due to the vast size and dynamic nature of the Web. To automatically evaluate Web search engines, a method using online taxonomies that were created as part of Open Directory Project (ODP) is described in [Beitzel et al., 2003b]. Online directories were used as known relevant items for a query. If a query matches either the title of the item stored or the directory file name containing a known item then it is considered a match. The authors compared the system rankings achieved using this automated approach versus a limited scale, human user based system rankings created using multiple individual users. The two sets of rankings were statistically identical.

8.2.2 High Precision Search

Another concern in evaluating Web search engines is the differing measures of success as compared to traditional environments. Traditionally, precision and recall measures are the main evaluation metrics, while response time and space requirements are likely addressed. However, in the Web environment, response time is critical. Furthermore, recall estimation is very difficult, and precision is of limited concern since most users never access any links that appear beyond the first answer screen (first ten potential reference links). Thus, Web search engine developers focus on guaranteeing that the first results screen is generated quickly, is highly accurate, and that no severe accuracy mismatch exists. For example, in [Ma et al., 2003], text is efficiently extracted from template generated Web documents; the remainder of the frame or frames are discarded to prevent identifying a document as relevant as a result of potentially an advertisement frame matching the query. In [Beitzel et al., 2004a], efficient, high-precision measures are used to quickly sift and discard any item that is not with great certainty relevant as a top-line item to display in a current news listing service.

8.2.3 Query Log Analysis

In summary, although similar and relying on much the same techniques as used in traditional information retrieval system domains, the Web environment provides for many new opportunities to revisit old issues particularly in terms of performance and accuracy optimizations and evaluation measures of search accuracy. In that light, recently, an hourly analysis of a very large topically categorized Web query log was published [Beitzel et al., 2004b]. Using the results presented, it is possible to generate many system optimizations. For example, as indicated in the findings presented, user request patterns repeat according to the time of day and day of week. Thus, depending on the time of day and day of week, it is possible to pre-cache likely Web pages in anticipation of a set of user requests. Thus, page access delays are reduced increasing system throughput. Furthermore, in terms of accuracy optimization, it is likewise possible to adjust the ranking measures to better tune for certain anticipated user subject requests. In short, many optimizations are possible. What optimizations can you come up with using such logs? What measures would you use to demonstrate success? We are sure that in the next edition of the book, many such measures and optimizations will be described.

8.2.4 Page Rank

We close this section on Web search with the most popular algorithm for improving Web search. This PageRank algorithm (named after Page) was first described in [Brin and Page, 2000]. It extends the notion of hubs and authorities in the Web graph originally described in [Kleinberg, 1999]. PageRank is at the heart of the popular Web search engine, Google. Essentially, the PageRank algorithm uses incoming and outgoing links to adjust the score of a Web page with respect to its popularity, independent of the user's query. Hence, if a traditional retrieval strategy might have previously ranked two documents equal, the PageRank algorithm will boost the similarity measure for a *popular* document. Here, *popular* is defined as having a number of other Web pages link to the document. This algorithm works well on Web pages, but has no bearing on documents that do not have any hyperlinks. The calculation of PageRank for page A over all pages linking to it $D_1...D_n$ is defined as follows:

$$PageRank(A) = (1-d) + d \sum_{D_1 \ldots D_n} \frac{PageRank(D_i)}{C(D_i)}$$

where $C(D_i)$ is the number of links out from page D_i and d is a dampening factor from 0-1. This dampening factor serves to give some non-zero PageRank to pages that have no links to them. It also smooths the weight given to other links when determining a given page's PageRank. This significantly affects the time needed for PageRank to converge. The calculation is performed iteratively. Initially all pages are assigned an arbitrary PageRank. The calculation is repeated using the previously calculated scores until the new scores do not change significantly. For the example in Figure 8.2, using the common dampening factor of 0.85 and initializing each PageRank to 1.0, it took 8 iterations before the scores converged.

Figure 8.2. Simple PageRank Calculation

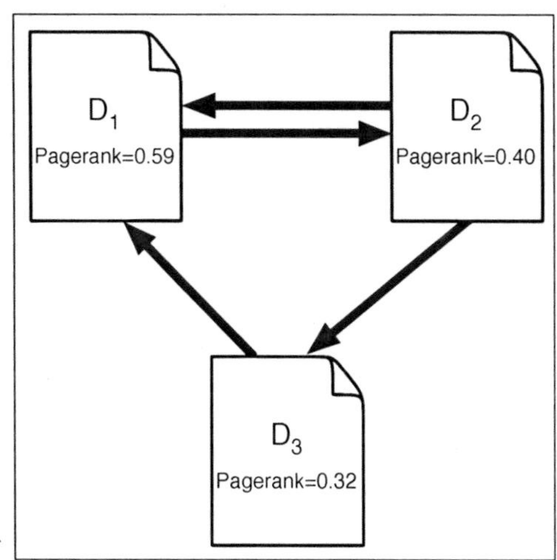

8.2.5 Improving Effectiveness of Web Search Engines

Using a Web server to implement an information retrieval system does not dramatically vary the types of algorithms that might be used. For a single machine, all of the algorithms given in Chapter 5 are relevant. Compression of the inverted index is the same, partial relevance ranking is the same, etc. However, there were and are some efforts specifically focused on improving the performance of Web-based information retrieval systems.

In terms of accuracy improvements, it is reasonable to believe that by sending a request to a variety of different search engines and merging the obtained results one could improve the accuracy of a Web search engine. This indeed was proposed as early as TREC-4 . Later, in the CYBERosetta prototype [Desantis et al., 1996] system developed by the Software Productivity Consortium (SPC) for use by DARPA, identical copies of a request were simultaneously sent to multiple search servers. After a timeout limit was reached, the obtained results were merged into a single result and presented to the user.

8.3 Result Fusion

Fusing result sets as a means to improve accuracy became of wide academic research interest shortly after Lee [Lee, 1997] hypothesized on what conditions yielded successful fusion. That is, Lee used several common result fusing heuristics to merge results obtained from multiple independent search engines and demonstrated that relevant documents had a greater level of overlap than the set of non-relevant documents. His findings demonstrated that using the CombMNZ fusion heuristic resulted in higher retrieval accuracy than any of the individual search engines used. Aloui, et. al. expanded the work of Lee and concluded that to best capitalize on result fusion techniques, the individual search engines used had to greatly differ in their processing strategies and utilities [Alaoui et al., 1998].

Recently, in [Chowdhury et al., 2001, Beitzel et al., 2003a] a study revisiting the Lee fusion hypothesis was conducted. In this study, unlike in Lee's original study, all the system parameters, e.g., stemmers, parsers, stop-word list, etc., were kept constant and only the similarity measures used were varied. Furthermore, also unlike the Lee study, only the top existing similarity measures were used. The results demonstrated that the overlap difference between relevant and non-relevant documents that Lee described was far less significant when these new measures were used. Surprisingly, it was other system parameters that affected the overall fusion gains with greater impact than the initially postulated similarity measured used.

This observation relied upon using newly available highly accurate similarity measures. From the findings, it was postulated that over the years, given the accuracy improvement of the similarity measures, there remained only an insignificant difference between the result sets obtained using any of the better measures. Given only a slight difference between the result sets available, fusion, at least in that form, yielded only minimal improvements if not an actual reduction in retrieval accuracy. This makes sense when one considers that retrieval strategies have evolved over time to include useful features that were first generated for use with another strategy. Incorporation of term frequency and document length are now common across all retrieval strategies. Hence, as these strategies have evolved, it is not too surprising that they return very similar documents. This certainly reduces the likelihood that fusing retrieval strategies will yield improved effectiveness.

In terms of efficiency, in [Liu et al., 1996], an effort to enhance Web server performance improvements is described. They discussed the use of pre-started processes, or *cliettes*, to avoid the start-up costs of starting processes from a typical common gateway interface (CGI). This was used to implement a prototype system that provides search access to eight library collections.

Most current Web servers use a very detailed, full-text index, but if the Web continues to grow it may not be practical to use a single index. Early work in the area of Web-based distributed query processing was done by [Duda and Sheldon, 1994] in which a system that used the Wide Area Information Service (WAIS) only sent queries to certain servers based on an initial search of the content of those servers. The content was described by some specific fields in the documents that exist on each server such as *headline* of a news article or *subject* of an e-mail message. The use of a content index is the middle ground between sending the request to all of the servers, or providing a very detailed full-text index, and sending the request to only those servers that match the index.

More work done for the Glossary-of-Servers Server (GlOSS) builds a server that estimates the best server for a given query, based on the vector-space model [Gravano and Garcia-Molina, 1995]. The query vector is matched with a vector that characterizes each individual server. The top n servers are then ranked and searched. Several means of characterizing a server are explored. The simplest is to sum the *tf-idf* weights of each term on a given server and normalize based on the number of documents on the server. This yields a centroid vector for each server. A *tf-idf* vector space coefficient (as described in Section 2.1) can then be used to rank the servers for a given query. Different similarity coefficient thresholds at which a server is considered a possible source and assumptions used to estimate which databases are likely to contain all of the terms in the query are also used. It is estimated that the index on the GlOSS server is deemed to be only two percent of the size of a full-text index.

Query processing using a full-text index on a Web server can be done with any of the combination of strategies and utilities described in Chapters 2 and 3. However, an additional strategy based on the use of hypertext links found on Web pages has been investigated [Yuwono and Lee, 1996]. In this work, a strategy referred to as *vector spreading activation* was investigated in which documents were ranked based on a match with a term in a simple query. Additionally, documents that contained links to the original result set were added to the result set. The weight of the new *linked* documents was scaled to be less than the weight of the documents in the original result set. Experiments with scaling factors of zero and 0.5, with increments of 0.1, showed that 0.2, was the best scaling factor. Vector spreading activation was shown to be slightly better than *tf-idf* when average precision was measured for a small test collection of only 2,393 Web pages. Additionally, this system did not use a full-text index. The indexer uses only HTML tokens such as terms in boldface or italics, the first sentence of every list item, titles, all-level headings, and anchor hypertexts.

What, by necessity, differs in the Web based search engine domain from the traditional information retrieval system environment is the means to evaluate individual systems. In conventional environments, a standard benchmark query and data mix is used to compare across systems. In the Web domain, however, each search engine indexes only a portion of the available data, and the portions do not necessarily overlap nor do they necessarily index even the same version (different time period) of the data where they do indeed overlap.

8.4 Peer-to-Peer Information Systems

We now turn our focus to an emerging field, a cross between the networking domain and the information retrieval discipline, namely Peer-to-Peer (P2P) architectures. By definition, Peer-to-Peer architectures are distributed environments where each node in the network is potentially a source for information (a server), a client in need of information (a client), and an intermediate router (a router) of information. Each node is independent and the system operates in a purely decentralized manner. In the realm of information retrieval systems, the provided resources are in the form of searchable data.

The main characteristics of P2P systems are their ad-hoc nature and durability. P2P systems can gracefully handle the joining and leaving of nodes from the system. The resources offered by these nodes are dynamically added or removed from the system as necessary. Furthermore, the failure of a single node does not destroy the overall system.

The origin of the P2P movement is often attributed to Napster, the music file sharing system, although Napster actually relied on a centralized implementation. That is, Napster was not decentralized, and hence, was not peer-to-peer in the pure sense of the definition. However, Napster did offer P2P functionality in that users could dynamically share files with others. Besides the inherent single point of contention in terms of performance and reliability, Napster's centralized implementation eventually doomed it to legal action, and today, Napster no longer exists in its original form. The demise of Napster taught enthusiasts a lesson. In response, they created the Gnutella protocol [V0.4, 2004], which is truly P2P, and serves as the basis of much of today's P2P research. (A later version of the Gnutella protocol [V0.6, 2004] also exists and extends P2P architectures to include hierarchies. This protocol and its applications are discussed later.)

Systems based on the Gnutella (Version 0.4) protocol generally provide only primitive search capability. That is, they generally rely on exact name search typically accomplished via sub-string matching. Specifically, a query matches a file if all the terms in the query are sub-strings of the file's metadata. Files that are returned to the client are grouped based on the similarity of their metadata. There is currently no accepted way of ranking these groups. The client picks one of these groups, and downloads the associated file from a corresponding server [Rohrs, 2000, Rohrs, 2001].

There are other problems associated with the majority of the Gnutella (Version 0.4) based P2P information retrieval systems. These include global networking flooding and non-deterministic, poor accuracy search results. Since P2P information retrieval systems are, by definition, decentralized, for every search request, messages are sent to all nodes potentially possessing relevant documents. Since only limited search and document ranking capabilities exist at the nodes, any potentially relevant document is sent to the requesting nodes. Given the number of potentially relevant documents, the resulting network traffic overwhelms the network resources. This condition is referred to as global network flooding. To reduce the traffic, [Yu et al., 2003] developed a results filtering and merging technique where nodes collect information about their neighbors contents. Thus, when potential results to a request arrive at an intermediate node, only merged and filtered results are propagated back to the requesting node. A recent merging technique for hierarchical peer-to-peer networks is given in [Lu and Callan, 2004].

Another approach to reduce network traffic is to selectively transmit the request to only a limited set of target nodes. This approach suffers from potentially non-deterministic or poor result generation. Since only a limited number of nodes are accessed, depending on network conditions, different results may be obtained each time a request is made, hence the non-determinism. Furthermore, poor selection of the target nodes is likely to result in poor search accuracy. Hewlett Packard Company's PeerSearch [Tang et al., 2002, Tang et al., 2003] reduces the risk of poor target node selection by mapping the index and routing the queries according to a logical mapping of the vector space model retrieval coordinates onto the network. Thus, semantically near items should be mapped near each other, reducing the traffic.

Recently, a newer version of the Gnutella protocol [V0.6, 2004] was released. In this version, logical hierarchies are supported. That is, in the original P2P architecture models, all nodes were logically equivalent in function, and all information was decentralized. In this later protocol, some nodes act as *leaves* (client and server nodes) whereas other nodes serve as *directory nodes* providing no content but rather serving as a global directory for the content of their associated leave nodes. These hybrid networks, a composition of decentralized and centralized repositories, are providing additional opportunities for retrieval. Using these directory nodes, it is possible to more accurately access content and selectively choose proper target nodes. In [Liu and Callan, 2003], the authors propose and evaluate a P2P information retrieval system for such networks. The results presented demonstrated that by relying on the information in the directory nodes, network traffic is significantly reduced while accuracy is minimally compromised.

Some of the current academic P2P systems that are available are Edutella [Nejdl et al., 2002] and PeerDB [Ng et al., 2003]. These systems, however, are mainly focused on standardizing interfaces and query languages for Internet accessible services. Their goal is to create a P2P supercomputing or federated database system, not an information retrieval system.

Other research in P2P systems focuses on bandwidth efficiency. Rather than on relying on the Gnutella protocol, more intelligent routing protocols are presented [Ratnasamy et al., 2001, Sripanidkulchai et al., 2003, Stoica et al., 2001]. These efforts focus on improving response time, but do not improve the way that queries are answered and how results are ranked.

8.4.1 Example: Peer-to-Peer Information Retrieval System

In PIRS [Yee and Frieder, 2004], a P2P Information Retrieval System built on top of Gnutella, the primary goal is to enhance the search effectiveness by increasing the variety of system supported queries and improving the ranking mechanism. Improving the variety of queries that can be answered relies on building a corpus of metadata that reflects users' query patterns. Currently, the songs found on a typical Gnutella network contain metadata that are machine generated (e.g., using ID3 data [Nilsson, 2004] from Web sites such as freedb.org). A user who is unaware of the metadata annotation conventions, or deliberately poses a vague query, will not be able to find desired files. For example, a query for a "local Chicago band" will return nothing meaningful in the Gnutella network, whereas a query for " The Off-key Singing Trio" will.

PIRS solves this problem by forcing the client to randomly copy metadata from all the servers in the group from which the file was selected. This form of metadata copying significantly improves the number of queries that are satisfied.

PIRS ranks groups of files, not individual files, using the aggregate metadata of the group. It uses four ranking criteria:

- **Term Frequency** - measures the total number of times a query term appears in a group's metadata
- **Inverse Term Frequency** - measures term frequency, where each term's contribution is normalized by the inverse of its frequency over all groups
- **Precision** - measures the ratio of query term frequency and the total number of terms in the group
- **Group Size** - measures the total number of files in the group

Experimental results show that group size outperforms the other ranking criteria. There are two reasons for its effectiveness: a large group suggests that a file has a large degree of support for matching with a query; and a large group suggests that the file is popular in general, and is therefore a good download candidate. Overall, the use of random sampling, and group size ranking improves the query performance by an order of 30% over other combinations of metadata copying, and result ranking.

8.5 Other Architectures

In addition to the peer-to-peer architectures, some additional core distributed architectures exist. These include the shared disk architecture and the distributed data architecture. In each case, the notion is that the search is being done by multiple retrieval servers. If the search was being done by a single large machine with multiple processors then it would be a *parallel information retrieval search* (see Chapter 7).

8.5.1 Shared Disk Architecture

Even with numerous distributed processors, it is possible to link them all to a single shared disk. Incoming documents might be farmed out to the different servers for indexing, but all of the final index is stored in a single storage array. Queries can be processed by different servers, but they all access the index on the single storage array. The storage area becomes a significant point of contention, and it can result in degraded efficiency. The advantage is that even though the storage area can be a single point of failure, it is possible to use an additional storage array as a backup. The two storage areas can be synchronized at index time, and should a disk failure occur, the backup storage area can be immediately used.

If a processor crashes, it is only processing queries so users are not impacted at all. The entire index remains available to all users. Hence, reliability can be quite good with this architecture.

8.5.2 Distributed Disk Architecture

Here, each server has its own local disk, and the index is spread across the local disks. At index time, the document collection can be partitioned into the different servers, and they can all create the index in parallel and store their portion on their own local drives. Queries are also distributed across servers. Issued queries are sent to the processors that contain the posting list(s) that are requested. For common terms, this may be many different processors, but for an uncommon term, it may only be a small number of processors.

With this approach, there is no single point of resource contention; so it is extremely efficient. If a processor crashes, however, the portion of the index that is maintained by that processor is unavailable. For Web search applications this may be a reasonable tradeoff, and users do not need to be informed about the missing documents for a given query. For a mission-critical search engine, it is crucial to find all relevant documents. Simply ignoring some documents because a server is down is not acceptable. Building processor redundancy into this architecture requires doubling the number of machines, which may be very expensive.

Hence, the distributed architecture is typically viewed as more efficient than a shared disk architecture but less reliable.

8.6 Summary

This chapter focused on searching document collections that are physically distributed as well as search of document collections using a collection of separate machines. A Web search engine is inherently an example of a distributed information retrieval system since the actual documents are stored in servers around the world.

We started with a theoretical model of distributed information retrieval system and then moved into a brief discussion of recent work on distributed search strategies as well as very recent work on the use of peer-to-peer systems for information retrieval. Finally, we discussed other viable distributed architectures.

It is reasonable to expect that as cross-language information retrieval continues to grow and as more countries increase their stores of electronically available document collections, the need for highly effective, highly efficient distributed search systems will continue to increase.

8.7 Exercises

1 Develop a distributed IR algorithm that stores equally sized portions of an inverted index on separate machines. Compute the communications overhead required by your approach.

2 Describe the effects of document updates on a distributed information retrieval algorithm described in this chapter.

3 Recently Web search engines are facing the problem that developers of Web pages are adding terms that are commonly queried just to draw attention to their page. A user might add *Disneyland* to a page about *kitchen plumbing*. Develop a heuristic to circumvent this problem—talk about how your approach will avoid a reduction in effectiveness for a "normal" or untampered document collection.

Chapter 9

SUMMARY AND FUTURE DIRECTIONS

We described a variety of search and retrieval approaches, most of which primarily focused on improving the accuracy of information retrieval engines. Unlike other search and retrieval domains, e.g., traditional relational databases, the accuracy of retrieval is not constant. That is, in the traditional relational database domain all techniques result in perfect accuracy. Hence, the main concern, in terms of performance evaluation, is the overall system throughput and the individual query performance.

In the information retrieval domain, accuracy varies as the associated precision and recall measures of all engines are both approach and data dependent. Thus, all information retrieval performance evaluation must account for both the resulting accuracy, as well as the associated processing times. In both database and information retrieval systems performance evaluation, commonly referred to as *benchmarking*, must also take storage overhead into account. Given the continuing improvements in storage technology coupled with the ongoing reduction in cost, relatively little attention is focused on storage overhead reduction as compared to improving computational time, and where appropriate, accuracy demands.

To assess the performance of database systems, many benchmarks were developed. Many of these benchmarks are in commercial use. Examples include the TPC family of benchmarks [Kohler, 1993]. Until the early 1990's, little emphasis was placed on the development of benchmarks for uniform evaluation of the performance of information retrieval approaches or engines. The datasets used in the evaluation of information retrieval systems were small in size, often on the order of megabytes, and the mix of queries studied were limited in domain focus, number, and complexity.

In 1985, Blair and Maron [Blair and Maron, 1985] authored a seminal paper that demonstrated what was suspected earlier: performance measurements obtained using small datasets were not indicative for larger document collections. In the early 1990's, the United States National Institute of Standards and Technology (NIST), using the text collection created by the United States Defense Advanced Research Project Agency (DARPA), initiated a conference to support the collaboration and technology transfer between academia, industry, and government in the area of text retrieval. The conference, named the Text REtrieval Conference (TREC) aimed to improve evaluation methods and measures in the information retrieval domain by increasing the research in information retrieval using relatively large test collections on a variety of datasets.

TREC is an annual event held in November at NIST. Over the years, the number of participants has steadily increased and the types of tracks have greatly varied. In its most recent 2003 incarnation, the twelfth conference, TREC consisted of six tracks, namely Genomics, HARD, Novelty, Question Answering, Robust Retrieval, and Web. The specifics of each track are not relevant since the tracks are continuously modified. Suffice to say that the type of data, queries, evaluation metrics, and interaction paradigms (with or without a user in the loop) vary greatly. The common theme of all tracks is to establish an evaluation corpus to be used in evaluating search systems.

Conference participation procedures are as follows. Initially a call for participation is announced. Those who participate eventually define the specifics of each task. Documents and topics (queries) are procured, and each participating team conducts a set of experiments. The results are submitted for judgment. Relevance assessments are obtained, and the submitted results are evaluated. The findings are evaluated, summarized, and presented to the participants at the annual meeting. After the meeting, all participants submit their summary papers, and a TREC conference proceeding is published.

Early TREC forums used data on the order of multiple gigabytes. Representative collection statistics are listed in Table 9.1. A sample document from the above collection is presented in Figure 9.1. A sample query is illustrated in Figure 9.1.

Today, the types of data vary greatly, depending on the focus of the particular track. Likewise, the volumes of data vary. At the writing of this second edition, a terabyte data collection is proposed for one of the 2005 TREC tracks with a preliminary collection somewhat in excess of 400 GB to be used in 2004. Thus, within roughly a decade, the collection sizes will grow by three orders of magnitude from a couple of gigabytes to a terabyte. This growth of data might necessitate new evaluation metrics and approaches.

Throughout its existence, interest in TREC activities has steadfastly increased. With the expanding awareness and popularity of distributed information retrieval engines, e.g., the various World Wide Web search engines, the number of academic and commercial TREC participants continues to grow. Given this increased participation, more and more techniques are being developed and evaluated. The transfer of general ideas and crude experiments from TREC participants to commercial practice each demonstrates the success of TREC.

Table 9.1. Size of TREC data

Disk	*Collection*	Size (MB)	Number of Documents	Median $\frac{Terms}{Doc}$	Mean $\frac{Terms}{Doc}$
1	*Wall Street Journal*, 1987—1989	267	98,732	245	434.0
1	*Associated Press*, 1989	254	84,678	446	473.9
1	*Computer Select*, Ziff-Davis	242	75,180	200	473.0
1	*Federal Register*, 1989	260	25,960	391	1,315.9
1	abstracts of US DOE	184	226,087	111	120.4
2	*Wall Street Journal*, 1990—1992	242	74,520	301	508.4
2	*Associated Press*, 1988	237	79,919	438	468.7
2	*Computer Select*, Ziff-Davis	175	56,920	182	451.9
2	*Federal Register*, 1988	209	19,860	396	1,378.1
3	*San Jose Mercury News*, 1991	287	90,257	379	453.0
3	*Associated Press*, 1990	237	78,321	451	478.4
3	*Computer Select*, Ziff-Davis	345	161,021	122	295.4
3	*US Patents*, 1993	243	6,711	4,425	5,391
4	*Financial Times*, 1991—1994	564	210,158	316	412.7
4	*Federal Register*, 1994	395	55,630	588	644.7
4	*Congressional Record*, 1993	235	27,922	288	1,373

Over the years, the raw average precision numbers presented in the various TREC proceedings initially increased and then decreased. This appears to indicate that the participating systems have actually declined in their accuracy over some of the past years. In actuality, the queries and tasks have increased in difficulty. When the newer, revised systems currently participating in TREC are run using the queries and data from prior years, they tend to exhibit a higher degree of accuracy as compared to their predecessors. Any perceived degradation is probably due to the relative complexity increase of the queries and the tasks themselves.

We do not review the performance of the individual engines participating in the yearly event since the focus of this book is on algorithms, and the effects of the individual utilities and strategies are not always documented. Detailed

<DOC>
<DOCNO>WSJ880406-0090 </DOCNO>
<HL> AT&T Unveils Services to Upgrade Phone Networks Under Global Plan </HL>
<AUTHOR> Janet Guyon (WSJ Staff) </AUTHOR>
<DATELINE> NEW YORK </DATELINE>
<TEXT>
American Telephone & Telegraph Co. introduced the first of a new generation of phone services with broad implications for computer and communications equipment markets. AT&T said it is the first national long-distance carrier to announce prices for specific services under world-wide standardization plan to upgrade phone networks. By announcing commercial services under the plan, which the industry calls the Integrated Services Digital Network, AT&T will influence evolving communications standards to its advantage, consultants said, just as International Business Machines Corp. has created de facto computer standards favoring its products. . . .
</TEXT>
</DOC>

Figure 9.1. Sample TREC document

<top>
<num> Number: 168
<title> Topic: Financing AMTRAK
<desc> Description:
A document will address the role of the Federal Government in financing the operation of the National Railroad Transportation Corporation (AMTRAK)
<narr> Narrative:
A relevant document must provide information on the government's responsibility to make AMTRAK an economically viable entity. It could also discuss the privatization of AMTRAK as an alternative to continuing government subsidies given to air and bus transportation with those provided to AMTRAK would also be relevant.
</top>

Figure 9.2. Sample TREC query

information on each TREC conference is available in written proceedings or on-line at: trec.nist.gov.

TREC, although successful, does have its shortcomings. As noted, performance evaluation in retrieval systems involves both accuracy and performance assistance. TREC, however, only evaluates accuracy, paying little if any, significance to processing times and storage overheads. In terms of relevancy (accuracy), common TREC criticism focuses on the means of judging document-to-query relevancy.

Given the limited number of human document judgment analysts available to NIST, pooling is used to determine the relevant documents. Pooling, as now used in TREC [Harman, 1995], is the process of selecting top-ranked documents obtained from multiple engines, merging and sorting them, and retaining the remaining unique document identifiers as relevant documents (i.e., removing the duplicate document identifiers). Although relatively effective, pooling does result in several false-negative document ratings. To avoid such problems, recent work describes methods which avoid the need for pooling [Sanderson and Joho, 2004].

We also note that a new effectiveness measure has been proposed to be more resilient to problems with incompleteness in a pool. Pooling assumes that *most* relevant documents will be found. When that is not the case, average precision is not robust [Buckley and Voorhees, 2004]. Furthermore, average precision does not include a user preference. A document not found is treated the same as a document that is not relevant. A preference based measure focuses on the number of times judged nonrelevant documents are retrieved before relevant documents. Simply counting the number of non relevant before we hit a relevant document is not sufficient because of the vast differences in relevant documents available to a query. A query with one hundred relevant documents has a much higher chance of hitting a relevant document than one that has only one or two relevant documents. To normalize for the number of relevant documents, the following measure is proposed:

$$bpref = \frac{1}{r}\sum_{r}\left(1 - \frac{|n\ ranked\ higher\ than\ r|}{R}\right)$$

Another recently described form of evaluation uses term relevance as opposed to document relevance. Here, a list of relevant terms is identified for a given query and effectiveness is measured based on a system's ability to find terms in the list. Since, a set of terms can be defined for a query without detailed knowledge of a test collection, this approach has the potential of scaling to very large document collections [Amitay et al., 2004].

We note that the Cross-Language Evaluation Forum (CLEF) has followed the basic TREC style but focuses on cross-lingual evaluation (see Section 4.1). The CLEF Web site is **clef.iei.pi.cnr.it:2002**. Additionally, a new test collection of conversational speech was recently developed [Oard et al., 2004].

In spite of all the past successful research efforts, the domain of information retrieval is still in its infancy. Twenty years ago, the number of retrieval strategies could be counted on one hand. Most of the research literature focused on the four key retrieval strategies: the vector space, probabilistic, Boolean, and fuzzy-set. Since we developed our first edition of this book, language models were applied to the problem and the result is a ninth retrieval strategy.

Until recently, distributed information retrieval was only of theoretical interest. With the expansion of personal Internet use and the advent of the World Wide Web (WWW), distributed information retrieval, specifically search and retrieval of information across the WWW, is a daily practice.

Cross-language retrieval was just getting underway when we went to press with the first edition. Now it is a fairly mature area. It has taken us one step closer to a search environment that would allow a user to query a world wide document collection and obtain results in a single language.

We should also note that search of HTML pages is only one restricted type of search. Most large companies have search problems that cover large bodies of texts without hyperlinks (e.g.; Word documents, PowerPoint presentations, PDF files). The techniques that work well for Web search do not necessarily perform well for these data.

In terms of the research community, heightened interest is best demonstrated by the increased popularity of the NIST TREC activities. In its initial years, the number of participants in the TREC activities numbered less than thirty for most tasks. In the sixth NIST TREC meeting, the number of participants exceeded fifty. In the twelfth offering, the number of participants exceeded 100. The conference started with tests of only two Gigabytes of text (an amount which was very difficult for many researchers) and is now gearing up for a Terabyte of text.

Given the growing interest, future advances are clearly on the horizon. The question is which areas still need further investigation. We project future research using the same paradigm used throughout the book. That is, first we address strategies, followed by utilities and efficiency concerns. Issues involving parallelism and distributed processing conclude our projections.

Additional data strategies are still required. In the TREC activities, the average precision numbers rarely reach the forty percent mark for any task. Significantly improving these numbers requires new insight and potentially a new strategy. The past several years have resulted in a steady improvement in retrieval accuracy, but current results are still unacceptable. It is unlikely that even this continued improvement will result in significant strides to sufficiently improve retrieval accuracy. This is especially true when faced with vastly larger data sets. It is reasonable to suspect that simple pattern matching approaches will continue to stay at the existing plateau observed in TREC during the last two or three years. To go beyond this will likely require incorporation of more complex natural language processing. At present, recent work on information extraction and "light parsing" are just now becoming computationally feasible.

Additional strategies are also required to cope with the diversity of data presently available on-line. Throughout this book, we addressed only text oriented data. Given the adage that a picture is worth a thousand words, one must find a way of extracting and integrating the thousands of words portrayed by an image. Currently, information retrieval models do not support this. There are efforts that address the image integration issue, for example, IRIS (adapted as the IBM ImageMiner Project) [Alshuth et al., 1998]. However, they still do not fully integrate structured, text, and image data into a cohesive environment. It is reasonable to expect that the future will require an extended corpus consisting of integrated text with images. Such a corpus will make it possible to evaluate progress of new text and image retrieval algorithms.

It is possible to represent information retrieval processing utilities on a continuum where the two extremes are simple pattern matching and full natural language text processing. Currently, the majority of the utilities fall closer to the simple pattern matching end of the continuum. For example, both passage-based and n-gram techniques clearly focus on purely pattern matching analysis. Semantic networks and parsing techniques more closely align with natural language processing, but clearly do not support full content analysis as expected from natural language processing. It is our belief that to significantly increase the accuracy of retrieval, the semantic meaning of the text, in contrast to its denotational, or even worse, purely its character representation, must be extracted. When we went to press with the first edition, text extraction was a relatively new field. Now, there are a variety of commercial text extractors. The question still remains: How can these tools be used to improve information retrieval?

Parallel processing architectures are now widely available and are in daily use. They are no longer just research engines. Even our personal computers are configured as parallel processing engines. Thus, information retrieval applications must be developed to harness this parallel processing capability. In Chapter 7, we described some of the ongoing parallel processing efforts. None of these efforts, however, have demonstrated scalability to the thousands of nodes. None can handle a diversity of data formats, support multi-language retrieval, efficiently support all of the described retrieval strategies and utilities, provide multi-user concurrency with on-line recovery, and support a "plug-and-play" composition of strategies and utilities environment. Furthermore, with the diversity of the underlying models of parallel architectures, even if some solutions to the above concerns are available, they do not seamlessly port across multiple parallel architectures. Clearly, in the realm of parallelism in information retrieval, there is a wide area for further investigation.

With the continued advances in wireless technology, data are available not only on host computers, but also on mobile computing devices worldwide. This distributed nature introduces several issues not previously of much concern to the information retrieval domain. For example, due to the portable nature of the storage devices, most of the data are available only at uncertain time intervals. Furthermore, each search site has access to only limited information and this information can change rapidly. Thus, distributed information retrieval algorithms must account for these constraints. Some ongoing research efforts in the domains of distributed operating and database systems focus on related issues. An adaptation of some of the results from such efforts might be appropriate. To date, no information retrieval research efforts address these concerns.

Throughout this book, we have advocated a plug and play architecture for information retrieval. We described strategies, utilities, efficiency considerations, integration paradigms, and processing topologies for information retrieval. The primary problem for future information retrieval research investigation is: How does one achieve synergy in the composition of all of these factors?

References

[Abiteboul, 1997] Abiteboul, S. (1997). Querying semistructured data. In *Proceedings of the International Conference on Database Theory.*

[Adams, 1991] Adams, E. (1991). *A Study of Trigrams and Their Feasibility as Index Terms in a Full Text Information Retrieval System.* PhD thesis, George Washington University, Department of Computer Science.

[Adriani, 2000] Adriani, M. (2000). Dictionary-based CLIR for the CLEF multilingual track. In *Working Notes of the Workshop in Cross-Language Evaluation Forum (CLEF)*, Lisbon.

[Agun and Frieder, 2003] Agun, S. K. and Frieder, O. (2003). HAT: A hardware assisted top-doc inverted index component. In *ACM Twenty-Sixth Conference on Research and Development in Information Retrieval (SIGIR).*

[Aho and Corasick, 1975] Aho, A. and Corasick, M. (1975). Efficient string matching: An aid to bibliographic search. *Communications of the ACM*, 18:333–340.

[Al-Kharashi and Evens, 1994] Al-Kharashi, I. and Evens, M. (1994). Comparing words, stems, and roots as index terms in an arabic information retrieval system. *Journal of the American Society for Information Science*, 45(8):548–560.

[Al-Onaizan et al., 1999] Al-Onaizan, Y., Curin, J., Jahr, M., Knight, K., Lafferty, J., Melamed, I. D., Och, F. J., Purdy, D., Smith, N. A., and Yarowsky, D. (1999). Statistical machine translation, final report, JHU workshop. `http://www.clsp.jhu.edu/ws99/projects/mt/final_report/mt-final-report.ps`.

[Alaoui et al., 1998] Alaoui, S., Goharian, N., Mahoney, M., Salem, A., and Frieder, O. (1998). Fusion of information retrieval engines (FIRE). In *Proceedings of the International Conference on Parallel and Distributed Processing Techniques and Applications (PDPTA-98).*

[Aljlayl and Frieder, 2002] Aljlayl, M. and Frieder, O. (2002). On arabic search: Improving retrieval effectiveness via a light stemming approach. In *Proceedings of the ACM Eleventh Conference on Information and Knowledge Management*, Washington, DC.

[Aljlayl et al., 2002] Aljlayl, M., Frieder, O., and Grossman, D. (2002). On bidirectional English-Arabic search. *Journal of the American Society of information Science and Technology (JASIST)*, 53(13).

[Allan et al., 1995] Allan, J., Ballesteros, L., Callan, J.P., Croft, W.B., and Lu, Z. (1995). Recent experiments with INQUERY. In *Proceedings of the Fourth Text REtrieval Conference (TREC-4)*, pages 49–63.

[Alliance, 2004] Alliance, Globus (2004). The globus alliance.

[Alshuth et al., 1998] Alshuth, P., Hermes, T., Herzog, O., and Voigt, L. (1998). On video retrieval: Content analysis by Imageminer. In *Proceedings of the IS&T/SPIE Symposium on Electronic Imaging 98, Science and Technology, Multimedia Processing and Applications, Storage and Retrieval for Image and Video Databases*, volume 3312, pages 236–247.

[Amitay et al., 2004] Amitay, E., Carmel, D., Lempel, R., and Soffer, A. (2004). Scaling IR-system evaluation using term relevance sets. In *ACM 27th Conference on Research and Development in Information Retrieval (SIGIR)*, pages 10–17.

[Anh and Moffat, 2004] Anh, V.N. and Moffat, A. (2004). Inverted index compression using word-aligned binary codes. *Information Retrieval.* Available at http://www.kluweronline.com, pre-publication date April 2, 2004.

[Asokan et al., 1990] Asokan, N., Ranka, S., and Frieder, O. (1990). A parallel free text search system with indexing. In *Proceedings of the International Conference on Databases, Parallel Architectures, and their Applications (PARBASE-90)*, pages 519–534.

[Bailey and Hawking, 1996] Bailey, P. and Hawking, D. (1996). A parallel architecture for query processing over a terabyte of text. Technical report.

[Ballerini et al., 1996] Ballerini, J.P., Buchel, M., Domenig, R., Knaus, D., Mateev, B., Mittendorf, E., Schauble, P., Sheridan, P., and Wechsler, M. (1996). SPIDER retrieval system at TREC-5. In *Proceedings of the Fifth Text REtrieval Conference (TREC-5)*, pages 217–228.

[Ballesteros, 2001] Ballesteros, L. (2001). *Resolving ambiguity for cross-language information retrieval: A dictionary approach.* PhD thesis, University of Massachusetts Amherst.

[Ballesteros and Croft, 1997] Ballesteros, L. and Croft, B. W. (1997). Phrasal translation and query expansion techniques for cross-language information retrieval. In *Proceedings of the Twentieth Annual International ACM SIGIR Conference on Research and Development in Information Retrieval*, pages 84–91.

[Ballesteros and Croft, 1998] Ballesteros, L. and Croft, W. B. (1998). Resolving ambiguity for cross-language retrieval. In *Proceedings of the Twenty-First Annual International ACM SIGIR Conference on Research and Development in Information Retrieval*, pages 64–71.

[Baru et al., 1998] Baru, C., Gupta, A., Ludascher, B., Marciano, R., Papakonstantinou, Y., Velikhov, P., and Chu, V. (1998). XML-based information mediation with MIX. In *Proceedings of the ACM Special Interest Group on Management of Data (SIGMOD '98)*, pages 597–599.

[Bataineh et al., 1991] Bataineh, A., Ozguner, F., and Sarwal, A. (1991). Parallel boolean operations for information retrieval. *Information Processing Letters*, 39:99–108.

[Bataineh et al., 1989] Bataineh, A., Sarwal, Alok, Ozguner, F., and Dick, R. (1989). Parallel boolean operations for information retrieval. In *Conference on Hypercubes, Concurrent Computers, and Applications*, pages 445–448.

[Beckwith and Miller, 1990] Beckwith, R. and Miller, G. (1990). Implementing a lexical network. *International Journal of Lexicography*, 3(4):302–312.

[Beitzel et al., 2003a] Beitzel, S., Jensen, E., Chowdhury, A., Frieder, O., Grossman, D., and Goharian, N. (2003a). Disproving the fusion hypothesis: An analysis of data fusion via effective information retrieval strategies. In *ACM Eighteenth Symposium on Applied Computing (SAC)*, Melbourne, Florida.

[Beitzel et al., 2003b] Beitzel, S., Jensen, E., Chowdhury, A., Grossman, D., and Frieder, O. (2003b). Using manually-built web directories for automatic evaluation of known-item retrieval. In *Proceedings of the Twenty-Sixth Annual International ACM SIGIR Conference on Research and Development in Information Retrieval*, Toronto, Canada.

[Beitzel et al., 2004a] Beitzel, S., Jensen, E., Chowdhury, A., Grossman, D., and Frieder, O. (2004a). Evaluation of filtering current news search results. In *Proceedings of the 27th Annual International ACM SIGIR Conference on Research and Development in Information Retrieval*, pages 494–495, Sheffield, United Kingdom.

[Beitzel et al., 2004b] Beitzel, S., Jensen, E., Chowdhury, A., Grossman, D., and Frieder, O. (2004b). Hourly analysis of a very large topically categorized web query log. In *Proceedings of the 27th Annual International ACM SIGIR Conference on Research and Development in Information Retrieval*, pages 321–328, Sheffield, United Kingdom.

[Belew, 1989] Belew, R. (1989). Adaptive information retrieval. In *Proceedings of the Twelfth Annual International ACM SIGIR Conference on Research and Development in Information Retrieval*, pages 11–20.

[Bell et al., 1990] Bell, T.C., Cleary, J.G., and Witten, I.H. (1990). *Text Compression*. Prentice Hall, Englewood Cliffs, NJ.

[Berger and Lafferty, 1999] Berger, A. and Lafferty, J. (1999). Information retrieval as statistical translation. In *Proceedings of the 22nd Annual International ACM SIGIR conference on Research and Development in Information Retrieval*, pages 222–229.

[Berry, 1992] Berry, M. W. (1992). Large-scale sparse singular computations. *The International Journal of Supercomputer Applications*, 6(1):13–49.

[Bertoldi and Federico, 2003] Bertoldi, N. and Federico, M. (2003). ITC-irst at CLEF 2003: Monolingual, bilingual, and multilingual information retrieval. In *Workshop on Cross-Language Information Retrieval and Evaluation (CLEF)*, Darmstadt, Germany.

[Blair, 1974] Blair, D. (1974). SQUARE (Specifying QUeries as Relational Expressions) as a document retrieval language. Unpublished working paper, University of California, Berkeley.

[Blair, 1988] Blair, D. (1988). An extended relational document retrieval model. *Information Processing and Management*, 24(3):349–371.

[Blair and Maron, 1985] Blair, D.C. and Maron, M.E. (1985). An evaluation of retrieval effectiveness for a full-text document-retrieval system. *Communications of the ACM*, 28(3):289–299.

[Blandford and Blelloch, 2002] Blandford, D. and Blelloch, G. (2002). Index compression through document reordering. In *Proceedings of the 2002 IEEE Data Compression Conference (DCC'02)*.

[Bleir, 1967] Bleir, R.F. (1967). Treating hierarchical data structures in the SDC time-shared data management system (TDMS). In *Proceedings, 22nd ACM National Conference*, pages 41–49.

[Boag et al., 2003] Boag, S., Chamberlin, D., Fernandez, M., Florescu, D., Robie, J., Simeon, J., and Stefanescu, M. (2003). XQuery 1.0: A query language for XML. W3C working draft. Available from http://www.w3.org/TR/xquery.

[Bond and Reddaway, 1993] Bond, N. and Reddaway, S. (1993). A massively parallel indexing engine using DAP. *Cambridge Parallel Processing. Technical Report.*

[Bonifati and Ceri, 2000] Bonifati, A. and Ceri, S. (2000). Comparitive analysis of five XML query languages. *SIGMOD Record*, 29(1):68–79.

[Boughanem and Soule-Depuy, 1997] Boughanem, M. and Soule-Depuy, C. (1997). Mercure at TREC-6. In *Proceedings of the Sixth Text REtrieval Conference (TREC-6)*, pages 187–193.

[Boyer and Moore, 1977] Boyer, R.S. and Moore, J.S. (1977). A fast string searching algorithm. *Communications of the ACM*, 20(10):762–772.

[Breslauer and Galil, 1991] Breslauer, D. and Galil, Z. (1991). Parallel string matching algorithms. *Carnegie-Mellon University. Technical Report: CUCS-002-92.*

[Brill, 1992] Brill, Eric (1992). A simple rule-based part of speech tagger. *Proceedings of the Third Conference on Applied Computational Linguistics*, pages 152–155.

[Brin et al., 1995] Brin, S., Davis, J., and Garcia-Molina, H. (1995). Copy detection mechanisms for digital documents. In *Proceedings of the ACM Special Interest Group on Management of Data (SIGMOD)*.

[Brin and Page, 2000] Brin, S. and Page, L. (2000). The anatomy of a large-scale hypertextual web search engine. Technical report, Stanford University.

[Broder, 1998] Broder, A. (1998). On the resemblance and containment of documents. In *In SEQS: Sequences 91*.

[Broder et al., 1997] Broder, A., Glassman, S., Manasse, M., and Zweig, Geoffrey (1997). Syntactic clustering of the web. Technical Report 1997-015, Digital Equipment Corporation, Systems Research Center (SRC).

[Broglio et al., 1994] Broglio, J., Callan, J., Croft, W.B., and Nachbar, D. (1994). Document retrieval and routing using the INQUERY system. In *Proceedings of the Third Text REtrieval Conference (TREC-3)*, pages 29–38.

[Brown et al., 1990] Brown, P., Cocke, J., Pietra, S. Della, Pietra, V. Della, Jelinek, F., Lafferty, J., Mercer, R., and Roossin, P. (1990). A statistical approach to machine translation. *Computational Linguistics*, 16(2):79–85.

[Brown et al., 1991] Brown, P., Lai, J., and Mercer, R. (1991). Aligning sentences in parallel corpora. In *Proceedings of the 29th Annual Meeting of the ACL*, pages 169–176, Berkeley, CA.

[Brown et al., 1993] Brown, P., Pietra, S. Della, Pietra, V. Della, and Mercer, R. (1993). The mathematics of statistical machine translation: Parameter estimation. *Computational Linguistics*, 19(2):262–311.

[Buckley et al., 2000] Buckley, C., Cardie, C., Mardis, S., Mitra, M., Pierce, D., Wagstaff, K., and Walz, J. (2000). The smart/empire tipster ir system. In *TIPSTER Phase III Proceedings, Morgan Kaufmann.*

[Buckley et al., 1994] Buckley, C., Salton, G., Allan, J., and Singhal, A. (1994). Automatic query expansion using SMART: TREC-3. In *Proceedings of the Third Text REtrieval Conference (TREC-3)*, pages 69–80.

[Buckley et al., 1995] Buckley, C., Singhal, A., Mitra, M., and (G. Salton) (1995). New retrieval approaches using SMART: TREC-4. In *Proceedings of the Fourth Text REtrieval Conference (TREC-4)*, pages 25–48.

[Buckley and Voorhees, 2004] Buckley, C. and Voorhees, E. (2004). Retrieval evaluation with incomplete information. In *ACM 27th Conference on Research and Development in Information Retrieval (SIGIR).*

[Buneman et al., 1996] Buneman, P., Davidson, S., Hillebrand, G., and Suciu, D. (1996). A query language and optimization techniques for unstructured data. In *Proceedings of International Conference on Management of Data (ACM-SIGMOD)*, pages 505–516.

[Burgin, 1995] Burgin (1995). The retrieval effectiveness of five clustering algorithms as a function of indexing exhaustivity. *Journal of the American Society for Information Science*, 46(8):562–572.

[Callan, 1994] Callan, J.P. (1994). Passage-level evidence in document retrieval. In *Proceedings of the Seventeenth Annual International ACM SIGIR Conference on Research and Development in Information Retrieval*, pages 302–310.

[Callison-Burch and Osborne, 2003] Callison-Burch, Chris and Osborne, Miles (2003). Building and using parallel texts: Data driven machine translation and beyond. In *Proceedings of the North American Association of Computation Linguistics (NAACL) : Workshop on Building and Using Parallel Texts: Data Driven Machine Translation and Beyond.*

[Cancedda et al., 2003] Cancedda, N., Dejean, H., Gaussier, E., Renders, J., and Vinokourov, A. (2003). Report on CLEF-2003 experiments: Two ways of extracting multilingual resources from corpora. In *Proceedings of the CLEF 2003 Cross-Language Text Retrieval System Evaluation Campaign.*

[Carbonell et al., 1997] Carbonell, J., Yang, Y., Frederking, R., Brown, R., Geng, Y., and Lee, D. (1997). Translingual information retrieval: A comparative evaluation. In *Proceedings of the Fifteenth International Joint Conference on Artificial Intelligence (IJCAI-97)*, pages 708–715.

[Carmel et al., 2001] Carmel, D., Cohen, D., Fagin, R., Farchi, E., Herscovici, M., Maarek, Y. S., and Soffer, Aya (2001). Static index pruning for information retrieval systems. In

Proceedings of the 24th annual international ACM SIGIR conference on Research and development in information retrieval, pages 43–50.

[Carreras et al., 2002] Carreras, X., Marques, L., and Padro, L. (2002). Named entity extraction using AdaBoost. In *Proceedings of CoNLL-2002*, pages 167–170, Taipei, Taiwan.

[Cavnar, 1993] Cavnar, W. (1993). N-gram based text filtering for TREC-2. In *Proceedings of the Second Text REtrieval Conference (TREC-2)*, pages 171–179.

[Cavnar and Vayda, 1993] Cavnar, W. and Vayda, A. (1993). N-gram based matching for multifield database access in postal applications. In *Proceedings of the Second Annual Symposium on Document Analysis and Information Retrieval*, pages 287–297.

[Charniak, 1993] Charniak, E. (1993). *Statistical Language Learning*. The MIT Press, Cambridge, MA.

[Chen and Gey, 2002] Chen, A. and Gey, F. (2002). Building an arabic stemmer for information retrieval. In *Proceedings of the Eleventh Text REtrieval Conference (TREC-2002)*.

[Chen and Gey, 2003] Chen, A. and Gey, F. (2003). Experiments on cross-language and patent retrieval at NTCIR-3 workshop. In *Proceedings of the NTCIR-3 Workshop*.

[Chen, 1995] Chen, H. (1995). Machine learning for information retrieval: Neural networks, symbolic learning, and genetic algorithms. *Journal of the American Society for Information Science*, 46(3):194–216.

[Chen and Lynch, 1992] Chen, H. and Lynch, K. J. (1992). Automatic construction of networks of concepts characterizing document databases. *IEEE Transactions on Systems, Man, and Cybernetics*, 22(5):885–902.

[Chen et al., 1993] Chen, H., Lynch, K. J., Basu, K., and Ng, T. (1993). Generating, integrating, and activating thesauri for concept-based document retrieval. *IEEE Expert*, 8(2):25–34.

[Chen and Ng, 1995] Chen, H. and Ng, T. (1995). An algorithmic approach to concept exploration in a large knowledge network (automatic thesaurus consultation): Symbolic branch and bound search versus connectionist hopfield net activation. *Journal of the American Society for Information Science*, 46(5):348–369.

[Chen et al., 1995] Chen, H., Yim, T., and Frye, D. (1995). Automatic thesaurus generation for an electronic community system. *Journal of the American Society for Information Science*, 46(3):175–193.

[Chen, 1976] Chen, P. (1976). The entity relationship model—toward a unified view of data. *ACM Transactions on Database Systems*, 1(1):9–36.

[Chen and Wang, 1995] Chen, S. and Wang, Jeng-Yih (1995). Document retrieval using knowledge-based fuzzy information retrieval techniques. *IEEE Transactions on Systems, Man, and Cybernetics*, 25(5):793–803.

[Chen and Goodman, 1998] Chen, S. F. and Goodman, J. (1998). An empirical study of smoothing techniques for language modeling. Technical Report TR-10-98, Harvard University.

[Cho et al., 1999] Cho, J., Shivakumar, N., and Garcia-Molina, H. (1999). Finding replicated web collections. In *Proceedings of the ACM SIGMOD Conference on Management of Data (SIGMOD '99)*, pages 355–366.

[Chowdhury et al., 2001] Chowdhury, A., Frieder, O., Grossman, D., and McCabe, M.C. (2001). Analyses of multiple-evidence combinations for retrieval strategies. In *Proceedings of the Twenty-Fourth Annual International ACM SIGIR Conference on Research and Development in Information Retrieval*, New Orleans, Louisiana.

[Chowdhury et al., 2002] Chowdhury, A., Frieder, O., Grossman, D., and McCabe, M.C. (2002). Collection statistics for fast duplicate document detection. *ACM Transaction on Information Systems*, 20(2):171–191.

[Chowdhury and Pass, 2003] Chowdhury, Abdur and Pass, Greg (2003). Operational requirements for scalable search systems. In *Proceedings of the 2003 International ACM CIKM Conference on Information and Knowledge Management*, pages 435–442.

[Church, 1988] Church, K. (1988). A stochastic parts program and noun phrase parser for unrestricted text. In *Proceedings of the Second Conference on Applied Natural Language Processing*, pages 136–143.

[Cockshott, 1989] Cockshott, P. (1989). Disadvantages of parallelism in text retrieval. In *Proceedings of the IEE Colloquium on Parallel Techniques for Information Retrieval Digest*, pages 377–387.

[Codd, 1970] Codd, E. (1970). A relational model for large shared data banks. *Communications of the ACM*, 13(6):377–387.

[Cohen, 1995] Cohen, J. (1995). Highlights: Language and domain-independent automatic indexing terms for abstracting. *Journal of American Society for Information Science*, 46(3):162–174.

[Cohen and Kjeldsen, 1987] Cohen, P.R. and Kjeldsen, R. (1987). Information retrieval by constrained spreading activation in semantic networks. *Information Processing and Management*, 23(4):255–268.

[Connell et al., 1996] Connell, W. O., Ieong, I.T, Schrader, D., Watson, C., Biliris, A., Choo, S., Colin, P., Linderman, G., Panagos, E., Wang, J., and Walter, T. (1996). A teradata content-based multimedia object manager for massively parallel architectures. In *Proceedings of the 1996 ACM Special Interest Group on the Management of Data (SIGMOD)*, pages 68–78.

[Conrad et al., 2003] Conrad, J., Guo, X., and Schriber, C. (2003). Online duplicate document detection: signature reliability in a dynamic retrieval environment. In *Twelfth International Conference on Information and Knowledge Management (CIKM)*, pages 443–452.

[Conrad and Schriber, 2004] Conrad, J. and Schriber, C. (2004). Constructing a text corpus for inexact duplicate detection. In *ACM 27th Conference on Research and Development in Information Retrieval (SIGIR)*, pages 582–583.

[Cooper et al., 2002] Cooper, J., Coden, A., and Brown, E. (2002). A novel method for detecting similar documents. In *Proceedings of the 35th Hawaii International Conference on System Sciences (HICSS)*.

[Cooper, 1991] Cooper, W.S. (1991). Some inconsistencies and misnomers in probabilistic information retrieval. In *Proceedings of the Fourteenth Annual International ACM SIGIR Conference on Research and Development in Information Retrieval*, pages 57–62.

[Cooper et al., 1992] Cooper, W.S., Gey, F., and Dabney, D. (1992). Probabilistic retrieval based on staged logistic regression. In *Proceedings of the Fifteenth Annual International ACM SIGIR Conference on Research and Development in Information Retrieval*, pages 198–210.

[Craswell et al., 2002] Craswell, N., Hawking, D., Krumpholz, A., Mathieson, I., Thom, J.A., Vercoustre, A.-M., Wilkins, P., and Wu, M. (2002). Xml document retrieval with padre. In *Proceedings of the Seventh Australian Document Computing Symposium*.

[Crawford, 1981] Crawford, R. (1981). The relational model in information retrieval. *Journal of the American Society for Information Science*, pages 51–64.

[Crestani, 1994] Crestani, F. (1994). Comparing neural and probabilistic relevance feedback in an interactive information retrieval system. In *Proceedings of the IEEE International Conference on Neural Networks*, pages 3226–3230.

[Cringean et al., 1990] Cringean, J., England, R., Manson, G., and Willett, P. (1990). Parallel text searching in serial files using a processor farm. In *Proceedings of the Thirteenth Annual ACM SIGIR Conference on Research and Development in Information Retrieval*, pages 429–445.

[Cringean et al., 1991] Cringean, J., England, R., Manson, G., and Willett, P. (1991). Nearest-neighbour searching in files of text signatures using transputer networks. *Electronic Publishing–Origination, Dissemination, and Design*, 4(1):185–202.

[Croft and Harper, 1979] Croft, W.B. and Harper, D.J. (1979). Using probabilistic models of document retrieval without relevance information. *Journal of Documentation*, 35(4):282–295.

[Croft and Xu, 1994] Croft, W.B. and Xu, Jinxi (1994). Corpus-specific stemming using word form co-occurence. In *Proceedings for the Fourth Annual Symposium on Document Analysis Information Retrieval*, pages 147–159.

[Crouch et al., 1994] Crouch, C., Crouch, D., and Nareddy, K. (1994). Associative and adaptive retrieval in a connectionist system. *International Journal of Expert Systems*, 7(2):193–202.

[Crouch, 1989] Crouch, C.J. (1989). A cluster-based approach to thesaurus construction. In *Eleventh International ACM SIGIR Conference on Research and Development in Information Retrieval*, pages 309–320.

[Crouch, 1990] Crouch, C.J. (1990). An approach to the automatic construction of global thesauri. *Information Processing and Management*, 26(5):629–640.

[Cucerzan and Yarowsky, 1999] Cucerzan, S. and Yarowsky, D. (1999). Language independent named entity recognition: Combining morphological and contextual evidence. In *Joint SIGDAT Confernce on EMNLP and VLC*.

[Cutting et al., 1992] Cutting, D.R., Karger, D.R., Pedersen, J.O., and Tukey, J.W. (1992). Scatter/gather: A cluster-based approach to browsing large document collections. In *Proceedings of the Fifteenth Annual International ACM SIGIR Conference on Research and Development in Information Retrieval*, pages 318–329.

[Dai et al., 1999] Dai, Y., Khoo, C., and Loh, T. (1999). A new statistical formula for chinese text segmentation incorporating contextual information. In *Proceedings of the 21st Annual International ACM SIGIR Conference on Research and Development in Information Retrieval*, pages 82–89.

[Damashek, 1995] Damashek, M. (1995). Gauging similarity via n-grams: Language independent categorization of text. *Science*, 267(5199):843–848.

[D'Amore and Mah, 1985] D'Amore, R. and Mah, C. (1985). One-time complete indexing of text: Theory and practice. *Eighth Annual ACM SIGIR Conference on Research and Development in Information Retrieval*, pages 155–164.

[Darwish and Oard, 2003] Darwish, K. and Oard, D. (2003). CLIR experiments at Maryland for TREC-2002: Evidence combination for arabic-english retrieval. In *Proceedings of the Text Retrieval and Evaluation Conference (TREC-2003)*.

[Date, 1994] Date, C. (1994). *An Introduction to Database Systems*. Addison-Wesley.

[Davis and Ogden, 1997] Davis, M. W. and Ogden, W.C. (1997). Free reosurces and advanced alignment for cross-language text retrieval. In *Proceedings of the Sixth Text REtrieval Conference (TREC-6)*.

[Deerwester et al., 1990] Deerwester, S., Dumais, S.T., Furnas, G.W., Landauer, T.K., and Harshman, R. (1990). Indexing by latent semantic analysis. *Journal of the American Society for Information Science*, 41(6):391–407.

[DeHaan et al., 2003] DeHaan, D., Toman, D., Consens, M., and Özsu, M. (2003). A comprehensive XQuery to SQL translation using dynamic interval encoding. In *Proceedings of the ACM Special Interest Group on Management of Data (SIGMOD)*, San Diego, California.

[Demner-Fushman and Oard, 2003] Demner-Fushman, D. and Oard, D. W. (2003). The effect of bilingual term list size on dictionary-based cross-language information retrieval. In *Proceedings of the 36th Hawaii International Conference on System Sciences*.

[Dempster et al., 1977] Dempster, A. P., Laird, N. M., and Rubin, D. B. (1977). Maximum-likelihood from incomplete data via the EM algorithm. *Journal of the Royal Statistical Society*, 39:1–38.

[DeRose, 1988] DeRose, S. (1988). Grammatical category disambiguation by statistical optimization. *Computational Linguistics*, 14(1):31–39.

[Desai et al., 1987] Desai, B.C., Goyal, P., and Sadri, F. (1987). Non-first normal form universal relations: An application to information retrieval systems. *Information Systems*, 12(1):49–55.

[Desantis et al., 1996] Desantis, R., Frieder, O., and Moini, A. (1996). The CYBERosetta architecture. *Software Productivity Consortium, Internal Report*.

[Deutsch et al., 1999] Deutsch, A., Fernandez, M., Florescu, D., Levy, A., and Suciu, D. (1999). A query language for XML. In *Proceedings of the International World Wide Web Conference.*

[Dubes and Jain, 1988] Dubes, R.C. and Jain, A.K. (1988). *Algorithms for Clustering Data.* Prentice Hall.

[Duda and Sheldon, 1994] Duda, A. and Sheldon, M. (1994). Content routing in a network of WAIS servers. In *Proceedings of the IEEE Fourteenth International Conference on Distributed Computing Systems*, pages 124–132.

[Dumais et al., 1997] Dumais, S., Letsche, T., Littman, M., and Landauer, T. (1997). Automatic cross-language retrieval using latent semantic indexing. In *In AAAI Symposium on CrossLanguage Text and Speech Retrieval. American Association for Artificial Intelligence.*

[Dumais, 1994] Dumais, S. T. (1994). Latent semantic indexing (LSI): TREC-3 report. In *Proceedings of the Third Text REtrieval Conference (TREC-3)*, pages 219–230.

[El-Hamdouchi and Willett, 1986] El-Hamdouchi, A. and Willett, P. (1986). Hierarchic document clustering using ward's method. In *Proceedings of the Ninth Annual International ACM SIGIR Conference on Research and Development in Information Retrieval*, pages 149–156.

[El-Hamdouchi and Willett, 1989] El-Hamdouchi, A. and Willett, P. (1989). Comparison of hierarchic agglomerative clustering methods for document retrieval. *The Computer Journal*, 32(3):220–226.

[Elias, 1975] Elias, P. (1975). Universal codeword sets and representations of the integers. *IEEE Transactions on Information Theory*, IT-21(2):194–203.

[Elmasri and Navathe, 1994] Elmasri, R. and Navathe, S. (1994). *Fundamentals of Database Systems.* Addison-Wesley.

[Evans and Ghanemi, 1988] Evans, D. and Ghanemi, S. (1988). Parallel string matching algorithms. *Kybernetes*, 17(3):32–34.

[Federico and Bertoldi, 2002] Federico, M. and Bertoldi, N. (2002). Statistical cross-language information retrieval using n-best query translations. In *Proceedings of the 25th ACM SIGIR Conference on Research and Development in Information Retrieval*, pages 167–174.

[Fetterly et al., 2003] Fetterly, D., Manasse, M., and Najork, M. (2003). On the evolution of clusters of near-duplicate web pages. In *Proceedings of the First Latin American Web Congress*, page 37Ů45.

[Florescu and Kossman, 1999] Florescu, D. and Kossman, D. (1999). Storing and querying XML data using an RDBMS. *IEEE Data Engineering Bulletin*, 22(3):27–34.

[Flynn, 1972] Flynn, M.J. (1972). Some computer organizations and their effectiveness. *IEEE Transactions on Computers*, 21(9):948–960.

[Fontaine, 1995] Fontaine, Anne (1995). Sub-element indexing and probabilistic retrieval in the POSTGRES database system. Master's thesis, University of California, Berkeley.

[Foster, 2002] Foster, I. (2002). The grid: A new infrastructure for 21st century science. *Physics Today*, 55(2):42–47.

[Foster et al., 2001] Foster, I., Kesselman, C., and Tuecke, S. (2001). The anatomy of the grid: Enabling scalable virtual organizations. *International Journal of Supercomputing*, 15(1).

[Fox, 1990] Fox, C. (1990). A stop list for general text. *SIGIR Forum*, 24(1):19–35.

[Fox, 1983a] Fox, E.A. (1983a). *Extending the Boolean and Vector Space Models of Information Retrieval with P-Norm Queries and Multiple Concept Types.* PhD thesis, Cornell University.

[Fox, 1983b] Fox, E.A. (1983b). Some considerations for implementing the SMART information retrieval system under UNIX. Technical Report TR83-560, Cornell University.

[Frakes and Baeza-Yates, 1993] Frakes, W. and Baeza-Yates, R. (1993). *Information Retrieval: Data Structures and Algorithms.* Prentice-Hall, Inc.

[Francis and Kucera, 1982] Francis, W. and Kucera, H. (1982). *Frequency Analysis of English Usage. Lexicon and Grammer.* Houghton Mifflin.

[Frieder et al., 2000a] Frieder, O., Chowdhury, A., Grossman, D., and Frieder, G. (2000a). Efficiency considerations for scalable information retrieval servers. *Journal of Digital Information.*

[Frieder et al., 2000b] Frieder, O., Chowdhury, A., Grossman, D., and McCabe, M. C. (2000b). On the integration of structured data and text: A review of the sire architecture. In *Proceedings of the DELOS Workshop on Information Seeking, Searching, and Querying in Digital Libraries.*

[Frieder et al., 2003] Frieder, O., Grossman, D., and Chowdhury, A. (2003). On scalable information retrieval systems (invited keynote). In *IEEE Second International Symposium on Network Computing and Applications (NCA).*

[Fuhr, 1992] Fuhr, Norbert (1992). Probabilistic models in information retrieval. *The Computer Journal*, 35(3):243–255.

[Fung, 1998] Fung, P. (1998). A statistical view on bilingual lexicon extraction: From parallel corpora to non-parallel corpora. In *Machine Translation and the Information Soup, Third Conference of the Association for Machine Translation in the Americas (AMTA)*, Lecture Notes in Computer Science, pages 1–17.

[Gale and Church, 1991] Gale, W. and Church, K. (1991). A program for aligning sentences in bilingual corpora. In *Proceedings of the 29th Annual Meeting of the ACL*, Berkeley, CA.

[Galil, 1979] Galil, Z. (1979). On improving the worst-case running time of the Boyer-Moore string matching algorithm. *Communications of the ACM*, 22(9):505–508.

[Garcia-Molina et al., 1996] Garcia-Molina, H., Gravano, L., and Shivakumar, N. (1996). dscam: Finding document copies across multiple databases. In *Proceedings of the 4th International Conference on Parallel and Distributed Systems (PDIS 96).*

[Garcia-Molina et al., 1997] Garcia-Molina, H., Papakonstantinou, Y., Quass, D., Rajamaran, A., Sagiv, Y., Ullman, J., Vassalos, V., and Widom, J. (1997). The TSIMMIS approach to mediation: Data models and languages. *Journal of Intelligent Information Systems*, 8.

[Gauch and Wang, 1996] Gauch, S. and Wang, J. (1996). Corpus analysis for TREC-5 query expansion. In *Proceedings of the Fifth Text REtrieval Conference (TREC-5)*, pages 537–546.

[Ghose and Dhawle, 1977] Ghose, A. and Dhawle, A. (1977). Problems of thesaurus construction. *Journal of the American Society for Information Science*, 28(4):211–217.

[Giger, 1988] Giger, H.P. (1988). Concept based retrieval in classical IR systems. In *Eleventh International ACM SIGIR Conference on Research and Development in Information Retrieval*, pages 275–289.

[Goda et al., 2001] Goda, K., Tamura, T., Kitsuregawa, M., Chowdhury, A., and Frieder, O. (2001). Query optimization for vector space problems. In *Proceedings of the 24th Annual International ACM SIGIR Conference on Research and Development in Information Retrieval*, pages 416–417.

[Goharian et al., 2004] Goharian, N., Grossman, D., Raju, N., and Frieder, O. (2004). Migrating information retrieval from the graduate to the undergraduate curriculum. *Journal of Information Systems Education*, 15(1).

[Goldfarb, 1990] Goldfarb, C. (1990). *The SGML Handbook*. Oxford University Press.

[Goldman et al., 1999] Goldman, R., McHugh, J., and Widom., J. (1999). From semistructured data to XML: Migrating the lore data model and query language. In *Proceedings of the Second International Workshop on the Web and Databases (WebDB '99)*, Philadelphia, Pennsylvania.

[Goldsmith, 2001] Goldsmith, J. (2001). Unsupervised learning of the morphology of a natural language. *Computational Linguistics*, 27(2):153–198.

[Gollins and Sanderson, 2004] Gollins, T. and Sanderson, M. (2004). Improving cross language information retrieval with triangulated translation. In *Proceedings of the 24th Annual International ACM SIGIR Conference on Research and Development in Information Retrieval.*

[Gomez, 1988] Gomez, F. (1988). WUP: a parser based on word usage. In *Seventh Annual International Phoenix Conference on Computers and Communications*, pages 445–449.

[Gomez and Segami, 1989] Gomez, F. and Segami, C. (1989). The recognition and classification of concepts in understanding scientific texts. *Journal of Experimental Theoretical Artificial Intelligence*, pages 51–77.

[Gomez and Segami, 1991] Gomez, F. and Segami, C. (1991). The recognition and classification of concepts in understanding scientific texts. *IEEE Transactions on Systems, Man and Cybernetics*, 21(3):644–659.

[Gordon, 1988] Gordon, M. (1988). Probabilistic and genetic algorithms for document retrieval. *Communications of the ACM*, 31(10):1208–1218.

[Gordon, 1997] Gordon, M. (1997). It's 10 a.m. do you know where your documents are? The nature and scope of information retrieval problems in business. *Information Processing and Management*, 33(1):107–121.

[Grabs et al., 2001] Grabs, T., Böhm, K., and Schek, H.J. (2001). High-level parallelisation in a database cluster: a feasibility study using document services. In *Proceedings of the IEEE Seventeenth International Conference on Data Engineering (ICDE2001).*

[Grauer and Messier, 1971] Grauer, R.T. and Messier, M. (1971). *The SMART Retrieval System—Experiments in Automatic Document Processing*, chapter An Evaluation of Rocchio's Clustering Algorithm, pages 243–264. Prentice Hall.

[Gravano and Garcia-Molina, 1995] Gravano, L. and Garcia-Molina, H. (1995). Generalizing GIOSS to vector-space databases and broker hierarchies. In *Proceedings of the 21st International Conference on Very Large Database Conference*, pages 78–89.

[Greiff, 1996] Greiff, W. (1996). Computationally tractable, conceptually plausible classes of link matrices for the Inquery inference network. Technical Report TR96-66, University of Massachusetts, Amherst.

[Greiff et al., 1997] Greiff, W.R., Croft, W.B., and Turtle, H. (1997). Computationally tractable probabilistic modelling of boolean operators. In *Proceedings of the 20th Annual International ACM SIGIR Conference on Research and Development in Information Retrieval*, pages 119–128.

[Gropp and Lusk, 1998] Gropp, W. and Lusk, E. (1998). User's guide for MPICH, a portable implementation of MPI. Technical report, Mathematics and Computer Science Division, Argonne National Laboratory, University of Chicago.

[Grossman, 1995] Grossman, D. (1995). *Integrating Structured Data and Text: A Relational Approach.* PhD thesis, George Mason Univeristy.

[Grossman et al., 1997] Grossman, D., Frieder, O., Holmes, D., and Roberts, D. (1997). Integrating structured data and text: A relational approach. *Journal of the American Society for Information Science*, 48(2):122–132.

[Grossman et al., 1994] Grossman, D., Holmes, D., and Frieder, O. (1994). A parallel DBMS approach to IR. *The Third Text REtrieval Conference*, pages 279–288.

[Grossman et al., 1995] Grossman, D., Holmes, D., and Frieder, O. (1995). A dbms approach to ir in trec-4. In *Proceedings of the Fourth Text REtrieval Conference (TREC-4).*

[Guha et al., 1988] Guha, S., Rastogi, R., and Shim, K. (1988). Cure: An efficient clustering algorithm for large databases. In *Proceedings of the 1998 ACM-SIGMOD Special Interest Group on Management of Data*, pages 73–84.

[Guiasu and Shenitzer, 1985] Guiasu, S. and Shenitzer, A. (1985). The principle of maximum entropy. *Mathmatical Intelligencer*, 7(1).

[Gupte and Frieder, 1995] Gupte, A.V. and Frieder, O. (1995). Compression within a context-sensitive commercial random access domain: An industrial case study. *Information Processing and Management*, 31(4):573–591.

[Gutmann and Bell, 1994] Gutmann, P.C. and Bell, T.C. (1994). A hybrid approach to text compression. In *Proceedings of the Data Compression Conference DCC '94*, pages 225–233.

[Haddouti, 1999] Haddouti, H. (1999). Survey: Multilingual text retrieval and access. *UNESCO Press.*

[Harman, 1988] Harman, D. (1988). Towards interactive query expansion. In *Eleventh International ACM SIGIR Conference on Research and Development in Information Retrieval*, pages 321–331.

[Harman, 1992] Harman, D. (1992). Relevance feedback revisited. In *Proceedings of the Fifteenth Annual International ACM SIGIR Conference on Research and Development in Information Retrieval*, pages 1–10.

[Harman, 1995] Harman, D. (1995). The TREC conferences. In *Proceedings of the Hypertext - Information Retrieval - Multimedia: Synergieeffekte Elektronischer Informationssysteme (HIM'95)*, pages 9–28.

[Harman and Buckley, 2004] Harman, D. and Buckley, C. (2004). The NRRC reliable information access (RIA) workshop. In *ACM 27th Conference on Research and Development in Information Retrieval (SIGIR)*, pages 528–529.

[Hawking et al., 2000] Hawking, D., Bailey, P., and Craswell, N. (2000). Efficient and flexible search using text and metadata. Technical Report TR2000-83, Department of Computer Science CSIRO Matematical and Information Sciences.

[Hawking, 1991] Hawking, D.A. (1991). High speed search of large text bases on the fujitsu cellular array processor. In *Proceedings of the Fourth Australian Supercomputing Conference*, pages 83–90.

[Hawking, 1994a] Hawking, D.A. (1994a). The design and implementation of a parallel document retrieval engine. Technical report.

[Hawking, 1994b] Hawking, D.A. (1994b). Padre - a parallel document retrieval engine. In *Proceedings of the Third Fujitsu Parallel Computing Workshop*.

[Heintze, 1996] Heintze, N. (1996). Scalable document fingerprinting. In *In Proceedings of the USENIX Work-shop on Electronic Commerce*.

[Hiemstra and Kraaij, 1998] Hiemstra, D. and Kraaij, W. (1998). Twenty-one at TREC-7: Ad-hoc and cross-language track. In *Proceedings of Seventh Text REtrieval Conference (TREC-7)*, pages 227–238.

[Hiemstra et al., 2004] Hiemstra, D., Robertson, S., and Zaragoza, H. (2004). Parsimonious language models for information retrieval. In *ACM 27th Conference on Research and Development in Information Retrieval (SIGIR)*, pages 178–185.

[Hines and Harris, 1971] Hines, T.C. and Harris, J. L. (1971). Columbia University School of Library Service System for Thesaurus Development and Maintenance. *Information Storage and Retrieval*, 7(1):39–50.

[Hoad and Zobel, 2002] Hoad, T. and Zobel, J. (2002). Methods for identifying versioned and plagiarism documents. *Journal of the American Society for Information Science and Technology (JASIST)*.

[Hodjat et al., 2003] Hodjat, B., Franco, H., Bratt, H., and Precoda, K. (2003). Iterative statistical language model generation for use with an agent-oriented natural language interface. In *10th International Conference on Human-Computer Interaction*.

[Hofland, 1996] Hofland, K. (1996). A program for aligning English and Norwegian sentences. *Research in Humanities Computing*, pages 165–178.

[Hollaar and Haskins, 1984] Hollaar, L. and Haskins, R. (1984). Method and system for matching encoded characters. *U.S. Patent Number 4,450,520*.

[Hollaar and Haskins, 1991] Hollaar, L. and Haskins, R. (1991). Implementation and evaluation of a parallel text searcher for very large text databases. In *Proceedings of the 25th International Conference on System Sciences*, volume 1, pages 300–307.

[Holmes, 2004] Holmes, David (2004). Personal communication with David Holmes.

[Horspool, 1983] Horspool, R.N. (1983). Practical fast searching in strings. *Software Practice and Experience*, 10(6):501–510.

[Hull and Grefenstette, 1996] Hull, D. and Grefenstette, G. (1996). Querying across langages: a dictionary-based approach to multilingual information retrieval. In *Proceedings of the Nineteenth Annual International ACM SIGIR Conference on Research and Development in Information Retrieval*, pages 46–57.

[Hurson et al., 1990] Hurson, A.R., Miller, L.L., Pakzad, S.H., and Cheng, Jia-bing (1990). Specialized parallel architectures for textual databases. *Advances in Computers*, 30:1–37.

[Ives et al., 1999] Ives, Z. G., Florescu, D., Friedman, M., Levy, A., and Weld, D. S. (1999). An adaptive query execution system for data integration. In *Proceedings of the ACM SIGMOD Conference on Management of Data (SIGMOD '99)*, Philadelphia, Pennsylvania.

[Jelinek and Mercer, 1980] Jelinek, F. and Mercer, R. (1980). *Interpolated Estimation of Markov Source Parameters from Sparse Data*, pages 381–402. Noth-Holland Publishing Company, North Holland, Amsterdam.

[Jensen et al., 2002] Jensen, Eric C., Beitzel, Steven M., Pilotto, Angelo J., Goharian, Nazli, and Frieder, Ophir (2002). Parallelizing the buckshot algorithm for efficient document clustering. In *Proceedings of the Eleventh International Conference on Information and Knowledge Management (CIKM)*, pages 684–686. ACM Press.

[Kamps et al., 2004] Kamps, J., deRijke, M., and Sigurbjoernsson, B. (2004). Length normalization in XML retrieval. In *ACM 27th Conference on Research and Development in Information Retrieval (SIGIR)*, pages 80–87.

[Kamps et al., 2003] Kamps, J., Monz, C., de Rijke, M., and Sigurbjornsson, B. (2003). The university of amsterdam and CLEF 2003. In *Proceedings of the CLEF 2003 Cross-Language Text Retrieval System Evaluation Campaign.*

[Kanne and Moerkotte, 2000] Kanne, C. and Moerkotte, G. (2000). Efficient storage of XML data. In *Proceedings Of the 16th International Conference On Data and Knowledge Engineering (ICDE).*

[Kantor, 1994] Kantor, P. (1994). *Information Retrieval Techniques*, volume 29, chapter 2, pages 53–90. Learned Information, Inc.

[Karp and Rabin, 1987] Karp, R. and Rabin, M. (1987). Efficient randomized pattern-matching algorithms. *IBM Journal of Research and Development*, 31(2):249–260.

[Katz, 1987] Katz, S.M. (1987). Estimation of probabilities from sparse data for the language model component of a speech recognizer. *IEEE Transactions on Acoustics, Speech and Signal Processing*, ASSP-35:400–401.

[Khoja and Garside, 1999] Khoja, S. and Garside, R. (1999). Stemming arabic text. Technical report, Computing Department, Lancaster University.

[Kim and Kim, 1990] Kim, Y.W. and Kim, J.H. (1990). A model of knowledge based information retrieval with hierarchical concept graph. *Journal of Documentation*, 46(2):113–136.

[Kishida and Kando, 2003] Kishida, K. and Kando, N. (2003). Two stage refinement of query translation for pivot language approach to cross-lingual information retrieval: A trial at CLEF 2003. In *Proceedings of the CLEF 2003 Cross-Language Text Retrieval System Evaluation Campaign*.

[Kjeldsen and Cohen, 1987] Kjeldsen, R. and Cohen, P.R. (1987). The evolution and performance of the GRANT system. *IEEE Expert*, 2(2):73–79.

[Kjell et al., 1994] Kjell, B., Woods, W., and Frieder, O. (1994). Discrimination of authorship using visualization. *Information Processing and Management*, 30(1):141–150.

[Kleinberg, 1999] Kleinberg, J. (1999). Authoritative sources in a hyperlinked environment. *Journal of the ACM*, 46.

[Knuth et al., 1977] Knuth, D., Morris, J., and Pratt, V. (1977). Fast pattern matching in strings. *SIAM Journal of Computing*, 6(2):323–350.

[Kohler, 1993] Kohler, W. (1993). TPC: Transaction Processing performance Council. *Capacity Management Review*, 21(9):5–6.

[Kolcz et al., 2004] Kolcz, A., Chowdhury, A., and Alspector, J. (2004). Improved stability of i-match signatures via lexicon randomization. Technical Report Internal Report, AOL.

[Kowalski and Maybury, 2000] Kowalski, G. and Maybury, M. (2000). *Information Storage and Retrieval Systems: Theory and Implementation*. Kluwer Academic Publishers, Boston, MA.

[Kraft et al., 1994] Kraft, D., Petry, F., Buckles, B., and Sadasivan, T. (1994). The use of genetic programming to build queries for information retrieval. In *Proceedings of the IEEE Symposium on Evolutionary Computation*, pages 468–473.

[Kristensen, 1993] Kristensen, J. (1993). Expanding end-users' query statements for free text searching with a search-aid thesaurus. *Information Processing and Management*, 29(6):733–744.

[Krovetz, 1993] Krovetz, R. (1993). Viewing morphology as an inference process. In *Proceedings of the Sixteenth Annual International ACM SIGIR Conference on Research and Development in Information Retrieval*, pages 191–202.

[Krovetz and Croft, 1989] Krovetz, R. and Croft, W. (1989). Word sense disambiguation using machine-readable dictionaries. In *Proceedings of the Twelfth Annual International ACM SIGIR Conference on Research and Development in Information Retrieval*, pages 127–136.

[Kukich, 1992] Kukich, K. (1992). Techniques for automatically correcting words in text. *ACM Computing Surveys*, 24(4):377–439.

[Kwok, 1990] Kwok, K. (1990). Experiments with a component theory of probabilistic information retrieval based on single terms as document components. *ACM Transactions on Office Information Systems*, 8(4):363–386.

[Kwok, 1989] Kwok, K.L. (1989). A neural network for probabilistic information retrieval. In *Proceedings of the Twelth Annual International ACM SIGIR Conference on Research and Development in Information Retrieval*, pages 21–30.

[Kwok, 1995] Kwok, K.L. (1995). A network approach to probabilistic information retrieval. *ACM Transactions on Information Systems*, 13(3):324–353.

[Larkey et al., 2002a] Larkey, L., Allan, J., Connell, M., Bolivar, C., and Wade, C. (2002a). UMass at TREC-2002: Cross language and novelty tracks. In *Proceedings of the Text Retrieval and Evaluation Conference (TREC-2002)*.

[Larkey et al., 2002b] Larkey, L., Ballesteros, L., and Connell, M.E. (2002b). Improving stemming for arabic information retrieval: Light stemming and co-occurrence analysis. In *Proceedings of the 25th Annual International ACM SIGIR Conference on Research and Development in Information Retrieval*, pages 275–282.

[Larkey and Connell, 2000] Larkey, L. S. and Connell, M. E. (2000). Arabic information retrieval at umass in TREC-10. In *Proceedings of the Text Retrieval and Evaluation Conference (TREC-2000)*.

[Larsen and Aone, 1999] Larsen, B. and Aone, C. (1999). Fast and effective text mining using linear-time document clustering. In *Proceedings of the 5th ACM-SIGKDD Special Interest Group on Knowledge and Data Discovery*, pages 16–22.

[Lavrenko and Croft, 2001] Lavrenko, V. and Croft, W. B. (2001). Relevance-based language models. In *Proceedings of the 24th ACM SIGIR Conference on Research and Development in Information Retrieval*, pages 120–127.

[Lavrenko et al., 2002] Lavrenko, V. A, Choquette, M., and Croft, W. B. (2002). Cross-lingual relevance models. In *Proceedings of the 25th Annual International ACM SIGIR Conference on Research and Development in Information Retrieval*, page 175=182.

[Lecroq, 1994] Lecroq, T. (1994). Experimental results on string matching. *Software Practice and Experience*, 25(7):727–765.

[Lee, 1995] Lee, D. (1995). Massive parallelism on the hybrid text-retrieval machine. *Information Processing and Management*, 31(6):815–830.

[Lee et al., 1997] Lee, D., Chuang, H., and Seamons, K. (1997). Document ranking and the vector-space model. *IEEE Software*, 14(2):67–75.

[Lee and Ren, 1996] Lee, D. and Ren, L. (1996). Document ranking on weight-partitioned signature files. *ACM Transactions on Information Systems*, 14(2):109–137.

[Lee, 1997] Lee, J. (1997). Analysis of multple evidence combinations. In *Proceedings of the 20th Annual International ACM SIGIR Conference on Research and Development in Information Retrieval*, pages 267–276.

[Lee et al., 1993] Lee, J.H., Kim, M.H., and Lee, Y.J. (1993). Information retrieval based on conceptual distance in is-a hierarchies. *Journal of Documentation*, 49(2):188–207.

[Lee et al., 1994] Lee, J.H., Kim, M.H., and Lee, Y.J. (1994). Ranking documents in thesaurus-based boolean retrieval systems. *Information Processing and Management*, 30(1):79–91.

[Leek et al., 2000] Leek, T., Jin, H., Sista, S., and Schwartz, R. (2000). The BBN crosslingual topic detection and tracking system. In *Working Notes of the Third Topic Detection and Tracking Workshop.*

[Lenat and Guha, 1989] Lenat, D. and Guha, R. (1989). *Building Large Knowledge-Based Systems.* Addison-Wesley.

[Letsche and Berry, 1997] Letsche, T. and Berry, M. (1997). Large-scale information retrieval with latent semantic indexing. *Information Sciences*, 100:105–137.

[Levenshtein, 1966] Levenshtein, V. I. (1966). Binary codes capable of correcting deletions, insertions and reversals. *Sov. Phys. Dokl.*, 6:707–710.

[Levow and Oard, 2000] Levow, G. and Oard, D. (2000). Translingual topic tracking with prise. In *Working Notes of the Third Topic Detection and Tracking Workshop.*

[Levow et al., 2004] Levow, G., Oard, D., and Resnik, P. (2004). Dictionary-based techniques for cross-language information retrieval. *Information Processing and Management (to appear).*

[Lewis and Sparck Jones, 1996] Lewis, D. and Sparck Jones, K. (1996). Natural language processing for information retrieval. *Communications of the ACM*, 39(1):92–101.

[Lin and Chen, 2003] Lin, W. and Chen, H. (2003). Merging restults by using predicted retreival effectiveness. In *Proceedings of the CLEF 2003 Cross-Language Text Retrieval System Evaluation Campaign.*

[Littman and Jiang, 1998] Littman, Michael L. and Jiang, Fan (1998). A comparison of two corpus-based methods for translingual information retrieval. Technical Report CS-98-11, Duke University.

[Liu and Callan, 2003] Liu, J. and Callan, J. (2003). Content-based retrieval in hybrid peer-to-peer networks. In *Proceedings of the ACM Conference on Information and Knowledge Management.*

[Liu et al., 2004] Liu, S., Liu, F., Yu, C., and Meng, W. (2004). An effective approach to document retrieval via utilizing WordNet and recognizing phrases. In *ACM 27th Conference on Research and Development in Information Retrieval (SIGIR)*, pages 266–272.

[Liu and Croft, 2004] Liu, X. and Croft, W.B. (2004). Cluster-based retrieval using language models. In *ACM 27th Conference on Research and Development in Information Retrieval (SIGIR)*, pages 186–193.

[Liu et al., 1996] Liu, Y., Dantzig, P., Wu, C., Challenger, J., and Ni, L. (1996). A distributed web server and its performance analysis on multiple platforms. In *Proceedings of the Sixteenth IEEE International Conference on Distributed Computing Systems*, pages 665–672.

[Loney, 1997] Loney, K. (1997). *Oracle 8 DBA Handbook.* Osborne McGraw-Hill.

[Lovins, 1968] Lovins, J. (1968). Development of a stemming algorithm. *Mechanical Translation and Computational Linguistics*, 11:22–31.

[Lu et al., 1996] Lu, A., Ayoub, M., and Dong, J. (1996). Ad hoc experiments using EUREKA. In *Proceedings of the Fifth Text REtrieval Conference (TREC-5)*, pages 229–239.

[Lu and Callan, 2004] Lu, J. and Callan, J. (2004). Merging retrieval results in hierarchical peer-to-peer networks. In *ACM 27th Conference on Research and Development in Information Retrieval (SIGIR)*, pages 472–473.

[Lu et al., 1997] Lu, Z., McKinley, K.S., and Cahoon, B. (1997). A performance evaluation of parallel information retrieval on symmetrical multiprocessors. Technical report, Department of Computer Science, University of Massachusetts.

[Lucarella and Morara, 1991] Lucarella, D. and Morara, R. (1991). FIRST: Fuzzy information retrieval systems. *Journal of Information Science*, 17(2):81–91.

[Luk et al., 2002] Luk, R., Leong, H.V., Dillon, T., Chan, A., Croft, B., and Allan, J. (2002). A survey in indexing and searching XML documents. *Journal of the American Society of Information Science and Technology (JASIST)*, 53(6):415–437.

[Lundquist et al., 1999] Lundquist, C., Frieder, O., Holmes, D., and Grossman, D. (1999). A parallel relational database management system approach to relevance feedback in information retrieval. *Journal of the American Society for Information Science*, 50(5).

[Lundquist et al., 1997] Lundquist, C., Grossman, D., and Frieder, O. (1997). Improving relevance feedback in the vector space model. In *Proceedings of the Sixth ACM Annual Conference on Information and Knowledge Management (CIKM '97).*

[Lynch and Stonebraker, 1988] Lynch, C. and Stonebraker, M. (1988). Extended user-defined indexing with application to textual databases. In *Proceedings of the Fourteenth International Conference on Very Large Databases*, pages 306–317.

[Ma et al., 2003] Ma, L., Goharian, N., Chowdhury, A., and Chung, M. (2003). Extracting unstructured data from template generated web documents. In *Proceedings of the ACM Conference on Information and Knowledge Management.*

[MacFarlane et al., 1999] MacFarlane, A., McCann, J.A., and Robertson, S.E. (1999). PLIERS: A parallel information retrieval system using mpi. In *PVM/MPI*, pages 317–324.

[MacFarlane et al., 1997] MacFarlane, A., Robertson, S.E., and McCann, J.A. (1997). Parallel computing in information retrieval - an updated review. *Journal of Documentation*, 53(3):274–315.

[MacKay and Peto, 1995] MacKay, D. and Peto, L. (1995). A hierarchical dirichlet language model. *Natural Language Engineering*, 1(3):289–307.

[Macleod, 1978] Macleod, I. (1978). A relational approach to modular information retrieval systems design. In *Proceedings of the ASIS Annual Meeting*, pages 83–85.

[Macleod, 1979] Macleod, I. (1979). SEQUEL as a language for document retrieval. *Journal of the American Society for Information Science*, 30(5):243–249.

[Macleod and Robertson, 1991] Macleod, K. and Robertson, W. (1991). A neural algorithm for document clustering. *Information Processing and Management*, 27(4):337–346.

[Mak et al., 1991] Mak, V., Lee, K.C., and Frieder, O. (1991). Exploiting parallelism in pattern matching: An information retrieval application. *ACM Transactions on Information Systems*, 9(1):52–74.

[Maloney and Niv, 1998] Maloney, J. and Niv, M. (1998). TAGARAB: A fast accurate arabic name recogniser using high precision morphological analysis. In *Proceedings of the Workshop on Computational Approaches to Semitic Languages*, Montreal, Canada.

[Manning and Schutze, 1999] Manning, C. and Schutze, H. (1999). *Foundations of Statistical Natural Language Processing*. The MIT Press.

[Manning, 1989] Manning, G. (1989). The use of the DAP, a massively parallel computing system, for information retrieval and processing. In *IEE Colloquium on Parallel Techniques for Information Retrieval Digest*, pages 28–32.

[Maron and Kuhns, 1960] Maron, M.E. and Kuhns, J.L. (1960). On relevance, probabilistic indexing and information retrieval. *Journal of the Association for Computing Machines*, 7:216–244.

[Martinez et al., 2003] Martinez, J., Roman, J., Fombella, J., Serrano, A., Ruiz, A., Martinez, P., Goni, J., and Gonzalez, J. (2003). Evaluation of MIRACLE approach results for CLEF 2003. In *Proceedings of the CLEF 2003 Cross-Language Text Retrieval System Evaluation Campaign*.

[Masand and Stanfill, 1994] Masand, B. and Stanfill, C. (1994). An information retrieval testbed on the CM-5. In *Proceedings of the Third Text REtrieval Conference (TREC-3)*, pages 117–122.

[Mayfield and McNamee, 2003] Mayfield, J. and McNamee, P. (2003). Single n-gram stemming. In *Proceedings of the 26th Annual International ACM SIGIR Conference on Research and Development in Information Retrieval*, pages 415–416.

[Mazur, 1984] Mazur, Z. (1984). On a model of distributed information retrieval systems based on thesauri. *Information Processing and Management*, 20(4):499–505.

[Mazur, 1988] Mazur, Z. (1988). Properties of a model of distributed homogeneous information retrieval based on weighted models. *Information Processing and Management*, 24(5):525–540.

[McCabe et al., 1999] McCabe, M., Chowdhury, A., Grossman, D., and Frieder, O. (1999). A unified environment for fusion of information retrieval approaches. In *Proceedings of the Eighth ACM Conference on Information and Knowledge Management (CIKM)*.

[McCabe et al., 2000] McCabe, M. C., Lee, J., Chowdhury, A., Grossman, D., and Frieder, O. (2000). On the design and evaluation of a multi-dimensional approach to information retrieval. In *Proceedings of the 23rd ACM SIGIR Conference on Research and Development in Information Retrieval*, pages 363–365.

[McCallum and Nigam, 1998] McCallum, A. and Nigam, K. (1998). A comparison of event models for Naïve Bayes text classification. In *AAAI-1998 Learning for Text Categorization Workshop*, pages 41–48.

[McHugh et al., 1997] McHugh, J., Abiteboul, S., Goldman, R., Quass, D., and Widom., J. (1997). Lore: A database management system for semistructured data. *SIGMOD Record*, 26(3):54–66.

[McKenzie et al., 1990] McKenzie, B.J., Harries, R., and Bell, T. (1990). Selecting a hashing algorithm. *Software Practice and Experience*, 20(2):209–224.

[McNally, 1997] McNally, J. (1997). *Informix Unleashed*. Sams.

[McNamee, 2001] McNamee, P. (2001). Experiments in the retrieval of unsegmented japanese text at the NTCIR-2 workshop. In *Proceedings of the Second NTCIR Workshop*, pages 157–162, Tokyo, Japan.

[McNamee and Mayfield, 2002a] McNamee, P. and Mayfield, J. (2002a). Comparing cross-language query expansion techniques by degrading translation resources. In *Proceedings of the 25th Annual International ACM SIGIR Conference on Research and Development in Information Retrieval*, pages 405–406.

[McNamee and Mayfield, 2002b] McNamee, P. and Mayfield, J. (2002b). Entity extraction without language-specific resources. In *Proceedings of the Sixth Conference on Natural Language Learning (CoNLL-2002)*.

[Melnik et al., 2000] Melnik, S., Garcia-Molina, H., and Paepcke, A. (2000). A mediation infrastructure for digital library services. In *Proceedings of ACM Digital Libraries*, San Antonio, Texas.

[Miller et al., 1999] Miller, D., Leek, T., and Schwartz, R. (1999). A hidden markov model information retrieval system. In *Proceedings of the 22nd Annual International ACM SIGIR Conference on Research and Developmentin Information Retrieval*, pages 214 – 221.

[Minker et al., 1972] Minker, J., Wilson, G., and Zimmerman, B. (1972). An evaluation of query expansion by the addition of clustered terms for a document retrieval system. *Information Storage and Retrieval*, 8(6):329–348.

[Minsky, 1975] Minsky, M. (1975). *The Psychology of Computer Vision*, chapter A Framework for Representing Knowledge, pages 211–277. McGraw-Hill Book Company.

[Moffat and Zobel, 1994] Moffat, A. and Zobel, J. (1994). Fast ranking in limited space. In *Proceedings of the Tenth IEEE International Conference on Data Engineering*, pages 428–437.

[Moffat and Zobel, 1996] Moffat, A. and Zobel, J. (1996). Self-indexing inverted files for fast text retrieval. *ACM Transactions on Information Systems*, 14(4):349–379.

[Mohan and Willett, 1985] Mohan, K.C. and Willett, P. (1985). Nearest neighbor searching in serial files using text signatures. *Journal of Information Science Principles and Practice*, 11(1):31–39.

[Navarro et al., 2000] Navarro, G., de Moura, E. Silva, Neubert, M., Ziviani, N., and Baeza-Yates, R. (2000). Adding compression to block addressing inverted indexes. *Journal of Information Retrieval*, pages 49–77.

[Nejdl et al., 2002] Nejdl, W., Wolf, B., Qu, C., Decker, S., Sintek, M., Naeve, A., Nilsson, M., Palmér, M., and Risch, T. (2002). Edutella: A P2P networking infrastructure based on rdf. In *Proceedings of the World Wide Web Conference*.

[Ney et al., 1994] Ney, H., Essen, U., and Kneser, R. (1994). On structuring probabilistic dependencies in stochastic language modeling. *Computer Speech and Language*, 8(1):1–38.

[Ng et al., 2003] Ng, W., Ooi, B. C., Tan, K., and Zhou, A. (2003). Peerdb: A P2P-based system for distributed data sharing. In *Proceedings of the IEEE International Conference on Data Engineering (ICDE)*.

[Niemi and Jarvelin, 1995] Niemi, T. and Jarvelin, K. (1995). A straightforward NF2 relational interface with applications in information retrieval. *Information Processing and Management*, 31(2):215–231.

[Nilsson, 2004] Nilsson, M. (2004). Id3v2 overview.

[Nunzio et al., 2003] Nunzio, G.M. Di, Ferro, N., Melucci, M., and Orio, N. (2003). The University of Padova at CLEF 2003: Experiments to evaluate probabilistic models for automatic stemmer generation and query word translation. In *Proceedings of the CLEF 2003 Cross-Language Text Retrieval System Evaluation Campaign*.

[Oard, 2003] Oard, D. (2003). When you come to a fork in the road, take it: Multiple futures for CLIR research. In *Proceedings of the SIGIR 2003 Workshop on the future of Cross-Language Information Retrieval*.

[Oard and Diekema, 1998] Oard, D. and Diekema, A. (1998). Cross-language information retrieval. *Annual Review of Information Science and Technology (ARIST)*, 33:223–256.

[Oard et al., 2000] Oard, D., Levow, G., and Cabezas, C. (2000). CLEF experiments at the University of Maryland: Statistical stemming and backoff translation strategies. In *Cross Language Information Retrieval and Evaluation: Workshop of Cross-Language Evaluation Forum, CLEF 2000*, pages 176–187, Lisbon, Portugal.

[Oard et al., 2004] Oard, D., Soergel, D., Doermann, D., Huang, X., Murray, G., Wang, J., Ramabhadran, B., Franz, M., Gustman, S., Mayfield, J., Kharevych, L., and Strassel, S. (2004). Building an information retrieval test collection for spontaneous conversational speech. In *ACM 27th Conference on Research and Development in Information Retrieval (SIGIR)*, pages 41–48.

[Oard, 2004] Oard, Doug (2004). Personal communication with David Grossman.

[Och and Ney, 2003] Och, F. and Ney, H. (2003). A systematic comparison of various statistical alignment models. *Computational Linguistics*, 29(1):19–51.

[Och and Ney, 2000a] Och, F.J. and Ney, H. (2000a). A comparison of alignment models for statistical machine translation. In *Proceedings of COLING 2000*, pages 1086–1090, Saarbrücken, Germany.

[Och and Ney, 2000b] Och, F.J. and Ney, H. (2000b). Improved statistical alignment models. In *Proceedings of the Association of Computing Linguistics*, pages 440–447, Hong Kong, China.

[Olson, 1995] Olson, C. F. (1995). Parallel algorithms for hierarchical clustering. *Parallel Computing*, 21:1313–1325.

[Osborn et al., 1997] Osborn, M., Strzalkowski, T., and Marinescu, M. (1997). Evaluating document retrieval in patent database: A preliminary report. In *Proceedings of the Sixth ACM International Conference on Information and Knowledge Management*, pages 216–221.

[Ozkarahan, 1995] Ozkarahan, E. (1995). Multimedia document retrieval. *Information Processing and Management*, 31(1):113–131.

[Paepcke et al., 2000] Paepcke, A., Baldonado, M., Chang, C.C.K., Cousins, S., and Garcia-Molina, H. (2000). Building the Infobus: A review of technical choices in the Stanford Digital Library Project. Technical Report TR-2000-50, Stanford University.

[Pearce and Nicholas, 1993] Pearce, C. and Nicholas, C. (1993). Generating a dynamic hypertext environment with n-gram analysis. In *Procedings of the Second International Conference on Information and Knowledge Management*, pages 148–153.

[Peat and Willett, 1991] Peat, H.J. and Willett, P. (1991). The limitations of term co-occurrence data for query expansion in document retrieval systems. *Journal of the American Society for Information Science*, 42(5):378–383.

[Petry et al., 1993] Petry, F.E., Buckles, B., Prabbu, D., and Kraft, D. (1993). Fuzzy information retrieval using genetic algorithms and relevance feedback. In *ASIS '93 Proceedings of the Fifty-Sixth Annual ASIS Meeting*, pages 122–125.

[Pirkola, 1998] Pirkola, A. (1998). The effects of query structure and dictionary setups in dictionary-based cross-language information retrieval. In *Proceedings of the 21st Annual International ACM SIGIR Conference on Research and Development in Information Retrieval*, pages 55–63.

[Pirkola et al., 2001] Pirkola, A., Hedlund, T., Keskustalo, H., and Järvelin, K. (2001). Dictionary-based cross-language information retrieval: Problems, methods, and research findings. *Information Retrieval*, 4:209–230.

[Pirkola et al., 2003] Pirkola, A., Toivonen, J., Keskustalo, H., Visala, K., and Jarvelin, K. (2003). Fuzzy translation of cross-lingual spelling variants. In *Proceedings of the 23rd Annual International ACM SIGIR Conference on Research and Development in Information Retrieval*, pages 345–352.

[Pogue and Willett, 1987] Pogue, C.A. and Willett, P. (1987). Use of text signatures for document retrieval in a highly parallel environment. *Parallel Computing*, 4(3):259–268.

[Pollock and Zamora, 1984] Pollock, J. and Zamora, A. (1984). Automatic spelling correction in scientific and scholarly text. *Communications of the ACM*, 27(4):358–358.

[Ponte and Croft, 1998] Ponte, J. M. and Croft, W. B. (1998). A language modelling approach to information retrieval. In *Proceedings of the 21st ACM SIGIR Conference on Research and Development in Information Retrieval*, pages 275–281.

[Porter, 1980] Porter, M. (1980). An algorithm for suffix stripping. *Program*, 14(3):130–137.

[Pulley, 1994] Pulley, E. (1994). A preprocessor for integrating structured data and text. Master's thesis, George Mason University.

[Qu et al., 2003a] Qu, Y., Grefenstette, G., and Evans, D. (2003a). Automatic transliteration for japanese-to-english text retrieval. In *Proceedings of the 23rd Annual International ACM SIGIR Conference on Research and Development in Information Retrieval*, pages 353–360.

[Qu et al., 2003b] Qu, Y., Grefenstette, G., and Evans, D. (2003b). Clairvoyance CLEF-2003 experiments. In *Proceedings of the CLEF 2003 Cross-Language Text Retrieval System Evaluation Campaign*.

[Quass et al., 1996] Quass, D., Widom, J., Goldman, R., Haas, K., Luo, Q., McHugh, J., Nestorov, S., Rajaraman, A., Rivero, H., Abiteboul, S., Ullman, J., and Wiener., J. (1996). LORE: A lightweight object REpository for semistructured data. In *Proceedings of the ACM SIGMOD International Conference on Management of Data*, Montreal, Canada.

[Rabbiner, 1989] Rabbiner, L. (1989). A tutorial on hidden markov models and selected applications in speech recognition. *Proceedings of the IEEE*, 77(2):257–286.

[Rada et al., 1987] Rada, R., Mili, H., Bicknell, E., and Blettner, M. (1987). Development and application of a metric on semantic nets. *IEEE Transactions on System, Man, and Cybernetics*, 19(1):17–30.

[Raghavan and Garcia-Molina, 2002] Raghavan, S. and Garcia-Molina, H. (2002). Integrating diverse information management systems: A brief survey. Technical Report TR-2001-57, Stanford University.

[Rasmussen and Willett, 1989] Rasmussen, E. and Willett, P. (1989). Efficiency of hierarchic agglomerative clustering using the ICL distributed array processor. *Journal of Documentation*, 45(1):1–24.

[Ratnasamy et al., 2001] Ratnasamy, S., Francis, P., Handley, M., Karp, R., and Shenker, S. (2001). A scalable content-addressable network. In *Proceedings of the ACM SIGCOMM*.

[Reddaway, 1991] Reddaway, S. (1991). High speed text retrieval from large databases on a massively parallel processor. *Information Processing and Management*, 27(4):311–316.

[Rijsbergen, 1977] Rijsbergen, C.J. Van (1977). A theoretical basis for the use of co-occurrence data in information retrieval. *Journal of Documentation*, 33(2):106–119.

[Robertson and Walker, 1994] Robertson, S. and Walker, S. (1994). Some simple effective approximations to the 2-Poisson model for probabilistic weighted retrieval. In *Proceedings of the Seventeenth Annual International ACM SIGIR Conference on Research and Development in Information Retrieval*, pages 232–241.

[Robertson and Walker, 1997] Robertson, S. and Walker, S. (1997). On relevance weights with little relevance information. In *Proceedings of the 20th Annual International ACM SIGIR Conference on Research and Development in Information Retrieval*, pages 16–24.

[Robertson et al., 1995] Robertson, S., Walker, S., Beaulieu, M.M., and Gatford, M. (1995). Okapi at TREC-4. In *Proceedings of the Fourth Text REtrieval Conference (TREC-4)*, pages 73–96.

[Robertson, 1977] Robertson, S.E. (1977). The probability ranking principle in IR. *Journal of Documentation*, 33(4):294–304.

[Robertson, 1990] Robertson, S.E. (1990). On term selection for query expansion. *Journal of Documentation*, 46(4):359–364.

[Robertson, 1997] Robertson, S.E. (1997). Overview of the okapi projects. *Journal of Documentation*, 53(1):3–7.

[Robertson and Sparck Jones, 1976] Robertson, S.E. and Sparck Jones, K. (1976). Relevance weighting of search terms. *Journal of American Society for Information Science*, 27(3):129–146.

[Rocchio, 1966] Rocchio, J. J. (1966). *Document Retrieval Systems—Optimization and Evaluation*. PhD thesis, Harvard.

[Rocchio, 1971] Rocchio, J. J. (1971). *The SMART Retrieval System Experiments in Automatic Document Processing*, chapter Relevance Feedback in Information Retrieval, pages 313–323. Prentice Hall.

[Rogati and Yang, 2004] Rogati, M. and Yang, Y. (2004). Resource selection for domain-specific cross-lingual IR. In *ACM 27th Conference on Research and Development in Information Retrieval (SIGIR)*, pages 154–161.

[Rohrs, 2000] Rohrs, C. (2000). Keyword matching in gnutella. http://www.limewire.org/project/www/KeywordMatching.htm.

[Rohrs, 2001] Rohrs, C. (2001). Search result grouping in gnutella. http://www.limewire.org/project/www/result_grouping.htm.

[Rosenfeld, 2000] Rosenfeld, R. (2000). Two decades of statistical language modeling: Where do we go from here. *Proceedings of the IEEE*, 88(8).

[Ruiz, 2003] Ruiz, M. (2003). Report on CLEF 2003 experiments at UB. In *Proceedings of the CLEF 2003 Cross-Language Text Retrieval System Evaluation Campaign*.

[Ruocco and Frieder, 1997] Ruocco, A. and Frieder, O. (1997). Clustering and classification of large document bases in a parallel environment. *Journal of the American Society for Information Science*, 48(10):932–943.

[Salton, 1969] Salton, G. (1969). A comparison between manual and automatic indexing methods. *Journal of American Documentation*, 20(1):61–71.

[Salton, 1970a] Salton, G. (1970a). Automatic processing of foreign language documents. *Journal of the American Society for Information Science*, 21(3):187–194.

[Salton, 1970b] Salton, G. (1970b). Automatic text analysis. *Science*, 168(3929):335–342.

[Salton, 1971a] Salton, G. (1971a). *The SMART Retrieval System—Experiments in Automatic Document Processing*, chapter New Experiments in Relevance Feedback, pages 337–354. Prentice Hall.

[Salton, 1971b] Salton, G. (1971b). *The SMART Retrieval System—Experiments in Automatic Document Processing*, chapter Negative Response Relevance Feedback, pages 403–411. Prentice Hall.

[Salton, 1971c] Salton, G. (1971c). *The SMART Retrieval System—Experiments in Automatic Document Processing*, chapter Information Analysis and Dictionary Construction, pages 115–142. Prentice Hall.

[Salton, 1971d] Salton, G. (1971d). *The SMART Retrieval System Experiments in Automatic Document Processing*, chapter Relevance feedback and the optimization of retrieval effectiveness, pages 324–336. Prentice Hall.

[Salton, 1988] Salton, G. (1988). Parallel text search methods. *Communications of the ACM*, 31(2):202–214.

[Salton, 1989] Salton, G. (1989). *Automatic Text Processing*. Addison-Wesley.

[Salton and Buckley, 1988] Salton, G. and Buckley, C. (1988). Term-weighting approaches in automatic text retrieval. *Information Processing and Management*, 24(5):513–523.

[Salton and Buckley, 1990] Salton, G. and Buckley, C. (1990). Improving retrieval performance by relevance feedback. *Journal of the American Society for Information Science*, 41(4):288–297.

[Salton and Lesk, 1968] Salton, G. and Lesk, M. E. (1968). Computer evaluation of indexing and text processing. *Journal of the ACM*, 15(1):8–36.

[Salton et al., 1975] Salton, G., Yang, C.S., and Wong, A. (1975). A vector-space model for automatic indexing. *Communications of the ACM*, 18(11):613–620.

[Sanderson, 1997] Sanderson, M. (1997). Duplicate detection in the reuters collection. Technical Report TR-1997-5, Department of Computing Science at the University of Glasgow, Glasgow, UK.

[Sanderson and Joho, 2004] Sanderson, M. and Joho, H. (2004). Forming test collections with no system pooling. In *ACM 27th Conference on Research and Development in Information Retrieval (SIGIR)*, pages 33–40.

[Sanderson and Rijsbergen, 1991] Sanderson, M. and Rijsbergen, C.J. Van (1991). NRT: News Retrieval Tool. *Electronic Publishing*, 4(4):205–217.

[Sang and Meulder, 2003] Sang, E. F. and Meulder, F. D. (2003). Introduction to the CoNLL-2003 shared task: Language-independent named entity recognition. In *Proceedings of CoNLL-2003*, pages 142–147, Edmonton, Canada.

[Schank, 1975] Schank, R.C. (1975). *Conceptual Information Processing*. Oxford, Amsterdam.

[Schank and Lehnert, 1977] Schank, R.C. and Lehnert, W. (1977). *Human and Artificial Intelligence*, chapter Computer Understanding of Stories, pages 135–139. North-Holland, Amsterdam.

[Schek and Pistor, 1982] Schek, H.J. and Pistor, P. (1982). Data structures for an integrated data base management and information retrieval system. In *Proceedings of the Eighth International Conference on Very Large Data Bases*, pages 197–207.

[Schmidt et al., 2000] Schmidt, A., Kersten, M., Windhouwer, M., and Waas, F. (2000). Efficient relational storage and retrieval of XML documents. In *Proceedings of the Third International Workshop on the Web and Databases*, pages 47–52.

[Schutze and Pedersen, 1997] Schutze, H. and Pedersen, J. (1997). A co-occurrence-based thesaurus and two applications to information retrieval. *Information Processing and Management*, 33(3):307–318.

[Schutze and Silverstein, 1997] Schutze, H. and Silverstein, C. (1997). Projections for efficient document clustering. In *Proceedings of the 20th Annual International ACM SIGIR Conference on Research and Development in Information Retrieval*, pages 74–81.

[Selinger, 1979] Selinger, P. (1979). Access path selection in a relational database management system. *IBM Technical Disclosure Bulletin*, 22(4):1657–1660.

[SHA1, 1995] SHA1 (1995). *Secure Hash Standard*. U.S Department of Commerce/National Institute of Standards and Technology (FIPS PUB 180-1).

[Shanmugasundaram et al., 1999] Shanmugasundaram, J., Tufte, K., He, G., Zhang, C., DeWitt, D., and Naughton, J. (1999). Relational databases for querying XML documents: Limitations and opportunities. In *Proceedings of the 25th Conference on Very Large Databases (VLDB).*

[Sheridan and Ballerini, 1996] Sheridan, P. and Ballerini, J. P. (1996). Experiments in multilingual information retrieval using the SPIDER system. In *Proceedings of the Nineteenth Annual International ACM SIGIR Conference on Research and Development in Information Retrieval*, pages 58–65.

[Sheridan et al., 1997] Sheridan, P., Wechsler, M., and Schauble, P. (1997). Cross-language speech retrieval: Establishing a baseline performance. In *Proceedings of the 20th Annual International ACM SIGIR Conference on Research and Development in Information Retrieval*, pages 99–108.

[Sherman, 1994] Sherman, Franklin (1994). Personal communication with David Grossman.

[Shin, 1998] Shin, D. (1998). BUS: An effective indexing and retrieval scheme in structured documents. In *Proceedings of International Conference on Digital Libraries.*

[Shivakumar and Garcia-Molina, 1996] Shivakumar, N. and Garcia-Molina, H. (1996). Building a scalable and accurate copy detection mechanism. In *Proceedings of the Second International Conference on Theory and Practice of Digital Libraries.*

[Shivakumar and Garcia-Molina, 1998] Shivakumar, N. and Garcia-Molina, H. (1998). Finding near-replicas of documents on the web. In *Proceedings of the Workshop on Web Databases (WebDB 98).*

[Shuey et al., 1997] Shuey, R., Spooner, D., and Frieder, O. (1997). *The Architecture of Distributed Computer Systems: A Data Engineering Perspective.* Addison Wesley.

[Silvestri et al., 2004] Silvestri, F., Orlando, S., and Perego, R. (2004). Assigning identifiers to documents to enhance to clustering property of fulltext indexes. In *ACM 27th Conference on Research and Development in Information Retrieval (SIGIR)*, pages 305–312.

[Singhal, 1997] Singhal, A. (1997). *Term Weighting Revisited.* PhD thesis, Cornell University.

[Smeaton et al., 1997] Smeaton, A., Kelledy, F., and Quinn, G. (1997). Ad hoc retrieval using thresholds, wsts for french monolingual retrieval, document-at-a-glance for high precision and triphone windows for spoken documents. In *Proceedings of the Sixth Text Retrieval Conference (TREC-6).*

[Smeaton and Rijsbergen, 1983] Smeaton, A.F. and Rijsbergen, C.J. Van (1983). The retrieval effects of query expansion on a feedback document retrieval system. *The Computer Journal*, 26(3):239–246.

[Somers, 2001] Somers, H. (2001). Bilingual parallel corpora and language engineering. In *Anglo-Indian Workshop Language Engineering for South-Asian Languages (LESAL).*

[Song and Croft, 1999] Song, F. and Croft, W.B. (1999). A general language model for information retrieval. In *Proceedings of the Eighth International Conference on Information and Knowledge Management (CIKM '99).*

[Sparck Jones, 1979a] Sparck Jones, K. (1979a). Experiments in relevance weighting of search terms. *Information Processing and Management*, 15(3):133–144.

[Sparck Jones, 1979b] Sparck Jones, K. (1979b). Search term relevance weighting given little relevance information. *Journal of Documentation*, 35(1):30–48.

[Sparck Jones and Barber, 1971] Sparck Jones, K. and Barber, E.O. (1971). What makes an automatic keyword classification effective? *Journal of the American Society for Information Science*, 22(3):166–175.

[Sparck Jones and Jackson, 1968] Sparck Jones, K. and Jackson, D. (1968). Some experiments in the use of automatically obtained term clusters for retrieval. *Mechanized Information Storage, Retrieval and Dissemination*, pages 203–212.

[Sparck Jones and Willett, 1997] Sparck Jones, K. and Willett, P. (1997). *Readings in Information Retrieval*. Morgan Kaufmann Publishers, Inc.

[Spink, 1994] Spink, A. (1994). Term relevance feedback and query expansion: Relation to design. In *Proceedings of the Seventeenth Annual International ACM SIGIR Conference on Research and Devlopment in Information Retrieval*, pages 81–90.

[Spink, 1995] Spink, A. (1995). Term relevance feedback and mediated database searching: Implications for information retrieval practice and systems design. *Information Processing and Management*, 31(2):161–171.

[SQL, 2003] SQL (2003). SQL Standard: Standard database languages - SQL, ISO, IEC 9075-*.

[Sripanidkulchai et al., 2003] Sripanidkulchai, K., Maggs, B., and Zhang, H. (2003). Efficient content location using interest-based locality in peer-to-peer systems. In *Proceedings of the IEEE INFOCOM*.

[Stanfill, 1990] Stanfill, C. (1990). Partitioned posting files: A parallel inverted file structure for information retrieval. In *Proceedings of the Thirteenth Annual ACM SIGIR Conference on Research and Development in Information Retrieval*, pages 413–428.

[Stanfill and Kahle, 1986] Stanfill, C. and Kahle, B. (1986). Parallel free-text search on the connection machine system. *Communications of the ACM*, 29(12):1229–1239.

[Stanfill and Thau, 1991] Stanfill, C. and Thau, R. (1991). Information retrieval on the connection machine: 1 to 8192 gigabytes. *Information Processing and Management*, 27(4):285–310.

[Stanfill et al., 1989] Stanfill, C., Thau, R., and Waltz, D. (1989). A parallel indexed algorithm for information retrieval. In *Proceedings of the Twelfth Annual ACM SIGIR Conference on Research and Development in Information Retrieval*, pages 88–97.

[Steinbach et al., 2000] Steinbach, M., Karypis, G., and Kumar, V. (2000). A comparison of document clustering techniques. In *Proceedings of the Knowledge Data and Discovery (KDD) Workshop on Text Mining*.

[Stoica et al., 2001] Stoica, I., Morris, R., Karger, D., Kaashoek, F., and Balakrishnan, H. (2001). Chord: A scalable peer-to-peer lookup service for internet applications. In *Proceedings of the ACM SIGCOMM*.

[Stone, 1987] Stone, H. (1987). Parallel querying of large databases: A case study. *Computer*, 20(10):11–21.

[Stonebraker et al., 1983] Stonebraker, M., Stettner, H., Lynn, N., Kalash, J., and Guttman, Antonin (1983). Document processing in a relational database system. *ACM Transactions on Office Information Systems*, 1(2):143–158.

[Strzalkowski et al., 1997] Strzalkowski, T., Lin, Fang, and Perez-Carballo, J. (1997). Natural language information retrieval TREC-6 report. In *Proceedings of the Sixth Text REtrieval Conference (TREC-6)*, pages 209–228.

[Sundheim, 1995] Sundheim, B.M. (1995). Overview of results of the MUC-6 evaluation. In *Proceedings of the Sixth Message Understanding Conference (MUC-6)*, pages 13–32.

[Tang et al., 2003] Tang, C., Xu, Z., and Dwarkadas, S. (2003). Peer-to-peer information retrieval using self-organizing semantic overlay networks. In *ACM SIGCOMM*.

[Tang et al., 2002] Tang, C., Xu, Z., and Mahalingam, M. (2002). Peersearch: Efficient information retrieval in peer-to-peer networks. Technical Report HPL-2002-198.

[Teuful, 1988] Teuful, B. (1988). Statistical n-gram indexing of natural language documents. *International Forum of Information and Documentation*, 13(4):3–10.

[Teuful, 1991] Teuful, B. (1991). Office document retrieval. *International Forum of Information and Documentation*, 16(4):15–19.

[Thorelli, 1962] Thorelli, Lars Erik (1962). Automatic correction of errors in text. *BIT*, 2:45–62.

[Tomasic and Garcia-Molina, 1993] Tomasic, A. and Garcia-Molina, Hector (1993). Performance of inverted indices in shared-nothing distributed text document information retreival systems. In *Proceedings of the Second International Conference on Parallel and Distributed Information Systems*, pages 8–17.

[TREC, 2003] TREC (2003). *NIST Special Publication 500-255 : The Twelfth Text REtrieval Conference (TREC 2003)*. NIST.

[Trotman, 2003] Trotman, A. (2003). Compressing inverted files. *Information Retrieval*, 6:5–19.

[Turski, 1971] Turski, W.M. (1971). On a model of information retrieval systems based on thesaurus. *Information Storage and Retrieval*, 7(201):201–205.

[Turtle, 1991] Turtle, H. (1991). *Inference Networks for Document Retrieval*. PhD thesis, University of Massachusetts, Amherst.

[Uratani and Takeda, 1993] Uratani, N. and Takeda, M. (1993). A fast string-searching algorithm for multiple patterns. *Information Processing and Management*, 29(6):775–791.

[V0.4, 2004] V0.4, Gnutella Protocol Specification (2004). Gnutella protocol specification v0.4.

[V0.6, 2004] V0.6, Gnutella Protocol Specification (2004). Gnutella protocol specification v0.6.

[Vercoustre et al., 2002] Vercoustre, A.-M., Thom, J.A., Krumpholz, A., Mathieson, I., Wilkins, P., Wu, M., Craswell, N., and Hawking, D. (2002). CSIRO INEX experiments: XML search using PADRE. In *Proceedings of the First Workshop of the INitiative for the Evaluation of XML Retrieval (INEX)*, pages 65–70.

[Veronis, 2000] Veronis, Jean (2000). *Parallel Text Processing: Alignment and Use of Translation Corpora*. Kluwer Academic Publishers.

[Vogel et al., 1996] Vogel, S., Ney, H., and Tillmann, C. (1996). HMM-based word alignment in statistical translation. In *Proceedings of COLING 1996*, pages 836–841, Copenhagen.

[Voorhees, 1986] Voorhees, E. (1986). Implementing agglomerative hierarchic clustering algorithms for use in document retrieval. *Information Processing and Management*, 22(6):465–476.

[Voorhees, 1993] Voorhees, E. (1993). On expanding query vectors with lexically related words. In *Proceedings of the Second Text REtrieval Conference (TREC-2)*, pages 223–231.

[Walden and Sere, 1988] Walden, M. and Sere, K. (1988). Free text retrieval on transputer networks. *Microprocessors and Microsystems*, 13(3):179–187.

[Wang et al., 1985] Wang, Y., Vandendorpe, J., and Evens, M. (1985). Relational thesauri in information retrieval. *Journal of the American Society for Information Science*, 36(1):15–27.

[White and Date, 1989] White, C. and Date, C.J. (1989). *A Guide to SQL/DS*. Addison-Wesley.

[Wilkinson, 1994] Wilkinson, R. (1994). Effective retrieval of structured documents. In *Proceedings of the Seventeenth Annual International ACM SIGIR Conference on Research and Devlopment in Information Retrieval*, pages 311–317.

[Willet, 1988] Willet, P. (1988). Recent trends in hierarchical document clustering: A critical review. *Information Processing and Management*, 24(5):577–597.

[Willett, 1988] Willett, P. (1988). Recent trends in hierarchic document clustering: A critical review. *Information Processing and Management*, 24(5):577–597.

[Willett, 1990] Willett, P. (1990). Document clustering using an inverted file approach. *Journal of Information Science*, 2:223–231.

[Winograd, 1983] Winograd, T. (1983). *Language as a Cognitive Process: Volume 1: Syntax*. Addison-Wesley.

[Witten et al., 1999] Witten, I., Moffat, A., and Bell, T. (1999). *Managing Gigabytes*. Van Nostrand Reinhold.

[Wong et al., 1985] Wong, S.K.M., Wojciech, Z., and Wong, P. (1985). Generalized vector space model in information retrieval. *Proceedings of the Eighth Annual International ACM SIGIR Conference on Research and Development in Information Retrieval*, pages 18–25.

[Wu and Salton, 1981] Wu, H. and Salton, G. (1981). The estimation of term relevance weights using relevance feedback. *Journal of Documentation*, 37(4):194–214.

[Xu and Weischedel, 1999] Xu, J. and Weischedel, R. (1999). TREC-9 cross-lingual retrieval at bbn. In *Proceedings of the Text REtrieval and Evaluation Conference (TREC-9)*.

[Xu et al., 2001] Xu, J., Weischedel, R., and Nguyen, C. (2001). Evaluating a probabilistic model for cross-lingual information retrieval. In *Proceedings of the 24th ACM SIGIR Conference on Research and Development in Information Retrieval*, pages 105–110.

[Xu et al., 2003] Xu, W., Liu, X., and Gong, Y. (2003). Document clustering based on non-negative matrix factorization. In *Proceedings of the 26th ACM SIGIR 2003 Conference on Research and Development in Information Retrieval*, pages 267–273.

[Xue and Converse, 2002] Xue, N. and Converse, S. (2002). Combining classifiers for chinese word segmentation. In *Proceedings of the SIGHAN Workshop*.

[Yang and Korfhage, 1993] Yang, J. and Korfhage, R. (1993). Effects of query term weights modification in document retrieval: A study based on a genetic algorithm. In *Proceedings of the Second Annual Symposium on Document Analysis and Information Retrieval*, pages 271–285.

[Yang and Korfhage, 1994] Yang, J.J. and Korfhage, R. (1994). Query modification using genetic algorithms in vector space models. *International Journal of Expert Systems*, 7(2):165–191.

[Yannakoudakis et al., 1982] Yannakoudakis, E.J., Goyal, P., and Huggill, J.A. (1982). The generation and use of text fragments for data compression. *Information Processing and Management*, 18(1):15–21.

[Yee et al., 1993] Yee, W., Wong, P., and Lee, D. (1993). Implementations of partial document ranking using inverted files. *Information Processing and Management*, 29(5):647–689.

[Yee and Frieder, 2004] Yee, W.G. and Frieder, O. (2004). The design of pirs, a peer-to-peer information retrieval system. In *Proceedings of the VLDB 2004 Second International Workshop On Databases, Information Systems and Peer-to-Peer Computing*. Springer-Verlag Lecture Notes in Computer Science.

[Yu et al., 2003] Yu, B., Liu, J., and Ong, C.S. (2003). Scalable P2P information retrieval via hierarchical result merging. Technical report, University of Illinois at Urbana-Champaign.

[Yu et al., 1983] Yu, C.T., Buckley, C., Lam, I.I., and Salton, G. (1983). A generalized term dependence model in information retrieval. *Information Technology: Research and Development*, 2(4):129–154.

[Yu et al., 1989] Yu, C.T., W, Meng, and Park, S. (1989). A framework for effective retrieval. *ACM Transactions on Database Systems*, 14(2):147–167.

[Yuwono and Lee, 1996] Yuwono, B. and Lee, D. (1996). Search and ranking algorithms for locating resources on the world wide web. In *Proceedings of the Twelfth IEEE International Conference on Data Engineering*, pages 164–171.

[Zadeh, 1965] Zadeh, L. A. (1965). Fuzzy sets. *Information Control*, 8:338–353.

[Zahariev, 2004] Zahariev, M. (2004). Automatic sense disambiguation for acronyms. In *ACM 27th Conference on Research and Development in Information Retrieval (SIGIR)*, pages 586–587.

[Zamora et al., 1981] Zamora, E.M., Pollock, J.J., and Zamora, A. (1981). The use of trigram analysis for spelling error detection. *Information Processing and Management*, 17(6):305–316.

[Zeng et al., 2004] Zeng, H.J., He, Q.C., Chen, Z., and Ma, W.Y. (2004). Learning to cluster web search results. In *ACM 27th Conference on Research and Development in Information Retrieval (SIGIR)*, pages 210–217.

[Zhai and Lafferty, 2001a] Zhai, C. and Lafferty, J. (2001a). Model-based feedback in the language modeling approach to information retrieval. In *Proceedings of the Tenth International Conference on Information and Knowledge Management (CIKM 2001)*.

[Zhai and Lafferty, 2001b] Zhai, C. and Lafferty, J. (2001b). A study of smoothing methods for language models applied to ad hoc information retrieval. In *Proceedings of the 24th ACM SIGIR Conference on Research and Development in Information Retrieval*, pages 334–342.

[Zhai and Lafferty, 2002] Zhai, C. and Lafferty, J. (2002). Two-stage language models for information retrieval. In *Proceedings of the 25th ACM SIGIR Conference on Research and Development in Information Retrieval*, pages 49–56.

[Zhang et al., 1996] Zhang, T., Ramakrishnan, R., and Livny, M. (1996). Birch: An efficient data clustering method for very large databases. In *Proceedings of 1996 ACM-SIGMOD Special Interest Group on Management of Data*, Montreal, Canada.

[Zhao and Karypis, 2002] Zhao, Y. and Karypis, G. (2002). Evaluations of algorithms for obtaining hierarchical clustering solutions. In *Proceedings of the 2002 ACM International Conference on Information and Knowledge Management (ACM-CIKM)*, Washington D.C.

[Zipf, 1949] Zipf, G.K. (1949). *Human Behaviour and the Principle of Least Effort*. Addison-Wessley.

[Zobel et al., 1992] Zobel, J., Moffat, A., and Sacks-Davis, R. (1992). An efficient indexing technique for full-text database systems. In *Proceedings of the Eighteenth International Conference on Very Large Databases*, pages 352–362.

[Zobel et al., 1995] Zobel, J., Moffat, A., Wilkinson, R., and Sacks-Davis, R. (1995). Efficient retrieval of partial documents. *Information Processing and Management*, 31(3):361–377.

Index

Printed in the United States
69231LVS00003B/14

9 781402 030048